FURTHER GERMAN

Paul Coggle
assisted by
Susanne Staab, MA

School of European and
Modern Language Studies
University of Kent at Canterbury

TEACH YOURSELF BOOKS

ABOUT THE AUTHOR

Paul Coggle has wide experience in teaching German at all levels. He taught both in a comprehensive school and at Cornell University, USA before joining the University of Kent, where he is now Senior Lecturer in German.

Mr Coggle has co-authored several German textbooks, including the *Ealing Course in German*. In 1988 he was elected a Fellow of the Royal Society of Arts. In 1992 he acted as series editor on a series of *Teach Yourself Beginner's* titles in French, German, Italian and Spanish; in 1994, again as series editor, on a series of *Teach Yourself Verbs* titles in French, German, Italian and Spanish.

Long-renowned as the authoritative source for self-guided learning – with more than 30 million copies sold worldwide – the *Teach Yourself* series includes over 200 titles in the fields of languages, crafts, hobbies, sports, and other leisure activities.

British Library Cataloguing in Publication Data
Coggle, Paul
Further German
I. Title
438.3

Library of Congress Catalog Card Number: 94–65935

First published in UK 1994 by Hodder Headline Plc, 338 Euston Road, London NW1 3BH

First published in US 1994 by NTC Publishing Group, 4255 West Touhy Avenue, Lincolnwood (Chicago), Illinois 60646 – 1975 U.S.A.

Typeset by Transet Ltd, Coventry, Warwickshire.
Printed in England by Cox & Wyman Ltd, Reading, Berkshire.

First published 1994
Impression number 10 9 8 7 6 5 4 3 2 1
Year 1998 1997 1996 1995 1994

CONTENTS

Symbols and abbreviations

This indicates dialogue.
This indicates that the cassette is needed for the section.
This indicates exercises – practise using the language.
This indicates key words or phrases.
This indicates grammar or explanations.
This indicates a section where you practise your reading skills of German and revise vocabulary from the same lesson.

*	conjugated with **sein**
Acc./Akk.	accusative/**Akkusativ**
adj. n.	adjectival noun
coll.	colloquial
Dat.	dative/**Dativ**
f.	feminine
Gen.	genitive/**Genitiv**
intr.	intransitive
Lit.	literally
m.	masculine
n.	neuter
Nom.	nominative/**Nominativ**
pl.	plural
sep.	separable
sing.	singular
str.	strong
tr.	transitive
wk.	weak
wk. n.	weak noun

INTRODUCTION

Who is this course intended for?

This is a complete course for students who already have basic German and who want to improve their skills of communication as well as to increase their knowledge of the language. For people who have completed a course such as *Teach Yourself German* or another beginner's course in German, *Teach Yourself Further German* offers ample opportunity to build on what they have learnt. Although the course has been designed specifically for studying alone the material and exercises also lend themselves to classroom use. Students taking evening classes in German, studying for GCSE or GCE Advanced Level, and other examinations where the emphasis is on acquiring communicative skills, will find plenty of material in this book to help them achieve their objectives. There is also considerable help with grammar points.

How to use this course

Each unit of the book is divided clearly into different sections. Here are some suggestions as to how to deal with each section:

Lernziele *Learning objectives*

In this brief section you will find a list of the main objectives of the unit in terms of language functions and grammar points. The language functions tell you what use of the language you will learn, such as: Expressing likes and dislikes, and agreeing and disagreeing. The grammar points show you how the language works and provide you with a framework for improving your accuracy. Read this section before you start, then look out in the rest of the unit for the **Lernziele** as they are introduced so that you can pay special attention to them.

Aufnahmen *Recordings*

There are between two and four recordings in each of the ten units of the course. The subject matter of the recordings for any given unit centres around the topic chosen for that unit. The title given to the unit provides an indication of the topic. Ideally, listen to each recording in turn before you read the printed version in the book. It is important to train yourself to listen and understand – not to become dependent on the printed text. After all, in real-life situations, German speakers do not provide you with a print-out of what they say to you!

Try listening for the gist of what is being said and then study the recordings in greater detail. At what point you actually study the printed text is of course up to you, but you should always work at the recording until you are confident that you can understand everything without referring to the text.

The **Bemerkungen** (*comments*) at the end of each recording provide help with vocabulary and background information on German life and culture. Further vocabulary assistance can be found in the glossary at the end of the book.

When you are satisfied that you have understood a recording, move on to the comprehension material usually: true/false statements (**Richtig oder falsch?**) or multiple choice questions (**Welche Antwort paßt?**). Occasionally you will also find an exercise for you to start producing some of the language you encounter in the recordings: to give the German equivalent of an English phrase (**Sagen Sie's auf Deutsch!**), or to supply complete sentences (**Vervollständigen Sie die Sätze!**). To check your answers refer to the **Lösungsteil** (*Key to the exercises*) at the end of the book.

Redewendungen *Phrases*

This section brings together examples of the language functions outlined in **Lernziele**. Some of the examples you will have encountered in the recordings; some will be new to you. Alternative forms are given to cover various degrees of formality. For more sophisticated interactions, it is important to have, at your disposal, the precise turn of phrase that suits your purpose at that given moment. Concentrated study on this section will assist you in achieving this level of command.

Included in this section there is often a list of vocabulary (**Vokabeln**) linked to the topic of the **Lektion**. Needless to say, it is important to take every opportunity to extend your vocabulary. You ought by the end of the course to have an active German vocabulary of about 5,000 words. You should also be able to recognise or work out the meaning of many more words. Use odd moments in the day, for instance when you are waiting for a bus, to learn and test yourself on vocabulary. Remember to learn the gender and plural of nouns and the principal parts of strong and irregular verbs.

Grammatische Hinweise *Grammar points*

Fundamental grammar points, many of which you may well have encountered at an earlier stage of learning, are revised and expanded upon. A certain amount of advanced grammar is also included. For more detailed accounts of specific grammar points, you are recommended to turn to a reference grammar book. Here are a few that you could use:

M. Durrell (1991) *Hammer's German Grammar and Usage*
Edward Arnold
M. Durrell (1992) *Using German – A guide to contemporary usage*
Cambridge University Press
N. Paxton (1986) *Teach Yourself German Grammar*
Hodder & Stoughton
G. Drosdowski (ed)(1984) *DUDEN 4: Die Grammatik*
Bibliographisches Institut

To achieve a high level of expertise in the use of grammar you will need all the practice you can get in listening, speaking, reading and writing.

Übungen *Exercises*

Each **Lektion** contains exercises which are designed to help you gain command of the various language functions, grammatical structures and vocabulary items as they are introduced. Care has been taken to provide a range of exercise types from those focusing on grammar to the purely communicative. You should also find that the first exercises in a unit require less in the way of production from you than do the later exercises. In most cases, you are expected to complete the exercises in writing and then to check your answers in the **Lösungsteil**. The interpreting exercises can, however, be tackled both orally and in writing.

For the more open-ended exercises one possible set of answers is provided in the **Lösungsteil**. You may find that your own answers differ from those given, but that yours are just as acceptable.

Höraufgabe *Listening exercise*

Because the ability to listen and understand is so important, you are offered at least one listening comprehension exercise in each unit. You should keep on listening and re-winding the tape until you have managed to understand the gist of what is being said. Transcripts of these listening exercises are provided in the back of the book, but they are meant to be referred to only after you have practised and extended your listening skills.

Lesetext *Reading text*

The **Lesetexte** consist of authentic written texts from a variety of sources. You do not need to understand every single word here but you will find most of the vocabulary that you need in the glossary. Do not hesitate to use a dictionary if you need to. The follow-up materials should help you to ensure that you have understood the main points of these texts.

The audio cassettes

The audio cassettes are an important part of the course, since they provide you with the opportunity to listen to German spoken by a variety of native speakers and to continue your work on German beyond the book. You can play the cassettes while you are doing other tasks which do not demand anything of you intellectually, such as when you are travelling to work, doing the ironing, cleaning the car and so on. Use every opportunity to listen and achieve greater exposure to spoken German.

Beyond the course materials

The German media

Radio and television are an important source of native-speaker German. You should find, as you progress with this course, that you can begin to tackle broadcasts aimed at a German-speaking audience. Try recording short programmes from the radio or television to start with and keep re-winding and playing back the recording so that you gradually build up your comprehension skills. If you live in the UK or Eire you will have no problem in receiving German television stations via a satellite dish. Many radio stations are also available via satellite. On ordinary radio, the **BBC World Service** frequently transmits in German on 648 kHz medium wave and **Deutsche Welle** can be found on 6075 kHz short wave. Many German-speaking stations can be picked up on medium wave after dark.

German newspapers and magazines are often available in UK supermarkets and newsagents. You will need to be patient and persistent in order to decipher the formal, complex German used in the quality press (publications such as *die Zeit*, *der Spiegel*, *Focus*, *Süddeutsche Zeitung*), but there is no doubt that you will significantly improve your command of German by regularly tackling articles of this kind. Popular illustrated magazines (such as *Stern* and *Bunte*) can also be useful sources of reading material.

Dictionaries

At this stage of your German studies, you will undoubtedly need a good general German-English, English-German dictionary, such as *The Oxford Duden German Dictionary* or *Collins German Dictionary*.

You must, however, bear in mind that no dictionary will give you all the information you want to know and all dictionaries need to be used with caution.

Qualifications

You may be interested in obtaining a qualification in German. The prospect of sitting an examination certainly provides an added stimulus to keep you studying. You need to look carefully at the syllabuses from a number of different examining boards and decide which one suits you best in terms of level, subject matter content and skills required.

Throughout the world the Goethe-Institut offers information on German language classes and on the internationally recognised Zertifikat Deutsch als Fremdsprache which is offered at several levels. If you do not know the address(es) of the Goethe-Institut in your country, contact the central administration in Munich. The address is: Goethe-Institut, Helene-Weber-Allee 1, Postfach 19 04 19, D- 80604 München, Germany.

At the national level, qualifications in German can, in most countries, be gained from a variety of examining boards. In England and Wales, there are the various GCSE and AS- and A-level examining boards, as well as such bodies as the London Chamber of Commerce (Foreign Languages at Work) and the Royal Society of Arts. Your local college should be able to tell you about the National Vocational Qualifications (NVQs).

Viel Spaß beim Lernen!

1
BERLIN IST EINE REISE WERT

Lernziele

In this unit you will learn how to

- ask the way
- give directions and advice for journeys
- ask and give times of departure and arrival
- form and use the cases

Aufnahmen

1 Fahren oder fliegen?

Silke Trebing aus Münster in Westfalen fragt ihren Freund Bernd Schulz, wie sie mit dem Wagen nach Berlin kommt. Bernd erklärt ihr den Weg auf der Autobahn, schlägt aber vor, daß sie lieber fliegen soll.

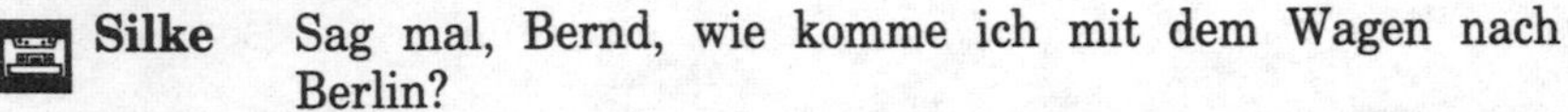

Silke Sag mal, Bernd, wie komme ich mit dem Wagen nach Berlin?

Bernd Also, wenn du Autobahn fährst, nimmst du von Münster die A1 in Richtung Hamburg. Am Autobahn-Kreuz Lotte–Osnabrück nimmst du die A30 in Richtung Bad Oeynhausen. Bei Bad Oeynhausen kommst du auf die A2 und fährst Richtung Hannover und Braunschweig. Die A2 führt dann direkt nach Berlin.

Silke Und wie lange brauche ich ungefähr für die ganze Fahrt?

Bernd Na, es kommt darauf an, wann du fährst, und ob der Verkehr ungehindert fließt, oder nicht. Heutzutage kommt es ja wegen Bauarbeiten oder einfach wegen hoher Verkehrsdichte sehr oft zu Stauungen.

Silke Ich habe vor, Freitag nach der Arbeit loszufahren.

Bernd Was?! Bist du verrückt? Mit deiner Ente brauchst du schon unter normalen Bedingungen fünf bis sechs Stunden für die 460 Kilometer nach Berlin. Am Wochenende wird es eine Ewigkeit dauern, bis du dorthin kommst. Fliegen wäre viel schneller und bequemer.

Silke Vielleicht hast du recht. Und ich hätte dann auch keine Parkprobleme in Berlin. Ich werde mich nach den Flügen erkundigen.

Bemerkungen

vorschlagen (ä, u, a) (sep.) *to suggest*. (In this book the abbreviation sep. is used to denote a 'separable verb', i.e. one whose prefix – (e.g. **vor**) can be separated from the main part of the verb)

die A1 German motorways are given the letter **A** (**Autobahn**) followed by a number. Federal highways (**Bundesstraßen**) are

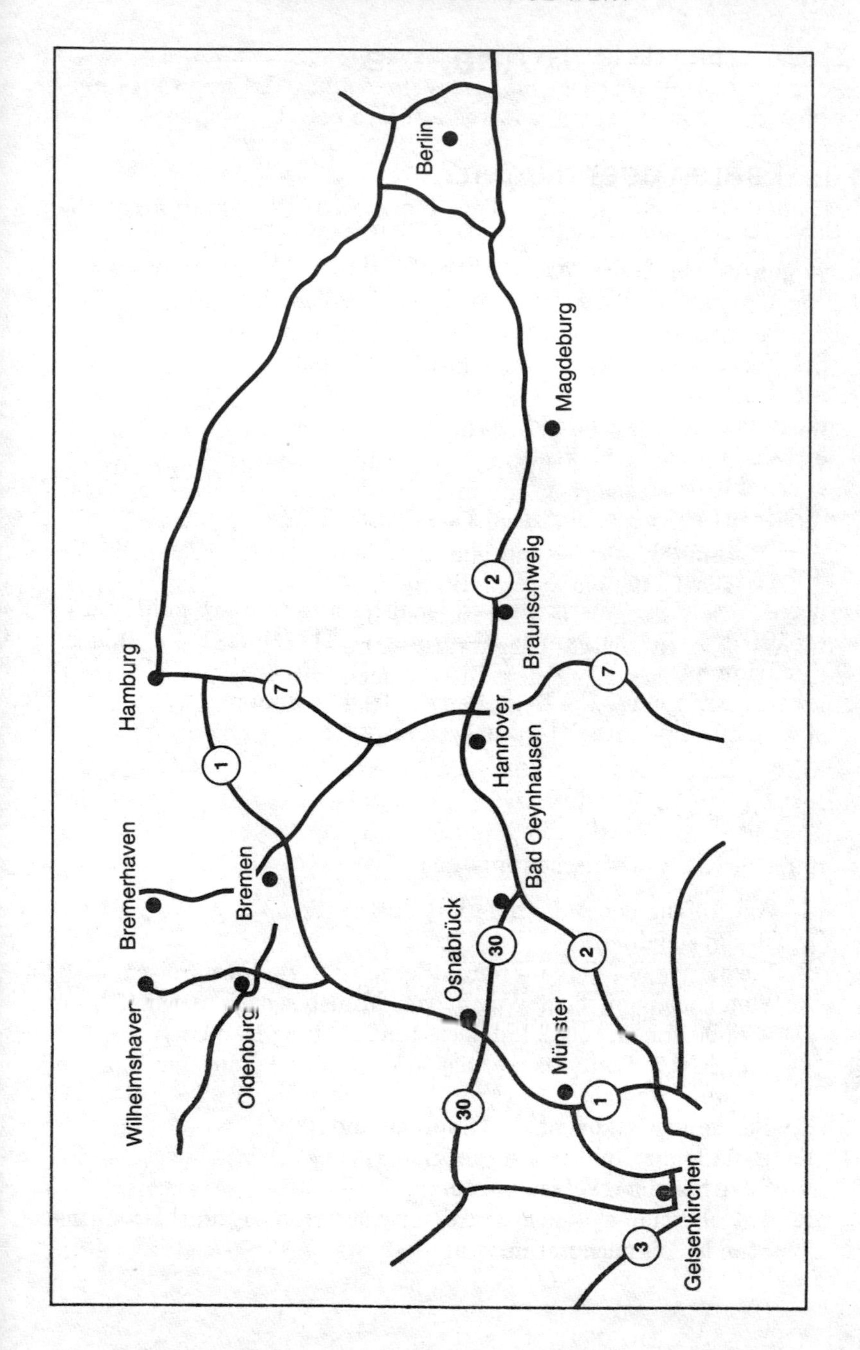
Berlin
Magdeburg
2
Braunschweig
Hamburg
7
7
1
Hannover
Bad Oeynhausen
Bremerhaven
Bremen
Osnabrück
30
2
Wilhelmshaver
Oldenburg
Münster
1
30
Gelsenkirchen
3

referred to by the letter **B** followed by a number
das Kreuz (**-e**) *four-way motorway interchange* (Lit. cross). A three-way interchange is referred to as **ein Dreieck** (Lit. a triangle)
führen *to lead*
es kommt darauf an *it depends*
fließen* (**ie, o, o**) *to flow*. (The * denotes that this verb forms the perfect tense with **sein**)
wegen (+ Gen./Dat.) *on account of, because of*. The dative is frequently used with **wegen** in colloquial German
die Bauarbeiten *roadworks* (Lit. building works)
die Verkehrsdichte *volume of traffic*
die Stauung (**-en**) *jam, tailback*
vorhaben (sep.) *to intend, plan*
losfahren* (sep.) *to set out*
verrückt *mad, insane*
die Ente (**-n**) *duck* (also used for a Citroën 2CV)
die Bedingung (**-en**) *condition*
die Ewigkeit *eternity*
wäre *would be*. This is a conditional form of the verb **sein** and is referred to in German as **Konjunktiv II**. (More about this in **Lektion 8**.)
hätte *would have*. The **Konjuktiv II** form of **haben**
sich erkundigen nach (+ Dat.) / **über** (+ Acc.) *to enquire about*

Richtig oder falsch?

Korrigieren Sie die falschen Aussagen.

1 Am Anfang der Aufnahme hat Silke vor, mit dem Wagen nach Berlin zu fahren.
2 Sie hat vor, mit ihrem Freund Bernd nach Berlin zu reisen.
3 Wenn man mit dem Wagen von Münster nach Berlin fahren will, fährt man zuerst auf der A1 in Richtung Hamburg.
4 Am Kreuz Lotte–Osnabrück nimmt man dann die A30 in Richtung Rheine.
5 Bei Hannover kommt man dann auf die A2.
6 Die A2 führt direkt nach Berlin.
7 Silke hat einen Volkswagen Golf.
8 Mit diesem Wagen braucht sie mindestens fünf bis sechs Stunden bis nach Berlin.

9 Wenn es auf der Autobahn zu Stauungen kommt, kann es natürlich viel länger dauern.
10 Nach ihrem Gespräch mit Bernd wird sich Silke nach Unterkunft in Berlin erkundigen.

2 Silke erkundigt sich nach den Flügen

Im Reisebüro fragt Silke Frau Jahn, ob sie am kommenden Freitag nach der Arbeit von Münster nach Berlin fliegen kann.

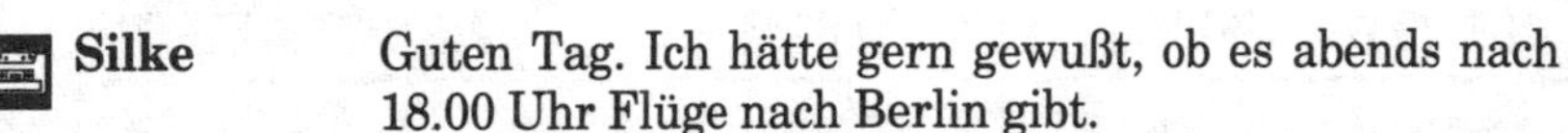

Silke Guten Tag. Ich hätte gern gewußt, ob es abends nach 18.00 Uhr Flüge nach Berlin gibt.

Frau Jahn Sonntags bis Freitags kann man um 19.20 Uhr mit British Airways ab Münster/Osnabrück nach Berlin Tegel fliegen. Sonnabends ist der letzte Flug um 14.20 Uhr. An welchem Tag wollten Sie denn fliegen?

Silke Am kommenden Freitag, wenn es geht. Um wieviel Uhr kommt die Maschine in Berlin Tegel an?

Frau Jahn Um 20.25 Uhr. Ich sehe mal auf dem Computer nach, ob noch Plätze frei sind. (*Sie sieht auf dem Computer nach.*) Ja, Sie haben Glück, es sind noch Plätze frei. Für wieviel Personen?

Silke Für mich alleine. Dann müßte ich auch noch wissen, ob ich Sonntag abend oder Montag früh zurückfliegen könnte.

Frau Jahn Also, Sonntag abends startet der letzte Flug um 17.40 Uhr und montags ist der erste Flug um 6.50 Uhr – Ankunft in Münster/Osnabrück um 8.00 Uhr.

Silke Mmm. 8.00 Uhr am Flughafen. Dann wäre ich erst gegen 9.00 Uhr im Büro. Aber ich glaube, das wäre nicht so schlimm, wenn ich noch vorher mit meiner Chefin rede. Was kostet der Hin- und Rückflug?

Frau Jahn 480 Mark.

Bemerkungen

Ich hätte gern gewußt Lit. I would have liked to know.
sonnabends *on Saturdays.* **Sonnabend** is frequently used in North Germany instead of **Samstag**
nachsehen (**ie**, **a**, **e**) (sep.) *to have a look* (*to see*)
Wieviel? *How much/many?* Some Germans use **Wie viele?** for

How many?, which is not incorrect, but should strictly speaking be reserved for the more emphatic utterances – **Wie viele Kinder hat er denn?** (*How many children has he got then for heaven's sake!?*) – according to *Duden*, the main authority on the German language

dann müßte ich wissen . . . *then I (would) need to know* . . .

die Ankunft *arrival*

vorher *in advance, beforehand*

der Hin- und Rückflug *return flight*

ABFLUG VON BERLIN						FLUGHAFEN						ANKUNFT IN BERLIN
6.35	TXL	Mo-Fr	BA	3181	7.50	**München**	6.35	Mo-Fr	LH	6650	TXL	**7.55**
6.40	TXL	Mo-Fr	LH	6651	8.00		7.00	Mo-Sa	BA	3198	TXL	**8.20**
8.25	TXL	Mo-Sa	BA	3182	9.40		7.35	Mo-Sa	LH	6252	TXL	**8.55**
8.40	TXL	täglich	LH	6655	10.00		7.00	Mo-Fr	NS	630	THF	**9.25**
10.00	THF	Mo-Fr	NS	631	11.45		8.35	täglich	LH	6654	TXL	**9.55**
10.40	TXL	täglich	LH	6659	12.00		8.45	Mo-Fr	BA	3182	TXL	**10.05**
11.45	TXL	täglich	LH	6665	13.05		10.25	Mo-Sa	BA	3184	TXL	**11.45**
12.40	TXL	So-Fr	LH	6661	14.00		10.35	täglich	LH	6658	TXL	**11.55**
13.55	THF	Mo-Fr	NS	635	15.40		11.45	Mo-Fr	NS	632	THF	**13.25**
14.40	TXL	täglich	LH	6663	16.00		12.35	täglich	LH	6660	TXL	**13.55**
16.40	TXL	täglich	LH	6667	18.00		13.40	täglich	LH	6664	TXL	**15.00**
17.00	TXL	So-Fr	BA	3193	18.15		14.35	So-Fr	LH	6662	TXL	**15.55**
17.55	TXL	So-Fr	LH	6269	19.15		16.10	Mo-Fr	NS	636	THF	**17.50**
18.15	THF	Mo-Fr	NS	637	20.45		16.35	täglich	LH	6666	TXL	**17.55**
18.40	TXL	täglich	LH	6671	20.00		18.35	So-Fr	LH	6670	TXL	**19.55**
19.55	TXL	So-Fr	LH	6273	21.15		18.55	So-Fr	BA	3194	TXL	**20.15**
20.35	TXL	So-Fr	BA	3197	21.50		20.05	So-Fr	LH	6272	TXL	**21.25**
20.35	TXL	So-Fr	LH	6675	21.55		20.35	täglich	LH	6674	TXL	**21.55**
6.50	TXL	Mo-Fr (Sa: 7.30)	BA	3161	8.00	**Münster/**	8.30	Mo-Fr (Sa: 9.10)	BA	3162	TXL	**9.35**
11.35	THF	Mo-Fr	VG	113	12.35	**Osnabrück**	14.20	Mo-Fr	VG	114	THF	**15.20**
17.40	TXL	So-Fr	BA	3165	18.50		19.20	So-Fr	BA	3166	TXL	**20.25**

Welche Antwort paßt?

1 Ist es möglich, abends nach Berlin zu fliegen?
- (*a*) Um 19.20 Uhr kann man mit BA nach Berlin Tegel fliegen.
- (*b*) Der erste Flug ist um 6.50 Uhr.
- (*c*) Die Maschine kommt um 8.00 Uhr in Berlin Tegel an.

2 An welchem Tag wollen Sie fliegen?
- (*a*) Nächste Woche.
- (*b*) Am kommenden Freitag.
- (*c*) Freitags.

3 Um wieviel Uhr kommt die Maschine in Berlin an?
- (*a*) Fünf bis sechs Stunden.

(*b*) Gegen 9.00 Uhr im Büro.
(*c*) Um 20.25 Uhr.

4 Sind noch Plätze frei?
(*a*) Ich sehe mal auf dem Computer nach.
(*b*) Sonntag abends ist der letzte Flug um 17.40.
(*c*) Diese Plätze sind alle besetzt.

5 Für wieviel Personen?
(*a*) Das wäre nicht so schlimm.
(*b*) Für den Rückflug.
(*c*) Für mich alleine.

6 Könnte ich Montag früh zurückfliegen?
(*a*) Das hätte ich gern gewußt.
(*b*) Sie haben Glück, es sind noch Plätze frei.
(*c*) Der erste Flug nach Münster startet um 6.50 Uhr.

3 Am Flughafen

Am Flughafen Tegel fragt Silke die Dame am Informationskiosk, wie Sie zu ihrem Hotel in der Güntzelstraße kommt.

Silke Ich hätte eine Frage, bitte. Wie komme ich am besten in die Stadt?
Dame Mit dem Bus. Vom Flughafen fahren Sie mit der 109 bis zum Bahnhof Zoo.
Silke Und wie teuer wär's mit einem Taxi?
Dame Das würde Sie ungefähr das Zehnfache der Busfahrt kosten. Wenn Sie aber viel Gepäck haben, lohnt es sich vielleicht, mit einem Taxi zu fahren.
Silke Nein, viel Gepäck habe ich nicht. Bloß muß ich vom Bahnhof Zoo noch ein bißchen weiter fahren. Mein Hotel liegt nämlich in der Güntzelstraße.
Dame Kein Problem! Vom Zoo sind es nur drei U-Bahn-Stationen bis zur Güntzelstraße.
Silke Wo ist die Bushaltestelle?
Dame Durch diesen Ausgang, dann nach links. Zirka 50 Meter geradeaus. Da sehen Sie dann die Haltestelle auf der rechten Seite.
Silke Und wo kann ich eine Fahrkarte lösen?
Dame Im Bus beim Fahrer.

Bemerkungen

mit der 109 The gender is feminine, as this is an abbreviation for **die Buslinie 109**

Bahnhof Zoo short for **Bahnhof Zoologischer Garten**. A major intersection of the mainline railway, the **U-Bahn** and the **S-Bahn**. It is also well known as a site of the seamier life of Berlin

die U-bahn short for **Untergrundbahn**. The **S-Bahn** or **Stadtbahn** (Lit. city train) also forms an important link in Berlin's transport system, together with the usual bus service

kosten note that **kosten** is one of the few verbs in German to take a double accusative: **Das kostet dich nur einen Anruf** (*That will only cost you a phone call*)

es lohnt sich (nicht) *it's (not) worth it*

Viel Gepäck habe ich nicht note the word order here: **Viel Gepäck** has been 'fronted', i.e. brought to the front of the sentence. This is a very typical German sentence pattern which is used to place the emphasis on the desired sentence element

nämlich *you see* (Lit. namely)

zirka *about*

geradeaus *straight on*

lösen *to buy*, *obtain* (a ticket)

Richtig oder falsch?

Korrigieren Sie die falschen Aussagen

1. Die Dame am Informationskiosk empfiehlt Silke, mit dem Bus in die Stadt zu fahren.
2. Vom Flughafen fährt sie mit der 99 bis zum Bahnhof Zoo.
3. Die Taxifahrt würde sie ungefähr das Fünffache der Busfahrt kosten.
4. Wenn man viel Gepäck hat, lohnt es sich manchmal, mit einem Taxi zu fahren.
5. Silke hat viel Gepäck.
6. Silkes Hotel liegt gleich am Bahnhof Zoo.
7. Vom Zoo sind es nur drei Minuten zu Fuß bis zur Güntzelstraße.
8. Die Fahrkarte kann sie im Bus lösen.

4 Silke will nach Charlottenburg

Silke möchte eine Freundin in der Danckelmannstraße im Stadtteil Charlottenburg besuchen. Sie fragt die Empfangsdame in ihrem

Hotel, wie sie am besten dorthin kommt.

Silke	Entschuldigen Sie, bitte. Können Sie mir sagen, wie ich am besten zur Danckelmannstraße komme?
Empfangsdame	Zur Danckelmannstraße? Ach ja, die liegt in Charlottenburg. Am besten fahren Sie also mit der U-bahn. Schauen Sie mal hier auf den Stadtplan.
Silke	Also, wir sind hier in der Güntzelstraße. Die nächste U-Bahn-Station liegt an der Kreuzung Bundesallee, nicht wahr?
Empfangsdame	Richtig. Sie nehmen also die U9 Richtung Oslauer Straße bis zum Zoo, und am Zoo steigen Sie um in die U1 Richtung Ruhleben. Dann sind es nur noch drei Stationen bis zum Sophie-Charlotte-Platz. Dort steigen Sie aus, und vom Sophie-Charlotte-Platz gehen Sie ungefähr fünf Minuten zu Fuß bis zur Danckelmannstraße.
Silke	Vielen Dank. Darf ich den Stadtplan mitnehmen?
Empfangsdame	Ja, natürlich. Bitte schön. (*Gibt ihr den Stadtplan.*) Ich wünsche Ihnen einen schönen Tag.
Silke	Danke schön.

Bemerkungen

die liegt in Charlottenburg note the colloquial use of **die** instead of **sie**; note also the use of **liegen** to denote location, where English would use the verb *to be*: *That's in Charlottenburg*.
schauen auf (+ Acc.) *to look at*
umsteigen* (sep.) *to change* (buses, trains, etc.)
aussteigen* (**ei, ie, ie**) (sep.) *to get off, out of* (a train, bus, car, etc.)
Can you spot the two examples of the command form (the imperative)? They are **Entschuldigen Sie** (*excuse*) and **Schauen Sie** (*look*). Some of the directions in this **Aufnahme** are given by using the present tense: **Sie fahren** (*you go*), **Sie steigen um** (*you change*), **Sie gehen** (*you walk*). When the subject **Sie** is not the first element in the main clause, the subject and verb are, as you know, inverted and might at first glance be taken for examples of the command form: **Am besten fahren Sie mit der U-bahn**.

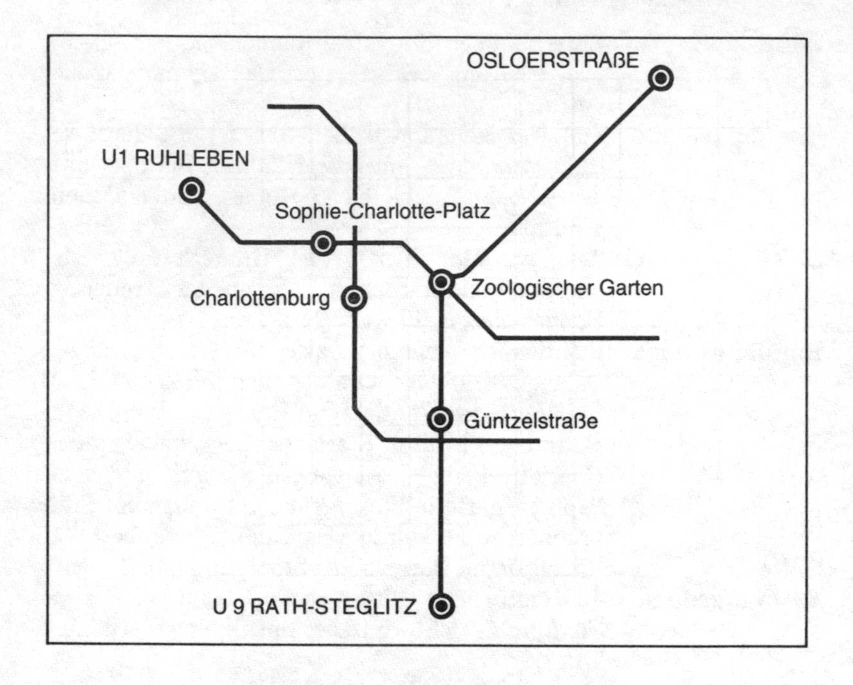

Rätsel

Fill in the boxes with the missing words. The name of one of Berlin's airports will be revealed vertically in the grid opposite (no. 11).

1 Die U-Bahn-Station Güntzelstraße liegt an der Kreuzung mit der ....
2 Silke beginnt ihre Frage mit dem Satz: .... Sie, bitte.
3 Zum Sophie-Charlotte-Platz nimmt Silke die U1 .... Ruhleben.
4 Die Empfangsdame wünscht Silke einen .... Tag.
5 Nach Charlottenburg fährt Silke am besten mit der ....
6 Silkes Freundin wohnt in der ....straße.
7 Von der U-Bahn-Station bis zur Wohnung von Silkes Freundin geht man ungefähr fünf Minuten zu ... .
8 Am Zoo muß Silke ....
9 Von der Güntzelstraße bis zum Zoo nimmt Silke die U9 Richtung .... Straße.
10 Silke fragt, ob sie den .... mitnehmen darf.

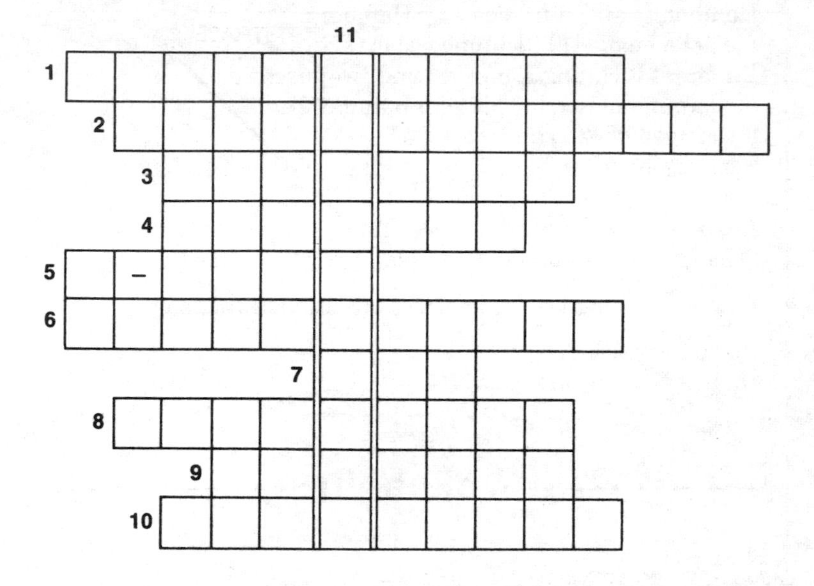

Redewendungen

- Announcing your intention to ask a question (the least formal version is listed first)

  Sag mal
  Sagen Sie mir, bitte, . . .
  Entschuldigen Sie, bitte.
  Können Sie mir sagen, . . .
  Ich hätte gern gewußt, . . .

- Asking for information

  Wie komme ich (am besten) in die Stadt?
  Was kostet die Busfahrt?
  Wie teuer wär's mit einem Taxi?
  Um wieviel Uhr startet die erste Maschine?
  Wann komme ich in Berlin an?
  Wo kann ich eine Karte lösen?

- Giving directions, offering advice

Du nimmst die A1 in Richtung Hamburg.
Sie nehmen die U9 Richtung Oslauer Straße.
Du fährst Richtung Hannover und Braunschweig.
Sie fahren mit der 109 bis zum Bahnhof Zoo.
Sie steigen am Zoo um.
Sie steigen am Sophie-Charlotte-Platz um.
Am besten fährst du mit der 109 bis zum Zoo.
Am besten fahren Sie mit einem Taxi.
Schauen Sie mal auf den Stadtplan.

- Expressing surprise at someone's intentions or actions

Bist du verrückt?!
Du bist ja wahnsinnig!

Vokabeln

Richtungen und Positionen (*Directions and positions*)

geradeaus	*straight on*	**gegenüber (von)** (+ Dat.)	*opposite*
links	*on the left*	**in der Nähe von** (+ Dat.)	*near*
rechts	*on the right*	**an der Ampel**	*at the traffic lights*
(nach) links	*to the left*	**an der Kreuzung**	*at the crossroads*
(nach) rechts	*to the right*	**um die Ecke**	*around the corner*

Gehen Sie hier geradeaus.
Nehmen Sie die erste Straße links.
Die Bäckerei ist das zweite Geschäft rechts.
Schau mal nach links!
Hier biegen Sie nach rechts ab.
Er wohnt gegenüber vom Rathaus.
Die Kirche ist in der Nähe vom Marktplatz.
An der Ampel biegt man nach links ab.
An der Kreuzung gehen Sie dann nach links.
Das Postamt finden Sie um die Ecke.

Grammatische Hinweise

Even advanced learners often need to be reminded of certain important points of grammar. Since cases fall into this category, it may be useful to take another look at them at this point. For quick reference purposes the forms of the definite and indefinite articles, possessive adjectives, and so on, in the various cases are given below.

1 Der, dieser *and* jener

		Singular		Plural
	Masculine	**Feminine**	**Neuter**	**All genders**
Nom.	der	die	das	die
	dieser	diese	dieses	diese
Acc.	den	die	das	die
	diesen	diese	dieses	diese
Gen.	des	der	des	der
	dieses	dieser	dieses	dieser
Dat.	dem	der	dem	den -n
	diesem	dieser	diesem	diesen -n

The endings on **jener**, **jene** and **jenes** are the same as those for **dieser**, **diese** and **dieses**.

2 Ein, kein *and* mein

		Singular		Plural
	Masculine	**Feminine**	**Neuter**	**All genders**
Nom.	ein	eine	ein	–
	kein	keine	kein	keine
Acc.	einen	eine	ein	–
	keinen	keine	kein	keine
Gen.	eines	einer	eines	–
	keines	keiner	keines	keiner
Dat.	einem	einer	einem	–
	keinem	keiner	keinem	keinen -n

The endings on **mein**, **dein**, **sein**, **ihr**, **Ihr**, **euer** and **unser** are the same as those for **ein** and **kein**.

3 The nominative

The nominative (**der Nominativ**) is used to indicate the subject of a verb:

Subject Nominative case	Verb	
Der letzte Flug (*m. sing.*)	startet	um 17.40 Uhr.
Mein Hotel (*n. sing.*)	liegt	in der Güntzelstraße.
Bernd und Silke (*pl.*)	wohnen	in Münster.

The nominative is also used after the verbs **bleiben**, **heißen**, **scheinen**, **sein** and **werden**:

Sie scheint eine gute Studentin zu sein.	*She seems to be a good student.*
Und du willst mein bester Freund sein!	*And you claim to be my best friend!*

4 The accusative

The accusative (**der Akkusativ**) is used (*a*) for the direct object of a verb and (*b*) after certain prepositions:

(*a*) Direct object

Subject Nominative case	Verb		Object Accusative case
Sie	sehen		die Haltestelle. (*f. sing.*)
Der Tourist	möchte		eine Fahrkarte (*f. sing.*) lösen.
Wir	hätten	dann	keine Parkprobleme. (*f. pl.*)
Der Gast	darf		den Stadtplan (*m. sing.*) mitnehmen.
Ich	wünsche	Ihnen	einen schönen Tag. (*m. sing.*)

Remember that the article or determiner (**ein**, **der**, **dieser**, **mein**, etc.) differs from the nominative form only with masculine singular nouns. The letter typical of the accusative masculine case is -**n**.

(*b*) Prepositions

The accusative is used with the following prepositions: **bis**, **durch**, **für**, **gegen**, **ohne**, **um**.

Also, **bis nächste Woche!**
Durch diesen Ausgang, dann nach links.
Wie lange brauche ich ungefähr **für die ganze Fahrt?**
Für mich alleine.
Ich habe nichts **gegen ihn**.
Ohne mich!
Das Postamt finden Sie **um die Ecke**.

5 The dative

The dative (**der Dativ**) is used (*a*) for the indirect object of a verb and (*b*) after certain prepositions:

(*a*) Indirect object

Subject **Nominative case**	**Verb**	**Indirect object** **Dative case**	**Direct object** **Accusative case**
Die Empfangsdame	erklärt	dem Gast (*m. sing.*)	den Weg.
Frau Werner	gibt	der Kundin (*f. sing.*)	einen Stadtplan.
Der Kellner	bringt	dem Herrn (*m. sing.*)	einen Kaffee.
Diese Mutter	erzählt	ihrem Kind (*n. sing.*)	eine Geschichte.
Ich	zeige	meinen Gästen (*m. pl.*)	die Stadt.

Note that certain verbs are followed by the dative, for example **danken, helfen** and **gefallen** (more on this on page 124).

The letters typical of the dative case are **-m** (for the masculine and neuter singular), **-r** (for the feminine singular) and **-n** (for the plural of all genders). Remember that in the dative plural the **-n** is added to the noun as well as the article or determiner, where possible.

(*b*) Prepositions

The dative is used with the following prepositions: **aus, außer, bei, gegenüber, mit, nach, seit, von, zu**

Aus ihrem Hotel kamen gerade Hunderte von Touristen.
Außer der Empfangsdame war niemand in der Eingangshalle.
Elke wohnt noch **bei ihren Eltern**.
Du bekommst eine Fahrkarte **beim Fahrer**.
Unser Hotel liegt **gegenüber dem Kino**.

Wie komme ich **mit dem Wagen** nach Berlin?
Mit deiner Ente brauchst du fünf bis sechs Stunden für die 460 Kilometer nach Berlin.
Wenn ich **mit meiner Chefin** rede . . .
Ich habe vor, Freitag **nach der Arbeit** loszufahren.
Ich werde mich **nach den Flügen** erkundigen.
Ich kenne Bernd und Silke **seit vielen Jahren**.
Vom Flughafen fahren Sie mit der 109 bis **zum Bahnhof Zoo**.
Heutzutage kommt es sehr oft **zu Stauungen**.

6 Accusative or dative?

With the following prepositions the accusative is used when direction is being indicated (answering the questions **wohin?**). The dative is used when position or location is being indicated (answering the question **wo?**): **an**, **auf**, **entlang**, **hinter**, **in**, **neben**, **über**, **unter**, **vor**, **zwischen**

Direction:
Wenn du **ans Kreuz Lotte–Osnabrück** kommst, nimmst du die A30.
Bei Bad Oeynhausen kommst du **auf die A2**.
Schauen Sie mal hier **auf den Stadtplan**.
Sie gehen **den Kurfürstendamm entlang** bis zur Uhlandstraße.
Wie komme ich am besten **in die Stadtmitte**?
Sie müssen **hinter das Hotel** fahren. Dort gibt es Parkplätze.
Normalerweise muß ich um 8.00 Uhr **ins Büro**.
Gehen Sie an der Ampel **über die Straße**.

Position / location:
Am Kreuz Lotte–Osnabrück nimmst du die A30.
An welchem Tag wollten Sie eigentlich fliegen?
Du fährst **auf der A2** bis nach Berlin.
Ich sehe mal **auf dem Stadtplan** nach.
Entlang dem Kurfürstendamm finden Sie viele Restaurants.
In der Stadtmitte findet man viele Geschäfte.
Hinter dem Hotel war ein schöner Garten.
Dann wäre ich erst gegen 9.00 Uhr **im Büro**.
Über der Straße hängt eine Lampe.

Unser Hotel liegt **zwischen dem Hauptbahnhof und einer Diskothek.**

7 The genitive

The genitive (**der Genitiv**) is used (*a*) to indicate possession and (*b*) after certain prepositions.

(*a*) Possession

The genitive covers what in English is expressed either by the 'possessive' '*s* or by *of*:

das Haus meines Bruders	*my brother's house*
am Ende des Monats	*at the end of the month*
das Auto unserer Freunde	*our friends' car*

The genitive is often avoided, particularly in informal German, by using the preposition **von** (+ Dat.):

Das Haus von meinem Bruder.
Das Auto von unseren Freunden.

(*b*) Prepositions

The genitive is used with the following prepositions: **angesichts**, **(an)statt**, **ausschließlich**, **außerhalb**, **beiderseits**, **bezüglich**, **diesseits**, **einschließlich**, **exklusiv**, **innerhalb**, **inklusiv**, **jenseits**, **laut**, **trotz**, **während**, **wegen:**

Angesichts des schlechten Wetters . . .	*In view of the bad weather . . .*
Diesseits der Grenze . . .	*On this side of the border . . .*
Einschließlich aller Steuern . . .	*Inclusive of all taxes . . .*
Trotz des Regens . . .	*In spite of the rain . . .*
Wegen hoher Verkehrsdichte . . .	*On account of the high volume of traffic . . .*
Während ihres Lebens . . .	*During her life . . .*

Informally and colloquially the dative is often used instead of the genitive with such prepositions as **trotz**, **wegen** and **während**:

Trotz dem schlechten Wetter . . .	*Despite the bad weather . . .*
Wegen dem Regen . . .	*On account of the rain . . .*
Während dem Krieg . . .	*During the war . . .*

Read through the **Aufnahmen** again, looking out specifically for examples of case and gender.

Übungen

1 Bestimmen Sie in den folgenden Sätzen den Dativ bzw. den Akkusativ. (*Identify the dative/accusative in the following sentences.*)

Beispiele

Heute abend gehe ich in das Theater.	in das Theater = Akk.
In diesem Theater wird oft Goethe gespielt.	in diesem Theater = Dat.
Die nette Dame erklärte mir den Weg.	mir = Dat.; den Weg = Akk.

(*a*) Wie komme ich mit dem Wagen nach Berlin?
(*b*) Wie lange brauche ich für die ganze Fahrt?
(*c*) Ich werde mich nach den Flügen erkundigen.
(*d*) Ohne dich ist es langweilig.
(*e*) Ich bin schon seit einer Stunde so müde.
(*f*) Ich brauche morgen früh einen Stadtplan.
(*g*) Hast du dir auch einen Kaffee bestellt?
(*h*) Kannst du mir vielleicht den Koffer tragen?
(*i*) Ich wünsche dir alles Gute.
(*j*) Wir haben auf unserer Reise so viel Spaß gehabt!

2 In the following hotel advertisement some of the articles (**ein**, **der**, etc.) and personal pronouns (**Sie**, **Ihnen**, etc.) have been erased. You are asked to supply the correct forms of the missing words. Since this is a grammar exercise in which gender and case are crucial to achieving accuracy, some vocabulary assistance is given below.

der Blick (-e) (**über** + Acc.) *view*
der See (-n) *lake*
der Bummel (-) *stroll*
der Luxus *luxury*
der Rahmen (-) *framework*
sich freuen auf (+ Acc.) *to look forward to*
unter (+ Dat.) *among*

25 JAHRE Inmitten der Metropole Berlin liegt das Hotel Seehof. Unsere romantische Seeterrasse und die Hotelzimmer bieten (*a*) (*b*) wunderschönen Blick über (*c*) Lietzensee und Entspannung nach (*d*) Stadtbummel.

In (*e*) First Class Hotel genießen Sie (*f*) exklusiven Luxus (*g*) 4-Sterne Oase mit sehr persönlicher Atmosphäre. Das Hotel Seehof Berlin bietet Tagungsgästen (*h*) idealen Rahmen für Geschäftstreffen jeder Art.

Wir freuen uns auf (*i*) Besuch!

Hotel Seehof Berlin am Lietzensee

Das Besondere unter (*j*)
Erstklassigen
Lietzensee-Ufer 11
14057 Berlin · Telefon 32 00 20
nahe ICC und Kurfürstendamm

3 Sehen Sie sich den Flugplan auf Seite 6 an. Eine Sekretärin ruft beim Reisebüro an, um sich für ihre Chefin nach den Flügen Berlin München zu erkundigen. Spielen Sie die Rolle vom Herrn im Reisebüro. Wenn Sie keine Kassette haben, schreiben Sie Ihre Antworten auf. Eine mögliche Lösung finden Sie im Lösungsteil.

Sekretärin Meine Chefin möchte am kommenden Mittwoch nach München fliegen. Wann geht die erste Maschine?

Sie (*a*)

Sekretärin Das ist natürlich mit Lufthansa, oder?

Sie (*b*)

Sekretärin Ach so, meine Chefin fliegt lieber mit Lufthansa. Gibt es denn mittwochs früh keinen Lufthansa-Flug?

Sie (*c*)
Sekretärin Wann landet die Maschine in München?
Sie (*d*)
Sekretärin Wann ist am gleichen Tag der letzte Flug zurück nach Berlin?
Sie (*e*)
Sekretärin Und die Ankunftszeit, bitte?
Sie (*f*)

4 You are living and working in Berlin. You need to make a business trip to Munich on Wednesday of next week. Before you phone your travel agent you decide to draw up in German a list of questions that you will want to ask. You will want to know when the first plane leaves for Munich, which airline (**die Fluglinie**) this is with, when this flight arrives in Munich, when the last Lufthansa flight leaves Munich for the return journey and when you will arrive back in Berlin.

When you write down your list of questions, leave room for the travel agent's answers. Using the flight schedule on page 6, write down what you think the travel agent would say. You should end up with a complete dialogue between yourself and the travel agent. A model version is given in the **Lösungsteil** but your own answers may vary slightly from those given.

5 Verbinden Sie die Satzpaare, um jeweils einen einzigen Satz zu bilden. Fangen Sie entweder mit **trotz** oder mit **wegen** an. (*Join the pairs of sentences to form a single sentence in each case. Start either with* ***trotz*** *or with* ***wegen****. Note that an adjective in a genitive phrase ends in* ***-en****.*)

Beispiele

Das Wetter ist so schlecht. Wir bleiben also heute zu Hause.
Wegen des schlechten Wetters bleiben wir heute zu Hause.
Der Preis ist zwar teuer. Wir wollen aber den neuen Mercedes kaufen.
Trotz des teu(e)ren Preises wollen wir den neuen Mercedes kaufen.

(*a*) Der Verkehr ist so dicht. Wir müssen also eine halbe Stunde früher abfahren.

(*b*) Dieser Stadtplan ist zwar gut. Wir finden den Weg aber nicht.

(c) Die Busfahrt nach Berlin ist zwar billig. Ich möchte aber lieber fliegen.
(d) Das Wetter ist so kalt. Wir wollen also heute nicht spazieren gehen.
(e) Die Maschine war zwar neu. Der Flug war aber sehr unbequem.
(f) Der Rückflug nach Münster ist Sonntag abend zwar spät. Ich möchte aber lieber dann als Montag früh zurückfliegen.
(g) Unsere finanziellen Probleme sind so schwierig. Wir können also dieses Jahr nicht in Urlaub fahren.
(h) Die Unterkunft ist zwar modern. Die Touristen finden diese Preise aber zu hoch.

6 With the assistance of the prompts in English play the role of the person giving directions. Note that in German street names ending in **-er** do not change their endings (**Konstanzer Straße, Düsseldorfer Straße**, etc.) but street names ending in **-isch** take the normal adjectival endings (e.g. **Gehen Sie rechts in die Bayerisch*e* Straße**, but **Wir sind hier in der Bayerisch*en* Straße**).

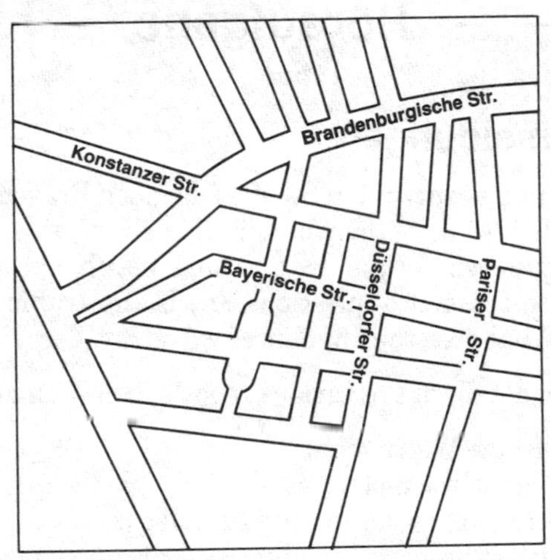

Tourist Entschuldigen Sie, bitte. Wie komme ich zur Pariser Straße?

Sie *Tell him that you're now in Brandenburgische Straße. Ask whether he can see the traffic lights at the next crossroads.*

Tourist Ja, die sehe ich.

Sie *Tell him to go right there into Düsseldorfer Straße. After about 300 metres he'll come to Konstanzer Straße. He should go over Konstanzer Straße, straight on for perhaps 300 metres further till he gets to Bayerische Straße. Then he should go left at this crossroads into Bayerische Straße.*

Tourist Moment, bitte. Was sagten Sie? Hier rechts, dann geradeaus bis zur Düsseldorfer Straße, über die Düsseldorfer Straße und weiter geradeaus bis zur Bayerischen Straße. Dann rechts.

Sie *Tell him, he doesn't go right but left into Bayerische Straße. Then about 1 km further on he'll come to Pariser Straße.*

Tourist Vielen Dank.

Sie *You say that he's welcome.*

Höraufgabe

Verkehrsmeldungen

Hören Sie zu und beantworten Sie die folgenden Fragen.

1 Even though some of the words in this short message will probably be unknown to you, you should be able to work out the answers to these two questions: (*a*) Is the traffic news good or bad? (*b*) What does the announcer wish travellers?

2 Fill in the details of the various reports (below and on page 24).

In North-Rhine Westphalia:
(*a*) Number of the motorway
(*b*) Direction of carriageway with tailback
(*c*) Length of tailback

In Baden-Württemberg (first report):
(*d*) Number of motorway
(*e*) Direction of carriageway with tailback
(*f*) Length of tailback

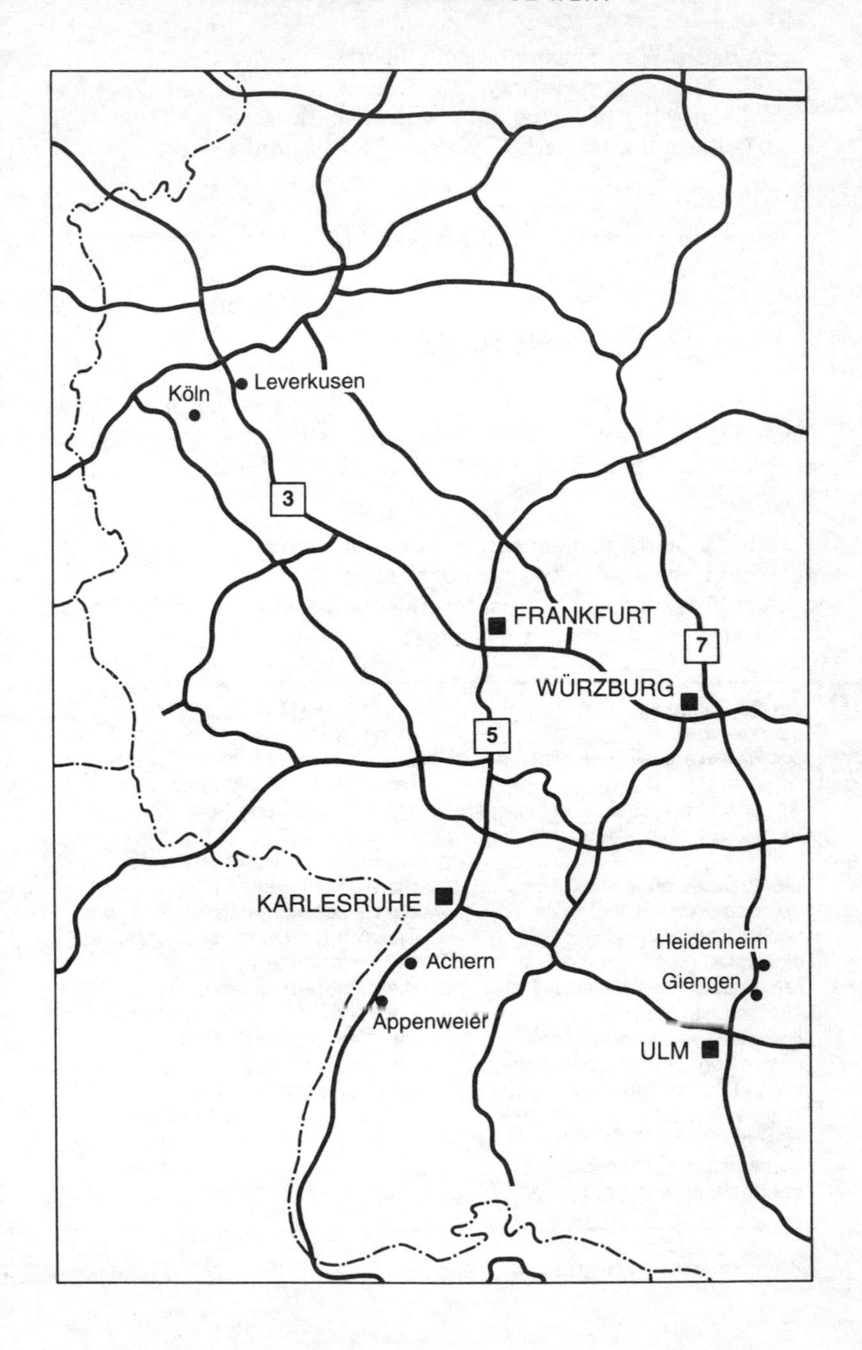
Köln
Leverkusen
3
FRANKFURT
7
WÜRZBURG
5
KARLESRUHE
Heidenheim
Achern
Giengen
Appenweier
ULM

In Baden-Württemberg (second report):
(*g*) Number of motorway
(*h*) Direction of carriageway with tailback
(*i*) Length of tailback

Lesetexte

1 Kurzreise nach Berlin

The leaflet opposite is advertising a short break in Berlin for people from Münster. Read the text to see what is on offer, paying special attention to the following points and noting the new vocabulary below:

- What is on the plan for the four days in Berlin.
- What is included in the price of the trip.
- Additional information concerning the booking of tickets for the theatre and other cultural events.

der EZ-Zuschlag *single-room supplement*
der Reiseverlauf *tour plan* (Lit. tour course)
Änderungen vorbehalten *subject to alteration* (Lit. alterations reserved)
die Zusteigemöglichkeit (-en) *pick-up point* (Lit. getting-on possibility)
einrichten (sep.) *to arrange*
reichhaltig *substantial, full* (referring to breakfast)
belegen *to occupy* (a room)
ansonsten *otherwise*
zur freien Verfügung (stehen) (*to be*) *at leisure* (Lit. at the free disposal)
gemeinsam *communal*
die Besichtigung (-en) *sightseeing*
die Führung (-en) *guided tour*
es empfiehlt sich . . . *. . . is recommended*
rechtzeitig *timely, in good time*
die Veranstaltung (-en) *event*
die Leistungen (f. pl.) *what is included* (Lit. achievements)
die Mahlzeit (-en) *meal*
die Reisebegleitung *courier in attendance* (Lit. tour accompaniment)
der Teilnehmer (-) *participant*
die Zahl (-en) *number*
erforderlich *required, necessary*
das Verkehrsamt *tourist information office*
das Kolpingwerk *Kolping organisation* (named after the Catholic priest Adolf Kolping 1813 – 1865, who founded the movement in 1849)

Now answer the questions on page 26.

KURZREISE BERLIN

BERLINFAHRT
21.–24. Oktober
Preis: 385,– – DM
EZ-Zuschlag
REISEVERLAUF
(Änderungen vorbehalten)

SONNTAG/MONTAGNACHT

Abfahrt um 1.00 Uhr.
Zusteigemöglichkeiten werden eingerichtet.

MONTAG BIS DONNERSTAG

Ankunft um 8.00 Uhr in Berlin zu einem reichhaltigen Frühstücksbuffet im Cafe Kranzler.
Zimmerbelegung. Kleine Stadtrundfahrt mit ersten wichtigen Informationen.
Ansonsten steht der Nachmittag zur freien Verfügung.
Abends gemeinsames Abendessen.

Große Stadtrundfahrt mit Besuchen und Besichtigungen.
Abends gemeinsames Abendessen.

Besichtigung des Schlosses Charlottenburg mit Führung.

Zur freien Verfügung,
Besuch in Potsdam.
Gem. Mittagessen, Rückfahrt.

Es empfiehlt sich eine rechtzeitige Buchung von Theaterkarten.

INFORMATIONEN UND ANFRAGEN

Theater- und Kulturprogramm über: Agentur Otfried Laur, Hardenbergstr. 7, 10623 Berlin, Tel. 030/3137007
Einstrittskarten für alle Veranstaltungen können dort bestellt werden!

Andere Informationen:
Verkehrsamt Berlin, Europa Center, Tel. 030/211234

LEISTUNGEN

Busfahrt hin und zurück,
3 Übernachtungen mit Frühstück,
1 Frühstücksbuffet am Ankunftsmorgen, 3 warme Mahlzeiten gem. Programm, Führungen und Besichtigungen gem. Programm, Reisebegleitung während der ganzen Reise, Komfort-Reisebus.

Eine Mindestteilnehmerzahl ist erforderlich!

„MIT KOLPING REISEN"
Kolpingwerk
Diözesanverband Münster
Krumme Str. 9
48143 Münster
Tel. 0251/4 24 38

Beantworten Sie die folgenden Fragen auf Englisch:

1 What is said about pick-up points for commencing the journey?
2 What is on the schedule for the day of arrival in Berlin?
3 On which days is dinner offered as part of the package?
4 On which day is neither lunch nor dinner offered?
5 What is planned for Wednesday?
6 What is on the schedule for Thursday before the return journey?
7 What seven items does the package include?
8 What recommendation is made concerning theatre tickets?
9 What condition is stated for the tour taking place?
10 Where can further information about Berlin be obtained from?

Stadtrundfahrten für Anspruchsvolle
Ostberlin, Westberlin und Umgebung exklusiv
im 8-Personen-Kleinbus einmal ganz anders erleben
KAIBEL & ERDMANN ☎ 686 00 62

Stadtrundfahrten individuell
im 8-Personen-Kleinbus Ost- oder Westteil Berlins und Umgebung mit
Kunick und Bürger
Sofortservice: Funktel. 0161/1 30 29 18 · Vorbestellung: (9) 5 61 46 79

SKIP - MIETWAGEN MIT CHAUFFEUR
KLEINBUSSE der EXTRA-KLASSE ! ! !
Bordservice • mobil phone & fax
auch MERCEDES-LIMOUSINEN verfügbar ! !
TEL.: 030/262 87 41
• Transfer
• ind. Ausflüge
• Reisen von u. nach Berlin
• Touristikbetreuung mit Stadtführer & Dolmetscher
SKIP • Thomas Moritz • Kurmärkische Str. 12 • 1000 Berlin 30

2 Eine Fahrt durch Berlin

Here is an advertisement for Berlin's public transport system. Read it through and see if you can make out the following:

- what a car driver visiting Berlin gets to see of the city.
- what impressions visitors have of Berlin if they use the various means of public transport.

- what the tip at the end of the advertisement draws attention to.

Berlin – ein bißchen von oben herab betrachtet

Der normale Berlin-Besucher besucht Berlin mit dem Auto. Natürlich sieht auch er viel von der Stadt, aber auf dem Weg von einer Sehenswürdigkeit zur anderen sieht er hauptsächlich hintere Stoßstangen. Anders der BVG-Benutzer: Vom Oberdeck des Busses blickt er ganz entspannt auf das Leben in der Stadt herab, beim U-Bahn-Fahren taucht er total in den Schnellkurs in ‚Berlinern als Muttersprache' ein, und wenn er mit der S-Bahn ins Grüne oder Blaue fährt, fährt er vorher noch mitten durch die Berliner Hinterhöfe. Am Ende hat er neben dem Touristen-Berlin so viel vom Berliner-Berlin gesehen, daß er normale Besucher der Stadt womöglich ein ganz klein wenig von oben herab betrachtet.

Besonderer Tip:
Mit dem BVG-24-Stunden-Ticket können Sie 24 Stunden lang alle Busse, alle U-, S- und Straßenbahnen und sogar die Linienschiffe der BVG benutzen.

betrachten *to look at, observe*
von oben herab betrachten *to look down on* (also: condescendingly)
die Sehenswürdigkeit (**-en**) *sight*
hauptsächlich *mainly*
die Stoßstange (**-n**) *bumper*
BVG *Berliner Verkehrs-Betriebe*
der Benutzer (-) *user*
das Oberdeck *top deck.* Berlin has double-decker buses
herabblicken auf (+ Acc.) (sep.) *to look down on*
entspannt *relaxed*
eintauchen* in (+ Acc.) (sep.) *to immerse* (oneself) *in*
der Schnellkurs *rapid course*
berlinern *to speak Berlin dialect*
die Muttersprache *mother tongue.* Compare **Deutsch als Fremdsprache** (*German as a foreign language*)
ins Grüne fahren* *to take a trip into the country(side)*
ins Blaue fahren* *to go on a mystery tour*
mitten durch (+ Acc.) *through the midst of*
der Hinterhof (¨**e**) *courtyard.* Many Berlin apartment blocks are built around inner courtyards
neben (+ Dat.) *near, next to;* here: *in addition to*
womöglich *possibly*
die Straßenbahn (**-en**) *tram*
das Linienschiff (**-e**) *company ship;* ship belonging to the Berlin transport system
benutzen *to use*

Beantworten Sie:

1 Womit besucht der normale Berlin-Besucher Berlin?
2 Was sieht er auf dem Weg von einer Sehenswürdigkeit zur anderen?
3 Von wo kann der BVG-Benutzer ganz entspannt auf das Leben in der Stadt herabblicken?
4 Wann taucht er total in den Schnellkurs in »Berlinern als Muttersprache« ein?
5 Womit kann der BVG-Benutzer ins Grüne oder ins Blaue fahren?
6 Was sieht man, wenn man mit der S-Bahn durch Berlin fährt?
7 Warum kann der BVG-Benutzer normale Besucher der Stadt womöglich ein ganz klein wenig von oben herab betrachten?
8 Womit kann man 24 Stunden lang alle Verkehrsmittel der BVG benutzen?

Testen Sie Ihr Wissen

Schätzen Sie: Wie lang ist das Autobahnnetz in Deutschland?

1 6500 Kilometer
2 8300 Kilometer
3 10 800 Kilometer

2
MEIN TAGESABLAUF

Lernziele

In this unit you will learn how to

- talk about daily routines
- express frequency and sequence of events
- form and use the present tense
- use pronouns – demonstrative and personal

Aufnahmen

1 Lorenz Müller: Universitätslehrer

Lorenz Müller, 26, Lehrer an der Friedrich-Schiller-Universität Jena, erzählt, wie sein Tagesablauf an Wochentagen und am Wochende aussieht.

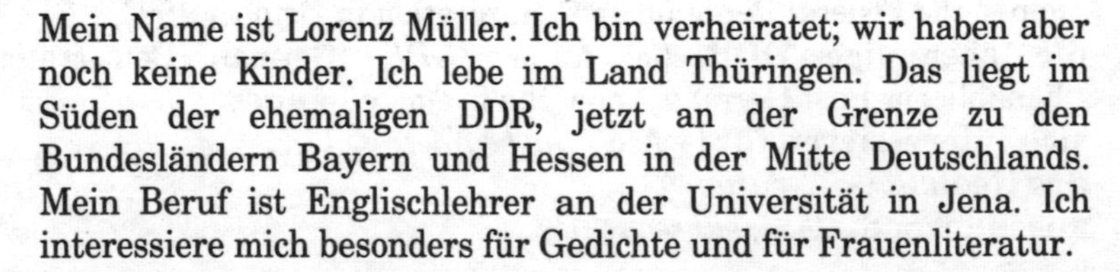

Mein Name ist Lorenz Müller. Ich bin verheiratet; wir haben aber noch keine Kinder. Ich lebe im Land Thüringen. Das liegt im Süden der ehemaligen DDR, jetzt an der Grenze zu den Bundesländern Bayern und Hessen in der Mitte Deutschlands. Mein Beruf ist Englischlehrer an der Universität in Jena. Ich interessiere mich besonders für Gedichte und für Frauenliteratur.

Mein Tagesablauf beginnt morgens gegen halb acht, wenn ich aufstehe, und anschließend frühstücke. Zum Frühstück esse ich normalerweise Brötchen mit Marmelade oder mit Nutella und trinke eine Tasse Kaffee, türkisch.

Meistens gehe ich aber dann erst mittags in die Stadt, in die Universität, weil meine Seminare erst später stattfinden. So habe ich also Zeit, am Vormittag zu Hause am Schreibtisch zu arbeiten, Seminare vorzubereiten, beziehungsweise zu lesen. Zur Arbeit fahre ich meistens mit dem Bus, aber manchmal laufe ich auch in die Stadt – es sind nur zehn Minuten zu Fuß.

Meine Seminare beginnen meistens erst am frühen Nachmittag oder sogar erst am frühen Abend. Mittagspause habe ich zwischen zwölf und zwei. Ich esse dann in der Mensa. Wenn ich keine Seminare habe, komme ich dann am frühen Nachmittag nach Hause, gehe einkaufen oder erledige, was sonst an Arbeit in der Wohnung anfällt. Am Abend lese ich ausgiebig die Zeitung, schaue Nachrichten im Fernsehen, manchmal dann noch einen Film. Gewöhnlich lese ich aber etwas, beziehungsweise höre Radio oder eine Schallplatte.

Am Wochenende besuchen wir öfters Freunde, gehen essen, besuchen die Schwiegereltern oder gehen ein wenig spazieren. Aber es muß auch all die Arbeit getan werden, die während der Woche liegengeblieben ist. Es wird gewaschen, saubergemacht, aufgeräumt.

Hobbys habe ich insofern keine, da glücklicherweise mein Beruf mein Hobby geworden ist. Ich beschäftige mich ausgiebig mit der Literatur und schreibe auch selbst.

Bemerkungen

der Tagesablauf *daily routine*
Thüringen one of the five new **Länder** or federal states which joined the Federal Republic upon unification in October 1990
die ehemalige DDR *the former GDR* (German Democratic Republic) or East Germany, now the five new **Länder**
sich interessieren für (+ Acc.) *to be interested in*
das Gedicht (-e) *poem*
anschließend *then, subsequently*

normalerweise *normally*
die Marmelade *jam*
meistens *mostly, usually*
erst mittags *not until lunchtime*
stattfinden (i, a, u) (sep.) *to take place*
vorbereiten (sep.) *to prepare*
beziehungsweise *alternatively*
zehn Minuten zu Fuß *a ten-minute walk*
sogar *even*
die Mensa *refectory, university dining-hall*
erledigen *to deal with, attend to*
sonst *otherwise*
anfallen (ä, ie, a) (sep.) *to come up* (of work)
ausgiebig *thoroughly*
öfters *fairly often*
die Schwiegereltern *parents-in-law*
tun (**u, a, a**) *to do*
liegenbleiben* (sep.) *to be left over, undone*
waschen (**ä, u, a**) *to wash*
saubermachen (sep.) *to clean*
aufräumen (sep.) *to clear up*

Note the special use of the passive in the three following examples:

es wird gewaschen *washing is done*; (here: *we do the washing*)
es wird saubergemacht *cleaning is done*; (here: *we do the cleaning*)
es wird aufgeräumt *clearing up is done*; (here: *we do the clearing up*)

glücklicherweise *fortunately*
sich beschäftigen mit *to concern oneself with*

Richtig oder falsch?

Korrigieren Sie die falschen Aussagen.

1 Lorenz ist verheiratet.
2 Er hat zwei Kinder.
3 Er lebt im Land Thüringen.
4 Das ist im Norden der ehemaligen DDR.
5 Er ist Englischlehrer von Beruf.
6 Er ist Lehrer an der Universität in Jena.
7 Er interessiert sich für Frauenliteratur.

8 Lorenz steht um halb sieben auf.
9 Zum Frühstück ißt er meistens Brötchen mit Marmelade oder Nutella.
10 Zum Frühstück trinkt er eine Tasse Tee.
11 Seine Seminare finden meistens erst am frühen Nachmittag oder sogar erst am frühen Abend statt.
12 Er hat deshalb Zeit, am Vormittag zu Hause im Garten zu arbeiten und einkaufen zu gehen.
13 Von zu Hause kann er in zehn Minuten in die Stadt laufen.
14 Zu Mittag ißt Lorenz zu Hause.
15 Am Abend liest er kurz die Zeitung.
16 Er hört Nachrichten im Radio.
17 Am Wochenende müssen Lorenz und seine Frau all die Arbeit erledigen, die sie während der Woche nicht gemacht haben.
18 Sein Beruf ist auch sein Hobby.

2 Corinnna Wolfram: Kellnerin

Corinna Wolfram ist 22 Jahre alt und arbeitet als Kellnerin in München. Sie ist vor zwei Jahren von Würzburg nach München gezogen.

Martina Corinna, du bist 22 Jahre alt, wohnst seit zwei Jahren in München und arbeitest als Kellnerin. Wie sieht eigentlich dein Tagesablauf aus?

Corinna Es kommt darauf an, ob ich Frühschicht oder Spätschicht arbeiten muß. Wir haben nämlich in der Gaststätte, wo ich arbeite, bis um Mitternacht durchgehend geöffnet. Wenn ich Spätschicht mache, komme ich erst gegen eins, halb zwei nach Hause. Ich stelle mich dann schnell unter die Dusche und gehe sofort ins Bett. Am nächsten Tag stehe ich dann meistens erst um neun oder halb zehn auf. Zum Frühstück trinke ich ein Glas Orangen- oder Grapefruitsaft und manchmal esse ich auch eine Scheibe Toast mit Marmelade oder Honig.

Martina Da hast du dann ein paar Stunden Freizeit, oder?

Corinna Ja. Bis 4.00 Uhr nachmittags kann ich machen, was ich will. Einmal in der Woche bringe ich meine Wäsche zum Waschsalon. Ab und zu räume ich mein Zimmer auf. Aber das nimmt nicht allzuviel Zeit in Anspruch.

Martina Was machst du also mit deiner Freizeit?

Corinna Zweimal in der Woche – montags und mittwochs – habe ich Englischstunden. Da wir in der Gaststätte so viele Ausländer haben, versuche ich, meine Englischkenntnisse aufzufrischen. Sonst gehe ich mit meinem Freund ins Kino oder wir fahren nach Starnberg zum Windsurfen auf dem Starnberger See.

Martina Und wie oft siehst du deine Eltern?

Corinna Höchstens viermal im Jahr zu Weihnachten und bei Geburtstagen. Die wohnen ja in Würzburg, was ziemlich weit weg ist.

Martina Und wie ist es mit dem Essen? Bekommst du deine Mahlzeiten hier im Restaurant umsonst?

Corinna Oh, ja. Das versteht sich von selbst. In meinem Zimmer habe ich nur eine Kochnische mit einer Heizplatte und einem kleinen Kühlschrank.

Bemerkungen

die Kellnerin (-nen) *waitress*
vor zwei Jahren (Dat.) *two years ago*
ziehen* (**ie, o, o**) *to move*
eigentlich *actually*
Wie sieht . . . aus? *What does . . . look like?*
Es kommt darauf an, ob . . . *It depends whether . . .*
die Schicht (**-en**) *shift*
die Gaststätte *public house, restaurant*
durchgehend geöffnet *open all day*
Ich stelle mich unter die Dusche. *I take a shower*. Note that while you can say in German **Ich nehme ein Bad**, you cannot use **nehmen** with **Dusche**. Instead you use a variety of expressions, such as the one here or **Ich dusche mich**
sofort *immediately*
der Saft *juice*
die Scheibe (**-n**) *slice*
der Honig *honey*
die Wäsche *washing, laundry*
der Waschsalon *launderette*
in Anspruch nehmen *to take up, make demands on*

allzuviel *too much*
versuchen *to try*
meine Englischkenntnisse (f. pl.) *my (knowledge of) English*
auffrischen (sep.) *to freshen up, polish up*
der Starnberger See a large lake about 20 km from Munich, renowned for its water sports
höchstens *at the most*
zu Weihnachten *at Christmas*
bei Geburtstagen *on birthdays*
umsonst bekommen *to get free of charge*
die Kochnische (**-n**) *small cooking area* (Lit. cooking niche)
die Heizplatte (**-n**) *hotplate*
der Kühlschrank (**¨e**) *refrigerator*

Welche Antwort paßt?

1 Corinna, seit wann wohnst du in München?
(*a*) Ich bin jetzt 22 Jahre alt.
(*b*) Ich bin vor zwei Jahren hierher gezogen.
(*c*) Höchstens viermal im Jahr.

2 Was machst du, wenn du nach der Spätschicht nach Hause kommst?
(*a*) Es kommt darauf an, ob ich Frühschicht oder Spätschicht mache.
(*b*) Bis 4.00 Uhr nachmittags kann ich machen, was ich will.
(*c*) Ich stelle mich unter die Dusche und gehe sofort ins Bett.

3 Warum machst du Englischstunden?
(*a*) Weil wir in der Gaststätte so viele Ausländer haben.
(*b*) Weil ich so gut Englisch spreche.
(*c*) Weil das nicht allzuviel Zeit in Anspruch nimmt.

4 Treibst du Sport?
(*a*) Ja, einmal in der Woche bringe ich meine Wäsche zum Waschsalon.
(*b*) Oh ja. Das versteht sich von selbst.
(*c*) Ja, ich gehe ziemlich oft zum Windsurfen.

5 Gehst du oft deine Eltern besuchen?
(*a*) Ja, jedes Jahr im Sommer fahre ich hin.
(*b*) Leider nur viermal im Jahr.

(*c*) Nein, sie wohnen in der nächsten Straße.

6 Bekommst du deine Mahlzeiten im Restaurant umsonst?
(*a*) Ja, das versteht sich auch von selbst.
(*b*) Ja, ich nehme meine Mahlzeiten mit ins Restaurant.
(*c*) Nein, im Restaurant gibt es nichts zum Essen.

Sagen Sie's auf Deutsch!

Which phrases in the recording with Corinna were used to express the following?

1 It (all) depends . . .
2 around one (o'clock)
3 I'll take a quick shower.
4 a slice of toast
5 now and again
6 four times a year at most
7 at Christmas
8 on birthdays

3 Frau Beitz: Rentnerin

Frau Beitz, 78, ist Rentnerin und Witwe. Sie wohnt allein in der Lübecker Innenstadt.

Paul Frau Beitz, Sie sind Rentnerin und wohnen hier allein. Wird Ihnen nicht manchmal langweilig?

Frau Beitz Aber nein! Mir wird nie langweilig. Es gibt ja allerhand zu tun. Meistens stehe ich schon um 7.00 Uhr auf. Ich hole dann ein paar Brötchen von der Bäckerei und koche Kaffee. Ich frühstücke ganz gemächlich – im Sommer sitze ich in der Morgensonne auf meinem Balkon. Anschließend lese ich die Zeitung. Ich interessiere mich nämlich sehr für Politik.

Paul Sehen Sie auch fern?

Frau Beitz Ja, aber erst abends, und dann nur selten. Während des Tages gehe ich lieber eine von meinen Freundinnen besuchen, oder wir gehen zusammen im Stadtpark spazieren. Gelegentlich esse ich in einem Restaurant zu Mittag.

Paul Haben Sie Familie?

Frau Beitz Ja, mein Sohn Helmut kommt mich fast immer am Wochenende besuchen. Er wohnt mit seiner Frau in Hamburg, also gar nicht weit weg. Wir machen dann samstags oder sonntags schöne Ausflüge in die Umgebung – mal die Ostseeküste entlang nach Wismar oder Rostock, mal in nördlicher Richtung nach Kiel oder Flensburg.

Paul Haben Sie irgendwelche Hobbys?

Frau Beitz Ich stricke gern. Ich bin gerade dabei, einen Pullover für meine Urenkelin zu stricken. Sie ist erst drei Jahre alt und wohnt in Osnabrück. Im März war ich eine Woche dort bei meiner Enkelin und ihrem Mann zu Besuch.

Paul Und was für Fernsehprogramme schauen Sie sich gerne an?

Frau Beitz Vor allem Nachrichtensendungen, Podiumsdiskussionen und Dokumentarfilme. Für Ratesendungen und Unterhaltungsserien habe ich gar kein Interesse.

Paul Und wann gehen Sie ins Bett?

Frau Beitz Normalerweise erst gegen Mitternacht. In meinem Alter braucht man ja nicht so lange schlafen!

Bemerkungen

die Rentnerin (**-nen**) *(female) pensioner*
die Witwe (**-n**) *widow*
Wird Ihnen nicht langweilig? *Don't you get bored?*
allerhand *all sorts (of things)*
Kaffee kochen *to make coffee*
gemächlich *leisurely*
fernsehen (sep.) (**ie, a, e**) *to watch television*
erst *not until, only*
gelegentlich *occasionally*
zu Mittag essen (**i, a, e**) *to eat lunch*
der Ausflug (**¨e**) *excursion, trip*
die Umgebung *surrounding area*
die Ostseeküste *Baltic Coast*
irgendwelch- *any . . . at all*
stricken *to knit*
ich bin gerade dabei . . . *I'm just (in the process of) . . .*
die Urenkelin (**-nen**) *great grand-daughter*
sich etwas anschauen *to watch something* (e.g. on TV)

die Nachrichtensendung (**-en**) *news* (*transmission*)
die Podiumsdiskussion (**-en**) *panel discussion*
der Dokumentarfilm (**-e**) *documentary* (*film*)
die Ratesendung (**-en**) *panel game*
die Unterhaltungsserie (**-n**) *soap opera*
das Alter (-) *age*

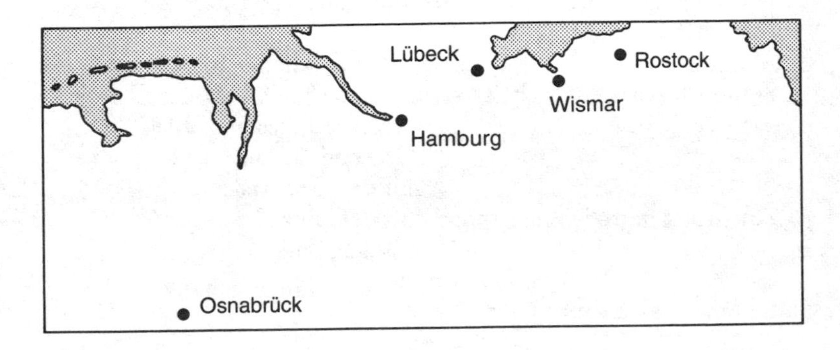

Wismar, Rostock Hanseatic ports, which – along with Lübeck and Hamburg – were formerly members of the Hanseatic League. This status is today reflected in the car registration codes for these cities (e.g. HH = Hansastadt Hamburg, HL = Hansastadt Lübeck, HWIS = Hansastadt Wismar)

Complete the sentences

Study the dialogue once more and then complete these phrases with the missing information.

1 Wird Ihnen nicht manchmal . . ?
2 Meistens stehe ich schon . . .
3 Im Sommer sitze ich in der Morgensonne . . .
4 Ich interessiere mich sehr . . .
5 Gelegentlich esse ich in einem Restaurant . . .
6 Wir machen samstags oder sonntags Ausflüge . . .
7 Ich bin gerade dabei, einen Pullover für meine Urenkelin . . .
8 Für Ratesendungen und Unterhaltungsserien habe ich . . .

Redewendungen

- Talking about daily routine

	um 6.00 Uhr	
Ich stehe	um halb acht	auf.
	gegen 9.00 Uhr	

	wasche	
Ich	dusche	mich. / Ich stelle mich unter die Dusche.
	bade	

	eine Scheibe Toast.
Zum Frühstück esse ich meistens	Brötchen mit Marmelade.
	Cornflakes mit Milch und Zucker.

	mit dem Fahrrad.
Zur Arbeit fahre ich meistens	mit dem Bus.
	mit dem Zug.

	im Restaurant.
Zu Mittag esse ich	in der Mensa.
	zu Hause.

	schaue ich Nachrichten im Fernsehen.
Am Abend	lese ich die Zeitung.
	höre ich Musik.

Erst gegen Mitternacht	gehe ich ins Bett.
Um 11.00 Uhr	gehe ich schlafen.
Schon um halb zehn	lege ich mich ins Bett.

- Frequency: saying how often you do something

Zur Arbeit fahre ich **meistens** mit dem Bus.	*I **usually*** (Lit. mostly) *go to work by bus.*
Aber **manchmal** laufe ich in die Stadt.	*But **sometimes** I walk into town.*
Am Wochenende besuchen wir **öfters** Freunde.	*At the weekend we **often** visit friends.*
Gewöhnlich lese ich etwas oder höre Musik.	***Usually** I read something or listen to music.*
Einmal in der Woche bringe ich meine Wäsche zum Waschsalon.	***Once a week** I take my washing to the launderette.*
Zweimal in der Woche habe ich Englischstunden.	***Twice a week** I have English lessons.*

Ich sehe meine Eltern **höchstens viermal im Jahr**.	*I see my parents **at the most four times a year**.*
Ab und zu räume ich mein Zimmer auf.	***Now and again** I clear up my room.*
Mir wird **nie** langweilig.	*I **never** get bored.*
Ich sehe **nur selten** fern.	*I **only seldom** watch TV.*
Gelegentlich esse ich in einem Restaurant zu Mittag.	***Occasionally** I eat lunch in a restaurant.*
Mein Sohn kommt mich **fast immer** am Wochenende besuchen.	*My son **nearly always** comes to visit me at the weekend.*
Normalerweise gehe ich erst gegen Mitternacht ins Bett.	***Normally** I don't go to bed till around midnight.*

Vokabeln

Words used to relate a sequence of events

zunächst *(at) first, initially*	**als nächstes** *next*
zuerst *(at) first*	**anschließend** *afterwards*
dann *then*	**zum Schluß** *finally*
danach *after that, then*	

Ich habe ihn **zunächst** nicht erkannt.
Zuerst haben wir etwas gegessen.
Dann haben wir uns unterhalten.
Danach haben wir Zeitung gelesen.
Als nächstes haben wir Kaffee getrunken.
Wir sind dann **anschließend** ins Theater gegangen.
Zum Schluß habe ich ihn wieder in sein Hotel gebracht.

Erst *and* schon

schon *already*	**erst** *only, not until*

Oft fahre ich schon um 6.00 Uhr los.
Meine Seminare beginnen erst am frühen Nachmittag.

Grammatische Hinweise

1 German Verbs

There are essentially three main groups of verbs in German: weak verbs, strong verbs and irregular verbs.

Weak verbs are those which, like **machen** and **spielen**, behave in a regular way and do not change their stems (in this case **mach-** and **spiel-**) to form their past tense. The main information about a given verb or its so-called principal parts are usually given as follows:

Infinitive	3rd person singular (present tense)	Past tense	Past participle
machen	macht	machte	gemacht
spielen	spielt	spielte	gespielt

Strong verbs are those which, like **fahren** and **brechen**, behave in a regular way, but undergo a vowel change in their stems to form their past tense. They sometimes undergo further vowel changes to form the past participle and the third person singular (i.e. the **er/sie/es** form) of the present tense:

Infinitive	3rd person singular (present tense)	Past tense	Past participle
fahren	f**ä**hrt	f**u**hr	gef**a**hren
brechen	br**i**cht	br**a**ch	gebr**o**chen

This information is often presented in abbreviated form as:

fahren (ä, u, a)　　　　brechen (i, a, o)

It is advisable to learn the principal parts of strong verbs by heart.

Irregular verbs are so-called because they behave in an unpredictable manner. While the number of irregular verbs in German is relatively small, these verbs are in frequent use and therefore need to be learned thoroughly. They can be divided into four main groups:

(*a*) **Haben**, **sein** and **werden**: these verbs are used not only on their own in their basic meanings but also as auxiliary verbs to form the compound tenses and the passive.

(*b*) The modal auxiliaries: these comprise the six modal auxiliaries, **können**, **müssen**, **wollen**, **dürfen**, **sollen** and **mögen**. The verb **wissen** also comes into this category because it behaves in a similar way to the modal auxiliaries.

(*c*) Irregular weak verbs: these undergo either a vowel or a vowel and a consonant change in their stem in the past tense and past participle, but in other respects behave like weak verbs – for example:

Infinitive	Present tense	Past tense	Past participle
denken	denkt	dachte	gedacht
kennen	kennt	kannte	gekannt
bringen	bringt	brachte	gebracht

(*d*) Irregular strong verbs: a few strong verbs undergo a consonant change as well as a vowel change in their stem in the past tense and past participle; for example:

Infinitive	Present tense	Past tense	Past participle
gehen	geht	ging	gegangen
stehen	steht	stand	gestanden
ziehen	zieht	zog	gezogen

Make sure you can not only recognise but also produce the various forms of irregular verbs in all four categories.

2 *Present tense*

You will by now probably feel relatively confident in the formation and use of the present tense in German. It may, however, be useful to have a reminder of the main points.

Formation

The present tense of German verbs is formed by adding the relevant endings to the stem. Take the infinitive, e.g. **machen**, **kommen**, remove the **-en** ending; **mach-** and **komm-**, and add the relevant endings (see overleaf):

Weak verbs	**Strong verbs**
mach-en	**komm-en**
ich mach-**e**	ich komm-**e**
du mach-**st**	du komm-**st**
er/sie/es mach-**t**	er/sie/es komm-**t**
wir mach-**en**	wir komm-**en**
ihr mach-**t**	ihr komm-**t**
sie/Sie mach-**en**	sie/Sie komm-**en**

Note that the singular form of **Sie** (the polite form for *you*) is omitted from the charts in this book. It is always the same as the third person plural **sie** form (*they*).

Some verbs need an extra **e** before the endings **-st** or **-t**:

antworten	du antwort**e**st	er/sie/es antwort**e**t	ihr antwort**e**t
finden	du find**e**st	er/sie/es find**e**t	ihr find**e**t
regnen	–	es regn**e**t	–

Others lose an **e** from the **-en** ending:

tun	wir tun	sie tun
klingeln	wir klingeln	sie klingeln
wandern	wir wandern	sie wandern

Verbs with a stem ending in **s**, **ss**, **ß**, **x** or **z** add only **-t** and not **-st** in the **du** form:

reisen	du reist	heizen	du heizt
küssen	du küßt		

Many strong verbs undergo a vowel change in the stem in the second and third person singular:

fallen	du fällst	er/sie/es fällt
fahren	du fährst	er/sie/es fährt
laufen	du läufst	er/sie/es läuft
helfen	du hilfst	er/sie/es hilft
essen	du ißt	er/sie/es ißt
geben	du gibst	er/sie/es gibt
sprechen	du sprichst	er/sie/es spricht
nehmen	du nimmst	er/sie/es nimmt
sehen	du siehst	er/sie/es sieht
lesen	du liest	er/sie/es liest

When the vowel change is **i** or **ie**, this is also present in the singular form of the imperative:

lesen	lies!
nehmen	nimm!
geben	gib!

Since it is not uncommon to hear advanced learners making errors with these forms, you would be well advised to make a conscious effort to learn them.

The present tense of **haben**, **sein** and **werden** is irregular:

haben	**sein**	**werden**
ich habe	ich bin	ich werde
du hast	du bist	du wirst
er/sie/es hat	er/sie/es ist	er/sie/es wird
wir haben	wir sind	wir werden
ihr habt	ihr seid	ihr werdet
sie/Sie haben	sie/Sie sind	sie/Sie werden

Modal verbs form their present tense differently from other verbs in that they do not add **-t** to the stem in the third person singular present tenses. In most cases these verbs also have a different vowel from the stem in the present tense singular:

	können	**müssen**	**wollen**	**dürfen**	**sollen**	**mögen**
ich	kann	muß	will	darf	soll	mag
du	kannst	mußt	willst	darfst	sollst	magst
er/sie/es	kann	muß	will	darf	soll	mag
wir	können	müssen	wollen	dürfen	sollen	mögen
ihr	könnt	müßt	wollt	dürft	sollt	mögt
sie/Sie	können	müssen	wollen	dürfen	sollen	mögen

Wissen forms its present tense in the same way as the modal verbs:

ich weiß	wir wissen
du weißt	ihr wißt
er/sie/es weiß	sie/Sie wissen

Uses of the present tense

The main use of the present tense is to refer to present, habitual or on-going actions, events or states:

Ich lese dein Buch.	*I am reading your book.*
Ute fährt oft nach Berlin.	*Ute often goes to Berlin.*
Du verstehst sehr gut Englisch.	*You understand English very well.*

The German present tense covers both the simple and the progressive forms of the English present tense:

Ich trinke Kaffee.	*I drink coffee (on a regular basis).* *I am drinking coffee (right now).*

The present tense is often used in German to refer to the future. In some cases German and English are similar in this use:

Morgen fliege ich nach Hamburg.	*I'm flying to Hamburg tomorrow.*
Dienstag um 10.00 Uhr bin ich verabredet.	*I have an appointment at 10.00 o'clock on Tuesday.*

However, the present tense is also used in German where its use in English would not be possible:

Ich bin in zehn Minuten wieder da.	*I'll be back in ten minutes.*
Ich sag's dir morgen.	*I'll tell you tomorrow.*
Weitere Informationen erhalten Sie beim Verkehrsamt.	*You'll get more information at the tourist office.*

The present tense is used in German to refer to those on-going actions, events or states which in English would require the use of some form of the past tense:

Kirsten wohnt schon lange in Ulm.	*Kirsten has been living in Ulm for a long time.*
Seit wann wartest du auf mich?	*How long have you been waiting for me?*
Seitdem ich ihn kenne, arbeitet er bei Bosch.	*Ever since I have known him he has been working for Bosch.*

Note that in this kind of sentence the present tense is used in conjunction with a phrase stating or enquiring about length of time.

As in English, the present tense can be used in German to achieve increased dramatic effect when narrating past events:

Stell dir vor, ich sitze gestern abend mit Silke im Kino, und plötzlich sagt sie mir, . . .

Just imagine, last night I'm sitting in the cinema with Silke and suddenly she says to me, . . .

3 Personal pronouns

Although the personal pronouns are encountered at an early stage in any German language course, they are a source of error for many an advanced learner. Particularly the distinction between the accusative and dative forms (where this exists) can lead to confusion.

Here they are for reference purposes:

	Singular				Plural			
	Nom.	**Acc.**	**Gen.**	**Dat.**	**Nom.**	**Acc.**	**Gen.**	**Dat.**
1st person	ich	mich	meiner	mir	wir	uns	unser	uns
2nd person (informal)	du	dich	deiner	dir	ihr	euch	euer	euch
2nd person (polite)	Sie	Sie (sich)	Ihrer	Ihnen (sich)	Sie	Sie (sich)	Ihrer	Ihnen (sich)
3rd person	er	ihn (sich)	seiner	ihm (sich)	sie	sie (sich)	ihrer	ihnen (sich)
	sie	sie (sich)	ihrer	ihr (sich)				
	es	es (sich)	seiner	ihm (sich)				

The forms in brackets are those which differ from the given forms when they are used reflexively:

Accusative

Jeden Tag wasche ich **ihn**.	*I wash him every day.*
Er wäscht **sich** nicht.	*He does not wash (himself).*
Wäscht er **Sie** jeden Tag?	*Does he wash you every day?*
Waschen Sie **sich** nicht?	*Don't you wash (yourself)?*

Dative

Ich wasche **ihm** die Haare.	*I wash his* (Lit. to him the) *hair.*
Er wäscht **sich** die Haare.	*He washes his* (Lit. to himself the) *hair.*
Wäscht er **Ihnen** die Haare?	*Does he wash your* (Lit. to you the) *hair?*

Wann waschen Sie **sich** die Haare? *When do you wash your* (Lit. to you the) *hair?*

Genitive: the genitive forms have been included in order to complete the overview of personal pronouns. In fact, they are not used in the everyday language and only rarely occur even in formal contexts.

An diesem Tag gedenken wir **ihrer**. *On this day we remember them.*

Use of *der, die* and *das*

In everyday speech, the **der/die/das** forms of the definite article are frequently used instead of **er/sie/es**:

Kennst du Karl? Oh ja **der** ist ein Freund von mir. **Den** kenne ich schon lange.
Was hältst du von Marga? **Die** ist ja sehr sympathisch. **Die** habe ich erst vorige Woche kennengelernt.

4 Subject–verb inversion

Subject–verb inversion is not unknown in English. It occurs, for instance, when we start a sentence with *Never* or *Hardly*:
Never has he spoken to me without complaining.
Hardly had I left the room, when I began to feel faint.

In German, this kind of inversion occurs whenever a sentence or main clause does not begin with the subject. Put another way, the finite verb has to be the second element in a main clause:

1st element	2nd element Verb		
Ich	fahre		morgen nach Weimar.
Morgen	fahre	ich	nach Weimar.
Nach Weimar	fahre	ich	morgen.

The first element in the main clause can be a subordinate clause. The finite verb in the main clause still has to be the second element:

Subordinate clause	Main clause Verb	Subject	
Weil es heute regnet,	fahren	wir	erst morgen nach Leipzig.

Almost any element of the sentence can be moved to first position (or 'fronted'). This characteristic of German will be looked at in more detail in **Lektion 9**. There is also more information on relative clauses in **Lektion 3**, pages 70–73, and other dependent (or subordinate) clauses in **Lektion 4**, pages 97–100.

Übungen

1 Ergänzen Sie den Lückentext. Diese Kundin findet schnell den richtigen Kühlschrank!

Verkäufer	Bitte schön. Wie kann ich . . . (*a*) . . . helfen?
Kundin	Ich suche . . . (*b*) . . . Kühlschrank. Können sie . . . (*c*) . . . welche zeigen?
Verkäufer	Ja, gern. Der von »Bosch« ist sehr gut. Gefällt er . . . (*d*) . . .?
Kundin	Ja, er gefällt . . . (*e*) . . . gut. Was kostet er?
Verkäufer	630 DM.
Kundin	Das ist . . . (*f*) . . . zu teuer! Haben . . . (*g*) . . . noch welche?
Verkäufer	Ja, sicher. Hier habe ich . . . (*h*) . . . für nur 420 DM.
Kundin	Ja, der ist gut. . . . (*i*) . . . nehme ich. Ich danke . . . (*j*) . . . für Ihre Hilfe.
Verkäufer	Nichts zu danken.

2 Stellen Sie Fragen in der **du**-Form.

Beispiel Morgen helfe ich Frau Renke beim Einkaufen.
Hilfst du ihr oft beim Einkaufen?

Note that all these verbs are 'strong' verbs and change their vowel in the second and third person singular present tense. If you are not sure of the forms, look them up in the **Glossar** at the end of the book.

(*a*) Übermorgen fahre ich nach Italien.
(*b*) Morgen früh laufe ich 2 Kilometer.
(*c*) Heute abend sehe ich fern.
(*d*) Im Oktober gebe ich eine Party.
(*e*) Nächste Woche nehme ich an einem Kongreß teil.

(*f*) Heute abend esse ich im Restaurant »La Taverna«.
(*g*) Morgen früh spreche ich mit dem Direktor.
(*h*) Morgen treffe ich Dieter zum Mittagessen.

3 Marianne redet mit ihrer Freundin über ihren Tagesablauf. Setzen Sie die Sätze in die richtige Reihenfolge.

(*a*) Ja, ich esse meistens in einem Restaurant eine warme Mahlzeit.
(*b*) Es kommt darauf an, ob ich arbeite oder ob ich frei habe.
(*c*) Und was machst du abends nach der Arbeit?
(*d*) Doch. Ich gehe gern windsurfen. Aber das mache ich am Wochenende oder in den Ferien.
(*e*) Meistens erledige ich, was an Arbeit in der Wohnung anfällt. Manchmal schaue ich auch fern oder stricke.
(*f*) Wie sieht eigentlich dein Tagesablauf aus?
(*g*) Wenn ich arbeite, stehe ich um 7.00 Uhr auf, wasche mich, frühstücke, und fahre mit dem Bus ins Büro.
(*h*) Wie ist es, wenn du arbeitest?
(*i*) Hast du sonst keine Hobbys?
(*j*) Ißt du in der Stadt zu Mittag?

4 Using all the places or buildings listed below, say where one can do the following:

Beispiel Wo kann man chinesisch essen?
Im Restaurant »Ming Jiauo«. (Note: **in** or **auf** + Dat.)

(*a*) Wo kann man Bücher leihen?
(*b*) Wo kann man Tennis spielen?
(*c*) Wo kann man italienisch essen?
(*d*) Wo kann man Geld wechseln?
(*e*) Wo kann man Bilder von Dürer sehen?

Restaurant »La Taverna«; Kunst-Galerie; Dresdner Bank; Stadtbücherei; Tennisplatz.

5 Using all the places or buildings listed below, say where one could go to do the following:

Beispiel Wohin geht man, wenn man schwimmen will?
Ins Schwimmbad. (Note: **in** or **auf** + Acc., **zu** + Dat.)

(*a*) Wohin geht man, wenn man eine Arbeit sucht?

(*b*) Wohin geht man, wenn man mit der Bahn fahren will?
(*c*) Wohin geht man, wenn man Fleisch kaufen will?
(*d*) Wohin fährt man, wenn man bergsteigen will?
(*e*) Wohin geht man, wenn man tanzen will?

Diskothek »Hot Live«; Bahnhof; Metzgerei; Arbeitsamt; Alpen.

6 Formen Sie die folgenden Sätze so um, daß der kursiv gedruckte Satzteil betont wird. (*Change the word order in the following sentences in such a way as to emphasise the word in italics.*)

Beispiel Ich habe *das* nicht gewollt./*Das* habe ich nicht gewollt.

(*a*) Ich interessiere mich besonders *für Gedichte und Frauenliteratur*.
(*b*) Morgens gegen halb acht beginnt *mein Tagesablauf*.
(*c*) Ich gehe aber *meistens* erst gegen Mittag in die Stadt.
(*d*) Ich laufe auch *manchmal* in die Stadt.
(*e*) Wir besuchen *am Wochenende* öfters Freunde oder gehen essen.
(*f*) Ich trinke Orangensaft *zum Frühstück*, oder eine Tasse Kaffee, und esse ein Brötchen mit Marmelade.
(*g*) Mein Freund und ich fahren am Wochende *zum Windsurfen* an den Starnberger See.
(*h*) Ich habe *in meinem Zimmer* nur eine Kochnische mit einer Heizplatte und einem kleinen Kühlschrank.
(*i*) Ich sitze *im Sommer* in der Morgensonne auf meinem Balkon.
(*j*) Ich gehe *während des Tages* öfters meine Freunde besuchen.

7 Complete the sentences, then fill in the missing words horizontally, overleaf. Corinna's workplace will be revealed vertically (*k*).

(*a*) Lorenz Müller interessiert sich besonders für ....
(*b*) Viele Leute trinken zum Frühstück gerne ....
(*c*) Corinna trinkt aber lieber .... .
(*d*) Frau Beitz ist Rentnerin und ..... .
(*e*) Ihr Sohn Helmut kommt sie oft am Wochenende ....
(*f*) .... ißt Lorenz meistens in der Mensa.
(*g*) Einmal in der Woche bringt Corinna ihre ..... . in den Waschsalon.

(*h*) Frau Beitz schaut sich ...... Nachrichtensendungen an.
(*i*) .... ist auch eines ihrer Hobbys.
(*j*) Corinna arbeitet als ....

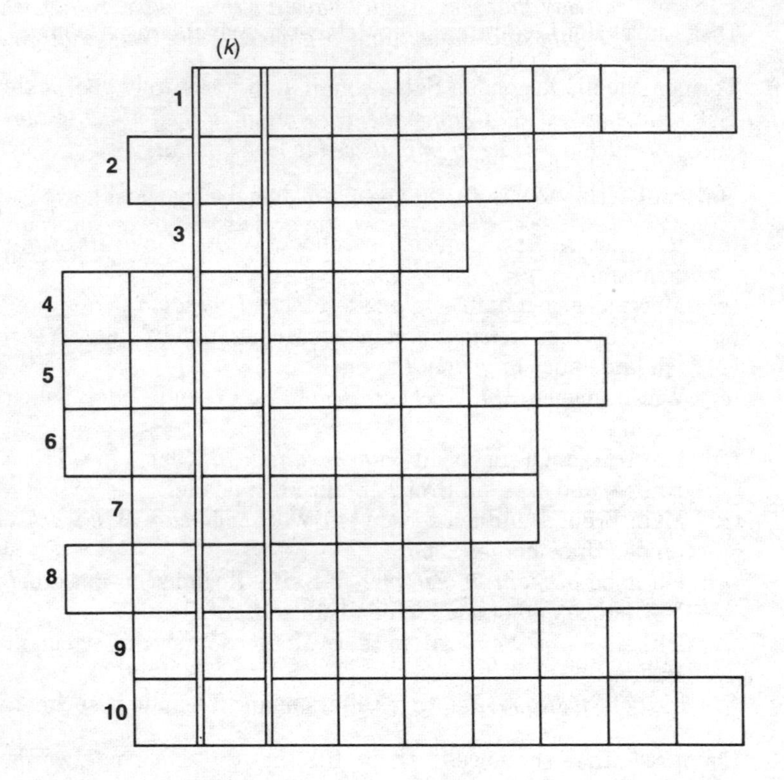

8 Sie reden mit einer Bekannten über Ihren Tagesablauf, Ihre Interessen und Ihre Hobbys. Vervollständigen Sie den Dialog mit Hilfe der auf Englisch gegebenen Hinweise. Verwenden Sie dabei die Vokabeln, die in den bisherigen Aufnahmen vorgekommen sind. (*Complete the dialogue with the assistance of the English prompts, using the vocabulary given in the previous recordings.*)

Bekannte Wann stehst du eigentlich morgens auf?
Sie *Tell her that it depends on whether you have to work*

or whether you have free time; that during the week you usually get up at around seven, at weekends usually at around ten.

Bekannte Was frühstückst du normalerweise?

Sie *Say that you usually have a cup of coffee, rolls with jam and butter, and a glass of juice, and that you read the paper.*

Bekannte Und was machst du am Abend, nach der Arbeit?

Sie *Tell her that you usually watch the news on TV, read a book or knit.*

Bekannte Und was machst du gerne am Wochenende?

Sie *Answer that you sometimes visit friends or your parents, go for a walk occasionally, or do the work that has been left during the week.*

Bekannte Siehst du deine Eltern öfters?

Sie *Explain that, unfortunately, you see them only three times a year at the most.*

Höraufgabe

Robert Paulsen: Tagesablauf

Robert Paulsen aus Jena erzählt über seinen Tagesablauf.

1 Give the details concerning Robert Paulsen.

(*a*) age
(*b*) marital status
(*c*) number of children
(*d*) age of children
(*e*) place of residence
(*f*) nationality
(*g*) occupation
(*h*) occupation of spouse

2 Beantworten Sie die folgenden Fragen.

(*a*) Wie unterscheidet sich der Tagesablauf eines Wissenschaftlers von dem eines Arbeiters?

(*b*) Wer bringt die Tochter in den Kindergarten?
(*c*) Wie kommt Robert Paulsen in die Uni?
(*d*) Wie ist in Deutschland die Einteilung im Studium?
(*e*) Was ist der Nachteil der flexibleren Arbeitszeit von Robert?
(*f*) Wann unterrichtet Robert am liebsten?
(*g*) Was macht Robert oft am Nachmittag?
(*h*) Was macht er am Nachmittag, wenn er nicht arbeitet?
(*i*) Woran arbeitet er im Moment besonders?
(*j*) Welche Hobbys hat er?

3 **Diktat** (*Dictation*): hören Sie sich die Aufnahme genau an und schreiben Sie dann mit: von »Frühstück esse ich . . . « bis » . . . stattfindet, nicht läßt«. Die korrekte Version des Diktats finden Sie fettgedruckt (*in bold print*) in **Transkriptionen der Höraufgaben**.

Lesetext

DIE MEISTEN NEHMEN DAS AUTO

Rund 12 Prozent der *Erwerbstätigen* können den Arbeitstag *streßfrei* beginnen: Sie stehen vom Frühstück auf, *öffnen* eine Tür und stehen schon *im Laden*, in der Werkstatt oder im Stall. Es sind *vor allem* die selbständigen Händler, Handwerker und Landwirte, die am Arbeitsplatz wohnen. *Alle übrigen* müssen sich *allmorgendlich* auf den Arbeitsweg machen. Weitaus die meisten – 56 Prozent - setzen sich *zu diesem Zweck* ins Auto. Dies nicht immer nur aus Bequemlichkeit. Nicht weniges wohnen vielmehr so weit *draußen*, daß oft gar keine andere Möglichkeit bleibt, als *mit eigenen PS zur Arbeit zu reiten*. Mit Bahn oder Bus kommt jeder/jede siebte – 14 Prozent – zur Arbeit. Am unabhängigsten von Staus oder Streiks sind jene, die zu Fuß (9 Prozent) oder mit dem Fahrrad (6 Prozent) ihrem Betrieb entgegenstreben. Sie können sich jeden Morgen in dem befriedigenden Gefühl auf ihren Arbeitsplatz fallen lassen, schon etwas für Gesundheit und Umwelt getan zu haben.

Statistische Angaben: „Verkehr in Zahlen“, eigene Berechnungen.

Globus, 9. Juni

rund *around*
der/die Erwerbstätige (-**n**) *gainfully employed person, working person*
der Arbeitstag (-**e**) *working day*
streßfrei *free of stress*
die Werkstatt (¨**en**) *workshop*
der Stall (¨**e**) *stable, sty*
vor allem *above all*
selbständig *self-employed; independent*
der Händler (-) *tradesman*
der Handwerker (-) *craftsman*
der Landwirt (-**e**) *farmer*
der Arbeitsplatz (¨**e**) *work-place*
allmorgendlich *every morning*
der Arbeitsweg (-**e**) *way to work*
weitaus *by far*
zu diesem Zweck *for that purpose*
der Zweck (-**e**) *purpose*
die Bequemlichkeit (-**en**) *laziness, idleness; comfort*
die Möglichkeit (-**en**) *possibility*
mit eigenen PS zur Arbeit zu reiten *to take your own car to get to work* (colloquial) (Lit. ride your own horse power to work)
der Stau (-**s**) *traffic jam*
der Streik (-**s**) *strike*
entgegenstreben (sep.) *to strive towards*
befriedigend *satisfactory*
sich fallen lassen *to let oneself fall*

1 Wer arbeitet wo? Ordnen Sie zu!

(*a*) im Stall	(i) der Händler
(*b*) im Laden	(ii) der Handwerker
(*c*) in der Werkstatt	(iii) der Landwirt

2 Sagen Sie es in Prozent! Ordnen Sie noch einmal zu!

(*a*) Zahl der Erwerbstätigen, die keinen Arbeitsweg zurücklegen müssen	(i) 14%
(*b*) Zahl derer, die mit dem Auto fahren	(ii) 6%
(*c*) Zahl derer, die mit der Bahn/ dem Bus fahren	(iii) 56%
(*d*) Zahl derer, die zu Fuß gehen	(iv) 9%
(*e*) Zahl derer, die mit dem Fahrrad fahren	(v) 12%

3 Finden Sie das passende Wort! Ordnen Sie die nachfolgenden Wörter den gleichbedeutenden Wörtern im Text (kursiv gedruckt / *printed in italics*) zu.

(*a*) außerhalb
(*b*) ohne Streß
(*c*) mit dem eigenen Auto zur Arbeit zu fahren
(*d*) Berufstätigen
(*e*) im Geschäft
(*f*) alle anderen
(*g*) dazu
(*h*) jeden Morgen
(*i*) aufmachen
(*j*) hauptsächlich

3
AUSBILDUNG UND STUDIUM

Lernziele

In this unit you will learn how to

- talk about training and courses of study
- ask questions and react to questions
- form and use the past and perfect tenses, and relative clauses

Aufnahmen

1 Banklehre

Birgit erklärt ihrem Onkel Heinz, der aus Argentinien bei der Familie in Berlin zu Besuch ist, warum sie eine Banklehre macht, obwohl sie gerne studiert hätte.

Heinz Deine Mutter hat mir gesagt, daß du bei der Deutschen Bank eine Lehre machst. Hast du denn nicht studieren wollen?

Birgit Eigentlich doch. Aber ich mußte auch einsehen, daß gerade hier in Deutschland für Akademiker Schwierigkeiten bestehen, Arbeit zu finden. Und ich wollte auf keinen Fall arbeitslos werden. Ich habe mich deshalb um eine Banklehre beworben.

Heinz Kennst du denn Leute, die studiert haben und nachher keine Stellung gefunden haben?

Birgit Oh, ja! Sehr viele sogar. Bei uns gibt es eben zu viele Studenten. Es hat ja jeder, der Abitur gemacht hat, das Recht auf ein Hochschulstudium, und die Universitäten sind deswegen überfüllt. In Berlin studieren zum Beispiel etwa 146 000 Menschen. In ganz Deutschland sind es ungefähr 1,8 Millionen. Die Wirtschaft kann so viele akademisch qualifizierte Leute einfach nicht aufnehmen.

Heinz Als ich aber vor drei Jahren hier war, hast du dich – wenn ich mich recht erinnere – für die englische Sprache besonders interessiert. Hast du das denn aufgeben müssen?

Birgit Aber gar nicht! Jeden Tag mache ich von meinen Englischkenntnissen Gebrauch. Und im Augenblick lerne ich intensiv italienisch, da ich im Oktober für ein ganzes Jahr zu unserer Zweigstelle in Florenz geschickt werde.

Heinz Hast du aber das Gefühl, daß du angemessen ausgebildet wirst?

Birgit Ganz sicher! Ich nehme regelmäßig an Kursen teil und werde dann so mit der Zeit mit allen Bereichen des Bankwesens vertraut.

Heinz Und du bedauerst es wirklich nicht, daß du nicht studiert hast?

Birgit Doch, ein bißchen! Aber ich bin ehrlich gesagt mit meinem Beruf sehr zufrieden.

Heinz Dann bin ich auch zufrieden!

Bemerkungen

die Banklehre *banking apprenticeship*
einsehen (**ie, a, e**) (sep.) *to recognise, acknowledge*
gerade hier in Deutschland *here in Germany of all places*
der Akademiker (-) (*MA*) *graduate*
bestehen (**e, a, a**) *to exist*
auf keinen Fall *under no circumstances*
sich bewerben (**i, a, o**) **um** (+ Acc.) *to apply for*

sogar *even*
das Abitur school-leaving examination, usually taken at 18 or 19. Often compared to A-levels in England and Wales.
das Hochschulstudium *study at an institution of higher education*. Everyone who gains the **Abitur** is entitled to higher education. The only bar is the **numerus clausus**, or quota system, in certain subjects.
aufnehmen (i, a, o) (sep.) *to accept, absorb*
sich erinnern (an + Dat.) *to remember*
aufgeben (i, a, e) (sep.) *to drop*
Gebrauch machen (von + Dat.) *to make use of*
die Zweigstelle (-n) *branch*
angemessen *appropriately*
ausbilden (sep.) *to train*
teilnehmen (i, a, o) (sep.) **an** (+ Dat.) *to take part in*
der Bereich (-e) *area*
das Bankwesen (-) *banking system*
vertraut mit (+ Dat.) *familiar with*
bedauern *to regret*
ehrlich gesagt *quite honestly* **zufrieden** *satisfied*

Richtig oder falsch?

Korrigieren Sie die falschen Aussagen.

1 Birgit macht eine Lehre bei der Dresdner Bank.
2 In Deutschland fällt es Akademikern schwer, Arbeit zu finden.
3 Birgit hat sich um eine Banklehre beworben, weil sie nicht arbeitslos werden wollte.
4 Birgit kennt nur wenige Leute, die studiert haben und nachher keine Arbeit gefunden haben.
5 In Deutschland hat jeder, der das Abitur gemacht hat, das Recht auf ein Hochschulstudium.
6 Die deutsche Wirtschaft braucht immer mehr akademisch qualifizierte Leute.
7 Birgit hat in ihrem Beruf leider keine Möglichkeit, von ihren Englischkenntnissen Gebrauch zu machen.
8 Birgit bereitet sich jetzt auf ein Jahr in Italien vor.
9 Durch die regelmäßige Teilnahme an Kursen wird Birgit allmählich mit allen Bereichen des Bankwesens vertraut.
10 Birgit bereut es überhaupt nicht, daß sie nicht studiert hat.

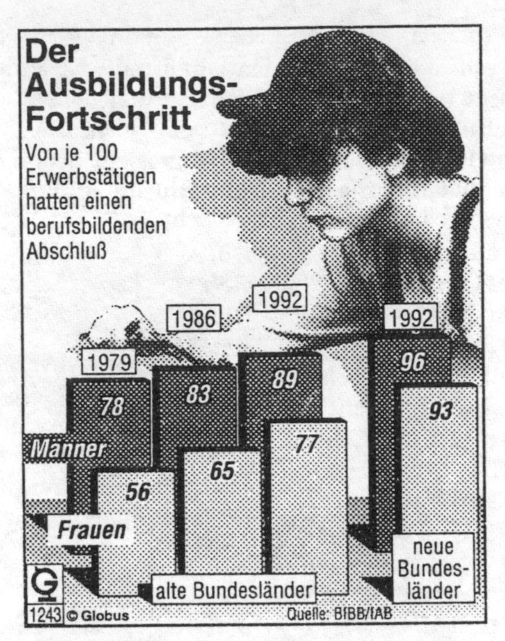

2 Hochschulstudium

Ilona lernt Vera beim Mittagessen in der Mensa kennen.

Ilona Ist hier noch frei?
Vera Ja, bitte schön. (*Pause*) Ich studiere Anglistik im vierten Semester. Was studierst du?
Ilona Chemie im neunten Semester. Ißt du jeden Tag hier in der Mensa zu Mittag?
Vera Nein. Es kommt darauf an, ob ich zu einem Seminar oder zu einer Vorlesung muß. Womöglich arbeite ich zu Hause und esse dann auch da zu Mittag.
Ilona Du hast aber Glück! Wir Chemie-Studenten müssen jeden Tag ins Labor. Versuche durchführen kann man ja eigentlich nur im Labor. Bald bin ich aber mit dem Studium fertig. Ende nächsten Semesters will ich das Staatsexamen ablegen.
Vera Und was möchtest du dann werden?
Ilona Ich werde mich um eine Stellung beim Umweltministerium bewerben. Die Konkurrenz ist zwar ziemlich stark, aber

vielleicht schaffe ich es trotzdem. Und du, was hast du vor?

Vera Ich möchte Gymnasiallehrerin für Englisch werden. Bis ich mit dem Studium fertig bin, wird hoffentlich wieder Nachfrage nach Lehrern bestehen.

Ilona Hast du auch in England studiert?

Vera Ja, ich habe vor zwei Jahren ein Jahr in Canterbury studiert. Es hat ungeheuer viel Spaß gemacht.

Bemerkungen

die Anglistik English language and literature

das Semester (-) *semester, term.* The German university year is divided into two terms or semesters (**Sommersemester** and **Wintersemester**). Eight semesters is the minimum time in which one can complete one's studies. Most students take much longer.

Was studierst du? note that even though they have just met, Ilona and Vera call each other **du**; this is normal practice between students

die Vorlesung (**-en**) *lecture*

Glück haben *to be lucky*

das Labor(**atorium**) *lab*(*oratory*)

der Versuch (**-e**) *experiment*

durchführen (sep.) *to conduct, carry out*

das Staatsexamen *state examination* (similar to the MA degree)

ablegen (sep.) *to sit, take* (an exam)

die Stellung (**-en**) *position*

das Umweltministerium *Ministry of the Environment*

die Konkurrenz *competition*

schaffen *to manage* (colloquial)

der Gymnasiallehrer (-) *teacher* at a **Gymnasium** or grammar school

die Nachfrage *demand*

ungeheuer *huge*(*ly*), *immense*(*ly*)

der Spaß *fun*

Welche Antwort paßt?

1 Entschuldigung, ist hier noch frei?
   (*a*) Ich studiere Anglistik im vierten Semester.
   (*b*) Ja, bitte schön.
   (*c*) Ich esse oft hier zu Mittag.

2 Und was studierst du, wenn ich fragen darf?
  (*a*) Ich muß jeden Tag ins Labor.
  (*b*) Ende nächsten Semesters will ich das Staatsexamen ablegen.
  (*c*) Chemie im neunten Semester.

3 Ißt du jeden Tag hier in der Mensa?
  (*a*) Es kommt darauf an.
  (*b*) Ich esse jeden Tag zu Hause.
  (*c*) Ich habe meistens Vorlesungen oder Seminare.

4 Und was möchtest du nach dem Studium werden?
  (*a*) Ich studiere Anglistik im vierten Semester.
  (*b*) Ich möchte mich um eine Stellung im Umweltministerium bewerben.
  (*c*) Versuche durchführen kann man eigentlich nur im Labor.

5 Hast du auch in England studiert?
  (*a*) Wir Chemie-Studenten müssen jeden Tag ins Labor.
  (*b*) Ja, ich habe vor zwei Jahren ein Jahr in Canterbury studiert.
  (*c*) Die Konkurrenz ist im Moment ziemlich stark.

Sagen Sie's auf Deutsch!

1 Is this seat taken?
2 I have been studying English literature and linguistics for one and a half years.
3 Aren't you lucky!
4 At the end of next term I intend to take my final exam.
5 And what would you like to be?
6 And what are your plans?
7 I would like to teach English in a grammar school.
8 . . . hopefully there will be a demand for English teachers again.
9 It was great fun.

3 Hauptschulabschluß – und dann?

Markus und Barbara werden beide im Juli ihren Qualifizierten Hauptschulabschluß machen, und haben vor ein paar Monaten angefangen, sich um eine Lehrstelle zu bewerben. In der Schule tauschen sie ihre Erfahrungen aus.

Markus Du, Barbara, hast du denn schon eine Lehrstelle in Aussicht nach dem Quali?

Barbara Bis jetzt leider noch nicht. Ich habe zwar schon zwei Vorstellungsgespräche gehabt, aber die Meister scheinen in die handwerklichen Fähigkeiten von Frauen immer noch ziemlich wenig Vertrauen zu haben, oder sie glauben, daß Frauen lieber heiraten und Kinder kriegen sollen.

Markus Wofür hast du dich denn eigentlich beworben?

Barbara Ich möchte unbedingt eine Schreinerlehre machen. So ein Bürojob liegt mir überhaupt nicht. Und als Schreinerin kann ich wenigstens auch ein bißchen kreativ arbeiten. Und wie sieht's bei dir aus?

Markus Ich habe mich um einen Ausbildungsplatz als Industriekaufmann beworben. Nächste Woche habe ich ein Vorstellungsgespräch bei einer großen Exportfirma.

Barbara Hast du denn da überhaupt eine Chance gegen die Leute mit Mittlerer Reife? Ich habe gehört, daß die Unternehmen im kaufmännischen Bereich immer weniger Hauptschulabgänger einstellen. Sogar Abiturienten bewerben sich ja zunehmend um diese Stellen!

Markus Das stimmt schon. Aber meine Zensuren sind ziemlich gut. Und außerdem habe ich in den Osterferien ein Praktikum bei eben diesem Unternehmen gemacht. Also glaube ich, daß ich eine gute Chance habe, genommen zu werden.

Barbara Und was machst du, wenn es nicht klappt?

Markus Dann werde ich wahrscheinlich die Mittlere Reife machen. Das wollten meine Eltern sowieso von Anfang an, weil sie der Meinung sind, daß der Quali heutzutage nichts mehr wert ist.

Bemerkungen

die Erfahrung (-en) *experience*
austauschen (sep.) *to exchange*
in Aussicht haben *to have the prospect of*
die Lehrstelle (-n) *training place*. Note that in Germany the majority of school-leavers embark on a three-year structured training programme, at the end of which there is a set of exams which

gives them qualified professional status

der Qualifizierte Hauptschulabschluß *secondary-school leaving certificate.* The compulsory minimum schooling period in Germany is nine years, at the end of which pupils are examined in the core subjects such as German, English and Mathematics; most young people then go on to do an apprenticeship

das Vorstellungsgespräch (**-e**) *job interview*

der Meister (-) *master craftsman*

handwerklich *technical* (of work done by a craftsman/woman)

die Fähigkeit (**-en**) *ability*

das Vertrauen *confidence, trust* **unbedingt** *absolutely*

die Schreinerlehre (**-n**) *carpentry apprenticeship*

der Schreiner (-) *carpenter* **das Büro** (**-s**) *office*

der Ausbildungsplatz (¨-e) *training place*

der Industriekaufmann / die Industriekauffrau person with three years' business training employed on the business side of an industrial company; at the end of the three years a professional exam is taken

die Mittlere Reife *secondary-school leaving certificate* taken after ten years of schooling; people either do an apprenticeship afterwards, or continue to attend school for two more years, after which they sit for the **Fachabitur**; this is narrower than the general **Abitur** taken at German grammar schools (**Gymnasien**) but nevertheless opens the door to higher education

kaufmännisch *commercial, business*

der Hauptschulabgänger(-)/**die Hauptschulabgängerin** (**-nen**) *secondary-school leaver* (after nine years)

der/die Abiturient(**-en**)/**-in**(**-nen**) student who has passed the general German **Abitur** exams (after 13 years)

die Zensur (**-en**) *mark, grade*

das Praktikum (**Praktika**) period of practical instruction/training undertaken while still at school/university; work placement

Richtig oder falsch?

Korrigieren Sie die falschen Aussagen.

1 Barbara hat schon eine Lehrstelle gefunden.
2 Sie hat bereits vier Vorstellungsgespräche gehabt.
3 Die Schreinermeister sind oft der Meinung, daß Frauen für diesen Beruf nicht geeignet sind.

4 Barbara hätte lieber einen Bürojob.
5 Markus will auch eine Schreinerlehre machen.
6 Er hat noch keinen Ausbildungsplatz gefunden.
7 Immer mehr Leute mit Mittlerer Reife oder Abitur bewerben sich für solche Stellen.
8 Markus hat daher keine Chance, einen Ausbildungsplatz als Industriekaufmann zu bekommen.
9 Er hat aber schon einmal ein Praktikum bei diesem Unternehmen gemacht.
10 Wenn er die Stelle nicht bekommt, wird er eine Lehre als Automechaniker machen.
11 Die Eltern von Markus wollen, daß er das Abitur macht.

Vervollständigen Sie die Sätze!

1 Hast du denn schon eine Lehrstelle . . .?
2 So ein Bürojob liegt . . .
3 Und wie sieht's . . .?
4 Ich habe mich um . . . beworben.
5 Hast du denn da überhaupt eine Chance . . .?
6 Und außerdem habe ich in den Osterferien . . .
7 Und was machst du, wenn . . .?

Redewendungen

- Ways of introducing a (perhaps intrusive) question

Darf ich Sie/dich mal etwas fragen?
Darf ich Ihnen/dir einmal eine Frage stellen?
Entschuldigen Sie, aber was ich Sie schon immer mal fragen wollte . . .
Ware es indiskret, wenn ich Sie nach (ihrem Privatleben) fragen würde?
Was ich mich schon lange gefragt habe: (sind Sie eigentlich verheiratet?)
Haben Sie sich nicht auch schon immer gefragt, (wie unsere Nachbarn ihr Geld verdienen)?
Ist es eigentlich wahr, daß (Sie viermal geschieden sind)?

Haben Sie auch schon gehört, daß (Herr Müller befördert worden ist)?

- Positive reactions to a question

  Ja.
  Ja, gerne.
  Oh, ja.
  Aber sicher.
  Ganz sicher sogar.
  Ja, das stimmt.
  Allerdings!
  Und ob!
  Sehr gut! / Ausgezeichnet!

- Negative reactions to a question

  Nein.
  Nein, danke.
  Oh, nein!
  Eigentlich nicht.
  Leider nicht.
  Aber gar nicht!
  Ganz und gar nicht!
  Unter keinen Umständen!
  Ach, du meine Güte! / Schrecklich!

- Vague or non-commital reactions

  Das mag schon stimmen.
  Kann sein.
  Ach, ja?
  Ist das so?
  Na, und?
  Und wenn schon!
  Dazu möchte ich eigentlich nichts sagen.
  Zu diesem Thema möchte ich mich nicht äußern.

Vokabeln

Studienfächer

Amerikanistik *American Studies*
Anglistik *English Language and Literature*
Biologie *Biology*
Chemie *Chemistry*
Computerwissenschaft *Computer Science*
Geisteswissenschaften *Humanities*
Germanistik *German Language and Literature*
Informatik *Information Technology*
Jura *Law*
Kunstgeschichte *History of Art*
Philosophie *Philosophy*
Physik *Physics*
Psychologie *Psychology*
Romanistik *Romance Languages and Literature*
Sozialwissenschaften *Social Sciences*
Soziologie *Sociology*
Wirtschaftswissenschaften *Economics*

Grammatische Hinweise

1 *Past tense*

Formation

To form the past tense – or imperfect as it is sometimes called – of weak verbs, add the appropriate endings, indicated in the box below, to the stem.

Because of the vowel changes that strong verbs undergo, the past tense form cannot usually be deduced from the infinitive and therefore has to be learned. The endings indicated in the box are added to the basic past tense form.

Weak verbs **spielen**	**Strong verbs** **fahren**
ich spiel-te	ich fuhr
du spiel-test	du fuhr-st
er/sie/es spiel-te	er/sie/es fuhr
wir spiel-ten	wir fuhr-en
ihr spiel-tet	ihr fuhr-t
sie/Sie spiel-ten	sie/Sie fuhr-en

As with the present tense, certain verbs need an extra **e** to 'oil the works':

arbeiten	ich arbeit**e**te	regnen	es regn**e**te
finden	du fand**e**st	lesen	du las**e**st

In the past tense, the irregular verbs **sein**, **haben** and **werden** behave as follows:

sein	**haben**	**werden**
ich war	ich hatte	ich wurde
du warst	du hattest	du wurdest
er/sie/es war	er/sie/es hatte	er/sie/es wurde
wir waren	wir hatten	wir wurden
ihr wart	ihr hattet	ihr wurdet
sie/Sie waren	sie/Sie hatten	sie/Sie wurden

The modal verbs (**können**, **müssen**, etc.) and **wissen** add the weak verb endings to the basic past tense form:

Ich konn-te	ich muß-te
ich woll-te	ich durf-te
ich moch-te	ich wuß-te

Ich konnte gestern nicht kommen. *I was not able to come yesterday.*
Wir mußten zu Hause bleiben. *We had to stay at home.*
Wußtet ihr das nicht? *Didn't you know that?*

2 Perfect tense

Formation

The perfect tense of most verbs is formed with the present tense of **haben** together with the past participle of the verb in question. The past participle is sent to the end of the sentence or clause:

Sie hat gestern hier gearbeitet. *She worked here yesterday.*
Ich habe dieses Buch gelesen. *I have read this book.*

A small group of verbs uses **sein** instead of **haben**:

Sie sind nach Italien gefahren. *They have gone to Italy.*
Wann ist er gekommen? *When did he come?*

Verbs that use **sein** are normally verbs of coming and going, appearing and disappearing, happening and staying:

Er ist spurlos verschwunden. *He has disappeared without trace.*
Er ist gestern gestorben. *He died yesterday.*
Wann ist es passiert? *When did it happen?*
Sie ist in Dresden geblieben. *She has stayed in Dresden.*

These verbs are asterisked (*) in the **Glossar** at the end of the book.

Past participles

Weak verbs: the past participles of weak verbs are formed by taking the stem of the verb and adding **ge**- at the front and -**t** at the end:

mach-en	**ge**-mach-**t**	spiel-en	**ge**-spiel-**t**

Certain verbs need an extra **e** to 'oil the works':

antworten	ge-antwort-**et**	regnen	ge-regn-**et**

Verbs that end in **-ieren** do not add a **ge**- at the front of the stem:

studier-en	studier-t	telefonier-en	telefonier-t

Strong verbs: the past participles of strong verbs have a **ge**- at the front and an **-en** at the end. The middle part has to be learned, but does bear some relationship to the infinitive:

fahren	**ge**-fahr-**en**	singen	**ge**-sung-**en**
bleiben	**ge**-blieb-**en**	brechen	**ge**-broch-**en**

Note that the past participle of **essen** needs an extra **-g-**:

essen	ge-**g**-essen

Irregular verbs: irregular weak verbs normally add a **ge**- at the front end and a **-t** at the end like other weak verbs, but they are similar to strong verbs in that the stem is often subject to a vowel change:

denken	ge-dach-t	bringen	ge-brach-t

The past participles of modal verbs are formed similarly:

können	ge-konn-t	müssen	ge-muß-t	wollen	ge-woll-t
dürfen	ge-durf-t	sollen	ge-soll-t	mögen	ge-moch-t

Note, however, that these past participles are used only when the modal verb stands on its own:

Ich habe es nicht gekonnt. — *I wasn't able to do it.*
Sie hat ihn gemocht. — *She liked him.*

When modal verbs are used together with another verb, the perfect tense is formed by the use of **haben** with a double infinitive construction.

Ich habe nicht mitgehen wollen.	*I didn't want to go along (with the others).*
Sie hat gestern arbeiten müssen.	*She had to work yesterday.*

It is even possible to find three infinitives together in sentences such as:

Hans hat nicht schwimmen gehen wollen.	*Hans didn't want to go swimming.*

***Sein, haben* and *werden*:** the past participles of **sein**, **haben** and **werden** are **gewesen**, **gehabt** and **geworden** respectively:

Sind Sie mal in Deutschland gewesen?	*Have you ever been to Germany?*
Wir haben viel Arbeit gehabt.	*We've had a lot of work.*
Wie sind sie so reich geworden?	*How did they become so rich?*

Separable verbs: the past participles of separable verbs, whether weak or strong, have the **-ge-** in between the separable particle and the verb:

abholen	ab-**ge**-holt	abfahren	ab-**ge**-fahren

Inseparable verbs: these do not add a **ge-** in order to form the past participle. The inseparable prefixes include: **be-**, **ent-**, **emp-**, **er-**, **ge-**, **miß-**, **ver-**, **wider-**, **zer-**:

beantworten	beantwortet	zerbrechen	zerbrochen

3 Uses of the past and perfect tenses

It is not easy to give hard and fast rules for the use of the past and perfect tenses. Generally speaking, however, the past tense is used in more formal contexts and the perfect tense in less formal and in colloquial contexts. In everyday spoken language, the perfect tense predominates. The past tense is used in the spoken language to some extent in Northern and Central Germany but is much less frequently heard in Southern Germany, Switzerland, Austria and South Tirol.

The past tense predominates in narrative fiction and non-fiction and in newspaper reporting. It is also widely used in formal speeches and lectures. The use of the past tense gives a certain distance from the events being referred to, whereas the use of the perfect tense suggests a greater degree of immediacy. It is nevertheless possible to find examples of both tenses in one and the same spoken or written text.

There is a tendency for newspaper reports to use the perfect tense for the first verb and the past tense for subsequent verbs:

Berufsbedingten Spürsinn **haben** Grenzbeamte am deutsch-schweizerischen Autobahnzollkontrollpunkt Weil **bewiesen**, als sie ein betagtes Ehepaar aus den Niederlanden **anhielten**. Aus dem Wagen **förderten** sie 104 Pakete Haschisch zutage . . . . Das Amtsgericht Lörrach **erließ** gegen den 67jährigen Mann und seine fünf Jahre ältere Frau Haftbefehl.

(*Westfälische Nachrichten*)

(*Border officials at the German-Swiss motorway checkpoint of Weil demonstrated professional intuition when they stopped an elderly married couple from the Netherlands. They produced 104 packs of hashish from the car. . . The Lörrach district court issued a warrant for the arrest of the 67-year-old man and his wife, who is five years his senior.*)

Certain verbs are more likely than others to be found in the past tense rather than the perfect tense. This is particularly the case with the modal verbs and **sein**, **haben** and **werden**:

Er wollte mich besuchen.	*He wanted to visit me.*
Sie war ein Jahr in Italien.	*She was in Italy for a year.*
Wir hatten kein Geld.	*We didn't have any money.*
Sie wurde ganz rot.	*She went all red.*

Nevertheless, it would also be possible to find:

Er hat mich besuchen wollen.
Sie ist ein Jahr in Italien gewesen.
Wir haben kein Geld gehabt.
Sie ist ganz rot geworden.

4 *Relative clauses*

Relative pronouns

Relative pronouns enable us to combine into one sentence two sets of information about one person or object:

Sentence 1 This book is not very interesting.
Sentence 2 I bought this book yesterday.

Combination of sentence 1 and sentence 2:

This book	that I bought yesterday	is not very interesting.
(*main clause*)	(*relative clause*)	(*main clause*)

Note that in the relative clause *this book* has been replaced by the relative pronoun *that*.

In English, it is often possible to omit the relative pronoun in a relative clause:

This book I bought yesterday is not very interesting.

It is not possible to omit relative pronouns in this way in German. Relative clauses must begin with a comma and end with either a comma, a full stop or a question mark.

Satz 1 Dieses Buch ist nicht sehr interessant.
Satz 2 Dieses Buch habe ich gestern gekauft.

Dieses Buch, **das** ich gestern gekauft habe, ist nicht sehr interessant.
(*Hauptsatz*) (*Relativsatz*) (*Hauptsatz*)

Note that the finite verb (in this case **habe**) is sent to the end of the relative clause.

Not only must the relative pronoun be retained in German, but any preposition connected with it must be placed at the beginning of the relative clause:

Satz 1 Wie heißt die Person?
Satz 2 Du bist mit der Person ins Kino gegangen.

Wie heißt die Person, **mit der** du ins Kino gegangen bist?
(*Präposition*)
(*Hauptsatz*) (*Relativsatz*)

While a similar structure is possible in English –

What is the name of the person **with whom** you went to the pictures?

– the most common spoken English version would be:

What is the name of the person you went to the pictures **with**?

Relative pronouns agree in number and gender with the noun they refer to. So, for instance, in the example sentence above, the pronoun **der** refers back to **die Person** (singular and feminine). In addition to number and gender, case also plays a role and in the example sentence just quoted the relative pronoun follows **mit**, which takes the dative. So the relative pronoun has to be dative, feminine, singular, i.e. **der**.

Here are examples of relative clauses which have occurred in the **Aufnahmen** for **Lektionen 1** and **2**:

Es muß all die Arbeit getan werden, **die** während der Woche liegengeblieben ist. (*nom., f., sing.*)
Kennst du denn Leute, **die** studiert haben und nachher keine Stellung gefunden haben? (*nom., plur.*)
Es hat ja jeder, **der** Abitur gemacht hat, das Recht auf ein Hochschulstudium. (*nom., m., sing.*)

Summary of relative pronouns

	Singular Masculine	**Plural Feminine**	**Neuter**	**All genders**
	Der Mann,	Die Frau,	Das Kind	Die Männer, Frauen, Kinder,
Nom.	der . . .	die . . .	das . . .	die . . .
Acc.	den . . .	die . . .	das . . .	die . . .
Gen.	dessen . . .	deren . . .	dessen . . .	deren . . .
Dat.	dem . . .	der . . .	dem . . .	denen . . .

Examples of relative pronouns in use

- Nominative

Wie hießt der Student, **der** bei Frau Werner wohnt?
Kennen Sie die Studentin, **die** bei Herrn Gruber wohnt?
Ich suche ein Haus, **das** nicht zu groß ist.
Wie heißen die Studenten, **die** dich gestern besucht haben?

- Accusative

Wie heißt der Ingenieur, für **den** du arbeitest?
Wo wohnt die alte Dame, **die** du jeden Tag besuchst?
Ist das nicht das Kind, **das** wir gestern gesehen haben?
Wo sind die Häuser, **die** die Firma Krause zu verkaufen hat?

- Genitive

Kennst du den Studenten, **dessen** Freundin bei Frau Huber wohnt?
Ist das nicht die Frau, **deren** Sohn in England studiert hat?
Das Buch, **dessen** Seiten zerrissen sind, werde ich nicht lesen.
Das sind Manuela und Daniel, **deren** Eltern in Namibia wohnen.

- Dative

Der Amerikaner, mit **dem** ich essen gegangen bin, ist sehr sympathisch.
Die Spanierin, mit **der** mein Bruder verheiratet ist, kommt aus Madrid.
Das Kind, **dem** ich 10 DM geschenkt habe, heißt Markus.
Die Freunde, bei **denen** wir in Rom gewohnt haben, kommen im Mai nach London.

Welch-

Welch- with the appropriate ending is occasionally used as a relative pronoun instead of **der**, **die** or **das**. It can be used to avoid repetition of forms, but such repetition is in general not considered to be particularly bad style:

Die, **welche** mitkommen wollen, müssen bis Dienstag unterschreiben.
or
Die (jenigen), **die** mitkommen wollen, müssen bis Dienstag unterschreiben.

Was

Was is used as a relative pronoun after such words as **alles**, **etwas**, **vieles**, **nichts**, **manches** and after indefinite neuter adjectival expressions, such as **das Beste**, **das Schlimmste**, **das Einfachste**:

Alles, was er sagte, war falsch. *Everything (that) he said was wrong.*

Es stimmte nichts, was er sagte.	*Nothing (that) he said was correct.*
Das Schlimmste, was mir je passiert ist, . . .	*The worst (thing) that ever happened to me . . .*

Note that, as with other relative clauses, **was** clauses need the appropriate punctuation.

Übungen

1 Using all 12 past participles from the list below, fill in the 12 gaps in the text.

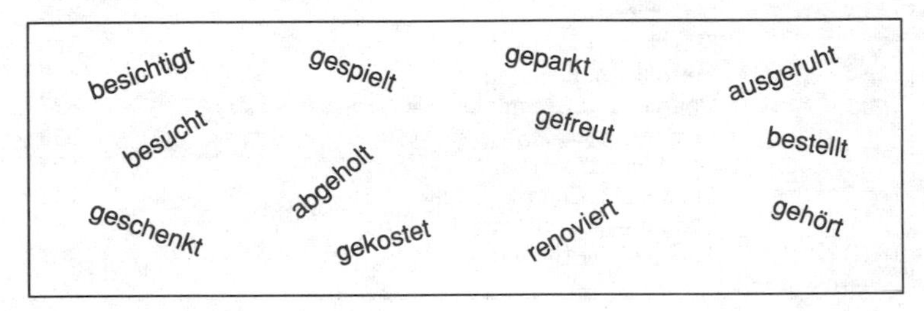

Gestern nachmittag hat Frank Jens seinen Freund Jan Frey vom Bahnhof . . . (*a*) . . . Frank hat seinen Wagen in einem Parkhaus im Stadtzentrum . . . (*b*) . . ., und sie haben dann die Paulskirche am Marktplatz . . . (*c*) . . . Die Kirche hat man vor ein paar Monaten . . . (*d*) . . . Im Café Sieben gegenüber von der Kirche haben sie sich eine Tasse Kaffee . . . (*e*) . . . und sich eine halbe Stunde . . . (*f*) . . . Der Kaffee war sehr teuer und hat Frank fast 5 DM . . . (*g*) . . . Nachher haben sie Franks Freundin Anna . . . (*h*) . . . Jan hat ihr Blumen . . . (*i*) . . ., und sie hat sich natürlich . . . (*j*) . . . Am Abend haben sie im Radio Musik . . . (*k*) . . . und Karten . . . (*l*) . . .

2 The extract overleaf is from the *Personal- und Vorlesungsverzeichnis* (catalogue of staff and lectures) of the Universität-Gesamthochschule Paderborn. Some of the subjects areas are immediately recognisable, others are not so clear. Match 12 of them with the appropriate English equivalents overleaf. You should in most instances be able to work out which is which from the component parts of the German titles.

Lehrveranstaltungen

Fachbereich		Seite
	Für Hörer aller Fachbereiche	205
(*a*)	Philosophie, Geschichte, Geographie, Religions- und Gesellschaftswissenschaften	213
(*b*)	Erziehungswissenschaft, Psychologie, Sportwissenschaft	229
(*c*)	Sprach- und Literaturwissenschaften	245
(*d*)	Kunst, Musik, Gestaltung	273
(*e*)	Wirtschaftswissenschaften	283
(*f*)	Physik	307
(*g*)	Architektur – Landespflege	373
(*h*)	Bauingenieurwesen	385
(*i*)	Landbau	415
(*j*)	Maschinentechnik I	315
(*k*)	Maschinentechnik II	395
(*l*)	Maschinentechnik III	419
(*m*)	Chemie und Chemietechnik	327
(*n*)	Elektrotechnik	339
(*o*)	Nachrichtentechnik	183
(*p*)	Elektrische Energietechnik	185
(*q*)	Mathematik – Informatik	353
(*r*)	Technischer Umweltschutz	201

(i) Agriculture
(ii) Economics
(iii) Telecommunications (technology)
(iv) Education
(v) Civil Engineering
(vi) Electrical Engineering
(vii) Technical Environmental Protection
(viii) Social Sciences
(ix) Landscaping
(x) Linguistics
(xi) History
(xii) Mechanical Engineering

3 Verbinden Sie die folgenden Sätze, indem sie das entsprechende Relativpronomen verwenden.

Beispiel Marianne wohnt in einem alten Haus. Das Haus gehört ihren Eltern.

Marianne wohnt in einem alten Haus, das ihren Eltern gehört.

(*a*) Peter ist Englischlehrer an einer deutschen Universität. Die Universität ist sehr alt.
(*b*) Birgits Tochter geht in einen Kindergarten. Der Kindergarten ist ganz in der Nähe.
(*c*) Am Wochenende machen wir die Hausarbeiten. Die Hausarbeiten sind während der Woche liegengeblieben.
(*d*) Corinna arbeitet als Kellnerin in einem Restaurant. Das Restaurant ist bis um Mitternacht durchgehend geöffnet.
(*e*) Corinna besucht nur selten ihre Eltern. Ihre Eltern wohnen sehr weit von ihr entfernt.
(*f*) Abends geht sie ab und zu mit ihrem Freund ins Kino. Das Kino bietet ein gutes Programm.
(*g*) Frau Beitz denkt oft an ihren Mann. Ihr Mann ist vor einigen Jahren verstorben.
(*h*) Im Sommer frühstückt sie auf ihrem Balkon. Der Balkon liegt in der Morgensonne.
(*i*) Am Wochenende kommt sie ihr Sohn Helmut besuchen. Ihr Sohn wohnt mit seiner Frau in Hamburg.
(*j*) Frau Beitz strickt gerade einen Pullover für ihre Urenkelin. Ihre Urenkelin wohnt in Osnabrück.

4 Bilden Sie Sätze im Perfekt mit Hilfe der Stichworte.

Beispiel
Ich/ München/ Anglistik studieren.
Ich habe in München Anglistik studiert.

(*a*) Ich/ fünf Jahre lang/ bei Freunden/ Schellingstraße/ wohnen.
(*b*) Ich/ meistens/ zu Fuß/ zur Uni gehen.
(*c*) Mittags/ ich/ Mensa/ essen.
(*d*) Oft/ ich/ Bibliothek/ arbeiten.
(*e*) Das Leben in München/ sehr gut/ gefallen.
(*f*) Ein Auslandsjahr/ ich/ in England/ verbringen.
(*g*) Dort/ ich/ viele britische Studenten/ kennenlernen.
(*h*) Ich/ Englischkenntnisse/ natürlich/ auch enorm verbessern.
(*i*) Eigentlich/ ich/ wollen/ in England bleiben.
(*j*) Ich/ aber/ zurückkommen/ und Staatsexamen ablegen.
(*k*) In Sommerferien/ immer/ Freunde in England/ besuchen.
(*l*) Vor drei Jahren/ sich bewerben um/ Stelle als Englischlehrerin.

5 Now imagine that you are at a greater distance in time from the above events and that you are recording them for more formal purposes. Use the past tense to achieve this effect.

6 Was hat Frank Bäcker in der letzten Zeit gemacht? Bilden Sie Sätze im Perfekt mit Hilfe der Stichworte.

Beispiel
Gestern abend – mit Freundin – Kino gehen
Gestern abend ist er mit seiner Freundin ins Kino gegangen.

(*a*) Sonntag nachmittag – mit Familie – spazieren gehen.
(*b*) Montag abend – bei Freundin – fernsehen.
(*c*) Dienstag – acht Stunden – Bibliothek arbeiten.
(*d*) Dienstag abend – Stadt – zu viel trinken.
(*e*) Mittwoch – sehr spät – aufstehen.
(*f*) Mittwoch nachmittag – Briefe schreiben.
(*g*) Donnerstag früh – nach Berlin fahren.
(*h*) In Berlin – viele Studienbücher kaufen.
(*i*) Bis 4.00 Uhr morgens – Diskothek – tanzen.
(*j*) Von fünf bis neun – bei Freund – auf Couch – schlafen.

7 The gaps in the following sentences will give you the words to fill into the grid horizontally. A word will be revealed vertically (*k*). It is something people need after leaving school.

(*a*) In einer .... werden junge Leute angemessen ausgebildet.
(*b*) Deshalb entscheiden sich viele Schulabgänger für eine Lehre, anstatt ein langes .... zu machen.
(*c*) Nach dem Staatsexamen .... oft keine Aussicht auf eine Stellung.
(*d*) Nach dem ...... kann man entweder studieren oder eine Lehre machen.
(*e*) Viel mehr Jugendliche machen heute die .... Reife, damit sie besser qualifiziert sind.
(*f*) Wenn man eine gute Stellung sucht, muß man heutzutage auch viel ..... haben.
(*g*) Eine Lehre als ....kaufmann/frau ist bei jungen Leuten auch sehr beliebt.
(*h*) Leider haben Jugendliche mit .... abschluß oft keine Chance gegen Leute mit Mittlerer Reife oder Abitur.
(*i*) Es hilft aber, wenn man gute .... hat.
(*j*) Im Ausland zu studieren macht .... viel Spaß.

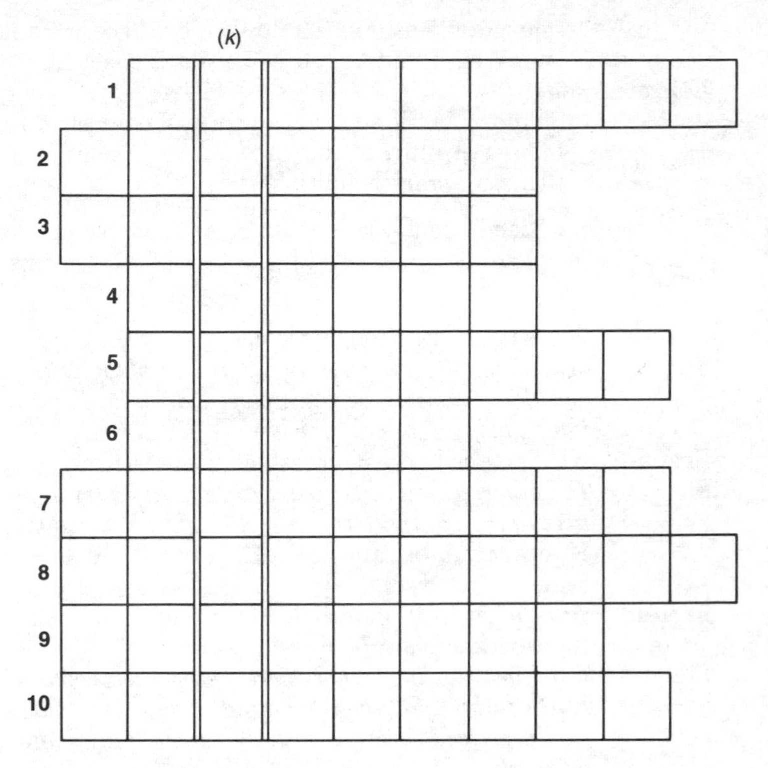

8 Jutta talks to her teacher about career plans after having done her **Mittlere Reife**. Complete the dialogue, playing the part of the teacher asking questions. There might be more than one possible answer, but you will find one possible solution in the key to the exercises. The type of questions you will need to ask occur in some form or other in the **Aufnahmen**.

Lehrerin (*a*)
Jutta Ich habe mich schon mehrmals beworben, aber bis jetzt habe ich leider noch keinen Ausbildungsplatz gefunden.
Lehrerin (*b*)
Jutta Ich habe mich um eine Stelle als Bankkauffrau beworben.
Lehrerin (*c*)
Jutta Ich weiß, daß die Konkurrenz groß ist, aber ich habe

sehr gute Zensuren, und außerdem habe ich schon einmal ein Praktikum bei einer Bank gemacht.

Lehrerin (*d*)

Jutta Dann werde ich mich um einen Ausbildungsplatz als Industriekauffrau bewerben. Da sind meine Chancen wahrscheinlich besser.

9 You talk to a friend about your career plans after having done A-Levels. Complete the dialogue with the help of the prompts in English.

Freund Was hast du denn jetzt nach dem Abitur vor?

Sie *Tell him that you actually wanted to study, but that you don't want to be unemployed afterwards, so you intend to do an apprenticeship.*

Freund Was für eine Lehre möchtest du denn machen?

Sie *Tell him that you really want to do a carpentry apprenticeship, but that the people who have done a* **Hauptschulabschuß** *or* **Mittlere Reife** *have a better chance there.*

Freund Warum bewirbst du dich denn nicht um eine Stelle als Industriekaufmann?

Sie *Tell him you know that more and more people with* **Abitur** *apply for these training places, but that you would prefer to work creatively rather than doing an office job.*

Freund Und was willst du machen, wenn es mit der Schreinerlehre nicht klappt?

Sie *Tell him that then, you want to study Biology and become a teacher, and that hopefully, when you have done your final exam, the demand for teachers will be higher once again.*

Höraufgabe

1 Auslandsstudium

Thomas und Stefan treffen sich nach einigen Jahren in ihrer Heimatstadt wieder, und unterhalten sich über die Vor- und

Nachteile eines Auslandsstudiums.

1 Wo hat Thomas studiert?
2 Was hat er studiert?
3 Im wievielten Semester ist Stefan?
4 Warum hat Thomas im Ausland studiert, und nicht in Deutschland?
5 Hat sich das Englisch von Thomas durch das Studium verbessert?
6 Sind die Vorlesungen und Seminare an deutschen Universitäten kleiner als an englischen Universitäten?
7 Hat Stefan viel Kontakt zu seinem Prof?
8 Warum will Stefan nicht im Ausland studieren?
9 Verlangen die deutschen Universitäten Studiengebüren?
10 Ist Thomas der Meinung, daß sich der finanzielle Aufwand gelohnt hat?

2 Studienkosten: ein Ost–West-Vergleich

Eine ostdeutsche Studentin (Damaris) die an der Humboldt-Universität Berlin studient spricht über ihr Studium nach der Wende.

1 Wieviel Jahre muß Damaris noch studieren, bevor sie mit ihrer Ausbildung vollkommen fertig ist?
2 Wie finanziert sie ihr Studium?
3 Muß sie das Geld, das sie bekommt, zurückzahlen?
4 Wovon hängt es ab, wieviel man von dem BaföG-Geld zurückzahlen muß?
5 Werden die ostdeutschen Studenten vom BaföG-Amt bevorzugt?
6 Welches sind die Unterschiede in der Behandlung von west- und ostdeutschen Studenten in Bezug auf das BaföG?
7 Warum bekommen ostdeutsche Studenten weniger BaföG als westdeutsche Studenten?
8 Ist es wahr, daß die Lebenshaltungskosten zwischen Ost- und Westdeutschland unterschiedlich sind?
9 Sind die Mieten in Westdeutschland höher oder niedriger als in Ostdeutschland?
10 Sind die Löhne in Ostdeutschland genauso hoch wie in Westdeutschland?

Lesetexte

1 Studienzeiten

ITALIENER STUDIEREN AM LÄNGSTEN

Am längsten brauchen die italienischen Studenten. Von der Immatrikulation bis zum bestandenen Examen gehen *im Durchschnitt* siebeneinhalb Jahre (also 15 Semester) drauf. *Nicht viel schneller schaffen* es ihre Kommilitonen in Frankreich. Auch die Studenten in Deutschland verbringen mit sieben Jahren überdurchschnittlich viel Zeit in Hörsälen, Seminaren und Bibliotheken – mehr jedenfalls als *vorgesehen*. Denn die sogenannte Regelstudienzeit – also die Zeit, in der man das Studium eigentlich *erfolgreich* bewältigen sollte – beträgt vier bis fünf Jahre. Das ist *genau* die Zeitspanne, die von den amerikanischen und japanischen Studenten bis zum Examen *benötigt* wird. Noch schneller sind die britischen Studenten. Sie schaffen ihr Pensum in *weniger als* vier Jahren.

Statistische Angaben: W. Kramer: Verkürzung der Bildungszeiten, Institut der deutschen Wirtschaft.

(*Globus*)

am längsten *longest*
bestanden *passed*
draufgehen *to go, elapse (of time)*
schaffen *to manage*
der/die Kommilitone/in (-n/-nen) *fellow student*
Zeit verbringen (i, a, a) *to spend time*
überdurchschnittlich *above average*
der Hörsaal (-äle) *lecture theatre*
das Seminar (-e) *seminar*
die Bibliothek (-en) *library*
vorgesehen *planned*
die Regelstudienzeit (-en) *period within which a university course should be completed*
bewältigen *to cope with*
das Pensum (-en) *amount of work, work quota*

1 Wer braucht wie lange? Ordnen Sie zu!

(*a*)	die italienischen Studenten	(i)	vier bis fünf Jahre
(*b*)	die französischen Studenten	(ii)	sieben Jahre
(*c*)	die deutschen Studenten	(iii)	siebeneinhalb Jahre
(*d*)	die amerikanischen Studenten	(iv)	vier Jahre oder weniger
(*e*)	die japanischen Studenten	(v)	fast siebeneinhalb Jahre
(*f*)	die britischen Studenten	(vi)	vier bis fünf Jahre

2 Wie lange ist die Regelstudienzeit an deutschen Universitäten?

3 Finden Sie jeweils ein passendes Wort im Text (kursiv gedruckt) für die nachfolgenden Wörter.

(*a*) durchschnittlich
(*b*) unter
(*c*) mit Erfolg
(*d*) die meiste Zeit
(*e*) gebraucht
(*f*) benötigen
(*g*) geplant
(*h*) bewältigen
(*i*) exakt
(*j*) ungefähr in derselben Zeit

2 Anzeige: das Arbeitsamt

HÄTTEN SIE DEN JUNGEN EINSTEIN ALS LEHRLING GENOMMEN?

Bekanntlich waren die Schulnoten Einsteins alles andere als befriedigend. Auch viele andere berühmte Beispiele – von Richard Wagner bis Robert Bosch und Thomas Mann – beweisen, daß die Schulleistung und die Lebensleistung nicht immer miteinander zu tun haben. Dies sollten Sie bei der Einstellung von Lehrlingen auch bedenken. Geben Sie schwächeren Schulabgängern eine Chance, vertrauen Sie auf die Leistungsbereitschaft von ausländischen Jugendlichen oder von Körperbehinderten.

Daß das Angebot an Lehrstellenbewerben so gering ist, liegt vor allem an der niedrigen Geburtenrate in den siebziger Jahren. Darum müssen Sie sich heute marktwirtschaftlich verhalten: Bieten Sie überzeugende Ausbildungskonzepte, laden Sie ein zu Schnupperlehre, Ferienjobs und Betriebsführungen. Und vor allem: Stellen Sie heraus, was Ihr Ausbildungsangebot besonders attraktiv macht. Bei allen Ihren Bemühungen unterstützt Sie gerne die Berufsberatung im Arbeitsamt. Rufen Sie an und bleiben Sie in ständigem Kontakt.

Hätten Sie . . . genommen? *Would you have taken . . ?* This is a form of the conditional (see **Lektion 9**)
bekanntlich *as is well known*
alles andere als *anything but*
beweisen (ei, ie, ie) *to prove*
miteinander zu tun haben *to have to do with each other*
der/die Bewerber/-in (-/**-nen**) *applicant*
niedrig *low*
die Geburtenrate (-n) *birth rate*
sich marktwirtschaftlich verhalten *to act according to the principles of the market economy*
die Schnupperlehre (-) programme which gives school leavers the opportunity to work in a company/ workshop for a short period of time in order to find out whether they would like to train there
die Betriebsführung (**-en**) *guided tour of a company*
herausstellen (sep.) *to stress*

1 Beantworten Sie die folgenden Fragen:
(*a*) Was beweisen die Schulnoten von berühmten Leuten wie Albert Einstein, Richard Wagner, Robert Bosch und Thomas Mann?
(*b*) Wem sollen die Unternehmen auch eine Chance geben?
(*c*) Warum ist das Angebot an Lehrstellenbewerbern so gering?
(*d*) Wie sollen sich die Unternehmen deshalb verhalten?
(*e*) Welche Angebote sollen die Unternehmen den jungen Lehrstellenbewerbern machen?
(*f*) Wer unterstützt die Unternehmen bei ihren Bemühungen?

2 Finden Sie zu den angegebenen Vokabeln das entsprechende Substantiv/Verb. Versuchen Sie zuerst, die Aufgabe ohne Wörterbuch zu lösen – nehmen Sie aber ruhig ein Wörterbuch zu Hilfe, wenn Sie es brauchen sollten!

Beispiel beweisen – der Beweis

(*a*) tun
(*b*) die Einstellung
(*c*) bedenken
(*d*) vertrauen
(*e*) das Angebot
(*f*) verhalten
(*g*) die Bemühungen
(*h*) unterstützen
(*i*) anrufen
(*j*) die Beratung

Das deutsche Bildungswesen

Weiterbildung

(allgemeine und berufsbezogene Weiterbildung in vielfältigen Formen)

		Berufsqualifizierender Studienabscluß
		Universität/ Technische Universität, Pädagogische Hochschule
Berufsqualifizierender Abschluß	Allgemeine Hochschulreife	**Fachhochschule**
		Verwaltungsfachhochschule
		Kunsthochschule
Fachschule	**Abendgymnasium/ Kolleg**	**Gesamthochschule**

Schuljahr						
	Berufsbildender Abschluß				Allgemeine Hochschulreife	
13	Mittlerer Bildungsabscluß	Fachhochschulreife			**Gymnasiale Oberstufe**	13
12	**Berufsausbildung in Betrieb u.**	**Berufs- aufbau- Schule**	**Berufs- fach- Schule**	**Fach- ober- Schule**	(Gymnasium, Berufliches- Gymnasium, Fachgymnasium,	12
11	**Berufsschule (Duales System)**				Gesamtschule)	11
10	Berufsgrundbildungsjahr					10

Abschlüsse an Hauptschulen nach 9 oder 10 Jahren / Realschulabschluß

Schuljahr						
10		10. Schuljahr				10
9	Sonderschule	**Hauptschule**	**Realschule**	**Gymnasium**	**Gesamtschule**	9
8						8
7						7
6		Orientierungs-Stufe				6
5		(schulformabhängig oder schulformunabhängig)				5
4	Sonderschule	**Grundschule**				4
3						3
2						2
1						1
	Sonderkindergarten	**Kindergarten**				

4
BERUF UND ARBEITSLOSIGKEIT

Lernziele

In this unit you will learn how to

- talk about jobs and conditions of work
- ask about and state intentions and plans for the future
- form and use the future tense
- form and use co-ordinating and subordinating conjunctions
- form and use comparatives and superlatives

Aufnahmen

1 Was sind Sie von Beruf?

Auf einem Flug von Stuttgart nach Budapest unterhalten sich Herr Krause und Frau Kubig über ihre Reiseziele und ihre Berufe.

Herr Krause Wohin fliegen Sie? Nach Budapest?
Frau Kubig Nein, nach Wien. Und Sie?
Herr Krause Ich fliege bis nach Budapest. Ich habe dort geschäftlich zu tun. Machen Sie Urlaub in Wien?

Frau Kubig Nein. Ich gehe zu einem Ingenieur kongreß. Ich bin nämlich Bauingenieurin.

Herr Krause Was?! Da muß ich aber staunen! Bauingenieur habe ich mir immer als Männerberuf vorgestellt.

Frau Kubig Ach nein. Wir bilden zwar immer noch nur eine kleine Minderheit, aber Frauen gibt es schon seit mehreren Jahren in diesem Beruf.

Herr Krause Ja, wenn man so ein bißchen genauer hinschaut, findet man heutzutage Frauen in fast jedem Beruf.

Frau Kubig Und was sind Sie von Beruf, wenn ich fragen darf?

Herr Krause Ich bin leitender Angestellter bei einer Firma, die Werkzeugmaschinen herstellt. Ich fliege nach Budapest, um Verhandlungen mit einer ungarischen Firma zu führen.

Frau Kubig Und wie gefällt Ihnen Ihr Beruf?

Herr Krause Eigentlich habe ich nur selten genügend Zeit, mir diese Frage zu stellen! Ich bin jetzt seit sieben Jahren bei der Firma Pfauter beschäftigt und bin im allgemeinen sehr zufrieden. Bloß möchte ich etwas mehr Zeit haben für meine Frau und meine Kinder.

Frau Kubig Zeitmangel ist ja eines der größten Probleme, wenn man berufstätig ist. Und Geschäftsreisen nehmen natürlich viel Zeit in Anspruch.

Herr Krause Sicher, aber für mich ist das Reisen einer der attraktivsten Aspekte meiner Arbeit.

Frau Kubig Für mich auch.

Bemerkungen

sich unterhalten über (+ Acc.) *to talk about*
Ich habe dort geschäftlich zu tun *I am going there for business purposes*
Urlaub machen *to go on holiday*
der Bauingenieur (**-e**) *civil engineer*
staunen über (+ Acc.) *to be amazed at*
die Minderheit (**-en**) *minority*
bilden *to form, constitute*
genau(er) hinschauen *to take a close(r) look*
der/die leitende Angestellte (**-n**) *executive, manager*
die Werkzeugmaschine (**-n**) *machine tool*

herstellen (sep.) *to produce*
die Verhandlung (**-en**) *negotiation*
nur selten *only occasionally*
beschäftigen *to employ*
ich bin beschäftigt bei (+ Dat.) *I am employed at*
im allgemeinen *in general*
der Zeitmangel (no pl.) *lack of time*
berufstätig sein *to be (gainfully) employed*
die Geschäftsreise (**-n**) *business trip*

Richtig oder falsch?

Korrigieren Sie die falschen Aussagen.

1 Herr Krause macht Urlaub in Wien.
2 Frau Kubig hat geschäftlich in Budapest zu tun.
3 Frau Kubig ist Bauingenieurin.
4 Herr Krause hat sich Bauingenieur immer als Männerberuf vorgestellt.
5 Es gibt mehr Frauen als Männer, die Bauingenieure sind.
6 Frauen gibt es heutzutage fast in jedem Beruf.
7 Herr Krause ist auch Bauingenieur.
8 Herr Krause mag seinen Beruf nicht sehr.
9 Sein Beruf läßt ihm sehr wenig Zeit.
10 Frau Kubig verreist sehr gerne geschäftlich.

2 Was machst du jetzt für eine Arbeit?

In der Untergrundbahn begegnen sich Gerd und Heiko zum ersten Mal nach ihrer Studienzeit.

Gerd Du, Heiko! Lange nicht gesehen! Wie geht's dir?
Heiko Hallo, Gerd! Gut, danke.
Gerd Und was machst du jetzt für eine Arbeit?
Heiko Ich unterrichte Deutsch als Fremdsprache im Sprachinstitut in der Herder Straße.
Gerd Und wie gefällt dir deine Arbeit?
Heiko Im allgemeinen sehr gut. Meine Studenten sind alle motiviert und fleißig, da sie es nötig haben, so schnell wie möglich die deutsche Sprache zu erlernen. Das einzige, was mir nicht so gut gefällt, ist die Bezahlung.

Gerd Wenn das so ist, kannst du denn daraus einen richtigen Beruf machen? Oder hast du noch was ganz anderes vor?

Heiko Naja, ich bin natürlich auf der Warteliste für eine Lehramtsstelle. Du weißt ja, daß ich eigentlich Gymnasiallehrer für Deutsch und Latein werden möchte. Aber da es momentan so viele Anwärter gibt, werde ich wohl noch mindestens ein bis zwei Jahre warten müssen. Und was machst du eigentlich zur Zeit?

Gerd Ich mache gerade meinen Zivildienst in einem Heim für körperlich und geistig behinderte Kinder. Ich bin ja, wie du weißt, Kriegsdienstverweigerer.

Heiko Das stelle ich mir ungeheuer schwierig vor – wie kommst du denn zurecht?

Gerd Es gefällt mir sehr gut – ich komme mir jedenfalls nützlicher vor, als wenn ich bei der Bundeswehr Schießübungen machen würde. Aber es ist auch oft unheimlich anstrengend und nervenaufreibend.

Heiko Das glaube ich dir! Wie lange mußt du denn noch machen?

Gerd Noch sechs Monate – das habe ich auch unserer Regierung zu verdanken! Als Zivi bist du ja auch noch drei Monate länger im Dienst als einer, der beim Bund seine Zeit absitzt.

Heiko Das fand ich auch schon immer ungerechtfertigt. Zumal die Belastung im Zivildienst wahrscheinlich viel größer ist! Und was hast du danach vor?

Gerd Ich möchte Sozialarbeiter werden. Im Raum Frankfurt werden zur Zeit viele Stellen für Sozialpädagogen angeboten.

Heiko Das ist sicher auch kein einfacher Job! Auf jeden Fall wünsche ich dir viel Glück dabei.

Bemerkungen

was für ein (**e/n**) *what kind of* (colloquial)

die Studienzeit (**-en**) *period of study*. Note that in Germany the minimum period of study is four and a half years (**neun Semester**), for natural sciences often much longer, and that the first degree (**das Staatsexamen**) is more or less equivalent to an MA

unterrichten *to teach, instruct*

die Fremdsprache (**-n**) *foreign language*

das Sprachinstitut (**-e**) *institute of languages*

gefallen (ä, ie, a) *to please*
motiviert *motivated*
fleißig *hard-working*
etwas nötig haben *to need something*
die Bezahlung (**-en**) *pay*
der Anwärter-/die Anwärterin (**-nen**) *candidate* (*for*)
der Zivildienst *community service*. In Germany, young men have the option of compulsory military service (12 months) or community service, which can be working in a hospital, with old or handicapped people (15 months); there are currently discussions as to whether young women should also do some kind of compulsory service after leaving school/university
körperlich / geistig behindert *physically / mentally handicapped*
der Kriegsdienstverweigerer (-) *conscientious objector*. It has become increasingly commonplace for young men to refuse to do military service and to take up community service instead – consequently it has also become easier and socially more acceptable for them to do so. Conscientious objectors used to be regarded as 'cowards'; today, the immense commitment required of community service workers is generally acknowledged
die Schießübung (**-en**) *shooting practice*
nervenaufreibend *nerve-racking*
jemandem etwas verdanken *to be indebted to someone for something*
der Zivi short for **Zivildienstleistender**, *person doing community service*
im Dienst sein *to be on duty, in service*
der Bund short for **die Bundeswehr**, *German federal army*
absitzen *to serve* (colloquial) (Lit. to sit out, sit through)
die Belastung (**-en**) *strain*
der Sozialarbeiter (-)/**die Sozialarbeiterin** (**-nen**) *social worker*
der Sozialpädagoge (**-n**)/**die Sozialpädagogin** (**-nen**) *person with a degree in social education*

Richtig oder falsch?

Korrigieren Sie die falschen Aussagen.

1 Heiko unterrichtet zur Zeit deutsche Literatur an der Universität.
2 Die Arbeit gefällt ihm nicht so gut, weil die Studenten nicht lernen wollen.

3 Heiko will eigentlich lieber Gymnasiallehrer für Deutsch und Latein werden.
4 Er muß aber noch lange auf einen Platz warten, weil er so schlechte Noten in seinem Examen hatte.
5 Gerd macht zur Zeit Zivildienst.
6 Er arbeitet in einem Altersheim.
7 Die Arbeit gefällt ihm überhaupt nicht.
8 Zivildienst dauert länger als Militärdienst.
9 Heiko glaubt, daß Zivildienst einfacher ist als Militärdienst.
10 Nach seinem Zivildienst will Gerd Sozialarbeiter werden.
11 Es gibt im Raum Frankfurt zur Zeit wenige Stellen für Sozialarbeiter.

Sagen Sie's auf Deutsch!

1 Long time, no see!
2 What kind of work are you doing at the moment?
3 in general
4 they need to
5 if that is the case
6 as you know
7 How are you getting on?
8 I really enjoy it.
9 I feel more useful than . . .
10 there are many jobs going

3 Arbeitslosigkeit

Renate und Klaus, zwei Arbeitslose aus Erfurt, lernen sich auf dem Arbeitsamt kennen. Sie reden über ihre Probleme und über mögliche Lösungen.

Renate Seit wann sind Sie arbeitslos?

Klaus Seitdem mein Betrieb vor sechs Monaten stillgelegt wurde. Ich war 18 Jahre lang Maschinist in einer Schuhfabrik, die nach der Wiedervereinigung nicht mehr konkurrenzfähig war.

Renate Ja, mir ist es ähnlich ergangen. Wir hatten in unserem Betrieb ein paar Monate Kurzarbeit und dann nach erfolglosen Verhandlungen mit einem westdeutschen Unternehmen kam die Stillegung.

Klaus Und beim jetzigen Wirtschaftsklima besteht kaum eine Chance, eine neue Stellung zu finden.

Renate Da haben Sie sicher recht! Deshalb denke ich daran, eine Stellung im Westen zu suchen.

Klaus Für mich wäre so was undenkbar. Ich habe hier meine ganze Familie und meinen Freundeskreis. Außerdem ist es gar nicht so leicht, im Westen eine erschwingliche Wohnung zu finden.

Renate Was werden Sie also tun? Hier bleiben und dahinvegetieren?

Klaus Ich habe vor, mich über Computer-Kurse zu erkundigen. Wenn ich auf diesem Gebiet Kenntnisse und Fertigkeiten vorweisen kann, habe ich vielleicht eine Chance auf Arbeit.

Renate Gute Idee! Arbeit mit Computern hat wenigstens Zukunft. Ich wünsche Ihnen viel Glück dabei.

Klaus Danke, und ich wünsche Ihnen eine erfolgreiche Zukunft im Westen.

Renate Vielen Dank.

Bemerkungen

das Arbeitsamt (**¨er**) *job centre*
reden über (+ Acc.) *to talk about*
der Betrieb (**-e**) *company, firm*
stillegen (sep.) *to close down.* Note that when three identical consonants come together, as here in **still-legen**, one of the consonants is dropped
der Maschinist (**-en**) *machinist*
mir ist es ähnlich ergangen *I found myself in a similar situation*
die Kurzarbeit (**-en**) *short-time working, short time*
erfolglos *unsuccessful*
die Stillegung (**-en**) *close-down, closure*
das Wirtschaftsklima (no. pl.) *economic climate*
eine Stellung suchen *to look for a position/job*
undenkbar *unthinkable*
der Freundeskreis (**-e**) *circle of friends.* Note that in Germany the word **Freund(in)** is used much more restrictively, i.e. only for

real friends, while in English the word friend is often used to refer to a mere acquaintance – **Bekannte(r)**.
erschwinglich *affordable*
dahinvegetieren (sep.) *to drag out a miserable existence* (colloquial)
erfolgreich *successful*

Richtig oder falsch?

Korrigieren Sie die falschen Aussagen.

1 Klaus ist seit zwei Jahren arbeitslos.
2 Er war Maschinist in einer Schuhfabrik.
3 Renate hat auch in einer Schuhfabrik gearbeitet.
4 Beim jetzigen Wirtschaftsklima ist es sehr einfach, eine neue Stellung zu finden.
5 Klaus möchte eine Stellung im Westen suchen.
6 Renate hat schon eine neue Stellung gefunden.
7 Im Westen sind Wohnungen sehr teuer.
8 Renate möchte auch noch ein paar Computer-Kurse machen.
9 Klaus hat viele Freunde im Westen.
10 Er möchte aber lieber im Osten bleiben.

Redewendungen

- Talking about plans for the future

Was hast du vor?
Was möchtest du werden?
Was für Pläne hast du für die Zukunft?
Was für Absichten hast du?
Was beabsichtigst du zu tun?
Was gedenkst du zu tun? (gehobene Sprache/ elevated speech)
Was führst du im Schilde (Umgangssprache/ colloquial speech)
Was steuerst du an?
Was hast du dir zum Ziel gesetzt?
Wofür hast du dich beworben?

- Asking about intentions

Was hast du denn (in den Sommerferien) vor?

Was haben Sie denn (für heute abend) geplant?
Wie lange beabsichtigen Sie denn, (in Deutschland zu bleiben)?
Wie werden Sie denn Ihren Urlaub verbringen/gestalten?
Wann werden Sie denn in Urlaub fahren?
Werden Sie nächste Woche (nach England fliegen)?
Denken Sie daran, (sich ein neues Auto zu kaufen)?
Beabsichtigen Sie, (Ihre Ferien zu Hause zu verbringen)?
Haben Sie vor, (im Sommer nach Italien zu fahren?)

- Stating intentions

Ich habe vor, (eine Woche zu meiner Schwester zu fahren).
Ich beabsichtige, (mir einen neuen Job zu suchen).
Ich werde voraussichtlich (morgen abend nicht zu Hause sein).
Ich will (heute nachmittag ins Schwimmbad gehen).
Ich möchte (in einer Stunde gehen).
Ich gedenke, (meine Tochter in Australien zu besuchen).
Ich plane, (an meinem Geburtstag eine große Feier zu veranstalten).

- Saying that a plan/intention will not/did not come about

Damit wird es nicht klappen.
Damit (Mit meinem Urlaub) hat es leider nicht geklappt.
Daraus wird leider nichts werden.
Daraus (Aus meiner Geburtstagsfeier) ist leider nichts geworden.
Das wird wahrscheinlich ins Wasser fallen.
Meine Pläne sind leider ins Wasser gefallen.
Das Fest wird wohl abgesagt werden.
Die Feier ist gerade abgesagt worden.
Das wird sich wohl in Luft auflösen.
Das hat sich leider in Luft aufgelöst.
Mein Plan ist leider durchkreuzt worden.

- Saying that you have changed your mind

Ich habe es mir anders überlegt.
Ich möchte das doch nicht machen.
Ich werde heute abend doch nicht kommen.
Ich habe meine Absichten/Pläne geändert.
Das paßt mir jetzt doch nicht so gut.
Das muß ich jetzt doch absagen.
Diese Einladung/Diesen Termin kann ich leider nicht wahrnehmen.

Vokabeln

Verbs and nouns of stating plans

vorhaben	das Vorhaben
beabsichtigen	die Absicht
planen	der Plan
wollen	der Wille
gedenken	das Gedenken

Collocations concerning plans

ein Vorhaben durchführen *to carry out a plan*
ein Vorhaben in die Tat umsetzen *to realise a plan, put a plan into action*
eine Absicht kundtun *to reveal an intention*
einen Plan fassen *to make a plan*
eine Absicht haben *to have an intention, intend*
einen Plan durchkreuzen *to thwart, frustrate a plan*
nach Plan verlaufen *to go according to plan*
seinen Willen durchsetzen *to get one's way*

Grammatische Hinweise

1 Future tense

Formation

The future tense in German is formed with the present tense of **werden** together with the infinitive of the verb in question:

ich werde spielen	wir werden spielen
du wirst spielen	ihr werdet spielen
er/sie/es wird spielen	sie/Sie werden spielen

Uses

The future tense has rather limited use in German. As already mentioned in **Lektion 2** (page 44), the present tense is used more widely in German than it is in English to refer to future time:

Morgen um diese Zeit sind wir in Berlin.	*We'll be in Berlin this time tomorrow.*
Wann sagst du mir, ob du kommst?	*When will you tell me whether you'll be coming?*

It is certainly possible to use the future tense in most instances where future time is being referred to, and this also applies to the example sentences above:

Morgen um diese Zeit werden wir in Berlin sein.
Wann wirst du mir sagen, ob du kommen wirst?

Nevertheless, the present tense is usually preferred so long as the context makes the time reference clear.

The future tense tends to be used for

predictions

Heute wird es nicht mehr regnen.	*It won't rain any more today.*
Das wirst du bereuen!	*You'll regret that!*

promises

Ich werde dir morgen im Geschäft helfen.	*I'll help you in the shop tomorrow.*
Ich werde nicht zu spät kommen.	*I won't be late.*

firm intentions

Ich werde im Sommer in Italien arbeiten.	*I'll work in Italy in the summer.*
Ich werde heute abend mitkommen.	*I'll come along this evening.*

supposition

Du wirst heute wohl nichts essen wollen.	*You'll no doubt not want to eat anything today.*
Du wirst wohl müde sein.	*You'll no doubt be tired.*

probability

Er wird wohl heute abend ankommen.	*He'll probably arrive this evening.*
Anna wird wohl krank sein.	*Anna must be ill.*

Note that the modal particle **wohl** is often used with the future tense to express supposition or probability.

2 *Uses of* wollen

There is a tendency for English speakers to want to use **wollen** as a future tense auxiliary. For example, they produce sentences such as **Ich will heute abend ins Kino gehen** which does not have the meaning *I shall go to the cinema this evening* but actually means *I* ***intend*** *going to the cinema this evening.*

The use of **wollen** to express intention is relatively common:

Wir wollen nächstes Jahr nach Japan fahren.	*We intend going to Japan next year.*
Heike und Stefan wollen im Juli heiraten.	*Heike and Stefan plan to get married in July.*

Other uses of **wollen** are to express desire or willingness:

Ich wollte ein neues Auto kaufen.	*I wanted to buy a new car.*
Wollt ihr uns helfen?	*Are you willing to help us?*

3 Zu + *infinitive clauses*

There are a few prepositions which can be used together with an infinitive to create an infinitive clause. **Um** is probably the most frequently encountered among these prepositions. Others are (**an**)**statt**, **außer** and **ohne**.

Um . . . zu . . . ((In order) *to . . .*)

Ich fliege nach Budapest, um Verhandlungen mit einer ungarischen Firma zu führen. (see **Lektion 4, Aufnahme 1**)	*I'm flying to Budapest* (*in order*) *to conduct negotiations with a Hungarian firm.*

Um . . . zu . . . can also be used as follows:

Dieses Spiel ist zu einfach, um interessant zu sein.	*This game is too simple to be interesting.*
Florian ist jetzt alt genug, um im Geschäft mitzuhelfen.	*Florian is old enough now to help in the shop.*

(An)statt . . . zu . . . (Instead of . . . -ing)

Anstatt mir zu helfen, lag er auf dem Boden und lachte.	*Instead of helping me he lay on the ground laughing.*

***Außer . . . zu . . .* (Except, in addition to)**

Außer einzukaufen, hat er nicht geholfen.	*Except for shopping, he did not help.*
Außer einzukaufen, hat er auch noch abgewaschen.	*In addition to shopping, he also washed up.*

***Ohne . . . zu . . .* (Without . . . -ing)**

Er aß weiter, ohne seinen Freunden zu helfen.	*He carried on eating, without helping his friends.*

***Zu . . .* (no preposition) (To . . ./of . . . -ing)**

Ich habe heute keine Zeit, ins Kino zu gehen.	*I have no time today to go to the cinema.*
Und beim jetzigen Wirtschaftsklima besteht kaum eine Chance, eine neue Stellung zu finden.	*And in the present economic climate there's next to no chance of finding a new job.*
Ich habe vor, mich über Computer-Kurse zu erkundigen. (see **Lektion 4**, **Aufnahme 3**)	*I intend informing myself (finding out) about computer courses.*

4 Dependent and independent clauses

If two sentences are joined together with a word such as *and* or *but* (so-called co-ordinating conjunctions) to form one sentence, the new sentence then consists of two clauses. Each clause is called an independent clause because it can stand on its own:

Sentence 1	We visited friends.
Sentence 2	Then we went to the cinema.

Combination of the two sentences:

We visited friends	and	then we went to the cinema.
(independent clause 1)		*(independent clause 2)*

If, however, two sentences are joined together with a so-called subordinating conjunction (such as *because* or *although*), with a relative pronoun (see **Lektion 3**, pages 70–73) or with **daß,** *that,* one clause becomes the main clause (**Hauptsatz**) and the other, the dependent or subordinate clause (**Nebensatz**):

Sentence 1 He stayed at home.
Sentence 2 He was ill.

Combination of the two sentences:

He stayed at home	because he was ill.
(*main clause*)	(*dependent clause*)

Note that the dependent clause, *because he was ill*, cannot stand on its own, except in answer to a question (such as *Why did he stay at home?*), whereas the main clause, *He stayed at home*, is a complete sentence in its own right.

Relative clauses (which were dealt with in **Lektion 3**, pages 70–73) are also dependent clauses.

Co-ordinating conjunctions

In German, the most common co-ordinating conjunctions that are used to link independent clauses are:

aber *but*
beziehungsweise (bzw.) *or*
entweder . . . oder . . . *either . . or . . .*
oder *or*
nicht . . . sondern . . . *not . . . but . . .*
und *and*

These are 'zero-rated' as far as word order is concerned, and the finite verb remains the second element in both clauses:

Ich möchte mit euch ins Theater gehen, aber ich kann heute nicht.
1 2 0 1 2

Marco arbeitete fünf Jahre lange in Deutschland, bzw. er wohnte fünf Jahre dort.

Entweder du gibst mir mein Portemonnaie zurück, oder ich gehe zur Polizei.

Morgen können wir zu Hause bleiben, oder du kannst mit Gerd nach München fahren.

Lars ist gestern nicht nach Leipzig geflogen, sondern er ist in Hamburg geblieben.

Wir sind essen gegangen, und wir haben dann einen Spaziergang durch den Park gemacht.

As in English, these conjunctions can also be used to link shorter elements than full sentences:

Ich wollte nicht Tee, sondern Kaffee.
Du kannst entweder Tee oder Orangensaft haben.

A further co-ordinating conjunction, **denn** (*because, for*), is sometimes found in written German. Unlike the subordinating conjunction **weil** (*because*), **denn** cannot be used to start a sentence:

Der junge Student verbrachte die Nacht auf dem Bahnhof, denn er hatte kein Geld für ein Hotelzimmer.

Subordinating conjunctions

The main subordinating conjunctions in German are:

als *when* (on *one* occasion)	**seit(dem)** *since*
bevor, ehe *before*	**sobald** *as soon as*
bis *until, by the time*	**solange** *as long as*
da *as*	**während** *while, whilst*
damit *so that*	**weil** *because*
daß *that*	**wenn** *when(ever), if*
indem *by + -ing*	**wie** *as*
nachdem *after*	**zumal** *especially as*
obwohl, obgleich *although*	

These conjunctions have the effect of sending the finite verb to the end of the subordinate clause:

Als ich heute aufgestanden **bin**,	konnte ich nichts essen.
(*subordinate clause*)	(*main clause*)

Ich möchte jetzt schlafen gehen, **damit** ich morgen nicht müde **bin**.
Ich weiß, **daß** du heute nicht kommen **kannst**.
Obwohl ich sehr müde **war**, mußte ich um 6.00 Uhr aufstehen.
Weil es **regnet**, werden wir zu Hause bleiben.
Wenn ich ihn **sehe**, ist er immer allein.
Zumal er so wenig Geld **verdiente**, wollte er nicht in einem teuren Restaurant essen.

Note that in colloquial German there is a tendency when using **weil** not to put the finite verb at the end of the sentence or clause:

Warum kommst du heute abend nicht mit?
Weil ich muß arbeiten.

Most Germans would deny that they do this, but in practice they frequently do. It is not something that you should copy.

Als, wenn, wann

Note the difference between **als** and **wenn**. **Als** (*when*) refers to one event in the past, whereas **wenn** means *if* or *when*(*ever*):

Als ich Marga sah, war sie allein.	*When I saw Marga she was alone.*
Wenn ich Marga sah, war sie allein.	*When(ever) I saw Marga she was alone.*
Wenn ich Marge sehe, ist sie immer allein.	*Whenever I see Marga, she is always alone.*
Wenn das Wetter morgen schön ist, werden wir nach München fahren.	*If the weather is good tomorrow, we'll be going to Munich.*

Wann? asks the question *When?* and can also be used in indirect questions (see below).

Indirect questions

Note that the verb also goes to the end of the clause in indirect questions:

Was willst du morgen machen?
Herr Kinski hat gefragt, **was** du morgen machen **willst**.

Wie geht es Werner und Inge?
Ich möchte wissen, **wie** es Werner und Inge **geht**.

Wann steht Markus morgens auf?
Ich weiß nicht, **wann** Markus morgens auf**steht**.

Direct questions which require a **ja/nein** response add **ob** (*whether*) in the indirect question form:

Kommst du morgen mit?
Wir möchten wissen, **ob** du morgen mit**kommst**.

5 Comparatives and superlatives

The comparative and superlative forms of adjectives are used to make comparisons and to express extremes. In German, the basic rule is to add **-er** to the adjective for the comparative form and **-st** for the superlative form. Adjectival endings are added to the comparative and superlative forms where required:

1 Dieses blaue Hemd ist billig.
2 Das grüne Hemd ist billig**er** als das blaue.
3 Das billig**ste** Hemd kostet nur 15 DM.

Note that **als** (*than*) is used, as in sentence 2 above, with the comparative **-er** form. Another kind of comparison can be expressed by using **genauso . . . wie . . .** (*just as . . . as . . .*):

Das Hotel Adler ist genauso teuer wie das Hotel Königsberg.

Some adjectives add an Umlaut in the comparative and superlative:

Hans ist klug.
Stefan ist kl**ü**ger als Hans.
Klaus ist der kl**ü**gste von allen.

Renate ist stark.
Karin ist st**ä**rker als Renate.
Laura ist die st**ä**rkste von allen.

Some adjectives lose an **e** in the comparative form:

teuer	teurer
dunkel	dunkler

Some adjectives add an extra **-e-** in the superlative:

süß	der/die/das süß**e**ste
alt	der/die/das ält**e**ste
spät	der/die/das spät**e**ste

Adjectives which have irregular forms in the comparative and superlative include (see overleaf):

gut	besser	der/die/das beste
hoch	höher	der/die/das höchste
nah	näher	der/die/das nächste

Adverbs

Most German adjectives can be used as adverbs. This also applies to the comparative and superlative forms. Note the use of **am** in the superlative form of adverbs:

Marga schwimmt gut.
Karin schwimmt besser als Marga.
Tanja schwimmt am besten von allen.

The adverbial form of the superlative is often used with **sein** (*to be*):

Dieser Student ist **am klügsten**. *This student is cleverest.*

Übungen

1 Hilda und Werner erzählen ihren Freunden von ihren Plänen für die kommenden Wochen. Setzen Sie die folgenden Sätze in die Gegenwart. (*Put the following sentences into the present tense.*)

(*a*) Morgen werden wir unsere Eltern besuchen.
(*b*) Am Dienstag werde ich im Garten arbeiten.
(*c*) Demnächst werden wir das Haus renovieren lassen.
(*d*) Ich werde bald mit meinem Englischkurs anfangen.
(*e*) Im Oktober werden wir nach England fahren.
(*f*) Im September wird Martin in die Schule kommen.
(*g*) In zwei Wochen werde ich meinen Job als Bedienung anfangen.
(*h*) Übermorgen werde ich zum Friseur gehen.
(*i*) Am Wochende werden wir zum Windsurfen gehen.
(*j*) Übrigens, das Abendessen wird gleich fertig sein!

2 Bilden Sie Sätze im Futur mit den angegebenen Satzteilen.

Beispiel
Ich/ fliege/ morgen/ Budapest.
Ich werde morgen nach Budapest fliegen.

(*a*) Frau Kubig/ gehen/ am Dienstag/ Ingenieurkongreß.
(*b*) Herr Krause/ dort/ Verhandlungen führen/ ungarische Firma.
(*c*) Ich/ Deutschunterricht geben/ ab September/ Sprachinstitut.
(*d*) Ich/ machen/ nächstes Jahr/ Zivildienst.
(*e*) Heiko/ arbeiten/ nach Studium/ als Lehrer.
(*f*) Danach/ er/ arbeiten/ als Sozialpädagoge.
(*g*) Wir/ werden/ Oktober/ arbeitslos.
(*h*) Ihr/ müssen kämpfen/ auf Arbeitsmarkt/ in Zukunft.
(*i*) Wir/ sich erkundigen nach/ Computer-Kursen/ morgen.
(*j*) Renate/ gehen/ bald/ Westen.

3 Zwei Freunde, die sich seit mehreren Jahren nicht gesehen haben, reden über ihre Arbeit. Setzen Sie die Sätze in die richtige Reihenfolge. (*Put the sentences into the right order*.)

(*a*) Ich war fünf Jahre lang leitender Angestellter in einer Kleiderfabrik, die aber stillgelegt wurde.
(*b*) Ach, ich bin vor zwei Monaten arbeitslos geworden, nachdem ich lange Zeit bei einer Firma gearbeitet habe, die Werkzeugmaschinen herstellt.
(*c*) Danach war ich acht Monate arbeitslos.
(*d*) Lange nicht gesehen! Was machst du denn jetzt beruflich?
(*e*) Und was hast du vorher gemacht?
(*f*) Nein, aber ich mache gerade Computer-Kurse, und hoffe, daß ich danach bessere Chancen habe.
(*g*) Und was machst du eigentlich jetzt beruflich?
(*h*) Da wünsche ich dir viel Glück!
(*i*) Und hast du Aussicht auf eine neue Stelle?
(*j*) Ich bin leitender Angestellter bei einer Schuhfabrik. Diese Stellung habe ich aber erst seit einem Jahr.

4 Formulieren Sie die folgenden Sätze um, indem Sie das Futur zusammen mit dem Wort **wohl** verwenden, um eine Vermutung zum Ausdruck zu bringen.

Beispiel
Heiko muß wahrscheinlich noch ein bis zwei Jahre auf eine Stelle warten.
Heiko wird wohl noch ein bis zwei Jahre auf eine Stelle warten müssen.

(*a*) Herr Krause fliegt wahrscheinlich zu Verhandlungen nach Budapest.

(*b*) Frau Kubig geht wahrscheinlich zu einem Ingenieurkongreß.
(*c*) Roland und Birgit fahren wahrscheinlich auch nächstes Jahr nach Ungarn in den Urlaub.
(*d*) Herr Falke hat wahrscheinlich eine sehr wichtige Stellung in der Firma.
(*e*) Dadurch hat er wahrscheinlich so wenig Zeit für seine Familie.
(*f*) Für viele Leute ist Reisen wahrscheinlich einer der attraktivsten Aspekte ihres Berufs.
(*g*) Jochen kommt wahrscheinlich aus Ostdeutschland.
(*h*) Du kannst Hans wahrscheinlich nicht verstehen.
(*i*) Ihr seid wahrscheinlich müde von der langen Fahrt.
(*j*) Man darf hier wahrscheinlich nicht parken.

5 Verbinden Sie die folgenden Sätze mit **da/weil/seit(dem)** oder **wenn**, je nach Bedeutung der beiden Sätze. Beachten Sie auch die veränderte Worstellung! Jede der Konjunktionen sollte zweimal verwendet werden. (*Use each of the conjunctions twice.*)

Beispiele
Er ist arbeitslos. Seine Firma hat zugemacht.
Er ist arbeitslos, weil/da/seit(dem) seine Firma zugemacht hat.
Ich kaufe für dich ein. Du gibst mir Geld.
Ich kaufe für dich ein, wenn du mir Geld gibst.

(*a*) Er fliegt oft nach Budapest. Er hat dort geschäftlich zu tun.
(*b*) Herr Krause ist erstaunt. Frau Kubig ist Bauingenieurin.
(*c*) Er ist erstaunt. Er hat sich Bauingenieur immer als Männerberuf vorgestellt.
(*d*) Herr Krause bringt seinen Kindern und seiner Frau immer etwas mit. Er geht auf Geschäftsreisen.
(*e*) Frau Kubig mag ihren Beruf. Sie kann viel reisen.
(*f*) Gerd will Sozialarbeiter werden. Er ist in zwei Monaten mit seinem Zivildienst fertig.
(*g*) Heiko unterrichtet an einem Sprachinstitut. Er ist mit seinem Studium fertig.
(*h*) Klaus ist arbeitslos. Seine Firma ist vor sechs Monaten stillgelegt worden.
(*i*) Sie ist einsam. Ihr Mann ist vor einiger Zeit gestorben.

6 Ergänzen Sie den Lückentext mit den Vokabeln aus **Lektion 4**. (*Complete the gaps in the text with the words given below, which all come from* **Lektion 4**. *Sometimes you will have to modify them slightly.*)

die Bezahlung, das Arbeitsamt, die Stillegung, eine Stellung suchen, die Kurzarbeit, berufstätig, die Geschäftsreise, der Betrieb, das Wirtschaftsklima, beschäftigt, die Arbeitslosigkeit.

Das .... in Deutschland ist im Moment nicht sehr gut. Besonders in Ostdeutschland ist die .... sehr groß, aber auch in Westdeutschland nimmt sie zu. Herr Werner ist .... Er ist bei einer westdeutschen Firma .... , die Werkzeugmaschinen herstellt. Letzte Woche war er auf einer .... in Ostdeutschland. Die .... in den ostdeutschen .... ist niedriger als in seinem Unternehmen. Weil die Werkzeugmaschinen in Ostdeutschland nicht konkurrenzfähig sind, machen die Angestellten dort oft schon .... , und nicht selten kommt dann die .... Viele Menschen in Ostdeutschland müssen sich dann eine neue .... Dabei hilft ihnen das ....

7 Bilden Sie Sätze mit **um . . . zu . . .** aus den folgenden Satzteilen.

Beispiel

Herr Krause/nach Budapest/ fliegen/ geschäftliche Verhand lungen/ führen.

Herr Krause fliegt nach Budapest, um geschäftliche Verhandlungen zu führen.

(*a*) Frau Kubig/ an einem Ingenieurskongreß/ nach Budapest/ teilnehmen/ fliegen.
(*b*) Wir/ nach Deutschland/ Verwandte/ fahren/ besuchen.
(*c*) Heiko/ Geld verdienen/ arbeiten/ in einem Sprachinstitut.
(*d*) Gerd/Sozialpädagogik/ werden/ Sozialarbeiter/ studieren.
(*e*) Renate/ sich erkundigen/ zum Arbeitsamt gehen/ nach freien Stellen.
(*f*) Klaus/ machen/ mehr Chancen haben/ einen Computer-Kurs.
(*g*) Renate/ Stellung finden/ gehen/ nach Westdeutschland.

8 You (Anna) meet an old friend, Anke, in town and exchange information about work. Complete the dialogue with the help of the prompts in English.

Anke Hallo, Anna. Lange nicht gesehen! Sag mal, was bist du jetzt von Beruf?

Sie *Tell her that you are a building engineer, that you are generally satisfied with it, that you especially like the travelling, but that one of the biggest problems is the lack of free time. Ask her what she is doing.*

Anke Ich war fünf Jahre lang leitende Angestellte bei einer Kleiderfabrik, die aber leider nicht mehr konkurrenzfähig war. Deshalb bin ich im Moment arbeitslos.

Sie *You say that you imagine that to be very difficult. Ask her how she is coping, and what she intends to do.*

Anke Beim jetzigen Wirtschaftsklima ist es schwer, eine Stellung zu finden. Ich möchte deshalb einen Computer-Kurs machen, und hoffe, daß ich dann bessere Chancen habe.

Sie *You say that this is a good idea, and that currently a lot of jobs are offered which demand knowledge in that field. Wish her good luck.*

Anke Vielen Dank!

Höraufgabe

Arbeitslosigkeit

Gerd aus Erfurt erzählt Regina von seinem Leben als Arbeitsloser.

Bemerkungen

die Arbeitslosigkeit (no pl.) *unemployment*
der/die Arbeitslose (**-n**) *unemployed man / woman*
seit wann? *since when?*
arbeitslos *unemployed*

zumachen (sep.) *to close down*
herstellen (sep.) *to produce*
konkurrieren *to compete*
das ist uns nicht gelungen *we did not succeed, we didn't manage that*
die Produktionsmethode (**-n**) *production method*
veraltet *outdated, old-fashioned*
die Nachfrage (**-n**) *demand*
das Produkt (**-e**) *product*
das Unternehmen (-) *company*
übernehmen (**i, a, o**), (sep.) *to take over*
das Übernahmeangebot (**-e**) *takeover bid*
reichlich *plenty*
der/die Interessent/in (**-en**) *interested person*
klarwerden (**i, u, o**), (sep.) (+ Dat.) *to realise*
man konnte sie vor Staub nicht mehr sehen *you could not see them for dust* (colloquial)
konkurrenzfähig *competitive*
der Arbeitsplatz (**¨e**) *job, position*
vorhaben (sep.) *to intend*
in naher Zukunft *in the near future*
der Fortbildungskurs (**-e**) *training course*
die Anforderung (**-en**) *demand*

1 Was wissen Sie über Gerd?
   (*a*) Seit wann ist Gerd arbeitslos?
   (*b*) Was war sein Beruf?
   (*c*) Warum hat seine Firma zugemacht?
   (*d*) Warum haben die Interessenten die Firma nicht übernommen?
   (*e*) Wie lange war Gerd bei dieser Firma?
   (*f*) Wie alt ist Gerd jetzt?
   (*g*) Hat er noch Hoffnung, einen Arbeitsplatz zu finden?
   (*h*) Was will er demnächst machen?

2 **Diktat:** Hören Sie sich die Aufnahme genau an und schreiben Sie mit: von »Seit wann sind Sie arbeitslos?« bis ». . . nur Westprodukte kaufen wollen«. Die korrekte Version des Diktats finden Sie fettgedruckt in **Transkriptionen der Höraufgaben**.

Lesetexte

1 Ein Traumjob

NUR DREI TAGE ARBEIT PRO MONAT

Ein Traumjob: nur drei Tage Arbeit im Monat, aber *volles Gehalt*. Mit etwas Glück sogar zwei Stufen über Tarif und *absolut* krisensicher.

Das gibt es nur im Öffentlichen Dienst, genauer, in den Kfz-Werkstätten der hessischen Polizei. Die 298 Handwerker in den 61 polizeieigenen Garagen zwischen Wiesbaden und Kassel *schieben schon seit Jahrzehnten eine ruhige Kugel*. Obendrein werden viele von ihnen für Qualifikationen bezahlt, die sie entweder gar nicht *besitzen* oder die gar nicht gefragt sind.

Ein Ende des Schlendrians hatte der Hessische Rechnungshof bereits 1974 angemahnt, doch *geschehen* ist seitdem nichts. Der neueste Jahresbericht, der demnächst dem Landtag vorgelegt wird, *moniert* wiederum: überhöhte Vergütungen, Unwirtschaftlichkeit und personelle Überbesetzung in den Werkstätten.

Während zum Beispiel in Hamburg ein Polizei-Mechaniker, statistisch gesehen, für 48 grüne Minnas *zuständig ist*, hat sein hessischer Kollege nur 14 Fahrzeuge zu *betreuen*. Ein Kfz-Handwerker aus der Wirtschaft, so der Rechnungshof, *schafft* dieses Pensum in drei Tagen pro Monat.

Jetzt will der Innenminister scharf reagieren: statt 14 soll jeder Polizei-Mechaniker *künftig* 15 Fahrzeuge warten.

(*Focus*)

der Tarif (-**e**) here: *agreed rate of pay*
die Stufe (-**n**) *step, level*
der Öffentliche Dienst *public service sector*
die Kfz-Werkstatt (¨**en**) *car repair workshop*
eine ruhige Kugel schieben *to take things easy*
obendrein *on top of that*
der Schlendrian *slackness (colloquial)*
der Hessische Rechnungshof *audit office of the state of Hesse*
der Jahresbericht (-) *annual report*
monieren *to criticise*
überhöht *excessively high*
die Vergütung (-en) *pay* (of a state employee)
die Unwirtschaftlichkeit *economic inefficiency*
die personelle Überbesetzung *overstaffing*
statistisch gesehen *statistically speaking*
die grüne Minna *colloquial expression for German police cars, which are green with white stripes*
betreuen *to look after*

1 Beantworten Sie die folgenden Fragen auf Englisch.

(*a*) What are the conditions of the dream job that is mentioned in the text?
(*b*) What employer are the mechanics working for?
(*c*) What are they criticised for?
(*d*) Has the criticism of the Hessische Rechnungshof had any effect so far?
(*e*) What points does this year's annual report raise?
(*f*) Is this situation the same in all the Länder of Germany?
(*g*) How does the performance of a mechanic employed with the police compare with that of a mechanic working in industry?
(*h*) What measure does the Interior Minister of Hesse intend to take to change that situation?

2 Finden Sie die Wörter im Text (kursiv gedruckt), die den nachfolgenden Wörtern sinngemäß entsprechen.

(*a*) haben
(*b*) bewältigt
(*c*) volle Bezahlung
(*d*) in Zukunft
(*e*) passiert
(*f*) vollkommen
(*g*) arbeiten schon seit über 20 Jahren zu wenig
(*h*) kritisiert
(*i*) verantwortlich ist
(*j*) überprüfen

2 Statistik: Europas Frauen im Beruf

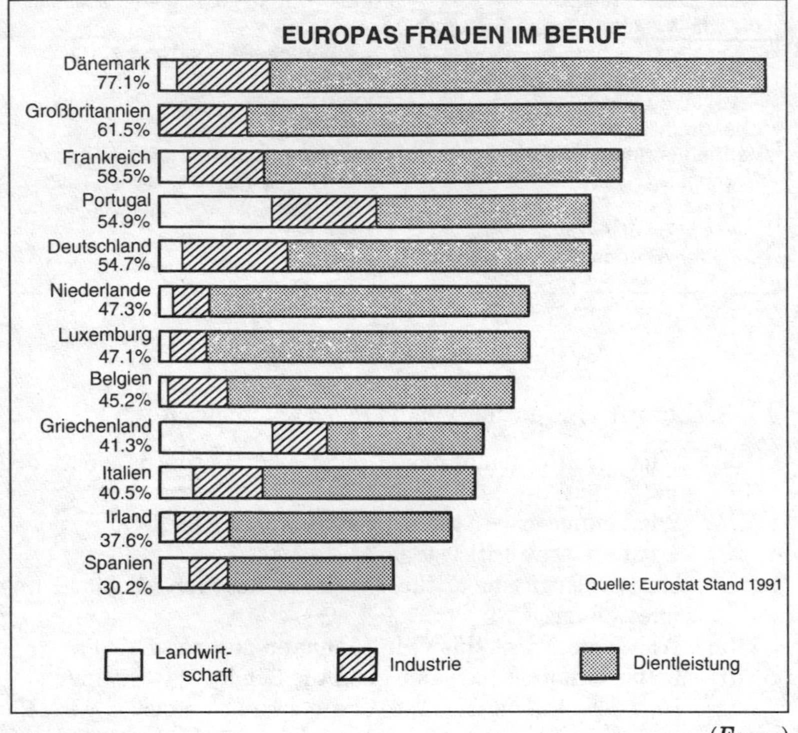

(*Focus*)

Verwenden Sie die Adjektive **hoch** und **niedrig** im Superlativ in Ihren Antworten!

1 Wo steht Spanien im Vergleich mit den anderen Ländern im Schaubild?
2 Und wo steht Dänemark?
3 In welchem Wirtschaftsbereich arbeitet in allen Ländern Europas der größte Anteil an Frauen?

5
FREIZEIT

Lernziele

In this unit you will learn how to

- talk about leisure activities
- ask about likes and dislikes
- express degrees of liking and disliking
- make suggestions
- use **lassen** and verbs followed by a preposition

Aufnahmen

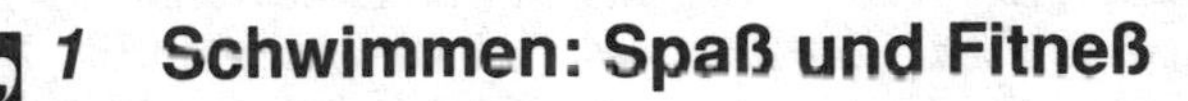

1 Schwimmen: Spaß und Fitneß

Martina unterhält sich mit Susanne über ihr langjähriges Hobby: das Schwimmen.

Martina Sag mal, Susanne, wie lange betreibst du denn dieses Hobby schon?

Susanne Also, meine Eltern haben mich schon mit fünf Jahren zum Schwimmunterricht geschickt, so daß ich natürlich in der Schule eine der besten im Schwimmunterricht war. Meine Lehrerin hat mir dann geraten, in einen Schwimmclub einzutreten.

Martina Und seit wann schwimmst du schon für diesen Club?

Susanne Seit zehn Jahren schon.

Martina Wie oft trainierst du denn da pro Woche?

Susanne Am Anfang trainiert man zweimal pro Woche eineinhalb Stunden. Dann, je nach Alter und Leistung, steigert sich das Trainingsprogramm: dreimal, viermal, fünfmal pro Woche. Und natürlich auch längere Trainingszeiten.

Martina Ist dir das denn niemals langweilig geworden?

Susanne Überhaupt nicht. Erstens trainiert man ja mit den anderen Schwimmern zusammen, und hat somit viel Spaß, und zweitens kommen dann ja auch die verschiedenen Wettkämpfe dazu. Da weiß man, wofür man trainiert hat. Auch wenn man nicht immer gewinnt.

Martina Bist du denn da nicht oftmals ziemlich ausgepumpt?

Susanne Eigentlich nicht. Das Trainingsprogramm steigert sich ja langsam, so daß ich jetzt daran gewöhnt bin, fünfmal pro Woche zu trainieren. Außerdem ist Schwimmen natürlich auch eine gute Methode, sich gesundheitlich fit zu halten. Es bringt den Kreislauf in Schwung, und ist der Sport, der die Gelenke am wenigsten belastet und dabei alle Muskeln des Körpers trainiert.

Martina Hast du jemals daran gedacht, aufzuhören?

Susanne Also vorerst nicht, denn ich finde, es hat eine Menge Vorteile: man ist mit jungen Leuten zusammen, hat eine sinnvolle Freizeitbeschäftigung, und hält sich obendrein noch fit. Mit den Wettkämpfen werde ich wohl aufhören, wenn ich zu studieren anfange, denn das nimmt fast jedes zweite Wochenende in Anspruch, und man ist oft auswärts. Aber das Schwimmen an sich werde ich immer betreiben – das kann man ja bis ins hohe Alter!

Bemerkungen

langjährig *of many years' standing, long-standing*
betreiben (ei, ie, ie) *to pursue* (of hobbies, etc.)
der Schwimmunterricht *swimming lessons*. Note that swimming is a major sport in Germany; swimming lessons in schools are com-

pulsory, and often children are advised by their PE teacher to join a swimming club; even in schools great emphasis is put on both correctness of style and on speed

eintreten (**i**, **a**, **e**), (sep.) **in** (+ Acc.) *to join*

sich steigern *to increase*

ausgepumpt *exhausted*

an etwas gewöhnt sein *to be used to something*

der Kreislauf *circulatory system*. This aspect of health is mentioned much more frequently in German than in English. A common diagnosis by German doctors is **Kreislaufstörungen** (Lit. circulatory disturbances)

das Gelenk (**-e**) *joint*

belasten *to strain*

auswärts *away, out of town*

Richtig oder falsch?

Korrigieren Sie die falschen Aussagen.

1. Susannes Eltern waren dagegen, daß sie schwimmen lernt.
2. Susannes Lehrerin hat ihr geraten, in einen Schwimmclub einzutreten.
3. Für diesen Club schwimmt sie schon seit fünf Jahren.
4. Als sie klein war, hat sie zweimal pro Woche trainiert.
5. Je nach Alter und Leistung steigert sich das Trainingsprogramm.
6. Das Training ist ihr oft ziemlich langweilig.
7. Die Wettkämpfe machen ihr besonders viel Spaß.
8. Nach dem Training fühlt sich Susanne oftmals ziemlich ausgepumpt.
9. Schwimmen ist eine der gesündesten Sportarten.
10. Außer dem gesundheitlichen Aspekt hat das Schwimmen keine Vorteile.
11. Wenn sie mit dem Studium beginnt, will Susanne mit den Wettkämpfen aufhören.
12. Schwimmen ist ein Sport, den man ab 50 nicht mehr betreiben sollte.

2 Wir sind immer unterwegs

Helga and Peter Schneider sind ein Ehepaar in den mittleren Jahren. Sie sind begeisterte Kegler, und ihr Hobby nimmt einen Großteil ihrer Freizeit in Anspruch, was sowohl Vor- als auch Nachteile hat.

An einem Samstagmorgen treffen sie eine alte Bekannte auf dem Markt.

Birgit Hallo, ihr beiden. Habt ihr nächstes Wochenende schon was vor? Alex und ich geben eine große Party.

Helga Toll, da kommen wir gern, nicht wahr, Peter?

Peter Vielen Dank für die Einladung, Birgit, aber . . . nächstes Wochenende sind Helga und ich mit dem Kegelclub in England, in unserer Partnerstadt. Hast du das etwa vergessen, Helga?

Birgit Könnt ihr das denn nicht mal ausfallen lassen? Wir haben doch so lange schon nicht mehr zusammen gefeiert.

Helga Ich weiß, Birgit. So ein Pech! Es tut uns ja auch wirklich leid . . . aber das ist schon seit Wochen geplant. Und du weißt ja, wie das ist in so einem Club – da kann man sich schlecht ausschließen, wenn solche Veranstaltungen organisiert werden. Das sagt uns auch nicht immer zu.

Birgit Habt ihr denn nie daran gedacht, auszutreten? Also, ich hätte davon schon längst genug. Da kann man sich ja gar nichts anderes mehr vornehmen außer Kegeln.

Peter Das ist eigentlich das einzige, was uns beiden nicht so gut gefällt. Aber es hat auch unheimlich viele Vorteile.

Helga Ja, das stimmt. Ich mag ganz besonders die gesellige Seite. Kegeln ist immer lustig, und man trifft öfters neue Leute, besonders wenn man auf Turniere geht.

Birgit Was, auf Turniere geht ihr auch noch? Da ist doch bestimmt eure ganze Freizeit verplant. Das wäre ganz und gar nicht nach meinem Geschmack. Ich habe gerne auch mal Zeit für mich selbst. So sehr eingebunden zu sein würde mir überhaupt nicht gefallen.

Helga Da hast du schon recht. Manchmal wird es uns ja auch zuviel. Ich habe zum Beispiel auch schon meinen Abendkurs in Französisch aufgegeben, weil es sich mit dem Kegeln am Mittwochabend überschneidet.

Peter Aber du darfst auch nicht vergessen, daß der Club viele interessante Unternehmungen organisiert, die uns beiden doch viel Spaß machen. Denk doch nur mal an die Städtereisen, die wir schon unternommen haben . . . und schließlich ist es ja auch eine sportliche Betätigung, die man bis ins hohe Alter betreiben kann.

Birgit Naja, jeder nach seinem Geschmack! Ich verstehe schon, warum euch das Kegeln Spaß macht, aber ich persönlich ziehe es vor, meine Freizeit selbst zu gestalten. Es ist mir lieber, flexibel zu sein und auch mal spontan was ganz anderes machen zu können. Außerdem habe ich es gerne, viele verschiedene Hobbys auszuüben, anstatt mich auf ein einziges zu konzentrieren.

Bemerkungen

unterwegs sein *to be on the move* (Lit. to be away)
eine Party geben *to give / throw a party*
der Kegelclub (**-s**) *bowling club*
die Partnerstadt (**-¨e**) *twin town*
etwas ausfallen lassen (**ä, ie, a**) *to skip something, give something a miss*
sich ausschließen (**i, o, o**) *to exclude oneself, not to take part in something*
das sagt uns nicht zu *that is not to our liking*
austreten (**i, a, e**) (sep.) (**aus** + Dat.) *to leave* (a club, society, etc.)
von etwas genug haben *to have enough of something*
sich etwas vornehmen (**i, a, o**) (sep.) *to plan something*
unheimlich viel *a great deal*
gesellig *sociable*
die Seite (**-n**) *aspect, side*
auf Turnier (**-e**) **gehen** *to take part in a tournament / competition*
verplanen *to book out completely, plan every minute*
das wäre nicht nach meinem Geschmack *that would not be to my taste*
zuviel werden *to become too much*
überschneiden (**ei, i, i**) *to clash, overlap*
vorziehen (**ie, o, o**) (sep.) *to prefer*
gestalten *to arrange*
es ist mir lieber *I prefer it*
ausüben (sep.) *to practise, do*
spontan *spontaneous(ly)*
sich konzentrieren (**auf** + Acc.) *to concentrate on something*

Richtig oder falsch?

Korrigieren Sie die falschen Aussagen.

1 Birgit und Alex geben in zwei Wochen eine große Party.

2 Helga und Peter sind an diesem Wochenende mit dem Kegelclub in Frankreich.
3 In einem Club kann man sich schlecht ausschließen, wenn solche Veranstaltungen geplant sind.
4 Helga und Peter ist es egal, daß sie sich fast gar nichts anderes vornehmen können.
5 Helga gefällt es besonders, daß man beim Kegeln neue Leute trifft.
6 Birgit geht auch gerne jedes Wochende auf Turniere.
7 Helga hat das Kegeln am Mittwochabend aufgegeben, weil es sich mit ihrem Französischkurs überschneidet.
8 Peter findet es sehr gut, daß der Club interessante Unternehmungen organisiert.
9 Kegeln ist eine Beschäftigung, die man nur als junger Mensch ausüben kann.
10 Birgit zieht es vor, ihre Freizeit selbst zu gestalten.

Sagen Sie's auf Deutsch!

1 Have you made any plans for the coming weekend?
2 Splendid, we'd love to come.
3 Can't you skip that for once?
4 What a pity!
5 That is not always to our liking.
6 Well, I would have had enough of that long ago.
7 That would not be at all to my taste.
8 You are right there.
9 But you must also not forget . . .
10 Just think of . . .
11 Well, each to their own!

3 Sport oder Kultur?

Marion und Cornelia sind Arbeitskolleginnen und verstehen sich gut, obwohl sie sehr unterschiedliche Interessen haben. An einem Abend möchte Marion Cornelia in die Oper einladen.

Marion Übrigens, Cornelia, ich habe zwei Karten für die Oper am Samstagabend. Hast du nicht Lust mitzukommen?
Cornelia Das ist ja sehr nett von dir, Marion, aber ehrlich gesagt interessiert mich die Oper nicht besonders. Ich bin zwar

schon kulturinteressiert, aber im allgemeinen ziehe ich sportliche Aktivitäten vor.

Marion Ach, komm, du mußt doch auch mal was anderes sehen als immer nur den Sportplatz! Ich meine, ich habe natürlich Verständnis dafür, wenn jemand Sport machen will, aber ich persönlich kann mich dafür gar nicht begeistern. Sport hat mich eigentlich schon immer gelangweilt.

Cornelia Das finde ich aber komisch. Sport hat doch so viel zu bieten. Man hält sich vor allem fit, übrigens auch geistig – man kann sich nämlich dabei wunderbar entspannen und abreagieren. Und außerdem kommt man mit vielen Leuten zusammen, sowohl wenn man aktiv Sport treibt, als auch wenn man nur als Zuschauer zu einem Fußballspiel geht.

Marion Also das käme mir nie in den Sinn. Fußball habe ich noch nie verstanden!

Cornelia Und was sind deine Vorlieben?

Marion Nun ja, ich interessiere mich eben für alles, was mit Kultur zu tun hat – in einer Großstadt wie München gibt es da ja alle Möglichkeiten. Ich bin gerne auf dem Laufenden, was die neuesten Filme, Theaterproduktionen und so weiter angeht. Was ich auch ganz toll finde ist, daß hier so viele Filme in der Originalsprache mit Untertiteln gegeben werden. Da kann ich wenigstens auch meine Sprachkenntnisse aufpolieren!

Marion Und magst du nur moderne Theaterstücke?

Cornelia Selbstverständlich schätze ich auch die Klassiker wie Goethe und Schiller. Abgesehen davon besuche ich auch regelmäßig Ausstellungen – letzten Sonntag war ich in der großen Impressionisten-Ausstellung, einfach fantastisch. Hier wird ja so viel Interessantes und Aufregendes geboten!

Cornelia Interessierst du dich auch für Musik?

Marion Sicherlich! Ich mag sowohl klassische als auch moderne Musik. Letzten Monat war ich erst wieder auf einem Konzert von Herbert Grönemeyer.

Cornelia Das hört sich ja alles sehr interessant an, aber ich finde doch, daß Sport auch einen sehr hohen Stellenwert hat. Mir wäre es zu einseitig, mich nur für einen Bereich zu interessieren.

Bemerkungen

die Karte (**-n**) *ticket*
kulturinteressiert *interested in the arts*
vorziehen (**ie, o, o**) (sep.) *to prefer*
der Sportplatz (¨**e**) *sports field*
das Verständnis *understanding*
Verständnis haben für (+ Acc.) *to understand something*
der Sport *sport*
Sport machen *to do/practise sport*
sich begeistern für (+ Acc.) *to be enthusiastic about*
bieten (**ie, o, o**) *to offer*
sich fit halten *to keep fit*
sich abreagieren (sep.) *to work off, calm down*
der Sinn (**-e**) *mind, sense*
in den Sinn kommen *to come to mind*
die Vorliebe (**-n**) *preference*
auf dem Laufenden sein *to be informed, up to date*
angehen (**e, i, a**) (sep.) *to concern*
der Untertitel (-) *subtitle*. Note that in Germany, most foreign language films are dubbed; subtitled films are the exception, and are shown in university towns or bigger cities
aufpolieren (sep.) *to brush up*
einen hohen/niedrigen Stellenwert haben *to have a high/low status*
einseitig *one-sided*

Welche Antwort paßt?

1 Hast du Lust, mit mir in die Oper zu gehen?
(*a*) In München wird ja viel in dieser Richtung geboten.
(*b*) Es ist relativ teuer, in die Oper zu gehen.
(*c*) Die Oper interessiert mich eigentlich nicht so sehr.

2 Warum magst du denn keinen Sport?
(*a*) Sport hat mich schon immer gelangweilt.
(*b*) Ich mache lieber Sport als zu lesen.
(*c*) Sport hat auch einen hohen Stellenwert.

3 Was sind deine Vorlieben?
(*a*) Ich habe zwei Karten für die Oper am Samstag.
(*b*) Ich halte mich immer gerne auf dem Laufenden.

(*c*) Ich mag alles gerne, was mit Kultur zu tun hat.

4 Magst du auch moderne Theaterstücke?
(*a*) Viele Leute mögen kein modernes Theater.
(*b*) Nein, ich ziehe die Klassiker vor.
(*c*) Ja, ich gehe oft ins Kino.

5 Interessierst du dich auch für Musik?
(*a*) Letzte Woche war ich in einer großen Ausstellung.
(*b*) Ja, ich interessiere mich sowohl für klassische als auch für moderne Musik.
(*c*) Nein, ich kann am Samstag leider nicht mit in die Oper gehen.

6 Findest du nicht, daß Sport auch einen hohen Stellenwert hat?
(*a*) Durch Sport kann man sich fit halten.
(*b*) Natürlich, aber ich interessiere mich eben nicht dafür.
(*c*) Sport ist eine Möglichkeit, neue Leute kennenzulernen.

Redewendungen

- Asking about likes

Was sind deine Vorlieben/Hobbys/Interessen?
Wie gefällt dir diese moderne Ausstellung?
Gefällt dir die neue Single von Herbert Grönemeyer?
Magst du nur moderne Theaterstücke?
Interessierst du dich auch für klassische Musik?
Würde es dir gefallen, mit mir in ein Konzert zu gehen?
Hättest du gerne dieses Buch?
Hast du Interesse an Sport?

- Expressing degrees of liking

Dieses Bild gefällt mir recht gut.
Moderne Malerei gefällt mir im allgemeinen sehr gut.
Ich habe klassiche Musik gerne.
Moderne Musik spricht mich besonders an.
Klassische Theaterstücke gefallen mir sehr.
Ich schätze Beethoven sehr.
Ich interessiere mich insbesondere für Sport.

Ich liebe klassische Literatur.
Ich schwärme für moderne Kunst.
Dieses Buch hat mich besonders begeistert.
Ich war von dieser Ausstellung sehr beeindruckt.

- Expressing degrees of disliking

Ich ziehe eigentlich die Oper dem Musical vor.
Diese Art von Musik spricht mich nicht besonders an.
Kriminalromane gefallen mir nicht so gut.
Diese Idee sagt mir nicht besonders zu.
Ich kann mit moderner Kunst nicht viel/überhaupt nichts anfangen.
Das ist/wäre ganz und gar nicht nach meinem Geschmack.
Das finde ich ja schrecklich/unmöglich.
Für Rockmusik kann ich mich ganz und gar nicht erwärmen/ begeistern.
Klassische Musik langweilt mich zu Tode.

- Making suggestions

Hast du mal daran gedacht, dir eine neue Frisur machen zu lassen?
Wie wäre es denn mit einem Kinobesuch heute abend?
Könntest du denn das nicht mal ausfallen lassen?
Hast du Lust, heute nachmittag mit mir ins Schwimmbad zu gehen?
Was hältst du von der Idee, am Wochenende wegzufahren?
Würdest du mit mir einen Tanzkurs machen?
Hättest du morgen abend Zeit für mich?
Wollen wir denn nicht mal zu viert ausgehen?
Was würdest du sagen, wenn ich dich zum Mittagessen einladen würde?
Laß uns doch jetzt gleich heimfahren!

Vokabeln

Vierzig Sportarten

Here are the names of 40 different sports. (Sorry if your own particular sport is missing!)

1	das Aerobic	21	die Leichtathletik
2	das Angeln	22	das Motorradrennen
3	das Autorennen	23	das Pferderennen
4	das Badminton (der Federball)	24	das Radfahren
5	der Basketball	25	das Reiten
6	das Bergsteigen	26	das Ringen
7	das Drachenfliegen	27	das Rodeln
8	der Eiskunstlauf	28	das Rollschuhlaufen
9	das Fallschirmspringen	29	das Rudern
10	das Fechten	30	das Schlittschuhlaufen
11	das Fitneßtraining	31	das Segeln
12	der Fußball	32	das Skateboardfahren
13	der Golf	33	das Skilaufen
14	das Hockey	34	das Squash
15	die Höhlenforschung	35	das Tauchen
16	das Jogging	36	das Tennis
17	das Judo	37	das Turnen
18	das Kanufahren	38	der Volleyball
19	das Karate	39	das Wandern
20	das Klettern	40	das Windsurfen

Try to match the following 24 English names of sports with their German equivalents. Some of the sports are too obvious to include in the English list, but learn the gender of even the easiest of nouns, e.g. ***das* Jogging**, to use the word correctly.

If there are some you just cannot work out, look up the answers.

(*a*)	(rock) climbing	(*i*)	tobogganing	(*q*)	fishing
(*b*)	caving	(*j*)	badminton	(*r*)	horse racing
(*c*)	diving	(*k*)	wrestling	(*s*)	mountain climbing
(*d*)	rambling	(*l*)	hang-gliding	(*t*)	riding
(*e*)	gymnastics	(*m*)	parachute jumping	(*u*)	canoeing
(*f*)	ice skating	(*n*)	sailing	(*v*)	roller skating
(*g*)	motorbike racing	(*o*)	fencing	(*w*)	skiing
(*h*)	rowing	(*p*)	figure skating	(*x*)	car racing

Grammatische Hinweise

1 *Uses of* lassen

The verb **lassen** is used in a number of different ways and with a number of different meanings. When used as a main verb on its own, **lassen** can be translated as (*a*) *to leave* and (*b*) *to stop*:

(*a*)	Du kannst deine Sachen hier lassen.	*You can leave your things here.*
	Laß mich nicht allein!	*Don't leave me alone!*
(*b*)	Laß das!	*Stop that!*
	Er kann das Rauchen nicht lassen.	*He can't stop smoking.*

Lassen can also be used with the meaning of *to allow / let*. In this case a second verb infinitive is normally required:

Laß mich bitte vorne sitzen!	*Let me sit in front, please!*
Meine Mutter läßt mich ihr Auto fahren.	*My mother lets me drive her car.*

The *allow / let* meaning of **lassen** can be extended to cover transitive uses of certain English verbs:

fallen (*to drop, fall*):

Ein Felsen fiel auf die Autobahn.	*A rock* ***dropped*** *on to the motorway.* (intr.)
Der Verbrecher ließ einen Felsen auf die Autobahn fallen.	*The criminal* ***dropped*** *a rock on to the motorway.* (tr.)

durchfallen (*to fail*):

Zwei Studenten sind bei der Prüfung durchgefallen.	*Two students* ***failed*** *the exam.* (intr.)
Wir haben zwei Studenten durchfallen lassen.	*We* ***failed*** *two students.* (tr.)

This also applies to **ausfallen** (*to not take place, be cancelled*);

Ihr Vortrag fällt heute aus.	*Her lecture* ***is cancelled*** *today.*
Sie mußte den Vortrag wegen einer Erkältung ausfallen lassen.	*She had* ***to cancel*** *the lecture because of a cold.*

Lassen can be used reflexively together with a second verb infinitive to express what can and cannot be done:

Wie läßt sich das erklären?	*How can that be explained?*

Ich lasse mich nur schwer überzeugen.	*I am difficult to convince.* (Lit. I allow myself to be convinced only with difficulty.)
Lassen Sie sich nicht durch seine Freundlichkeit irreführen.	*Don't be misled by his friendliness.*

This construction may often be used in preference to the passive:

Das läßt sich nicht machen. / Das kann nicht gemacht werden.
Diese Frage läßt sich nicht leicht beantworten. / Diese Frage kann nicht leicht beantwortet werden.

Lassen is used as a modal auxiliary together with a second verb infinitive to mean *to have / get something done*:

Wo läßt du dein Auto reparieren?	*Where do you get your car repaired?*
Wo kann ich mir die Haare schneiden lassen?	*Where can I get my hair cut?*
Laß mal den Kellner eine Flasche Wein bringen.	*Get the waiter to bring a bottle of wine.*

2 *Points to note about using* lassen

When **lassen** is used in the perfect tense together with another verb, a double infinitive construction results:

Hast du dir die Haare schneiden lassen?	*Have you had your hair cut?*

But, with verbs that have a close connection with **lassen**, – often written as one word in the infinitive form e.g. **liegenlassen**, **stehenlassen**, **fallenlassen** – the past participle form, **gelassen**, is sometimes used instead of the double infinitive construction:

Ich habe meinen Schirm irgendwo liegengelassen/ liegenlassen.	*I have left my umbrella (lying) somewhere.*
Sie hat eine beißende Bemerkung fallengelassen/ fallenlassen.	*She made a cutting remark.*

In dependent clauses, the finite verb form of **haben** does not go to the end of the clause, but appears before the double infinitive construction:

. . ., weil ich meinen Schirm irgendwo habe liegenlassen.
. . ., weil sie eine beißende Bemerkung hat fallenlassen.

However, the usual word order is employed when the **gelassen** form of the past participle is used:

. . ., weil ich meinen Schirm irgendwo liegengelassen habe.
. . ., weil sie eine beißende Bemerkung fallengelassen hat.

3 Verbs requiring a dative object

In German, a number of frequently used verbs require a dative object when speakers of English might expect to use an accusative object. These include:

antworten *to answer*	**gratulieren** *to congratulate*
begegnen *to meet* (by chance)	**helfen** *to help*
danken *to thank*	**raten** *to advice*
folgen *to follow*	**schaden** *to harm*

Ich habe **ihm** freundlich geantwortet.	*I answered him in a friendly manner.*
Wir sind **ihr** auf einer Party begegnet.	*We ran into her at a party.*
Er hat **mir** herzlich gedankt.	*He thanked me warmly.*
Sie folgte **ihrer Mutter** ins Haus.	*She followed her mother into the house.*
Wir haben **ihm** zum Geburtstag gratuliert.	*We congratulated him on his birthday.*
Kann ich **Ihnen** helfen?	*Can I help you?*
Ihm ist nicht zu raten.	*It is impossible to advise him.*
Rauchen schadet **der Gesundheit**.	*Smoking damages your health.*

Other verbs requiring a dative object include:

ähneln *to resemble*	**sich nähern** *to approach*
dienen *to serve*	**passen** *to suit*
drohen *to threaten*	**trauen** *to trust*
gehorchen *to obey*	**vorbeugen** *to prevent*
imponieren *to impress*	**widersprechen** *to contradict*

4 Verbs of increasing and decreasing

As in English, there are many verbs in German which express the notion of increasing and decreasing. You should distinguish between the transitive and the intransitive, e.g. **steigen** and **steigern**:

Die Mark steigt im Wert.	*The mark is increasing in value.*
Die Firma hat ihre Erträge um 10 Prozent gesteigert.	*The firm increased its profits by 10 per cent.*

Needless to say, verbs of increasing and decreasing are not all interchangeable. For detailed examples of how to use these verbs consult a bilingual reference work such as *Duden 2: Stilwörterbuch der deutschen Sprache*, (Bibliographisches Institut, Mannheim, 1988).

Here is a selection of the most commonly found verbs:

Increase

Transitive:

aufschlagen	anheben
erhöhen	erweitern
heraufsetzen	intensivieren
steigern	in die Höhe treiben
vergrößern	vermehren
verstärken	

Intransitive:

aufschlagen	sich erhöhen
hinaufgehen	klettern
steigen	sich vermehren
sich verstärken	wachsen
zunehmen	

Decrease

Transitive:

abschwächen	ermäßigen
senken	
herabsetzen	reduzieren
verkleinern	vermindern
verringern	

Intransitive:

abnehmen	nachlassen
schrumpfen	sich reduzieren
sich senken	sich vermindern
sich verringern	

Often a transitive verb can be made intransitive by the addition of a reflexive pronoun, e.g. **erhöhen/sich erhöhen**:

Die Regierung will die MWS (Mehrwertsteuer) erhöhen.	*The government wants to increase VAT.*
Die Produktionskosten erhöhen sich ständig.	*Production costs are constantly increasing.*

5 Verbs followed by a preposition

Many German verbs, like English verbs, are followed by a preposition. It is important to learn these verbs together with their preposition in order to be able to use them correctly, e.g. **warten auf** (*to wait for*), **abhängen von** (*to depend on*), **bestehen aus** (*to consist of*).

Many verbs in this category are reflexive. Here are just a few of them:

sich ärgern über (+ Akk.) *to be annoyed about*	**sich fürchten vor** (+ Dat.) *to be afraid of*
sich begeistern für (+ Akk.) *to be/get enthusiastic about*	**sich interessieren für** (+ Akk.) *to be interested in*
sich erinnern an(+ Akk.) *to remember*	**sich konzentrieren auf** (+ Akk.) *to concentrate on*
sich freuen auf (+ Akk.) *to look forward to*	**sich unterhalten mit** (+ Dat.) *to converse with*
sich freuen über(+ Akk.) *to be pleased about*	**sich verlassen auf** (+ Akk.) *to rely on*

Sie ärgerte sich über seine Abwesenheit.	*She was annoyed about his absence.*
Dafür kann ich mich nicht begeistern.	*I cannot get enthusiastic about that.*
Erinnerst du dich an ihn?	*Do you remember him?*

Ich freue mich auf deinen Besuch.	*I'm looking forward to your visit.*
Sie hat sich über seinen Besuch gefreut.	*She was pleased about his visit.*
Sie fürchtet sich vor mir.	*She's afraid of me.*
Er interessiert sich sehr für alte Bücher.	*He's very interested in old books.*
Ich muß mich auf meine Arbeit konzentrieren.	*I must concentrate on my work.*
Ich habe mich mit einem alten Freund unterhalten.	*I talked with an old friend.*
Auf ihn kannst du dich verlassen.	*You can rely on him.*

6 *Nouns and adjectives followed by a preposition*

Nouns and adjectives, like verbs, often need to be learned together with a preposition, e.g. **ein Beispiel für** (*an example of*), **ein Einwand gegen** (*an objection to*), **Angst vor** (*fear of*), **abhängig von** (*dependent on*), **gewöhnt an** (*used to*), **typisch für** (*typical of*).

Das ist ein gutes Beispiel für seine Arbeit.	*That is a good example of his work.*
Gegen seinen Vorschlag hat sie keine Einwände erhoben.	*She raised no objections to his suggestion.*
Er ist finanziell noch von seinen Eltern abhängig.	*He is financially still dependent on his parents.*
Dieses Werk ist typisch für das neunzehnte Jahrhundert.	*This work is typical of the nineteenth century.*

7 Da (r) + *preposition*

Look at these two examples using **sich erinnern an**:

Ich erinnere mich an ihn.	*I remember him.*
Ich erinnere mich nicht daran.	*I don't remember that.*

In the second example, **daran** (not **an es** or **an das**) is used because what is being referred to here is non-human. This **da**(**r**) + preposition construction (**daran**, **darauf**, **davor**, **dazu**, etc.) tends to be used instead of a preposition + pronoun construction in such cases. Note that the **r** is inserted before a vowel:

Gehen wir heute abend ins Kino?	*Are we going to the cinema this evening?*
Ja, ich freue mich schon darauf.	*Yes, I'm already looking forward to it.*
Interessierst du dich für Musik?	*Are you interested in music?*
Ja, ich interessiere mich sehr dafür.	*Yes, I'm very interested in it.*

A **da**(**r**) + preposition construction is also often used to provide the link between the main clause and the dependent or infinitive clause. Take, for example, the verb **denken an** (*to think of*). The linkword **daran** can be used to link two clauses:

Hast du jemals **daran** gedacht, aufzuhören? (**Lektion 5**, **Aufnahme 1**)

With some verbs, the inclusion of the **da**(**r**) + preposition is compulsory:

Habt ihr denn nie daran gedacht, auszutreten? (**Lektion 5**, **Aufnahme 2**)

In other cases it is optional:

Meine Lehrerin hat mir (dazu) geraten, in einen Schwimmclub einzutreten. (**Lektion 5**, **Aufnahme 1**)

The above examples all contain an infinitive clause. The **da(r)** + preposition construction can also be used to link other kinds of clauses:

Wir haben uns darüber gefreut, daß ihr gekommen seid.	*We were pleased that you came.*
Ich möchte mich danach erkundigen, ob Sie dieses Buch haben.	*I should like to enquire whether you have this book.*

A similar construction can be used with adjectives and nouns:

Hast du keine Einwände dagegen erhoben, daß deine Tochter allein wegfährt?	*Have you raised no objections to your daughter going away alone?*

Ich bin jetzt daran gewöhnt, fünfmal pro Woche zu trainieren.

Übungen

1 Kleine Gedächtnisstütze für die Reise!

Auto

Benzingutscheine
Reservekanister
Führerschein
Versicherung
Reisekarte
zusammenklappbare Stühle
Öl, Wasser, Luft überprüfen

Geld

Euroschecks
Kreditkarten

Toilettenartikel

Kulturbeutel
Fön
Wecker
Shampoo
Sonnenschutzcreme
Sonnenbrille
Sonnenhut
Badesachen
Taucherbrille
Bademantel

Sonstiges

Adressenliste
Schreibutensilien
Lesebrille, Reisebügeleisen
Lesestoff, Sprachlexikon
Wanderkarte
Dosenöffner
Reisespiele
Kamera, Filme
Walkman, Kassetten
Schuhputzzeug

Kleidung

leichte Kleidung
Strandkleidung
Kleidung für kühle Tage

Nachbarn benachrichtigen

Katze füttern
Blumen in Haus und
Garten gießen

der Dosenöffner (-)	*can-opener*	**das Bügeleisen (-)**	*iron*
der Gutschein (-e)	*voucher*	**der Reservekanister (-)**	*spare (petrol) can*
der Fön (-e)	*hair-dryer*		
der Wecker (-)	*alarm clock*		

Beantworten Sie die folgenden Fragen. In einigen Fällen ist zwar mehr als eine Antwort möglich. Im **Lösungsteil** finden Sie aber die nächstliegenden Antworten.

Beispiele
Wozu braucht man einen Dosenöffner?
Um Dosen zu öffnen.
Warum braucht man Benzingutscheine?
Damit man im Ausland verbilligtes Benzin kaufen kann.

Hier ein paar nützliche Redewendungen:

Benzin nachfüllen *to fill up with petrol*
sich vor etwas (+ Dat.) schützen *to protect oneself from something*
Wörter nachschlagen *to look up words*
sich die Haare trocknen *to dry one's hair*
Wanderwege finden *to find hiking routes*

(*a*) Wozu braucht man einen Fön?
(*b*) Warum braucht man Badesachen?
(*c*) Wozu braucht man einen Sonnenhut?
(*d*) Warum braucht man ein Sprachlexikon?
(*e*) Wozu braucht man Schuhputzzeug?
(*f*) Warum braucht man einen Wecker?
(*g*) Wozu braucht man eine Lesebrille?
(*h*) Wozu braucht man ein Reisebügeleisen?
(*i*) Wozu braucht man eine Wanderkarte?
(*j*) Warum braucht man einen Reservekanister?

2 Andreas wants to invite Michael to go to a football match with him, but Michael declines. Andreas then asks Michael about his leisure activities and interests. Complete the dialogue, playing the part of Andreas, who asks the questions. You will find possible solutions in the **Lösungsteil**.

Andreas (*a*)

Michael Danke, aber am Samstag habe ich schon was vor. Und ehrlich gesagt interessiere ich mich nicht besonders für Fußball.

Andreas (*b*)

Michael Doch, ich interessiere mich schon für Sport, aber eben nicht für Fußball. Ich schwimme zum Beispiel schon seit acht Jahren für einen Club, und dadurch ist fast meine ganze Freizeit verplant.

Andreas (*c*)

Michael Eigentlich nicht. Das Trainingsprogramm steigert sich ja langsam, so daß ich jetzt daran gewöhnt bin, viermal pro Woche zu trainieren.

Andreas (*d*)

Michael Also, vorerst nicht, denn es hat eine Menge Vorteile, und macht mir unheimlich viel Spaß.

Andreas (*e*)

Michael Es kommt darauf an. Ich interessiere mich für Theater und gehe auch ab und zu in eine Ausstellung, aber die Oper zum Beispiel interessiert mich überhaupt nicht.

3 Peter und Anneliese Beutner sind gerade aus dem Urlaub zurückgekommen, und haben sich überlegt, was sie alles erledigen müssen, bevor sie wieder anfangen zu arbeiten. Anneliese erzählt jetzt ihrer Freundin, Katja Grünemann, was gemacht werden muß. Katja fragt dann, von wem Anneliese bzw. Peter und Anneliese alles machen lassen wollen.
Stellen Sie gemäß den Beispielen Katjas Fragen. (*Ask Katja's questions in the manner demonstrated in the examples.*)

Beispiele

Anneliese Wir müssen unseren Wagen reparieren lassen.
Katja Von wem laßt ihr denn euren Wagen reparieren?
Anneliese Ich muß mir die Haare schneiden lassen.
Katja Von wem läßt du dir denn die Haare schneiden?

(*a*) Wir müssen unseren Garten herrichten lassen.
(*b*) Wir müssen unseren Hund impfen lassen.
(*c*) Ich muß mir einen neuen Hausschlüssel machen lassen.
(*d*) Ich muß meine Anzüge reinigen lassen.
(*e*) Wir müssen unsere Versicherungspolice verlängern lassen.
(*f*) Wir müssen unser Dach reparieren lassen.

(*g*) Ich muß mir den neuen Modekatalog schicken lassen.
(*h*) Ich muß meine Augen untersuchen lassen.
(*i*) Wir müssen unsere Stereoanlage überprüfen lassen.
(*j*) Ich muß meine Mitgliedskarte im Fitneßverein erneuern lassen.

4 Verbinden Sie die Satzteile!

There are admittedly several possibilities in some cases, but there is always one answer that is particularly suitable.

(*a*)	Ich interessiere mich dafür, . . .	(i)	unsere Kinder nur selten zu sehen.
(*b*)	Er konzentriert sich darauf, . . .	(ii)	mit seiner Frau zu sprechen.
(*c*)	Sie erinnert sich daran, . . .	(iii)	euch beide heute abend zu besuchen.
(*d*)	Wir freuen uns darauf, . . .	(iv)	wie schön früher alles war.
(*e*)	Sie raten ihm dazu, . . .	(v)	sein Projekt fertigzustellen.
(*f*)	Er hinderte sie daran, . . .	(vi)	einen Sprachkurs zu machen.
(*g*)	Ich denke daran, . . .	(vii)	wie ihre Examen ausgefallen sind.
(*h*)	Sie erkundigt sich danach, . . .	(viii)	Schlaftabletten zu nehmen.
(*i*)	Wir haben uns daran gewöhnt, . . .	(ix)	seine Karriere weiter zu verfolgen.
(*j*)	Er bestand darauf, . . .	(x)	mich um eine Stelle zu bewerben.

5 Complete the sentences below with vocabulary from this unit. By filling the grid opposite horizontally, the place where people go to do sport will be revealed vertically (*k*).

(*a*) Manche Leute ziehen es vor, ihre Freizeit selbst zu ....
(*b*) Sie können dann flexibel sein und auch mal .... was ganz anderes machen.
(*c*) Durch ..... hält man sich fit, trifft neue Leute und hat eine sinnvolle Freizeitbeschäftigung.
(*d*) Wenn man auf .... geht, weiß man, wofür man trainiert hat.
(*e*) Beim Sport muß man das Trainingsprogramm langsam ....
(*f*) Wenn man in einem Club Mitglied ist, ist es schwer, die

Freizeit nicht vollkommen zu ....

(*g*) Es gibt auch viele Leute, die Sport nicht mögen, und deren .... die Kultur ist.

(*h*) Es ist allerdings oft schwierig, für ein beliebtes Theaterstück eine ..... zu bekommen.

(*i*) Eine Großstadt wie London hat natürlich kulturell viel mehr zu ...... als eine kleinere Stadt.

(*j*) Aus diesem Grund gibt es viele Leute, die das Leben in der Stadt dem Landleben ....

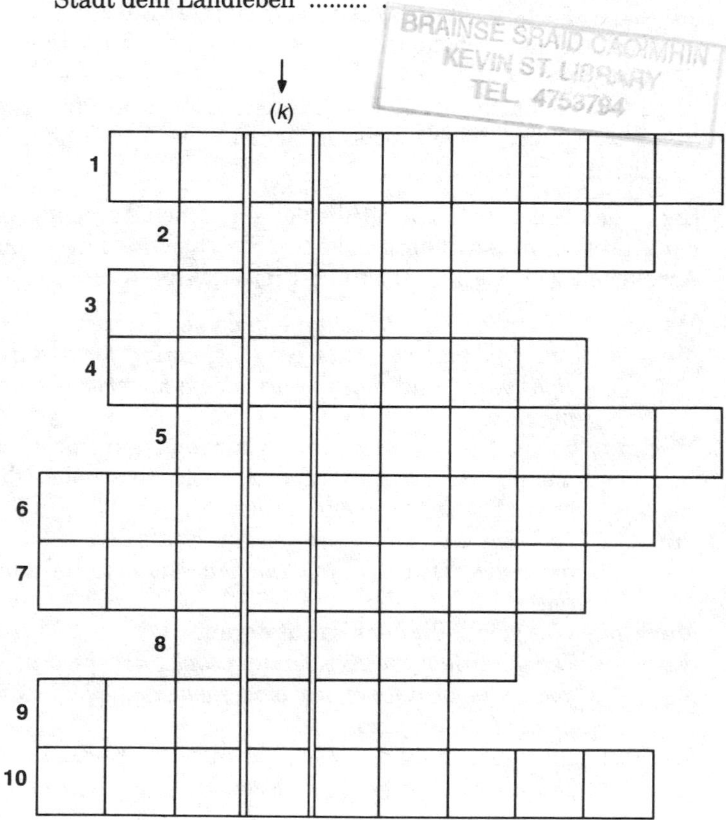

6 Formen Sie die folgenden Sätze um, wie im Beispiel angegeben.

Beispiel

Ich freue mich über deinen Besuch.

Ich freue mich darüber, daß du mich besuchst.

(*a*) Wir freuen uns auf euren Besuch.
(*b*) Er beschwert sich über den Lärm der Kinder.
(*c*) Sie dankte ihm für seine Bemühungen.
(*d*) Ich habe mich über die Unverschämtheit meines Nachbarn aufgeregt.
(*e*) Er bestand auf einer großen Geburtstagsfeier.
(*f*) Ich warte immer noch auf eine Entschuldigung von ihm.
(*g*) Sie war sehr traurig über den Verlust ihrer Eltern.
(*h*) Wir rechnen schon seit langem mit einer Einladung von euch.
(*i*) Ich habe ihn von der Richtigkeit meiner Aussage überzeugt.
(*j*) Wir glauben leider nicht mehr an eine Versöhnung mit unseren Freunden.

7 Ergänzen Sie den Dialog mit Hilfe der englischen Anregungen. In der Mittagspause unterhalten Sie sich mit einem Arbeitskollegen, Markus, über ihre Freizeitaktivitäten.

Markus Was machst du denn gerne in deiner Freizeit?
Sie *Tell him that you have been swimming for a club for eight years, and that you are also a member of a bowling club.*
Markus Soviel Sport – das wäre ganz und gar nicht nach meinem Geschmack! Da ist doch bestimmt deine ganze Freizeit verplant!
Sie *Tell him that sometimes you think that it is a little bit too much. However, you think it has a lot of advantages.*
Markus Was gefällt dir denn so gut daran?
Sie *Tell him that you meet many people, you keep fit and you get to see a lot of new places when going on tournaments with the clubs.*
Markus Interessierst du dich denn gar nicht für Kultur?
Sie *Tell him that you are interested in culture, but that you prefer sport.*
Markus Magst du denn zum Beispiel klassische Musik, oder Malerei?
Sie *Tell him that you prefer modern music, and that you also like to go to the cinema.*
Markus Naja, jeder nach seinem Geschmack!

Höraufgabe

Pläne für die Sommerferien

Sebastian und Jochen, zwei 18jährige Schüler, besprechen in ihrer Frühstückspause, was sie in den Sommerferien vorhaben.

Bemerkungen

Note that driving and dancing are two activities which exemplify the thoroughness with which the Germans go about a lot of things. Such activities are taught thoroughly and meticulous guidelines are set for them.

der Führerschein (**-e**) *driving licence*. Note that in Germany getting a driving licence is a much bigger undertaking than in Britain: you have to attend lessons in the theory of driving at a driving school (ten double lessons), at the end of which there is a written exam. Only after you have passed this exam are you allowed to take your practical driving exam, which consists of 30 – 40 minutes of driving either in town or on the motorway, or both

die Fahrschule (**-n**) *driving school*. These are the only places where you can learn to drive and attend the theory lessons

die Fahrerlaubnis *licence to drive*. Note that in Germany it is strictly forbidden to drive before having acquired a licence, even when accompanied by a licence-holder. Anyone caught driving without a licence is banned from driving for two years

die Stunde (**-n**) *lesson*. The average number of lessons is, as the dialogue says, 20; included in that are some compulsory lessons: one hour driving at night, two hours driving on country lanes outside town, and two hours on the motorway. Theoretically, of course, one could take the practical exam after these compulsory lessons, but people rarely do this

der Durchschnitt *average*

durchfallen* (**ä, ie, a**) (sep.) *to fail* (an exam)

der Deckel (-) *driving licence* (colloquial)

der Tanzkurs (**-e**) *dancing classes*. In Germany, dancing classes are very popular with teenagers, and are almost a 'must'; usually there are one or two dancing schools in any average-sized town, where people would enrol and do one or more courses. One ball is held half-way through the course, and another one at the end of the course, at which parents are usually present as well. However, young Germans tend to go to discos in their leisure time rather than to proper ballroom-dancing clubs. Nevertheless, most young people take a dancing course in the first place

die Hochzeit (**-en**) *wedding*

der Schritt (**-e**) here: *dancing step*

der Tanzclub (**-s**) *dance club*. This is the ideal place if you wish to pursue the sport further

1 Beantworten Sie die folgenden Fragen.

(*a*) In wieviel Tagen fangen für Sebastian und Jochen die Sommerferien an?
(*b*) Was will Sebastian in den Sommerferien machen?
(*c*) Was kann passieren, wenn man ohne Führerschein fährt?
(*d*) Wieviel Stunden braucht man in Deutschland im Durchschnitt für den Führerschein?
(*e*) Was hat Jochen für die Sommerferien geplant?
(*f*) Kann Sebastian auch tanzen?
(*g*) Wieviel Tanzkurse hat Jochen schon gemacht?
(*h*) Was will er nach dem dritten Tanzkurs machen?
(*i*) Was macht er außer Tanzen noch in seiner Freizeit?
(*j*) Was macht Sebastian gerne in seiner Freizeit?

2 Stellen Sie sich vor, Ihre Sommerferien fangen in einer Woche an. Schreiben Sie zehn Sätze darüber, was Sie in Ihren Ferien machen werden. Die folgenden Aktivitäten sollen in Ihren Sätzen vorkommen. Achten Sie darauf, das richtige Verb mit jeder Aktivität zu verwenden!

Beispiel
Freunde: In meinen Ferien werde ich Freunde besuchen.

(*a*) Schwimmbad
(*b*) Kino
(*c*) Tanzkurs
(*d*) Disco
(e) Tennis
(*f*) Konzert
(*g*) Eltern
(*h*) Führerschein
(*i*) Französisch
(*j*) Kochkurs

Lesetexte

1 Was Kinder wirklich sehen

FILME UND UNTERHALTUNG AM ABEND: SPANNENDER ALS LANGWEILIGE SERIEN AM NACHMITTAG

Die Politiker sehen's mit Stirnrunzeln, die Programm-Macher mit Gelassenheit: *Die beliebtesten Kindersendungen laufen im Abendprogramm, meist nach acht.* Der Spielfilm »Liebling, ich habe die Kinder geschrumpft« von der ARD in der Vorweihnachtszeit gezeigt, war mit 1,59 Millionen Zuschauern zwischen sechs und 13 Jahren der Hit der Kids im TV-Jahr 1992. An zweiter Stelle lag das Endspiel der Fußball-EM zwischen Deutschland und Dänemark, das 1,57 Millionen Kinder verfolgten. »Batman« sahen 1,22 Millionen.

Abgeschmettert: *Den Vorschlag der parlamentarischen Staatssekretärin im Bundesjugendministerium, Cornelia Yzer (31, ledig), einen eigenen Kinderkanal einzurichten, werteten deshalb ARD und ZDF als Botschaft aus dem Tal der Ahnungslosen.* Kommentar von ZDF-Pressesprecher Walter Kehr: »Das ignorieren wir nicht einmal.«

Kinder gucken nun mal nicht in erster Linie das, was speziell für sie erdacht wurde. Dabei gehören Programme im Ersten wie die »Sesamstraße« (in über 80 Ländern ausgestrahlt) oder die »Sendung mit der Maus« nach Einschätzung des ARD-Vorsitzenden Jobst Plog auch international »zu den Top-Angeboten des Genres«. *Beim ZDF verweist Redaktionsleiter Michael Albus nicht ohne Stolz auf Sendungen wie »Siebenstein«, »Löwenzahn« oder die werktäglichen Nachrichten für Kinder namens »Logo«. Die CDU-Politikerin Yzer glaubt dagegen, daß die Öffentlich-Rechtlichen ihren speziellen Erziehungs- und Bildungsauftrag hier »nicht erfüllen«.*

Neuer Sendeplatz: *Das ZDF überlegt unterdessen, wie es die jungen Zuschauer am Sonntag besser erreichen kann.* Falls die aufsichtsführenden Fernsehräte Ende Juni in Potsdam zustimmen, wandern die Kindersendungen vom frühen Nachmittag auf die Zeit von 10.00 Uhr bis 11.30 Uhr. Ab Oktober gäbe es dann, mit Blick auf die private Konkurrenz, eine öffentlich-rechtliche Kinderprogramm-Schiene – von der Wiederholung des »Disney-Clubs« in der ARD gegen 8.30 Uhr über den neuen ZDF-Termin bis zur »Sendung mit der Maus« um 11.30 Uhr im Ersten.

Ob früher oder später – bei den Programmleuten gilt immer noch das Wort von WDR-Fachmann Gert K. Müntefering: »*Kinderprogramm ist, was Kinder sehen.*«

TV-HITS DER KIDS '92

Titel der Sendung	Zuschauer zwischen 6 und 13 J. in Mio.
1. Liebling, ich habe die Kinder geschrumpft (ARD. 18.12.)	1,59
2. Fußballspiel Deutschland-Dänemark (ARD. 26.6.)	1,57
3. Wetten, daß . . .? (ZDF. 22.2.)	1,48
4. Wetten, daß . . .? (ZDF. 25.1.)	1,46
5. Asterix erobert Rom (ARD. 26.12.)	1,45

Quelle: GfK/ARD-Medienforschung

(*Focus*)

das Stirnrunzeln *frowning;* here: *disapproval*
die Gelassenheit *calmness, composure*
beliebt *popular*
die Kindersendung (**-en**) *children's programme*
das Abendprogramm (**-e**) *evening programme*
laufen (**ä, ie, au**) here: *to be on TV*
das Endspiel (**-e**) *final*
verfolgen *to follow, watch*
abschmettern (sep.) *to turn a deaf ear to someone*
der Vorschlag (**¨e**) *suggestion*
der/die parlamentarische Staatssekretär/-in (**-e/-nen**) *parliamentary secretary*
das Bundesjugendministerium (**-en**) *federal ministry for youth*

einrichten (sep.) *to establish*
werten *to judge, consider*
die Einschätzung (-en) *estimate*
verweisen auf (+ Acc.) *to point to*
der Stolz *pride*
werktäglich *during the week*
die Öffentlich-Rechtlichen *state television channels*
der Erziehungs- und Bildungsauftrag *task of training and educating*
der Sendeplatz (¨e) *place in the TV schedule*
die aufsichtsführenden Fernsehräte *committee members concerned with the supervision of TV programmes*
die Kinderprogramm-Schiene (-n) *range of children's programmes shown on various state TV channels*

1 Beanworten Sie die folgenden Fragen auf Englisch.

(*a*) What time are the programmes broadcast that children most like to watch?
(*b*) What kind of programmes are these?
(*c*) What is the reaction of politicians to this phenomenon?
(*d*) Do the programme co-ordinators think differently about it?
(*e*) What suggestion did Cornelia Yzer make to improve the situation?
(*f*) Was this suggestion received favourably by the co-ordinators?
(*g*) What programmes are there that have been made specifically for children?
(*h*) What does Cornelia Yzer accuse the state channels of?
(*i*) What measure does the ZDF intend to take to improve the attractiveness of its channel for children?
(*j*) What is the opinion of Gert K. Müntefering on this measure?

2 Finden Sie die Sätze im Text (kursiv gedruckt), die den nachfolgenden Sätzen sinngemäß entsprechen.

(*a*) Frau Yzer, CDU, ist der Meinung, daß die Fernsehanstalten Kindern nicht genug Erziehung und Bildung anbieten.
(*b*) Das Programm für Kinder wird von dem Geschmack der Kinder bestimmt.
(*c*) Frau Yzers Idee, ein eigenes Programm für Kinder anzubieten, wurde von den Fernsehanstalten als unrealistisch abgelehnt.
(*d*) Die Programme, die von Erwachsenen für Kinder gemacht werden, interessieren die Kinder oftmals nicht so sehr.
(*e*) Das ZDF versucht zur Zeit, eine Möglichkeit zu finden, wie

es die Kinder mehr für seine Sendungen interessieren kann.

(*f*) Die Programme, die Kinder am liebsten sehen, werden nicht nachmittags, sondern abends gezeigt.

(*g*) Das ZDF ist der Meinung, daß seine Kinderprogramme sehr gut sind.

2 Teletext

P257 257 3sat Do 9.09.93 15:07:09

3 Sat STRASSEN SCHWEIZ

ALLGEMEINE BEFAHRBARKEIT

Die Autobahnen und Hauptstrassen sind grösstenteils feucht oder nass.

Zum Teil muss auch mit Gewittern gerechnet werden.

Auf der Autobahn N 2, Bellinzona-Süd - Rivera behindert Nebel mit einer Sichtweite von 50 Metern den Verkehr.

Quelle: ACS/TCS/Polizei

What obstacles must drivers in Switzerland expect, according to this Teletext page?

6
TABAK UND ALKOHOL

Lernziele

In this unit you will learn how to

- ask opinions
- agree and disagree
- concede a point
- express lack of opinion or indifference
- use the passive

Aufnahmen

1 Jochen besteht auf seinem Recht

In der Mensa fragt Elke Dornbusch einen Kommilitonen, Jochen Fischer, nach seiner Meinung über das Rauchen in der Öffentlichkeit.

Elke	Bist du der Meinung, daß das Rauchen in der Öffentlichkeit verboten werden sollte?
Jochen	Ganz und gar nicht! Ich finde, die Antiraucherfanatiker sind schon zu weit gegangen mit ihren neurotischen Forderungen.
Elke	Was hältst du also von dem Argument, daß jeder das Recht haben sollte, reine Luft zu atmen?
Jochen	Das ist ja ein Witz! Ich als Radfahrer muß die ganzen Abgase von den vielen Autos einatmen. Wo bleibt denn da mein Recht auf reine Luft?
Elke	Da ist bestimmt 'was dran. Aber es gibt nur noch ein Unrecht mehr, wenn man sowohl Zigarettenrauch als auch Autoabgase atmen muß.
Jochen	Das ist mir egal. Solange die Autofahrer meine Luft verpesten, bestehe ich auf meinem Recht, auch in der Öffentlichkeit zu rauchen.
Elke	Und machst du dir um deine Gesundheit keine Sorgen?
Jochen	Nee, eigentlich nicht. Mir macht das Rauchen unheimlich viel Spaß. Und wenn ich ein paar Jahre früher sterbe, ist es mir schon recht so. Ich möchte sowieso nicht als alter Mann in einem Altensilo dahinvegetieren.

Bemerkungen

Note the words in this dialogue which are emotionally loaded, words which indicate the attitude of the speaker. For example, Jochen refers to the anti-smoking lobby as **Antiraucherfanatiker**, and with the word **Fanatiker** immediately condemns this group of people as over-ardent and near-insane. He further reveals his attitude by referring to their demands as **neurotisch**. When he is complaining about cars polluting the air, he uses the rather strong verb **verpesten**. The name Jochen chooses for an old people's home again reveals his attitude to such places. **Altensilo** is certainly derogatory and, some would say, offensive. He has rejected the standard expressions **Altersheim** and **Altenheim** as well as the euphemistic term **Seniorenheim**, which is preferred by many people nowadays. **Dahinvegetieren** is, of course, similarly dismissive.

bestehen (e, a, a) **auf** (+ Dat.) *to insist on*
die Forderung (-en) *demand*
rein *pure, clean*
atmen *to breathe*
der Witz (-e) *joke*
das Abgas (mostly pl.) *exhaust fumes*
das Recht (**auf** + Acc.) *right* (*to*)
Da ist bestimmt 'was dran *There's certainly something in that*
Es gibt nur noch ein Unrecht mehr *Two wrongs don't make a right*
verpesten *to pollute, foul up*
sich Sorgen machen um (+ Acc.) *to worry about*
es ist mir recht so *it's all right with me*
sowieso *in any case*
das Altensilo rather derogatory word for an old people's home
dahinvegetieren (sep.) *to vegetate* (*away*)

Richtig oder falsch?

Korrigieren Sie die falschen Aussagen.

1 Elke ist der Meinung, daß das Rauchen in der Öffentlichkeit verboten werden sollte.
2 Jochen ist auch sehr gegen das Rauchen.
3 Elke findet, daß jeder das Recht haben sollte, die Luft zu verpesten.
4 Jochen glaubt, daß die Autofahrer mehr im Unrecht sind als die Raucher.
5 Jochen macht sich große Sorgen um seine Gesundheit.
6 Deshalb will er das Rauchen aufgeben.
7 Er möchte noch lange leben.
8 Er möchte nicht in einem Altensilo dahinvegetieren.

Sagen Sie's auf Deutsch!

1 Not at all!
2 You must be joking!
3 Well, that's perhaps not altogether wrong.
4 I don't care.
5 I really enjoy smoking.
6 I'm quite happy with that.

MIR STINKT'S!

TANGRAM J 4

Ihnen auch? – Dann ist es Zeit mit dem RAUCHEN aufzuhören. Ihr Entschluß NICHTRAUCHER zu werden braucht einen verläßlichen PARTNER. **NICOBREVIN N** unterstützt zweifach: Medikamentös und durch Selbstkontrolle. **NICOBREVIN N** Kapseln enthalten kein Nikotin. Rezeptfrei in allen Apotheken – auch in Österreich und in der Schweiz. Empf. Preis für die 4-Wochen-Kur DM 36,–. **Nicht** teurer als 1 Woche Rauchen.

Nicobrevin N gegen das Rauchen.
INTER-BREVIPHARM GMBH, Postfach 1708, 61350 Bad Homburg v.d.H.

(*Bunte*)

2 Frau Merk spricht sich für ein Rauchverbot aus

In einer Gaststätte fragt Elke Dornbusch einen Gast, Frau Merk, nach ihrer Meinung zum Thema Rauchen in der Öffentlichkeit.

Elke Entschuldigen Sie bitte die Störung, aber darf ich Sie fragen, ob Sie für oder gegen ein Rauchverbot in Restaurants und Gaststätten sind?

Frau Merk Ich bin auf jeden Fall dafür. Ich finde, es ist eine Zumutung, wenn ich beim Essen durch das Rauchen von anderen Gästen gestört werde.

Elke Viele Gäste hier in der Gaststätte sagen aber, daß sie gerade dann rauchen möchten, wenn sie sich bei einem Glas Wein oder einer Tasse Kaffee entspannen.

Frau Merk Ja, das mag wohl sein. Solche Leute vergessen aber meistens, daß ihr Rauchen eine negative Einwirkung auf ihre Mitmenschen hat. Und es gibt ja Menschen, die einfach allergisch sind gegen Zigarettenrauch.

Elke Ja, aber sagen Sie ganz ehrlich, kann man wirklich ein totales Rauchverbot in allen Restaurants und Gaststätten verhängen?

Frau Merk Das wäre meines Erachtens nicht zu viel verlangt. Aber ich sehe auch ein, daß es noch eine Zeitlang dauern wird, bis diese Idee von der Mehrheit akzeptiert wird. Und in der Zwischenzeit wächst die Zahl der Restaurants, die das Rauchen entweder total oder zum Teil verbieten.

Bemerkungen

Note the very polite manner in which Elke approaches Frau Merk. It is important to know polite expressions for disturbing people and for interrupting them.

sich aussprechen (**i, a, o**) (sep.) **für** (+ Acc.) *to speak in favour of*
das Verbot (**-e**) *ban*
eine Zumutung *imposition, unreasonable demand*
beim Essen Lit. during the eating. In English, 'while I'm eating' would be preferred. German is renowned for making verbs into nouns (or 'normalising') in this way.
durch das Rauchen *by smoking*. see pages 156–7, for more information on the use of **durch**
gerade dann . . ., wenn *precisely at a time when . . .*
sich entspannen *to relax*
die Einwirkung auf (+ Acc.) *effect on*
der Mitmensch (**-en**) *fellow human being* (a 'weak noun' – see pages 188–90, for more about these)
ehrlich *honest(ly)*
meines Erachtens *in my estimation*
(**nicht**) **zu viel verlangt** (*not*) *asking too much*
eine Zeitlang *for a while*
die Mehrheit *majority*
die Zwischenzeit *meantime*
wachsen (**ä, u, a**) *to grow*
verbieten (**ie, a, o**) *to prohibit*

Richtig oder falsch?

Korrigieren Sie die falschen Aussagen.

1 Frau Merk ist der Meinung, daß jeder das Recht haben sollte, im Restaurant zu rauchen.
2 Sie raucht gerne beim Essen.
3 Viele Leute rauchen gerne bei einem Glas Wein oder einer Tasse Kaffee.
4 Es gibt viele Menschen, die gegen Zigarettenrauch allergisch sind.
5 Rauchen hat eine negative Einwirkung auf andere Menschen.
6 Frau Merk findet, daß man ein totales Rauchverbot in allen Restaurants und Gaststätten verhängen sollte.
7 Es gibt schon in den meisten Restaurants ein Rauchverbot.
8 Die Mehrheit der Leute akzeptiert das Rauchverbot in Gaststätten und Restaurants.

3 Kettenraucher wird Nichtraucher

Sascha Wagner aus München besucht seine alten Freunde, Antje und Frank Zehnder, in Hamburg.

Sascha Wie lange ist es eigentlich her, seit ihr mich in München besucht habt? Es ist jedenfalls schon lange her.

Antje Ja, das war im April vor drei Jahren. (*Sie bietet ihm eine Zigarette an.*) Möchtest du übrigens eine Zigarette?

Sascha Nein, danke. Ich habe vor anderthalb Jahren das Rauchen aufgegeben.

Frank Was?! Du warst doch immer Kettenraucher. Was ist denn passiert, daß du eine derart drastische Maßnahme ergriffen hast?

Sascha Na, als ich wegen ständiger Kopfschmerzen beim Arzt war, hat er Bluthochdruck festgestellt. Einen Zusammenhang mit dem Rauchen könne er nicht ausschließen, meinte er. Ich hab' also sofort angefangen, mir das Rauchen abzugewöhnen.

Antje Und war es denn nicht schwierig, diesen guten Vorsatz durchzuhalten?

Sascha Oh, doch! Ich bin auch zwei- oder dreimal rückfällig geworden. Aber bei jedem neuen Versuch ist in mir auch die

Entschlossenheit gewachsen, bis ich ehrlich sagen konnte, daß ich keine Lust mehr hatte zu rauchen.

Frank Prima, aber du hast doch nichts dagegen, wenn *wir* eine rauchen?

Sascha Überhaupt nicht. Ihr seid ja in der eigenen Wohnung. Dagegen kann ich nichts einwenden.

Bemerkungen

Note the use of **du**, **Sie** and **ihr** in the three dialogues. In **Aufnahme 1**, Elke calls Jochen **du** even though she doesn't know him. They are fellow students and therefore enjoy a certain solidarity. In **Aufnahme 2**, Elke and Frau Merk are strangers to each other and share no particular bond; consequently they refer to each other as **Sie**. The use of one form – either **du** or **Sie** – by both participants in a dialogue (as in **Aufnahmen 1** and **2**, above) is said to be 'symmetrical'. When one speaker uses **du** and the other uses **Sie** in return (for instance, when an adult and child who do not share family bonds address each other), the use is said to be 'asymmetrical'. In **Aufnahme 3**, Sascha uses **ihr** to Frank and Antje because he is on **du** terms with them both individually. **Ihr** is also sometimes used to ease the transition from **Sie** to **du**. For instance, one might start using **ihr** to a couple before saying **du** to them individually.

die Kette (-n) *chain*
jedenfalls *in any case*
übrigens *by the way*
vor anderthalb Jahren *18 months ago* (Lit. one and a half years ago)
passieren* *to happen*
derart *such* (Lit. of that kind)
eine Maßnahme ergreifen *to adopt/take a measure*
ständig *constant(ly)*
der Bluthochdruck *high blood pressure*
feststellen (sep.) *to ascertain*
der Zusammenhang *connection*
ausschließen (ie, o, o) (sep.) *to exclude*
könne note this use of **Konjunktiv 1** (see page 220) to convey reported speech
in Schwierigkeiten geraten* *to run into difficulties*
rückfällig werden* (i, u, o) *to relapse*
der Vorsatz *resolution, intention*
durchhalten *to see it through*
die Entschlossenheit *determination*
Ich habe keine Lust mehr *I don't want to any more*
Ich habe nichts dagegen *I don't mind* (Lit. I have nothing against it)
überhaupt nicht *not at all*
einwenden (e, a, a) (sep.) *to object*

Welche Antwort paßt?

1 Wie lange ist es eigentlich her, seit ihr mich in München besucht habt?
(*a*) Ich gehe jeden Mittag in die Mensa.
(*b*) Ich glaube, das ist jetzt drei Jahre her.
(*c*) Nein, danke.

2 Möchtest du übrigens eine Zigarette?
(*a*) Ich trinke keinen Alkohol.
(*b*) Nein, danke, ich habe das Rauchen aufgegeben.
(*c*) Ich rauche jeden Tag zehn Zigaretten.

3 Warum hast du denn das Rauchen aufgegeben?
(*a*) Mein Arzt hat es mir dringend geraten.
(*b*) Ich bin starker Raucher.
(*c*) Ich rauche am liebsten die teuren Zigaretten.

4 War es nicht schwer, das Rauchen aufzugeben?
(*a*) Immer mehr Menschen werden Nichtraucher.
(*b*) Ich habe nach drei Monaten wieder angefangen.
(*c*) Doch, schon. Aber ich habe es schließlich geschafft.

5 Hast du etwas dagegen, wenn ich rauche?
(*a*) Zigaretten werden immer teurer.
(*b*) Nein, natürlich nicht, es ist ja deine Wohnung.
(*c*) Ja, ich rauche auch morgens schon.

4 Nachrichtensendung: Gefahren des Alkoholismus

Auf einem Kongreß in Berlin hat der Präsident der deutschen Ärztekammer gestern vor den Gefahren des stark zunehmenden Alkoholismus gewarnt. Er wies darauf hin, daß das Problem unbemerkt von der Öffentlichkeit ständig anwachse. Die Zahl der Alkoholtoten liege etwa zehnmal so hoch wie die der Drogentoten. Insgesamt gebe es in Deutschland anderthalb bis zwei Millionen Alkoholkranke. Auch die Folgeschäden jahrelangen Alkoholmißbrauchs, wie Leberzirrhose, Hirnabbau und verschiedene Krebserkrankungen werden nach seiner Einschätzung von den meisten Menschen verkannt.

Der Präsident der Ärztekammer sieht vor allem in einer drastischen Verteuerung alkoholischer Getränke ein wirksames Mittel, den Alkoholkonsum zu drosseln. Jährlich würden für Alkohol und Zigaretten zwei Drittel der Beträge ausgegeben, die für die gesetzliche Krankenversicherung aufgebracht würden.

Bemerkungen

Note the formal style of this item from a radio newscast. Even though this is spoken language, the structure is more typical of the written language, since the text has in fact been written in order to be read aloud.

The following points are of particular interest:

1 The amount of information that is contained in each sentence.
2 The number of complex sentences, i.e. ones which contain a **daß** clause, a **zu** + infinitive clause, a relative clause (introduced by a relative pronoun, such as **der**, **die** or **das**).
3 The use of reported speech (noticeable in verbs such as **anwachsen**, **liegen**, etc.) See **Lektion 8** for further information on reported speech.
4 Use of the passive.
5 Use of the genitive.

die Kammer *chamber*
warnen vor (+ Dat.) *to warn against*
hinweisen (ei, ie, ie) auf (+ Acc.) (sep.) *to point out*
die Öffentlichkeit *the public*
anwachsen* (ä, u, a) (sep.) *to grow, increase*
der Folgeschaden (¨) *harmful effect*
der Mißbrauch *abuse*
die Leberzirrhose *cirrhosis of the liver*
der Hirnabbau *brain damage* (Lit. brain reduction)
der Krebs *cancer*
verkennen (e, a, a) *to fail to appreciate/ recognise*
die Verteuerung *price increase*
wirksam *effective*
das Mittel (-) *means*
drosseln *to reduce, cut* (Lit. throttle)
der Betrag (¨e) *amount*
gesetzlich *legal, statutory*
die Krankenversicherung *health insurance* (Lit. sickness insurance)
aufbringen (i, a, a) (sep.) *to raise, find* (money)

Richtig oder falsch?

Korrigieren Sie die falschen Aussagen.

1 Der Präsident der deutschen Ärztekammer hat vor den Gefahren des Rauchens gewarnt.
2 Die Öffentlichkeit weiß, daß starker Alkoholkonsum gefährlich sein kann.
3 Die Zahl der Drogentoten ist nicht so hoch wie die Zahl der Alkoholtoten.
4 In Deutschland gibt es relativ wenig Alkoholkranke.
5 Die meisten Menschen wissen nicht, daß zu starker Alkoholkonsum schwere Krankheiten zur Folge haben kann.
6 Der Präsident der Ärztekammer glaubt, daß der Alkoholkonsum weniger werden würde, wenn Alkohol teurer wäre.
7 Die Deutschen geben für Alkohol und Zigaretten mehr Geld aus als für ihre Krankenversicherung.

The genitive

Pick out all the examples of the genitive case in **Aufnahme 4**.

Redewendungen

- Asking opinions

  Was hältst du (davon)?
  Wie denkst du (darüber)?
  Was meinst du (dazu)?
  Wie ist deine Meinung (dazu)?
  Wie findest du das?

- Expressing agreement

  Da stimme ich mit dir (völlig) überein.
  Da bin ich ganz deiner Meinung.
  Ich bin der gleichen Meinung wie du.
  Ich teile deine Meinung.
  Darüber sind wir uns einig.

Da hast du (völlig) recht.
Das stimmt.
Richtig!

- Expressing disagreement

Da stimme ich nicht (ganz) mit dir überein.
Ich bin da (ganz) anderer Meinung.
Ich bin darüber anderer Meinung als du.
Hier gehen unsere Meinungen auseinander.
Darüber sind wir uns (leider) nicht einig.
Da hast du völlig unrecht.
Da liegst du völlig falsch.
Das stimmt nicht.
Unsinn!

- Conceding a point before going on to introduce a further argument

Das mag wohl sein, aber . . .
Da hast du vielleicht recht, aber . . .
Da ist bestimmt 'was dran, aber . . .
Das sehe ich schon ein, aber . . .
Sicher, aber . . .

- Expressing lack of opinion or indifference

Ich habe dazu keine Meinung.
Das ist mir egal.
Das ist mir (alles) Wurscht.
Das ist mir (alles) Schnuppe. (Berlin)
Na, und?
Na, und wenn schon!

Vokabeln

Kollokationen

The following are frequently used expressions in German. Most of the meaning is to be found in the nouns, but it is important to remember what verb goes with (or collocates with) each noun:

1	ein Verbot verhängen	14	einen Krieg führen
2	eine Maßnahme ergreifen	15	ein Geständnis ablegen
3	einen Vorsatz fassen	16	einen Einblick gewinnen
4	einen Vorsatz durchhalten	17	eine Rede halten
5	einen Versuch machen	18	die Initiative ergreifen
6	Geld ausgeben	19	eine Frage stellen
7	Geld aufbringen	20	in Lachen ausbrechen
8	einen Plan fassen	21	einen Besuch abstatten
9	ein Fest geben	22	jemandem Schaden zufügen
10	eine Mahlzeit einnehmen	23	einen Eindruck vermitteln
11	einen Platz einnehmen	24	ein Geschäft abschließen
12	einen Frieden schließen	25	einen Beitrag leisten
13	eine Gelegenheit beim Schopf fassen	26	einen Vergleich anstellen

Now match the English equivalents with the German collocations. Start with those that are immediately clear to you and then work the rest out by a process of elimination.

(*a*)	to spend money	(*n*)	to give an impression
(*b*)	to make a speech	(*o*)	to impose a ban
(*c*)	to have a meal	(*p*)	to find money
(*d*)	to make a resolution	(*q*)	to make a confession
(*e*)	to make a comparison	(*r*)	to make peace
(*f*)	to wage a war	(*s*)	to carry out a resolution
(*g*)	to conclude a deal	(*t*)	to burst out laughing
(*h*)	to gain an insight	(*u*)	to make a contribution
(*i*)	to adopt a measure	(*v*)	to ask a question
(*j*)	to occupy a place	(*w*)	to throw (give) a party
(*k*)	to conduct an experiment	(*x*)	to make a plan
(*l*)	to seize an opportunity (with both hands)	(*y*)	to do somebody harm
(*m*)	to pay a visit	(*z*)	to seize the initiative

Grammatische Hinweise

1 *The passive* (Das Passiv)

One area of grammar that needs frequent revision is the passive. Note the distinction is made between the active and the passive voice.

In the active voice, the initiator of an action, often referred to as the agent, is expressed as the subject of the sentence:

Florian und Elke besuchen an Wochenenden Frau Beitz in Lübeck.

subject	*verb*	*direct object*
initiators (agents)	*(active)*	*'sufferer'*

In the passive voice, however, the 'sufferer' of the action (normally the direct object in an active sentence) is expressed as the subject of the sentence:

Frau Beitz in Lübeck wird an Wochenenden (von Florian und Elke) besucht.

subject	*verb . . .*	*prepositional phrase /*	*. . . verb*
'sufferer'	*auxiliary (passive)*	*initiators*	*past participle*

Because in the passive the emphasis is taken away from the initiator, this element of the passive sentence is often omitted. Indeed, the initiator is often not known:

Mein Portemonnaie ist gestern gestohlen worden.	*My purse was stolen yesterday.*

It would be nice to know who the thief was! Or there is a desire not to mention who the initiator is:

Mein schöner, neuer Wagen ist kaputtgefahren worden.	*My lovely new car has been written off.*

Was it the speaker, or was it his/her spouse that wrote the car off? No blame is being apportioned here!

2 Forming the passive

The passive is formed with the auxiliary verb **werden** in the appropriate tense together with the past participle of the verb in question:

Present	Ich werde abgeholt.	*I am being picked up.*
Past	Ich wurde abgeholt.	*I was (being) picked up.*
Perfect	Ich bin abgeholt worden.	*I have been / was picked up.*

Note that in the perfect passive the past participle of **werden** is simply **worden** and has no **ge**- prefix.

Here is the sample verb **abholen** conjugated in the various tenses:

Indicative

Present
ich werde abgeholt
du wirst abgeholt
er/sie/es wird abgeholt
wir werden abgeholt
ihr werdet abgeholt
sie/Sie werden abgeholt

Past
ich wurde abgeholt
du wurdest abgeholt
er/sie/es wurde abgeholt
wir wurden abgeholt
ihr wurdet abgeholt
sie/Sie wurden abgeholt

Future
ich werde abgeholt werden
du wirst abgeholt werden
er/sie/es wird abgeholt werden
wir werden abgeholt werden
ihr werdet abgeholt werden
sie/Sie werden abgeholt werden

Perfect
ich bin abgeholt worden
du bist abgeholt worden
er/sie/es ist abgeholt worden
wir sind abgeholt worden
ihr seid abgeholt worden
sie/Sie sind abgeholt worden

Pluperfect
ich war abgeholt worden
du warst abgeholt worden
er/sie/es war abgeholt worden
wir waren abgeholt worden
ihr wart abgeholt worden
sie/Sie waren abgeholt worden

Future Perfect
ich werde abgeholt worden sein
du wirst abgeholt worden sein
er/sie/es wird abgeholt worden sein
wir werden abgeholt worden sein
ihr werdet abgeholt worden sein
sie/Sie werden abgeholt worden sein

Subjunctive (Konjunktiv I)

Present
ich werde abgeholt
du werdest abgeholt
er/sie/es werde abgeholt
wir werden abgeholt
ihr werdet abgeholt
sie/Sie werden abgeholt

Perfect
ich sei abgeholt worden
du sei(e)st abgeholt worden
er/sie/es sei abgeholt worden
wir seien abgeholt worden
ihr seiet abgeholt worden
sie/Sie seien abgeholt worden

Future
ich werde abgeholt werden
du werdest abgeholt werden
er/sie/es werde abgeholt werden
wir werden abgeholt werden
ihr werdet abgeholt werden
sie/SIe werden abgeholt werden

Subjunctive (Konjunktiv II)/Conditional	
Past	**Pluperfect**
ich würde abgeholt werden	ich wäre abgeholt worden
du würdest abgeholt werden	du wärest abgeholt worden
er/sie/es würde abgeholt werden	er/sie/es wäre abgeholt worden
wir würden abgeholt werden	wir wären abgeholt worden
ihr würdet abgeholt werden	ihr wäret abgeholt worden
sie/Sie würden abgeholt werden	sie/Sie wären abgeholt worden

See **Lektionen 8** and **9** for more on the subjunctive (**Konjunktiv I**) and **Konjunktiv II**/conditional.

3 Werden-Passiv *and* sein-Passiv

The passive using **werden** + past participle is the true passive. It is called the **Vorgangspassiv** or **werden-Passiv**. There is also the so-called **Zustandspassiv**, or **sein-Passiv**, which is formed with the verb **sein** + past participle.

In the **sein** passive, the past participle is used rather like an adjective:

Ich bin verletzt.	*I am wounded.*

For speakers of English, the distinction between the **sein** passive and the **werden** passive is less clear in the past tense:

Ich war verletzt.	*I was wounded.* (that is the state I was in)
Ich wurde verletzt.	*I was wounded.* (somebody wounded me)

4 *Subjectless passives*

The passive is sometimes used in German where in English it would be difficult, if not impossible, to do so. A number of examples of this construction occurred in **Lektion 2, Aufnahme 1**:

Es wird gewaschen.	*The washing gets done.*
Es wird saubergemacht.	*The cleaning gets done.*
Es wird aufgeräumt.	*The clearing up gets done.*

Es as a 'dummy subject'

In the above sentences, the grammatical subject is **es**, but this is often referred to as a 'dummy subject' since it does not stand in place of a specific noun. It can also disappear if another element is introduced in the first position in the sentence or clause:

Samstags wird saubergemacht.	*On Saturdays the cleaning gets done.*

The dummy subject can even be found when there is a 'real' subject in the sentence, as this example from **Lektion 2, Aufnahme 1** demonstrates:

Aber es muß auch all die Arbeit getan werden, die während der Woche liegengeblieben ist.

5 *Passive of dative verbs*

Verbs which in German are followed by the dative, such as **helfen** and **folgen** (see **Lektion 5**, page 124) cannot be made passive in the usual way. It is, however, possible to produce a kind of passive, if the dative object is retained:

Ihr wurde geraten, in einen Schwimmclub einzutreten.	*She was advised to join a swimming club.*
Mir wurde von einem Freund geholfen.	*I was helped by a friend.*
Ihnen wurde zur Geburt ihres ersten Kindes gratuliert.	*They were congratulated on the birth of their first child.*

Note that in this last sentence the subject (*they*) and verb (*were*) are both plural, whereas in German the verb (**wurde**) is singular because **Ihnen** is not the subject of the sentence but the dative object. All three sentences are, in fact, subjectless passives (referred to above).

6 *The passive agent* – von, durch *and* mit

As mentioned above, passive sentences do not have to include the initiator of the action, the **agent**. When, however, the agent is included it is normally introduced with the preposition **von**:

Mein Auto wurde von einem 16jährigen Schüler gestohlen.	*My car was stolen by a 16-year-old schoolboy.*

Even when the initiator is not clearly a human or animal agent, **von** is still used:

Das Haus wurde vom Blitz getroffen.	*The house was struck by lightning.*

Another preposition commonly associated with the passive is **durch**. Phrases introduced by **durch** indicate the means by which something was done. They do not normally refer to the initiator:

Der Verkehr wurde durch die Streikenden aufgehalten.	*The traffic was halted by (because of) the strikers.*

i.e. It was not necessarily the strikers' intention to stop the traffic, but this was the effect that the demonstration had.

Der Verkehr wurde von den Streikenden aufgehalten.	*The traffic was halted by the strikers.*

i.e. It was the strikers' (initiators) intention to stop the traffic.

It is possible for the two prepositions to appear in the same passive sentence:

Ich wurde von meiner Mutter durch einen langen Brief informiert.	*I was informed by my mother by means of a long letter.*

The preposition **mit** is used to indicate the instrument used to carry out an act:

Der alte Mann wurde mit einem Messer getötet.	*The old man was killed with (by) a knife.*

7 Active infinitive with passive meaning

A contrast exists between English, which uses the passive infinitive, and German, which uses the active infinitive, in such sentences as:

Das ist kaum zu glauben.	*That is scarcely to be believed.*

Dieses Fenster ist nicht zu öffnen.	*This window is not to be opened.*
Von ihm ist nichts Besseres zu erwarten.	*You cannot expect anything better from him.* (Lit. From him nothing better is to be expected.)

8 *Use of* man

The pronoun **man** is often used in German where a passive would be more common in English:

Hier spricht man Deutsch.	*German spoken here.*
Man glaubt, daß . . .	*It is thought that . . .*
So 'was macht man eben nicht.	*That sort is thing is just not done.*

Man is also used much more widely in other contexts than *one* is used in English:

So 'was vergißt man nicht so schnell.	*You don't forget something like that so quickly.*
Man darf nicht vergessen, daß er kein Deutsch spricht.	*You mustn't forget that he speaks no German.*

Übungen

1 Hier diskutieren zwei Freunde über die Risiken des Rauchens und des Trinkens. Setzen Sie die Sätze in die richtige Reihenfolge. Die Lösung finden Sie im **Lösungsteil**.

(*a*) Und hast du es geschafft?
(*b*) Bist du der Meinung, daß das Rauchen in der Öffentlichkeit verboten werden sollte?
(*c*) Naja, als ich beim Arzt war, hat er mich vor Herzinfarkt und Leberzirrhose gewarnt. Daraufhin habe ich das Trinken ganz schnell aufgegeben.
(*d*) Ja, auf jeden Fall. Ich selbst bin zwar Raucher, aber ich respektiere, daß andere Leute den Zigarettenrauch als störend empfinden.
(*e*) Nein, das habe ich mir völlig abgewöhnt.

(*f*) Und bist du nicht besorgt, daß das Rauchen deine eigene Gesundheit gefährden könnte?

(*g*) Wie hast du denn das geschafft?

(*h*) Doch, eigentlich schon. Ich weiß, daß es sehr schädlich ist, und habe auch versucht, es mir abzugewöhnen.

(*i*) Nein, leider nicht. Es macht mir eben unheimlich viel Spaß, und schmeckt mir auch so gut!

(*j*) Jetzt mal 'was anderes: trinkst du auch noch so viel wie früher?

2 Lesen Sie den folgenden Text und versuchen Sie alles zu verstehen. Vokabeln, die Sie nicht kennen, finden Sie im **Glossar**. Nach dem Text folgt eine kurze Übung:

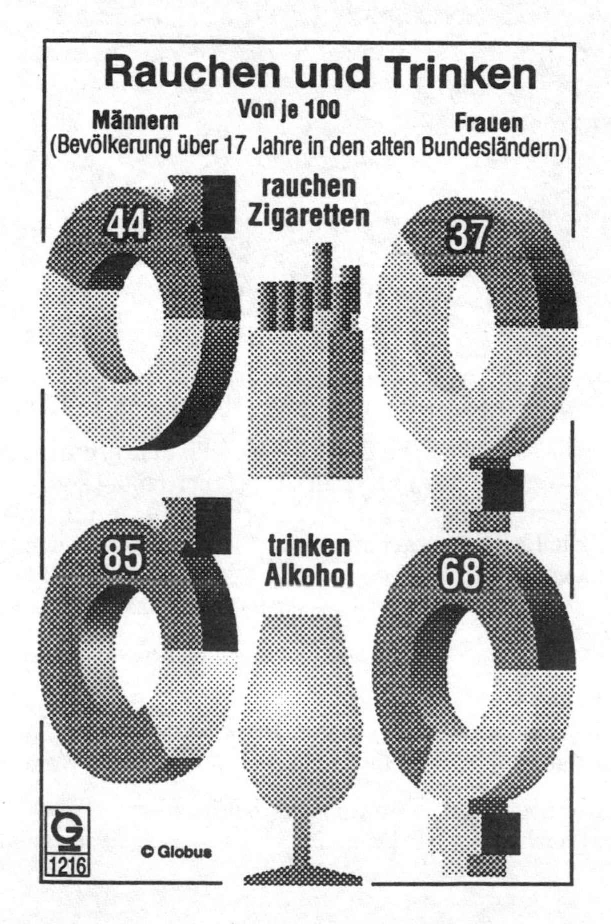

MÄNNER RÖGEN MEHR

Rauchen gefährdet die Gesundheit und ist obendrein teuer. Trotzdem rauchen in Westdeutschland 44 Prozent der Männer und 37 Prozent der Frauen Zigaretten. Vor allem bei den Männern gibt es viele *starke Raucher,* für die ein Päckchen pro Tag nicht ausreicht. Auch *beim Alkoholgenuß* liegen die Männer vorn, 85 Prozent trinken regelmäßig Bier oder Wein. Obwohl diese *Genußmittel* in Deutschland schon stark besteuert werden, wird immer wieder vorgeschlagen, *Raucher* und *Alkoholkonsumenten* mit *Sonderabgaben* zu belasten. Denn, *so lautet die Argumentation,* wer wissentlich seine Gesundheit schädigt, muß auch die finanziellen Folgen tragen, statt sie *der Allgemeinheit* aufzubürden.

Statistische Angaben: VERA-Studie, eigene Berechnungen

(*Globus*)

Ersetzen Sie die formalen Ausdrücke im Text (kursiv gedruckt) mit den angegebenen umgangssprachlichen Ausdrücken.

(*a*) wie es so schön heißt
(*b*) Leute, die stark rauchen
(*c*) allen anderen
(*d*) die Leute, die rauchen
(*e*) extra Steuern
(*f*) Produkte, die nicht lebensnotwendig sind
(*g*) die Leute, die trinken
(*h*) wenn man raucht, kann man krank werden
(*i*) was das Trinken angeht

3 Bilden Sie Passiv-Sätze aus den folgenden Aktiv-Sätzen.

Beispiele
Man sollte das Rauchen in der Öffentlichkeit verbieten.
Das Rauchen in der Öffentlichkeit sollte verboten werden.

Einige Leute halten ein Rauchverbot für falsch.
Ein Rauchverbot wird von einigen Leuten für falsch gehalten.

(*a*) Viele Leute empfinden das Rauchen in Lokalen als eine Belästigung.
(*b*) Manche Menschen genießen das Rauchen nach einer Mahlzeit.
(*c*) Man sollte ein totales Rauchverbot in allen Restaurants verhängen.
(*d*) Die Mehrheit der Leute akzeptiert diese Idee.
(*e*) Man sollte noch viel drastischere Maßnahmen gegen das Rauchen ergreifen.
(*f*) Man kann einen Zusammenhang zwischen dem Rauchen und Bluthochdruck nicht ausschließen.
(*g*) Man kann aber gegen das Rauchen in der eigenen Wohnung nichts einwenden.
(*h*) Die meisten Menschen verkennen die Gefahren des Alkoholismus.
(*i*) Die Deutschen geben jährlich eine ungeheure Summe für Alkohol und Zigaretten aus.
(*j*) Man sollte den Alkoholkonsum aus Gesundheitsgründen verringern.

4 Formen Sie die folgenden Sätze mit **man** um.

Beispiele
Die Leute verstehen oft nicht, was sie tun.
Man versteht oft nicht, was man tut.
Wir können diesen tragischen Unfall nur schwer vergessen.
Man kann diesen tragischen Unfall nur schwer vergessen.

(*a*) Bei uns zu Hause trinken wir öfters mal ein Glas Wein zum Essen.
(*b*) Deshalb sind wir aber noch lange nicht alkoholabhängig.
(*c*) Die Leute verkennen allerdings oftmals die Gefahren des Alkohols.
(*d*) In Deutschland geben die Leute viel zu viel Geld für Alkohol und Zigaretten aus.
(*e*) Die Menschen sollten sich mehr um ihre Gesundheit kümmern.
(*f*) In Deutschland rauchen auch viele Menschen oft zu viele Zigaretten.
(*g*) Die Lokalbesitzer sollten das Rauchen in den Restaurants verbieten.

(*h*) Die Menschen sollten auch viel mehr Rücksicht auf Nichtraucher nehmen.
(*i*) Die Regierung sollte Gesetze gegen das Rauchen erlassen.
(*j*) Die Bürger sollten ihr Geld für sinnvollere Dinge ausgeben.

5 Anita and Jürgen talk about health risks caused by smoking and drinking. Complete the dialogue with the help of the prompts in English.

Jürgen Sag mal, Anita, warum hast du denn plötzlich das Rauchen aufgegeben?

Anita *Tell him that you were concerned about your health; you had high blood pressure and your doctor said he could not exclude a link between that and the smoking. Also, your husband is allergic to smoke.*

Jürgen Stört es dich jetzt, wenn andere Leute in der Öffentlichkeit rauchen?

Anita *You say yes, very much. Tell him that you think smoking should be forbidden in public places, especially in restaurants when people are eating.*

Jürgen War es nicht schwierig, den guten Vorsatz durchzuhalten?

Anita *You say yes, you even relapsed two or three times, but then you were even more determined to give up smoking. Ask him whether he has reduced his alcohol consumption.*

Jürgen Ein wenig. Aber ich möchte es ganz aufgeben.

Anita *Ask him if he had been concerned about the harmful effects of alcohol abuse.*

Jürgen Ja. Das war auch der Grund, warum ich mich entschlossen habe, vollkommen aufzuhören. Ich habe nämlich Angst vor Krebs und Leberzirrhose.

6 Charles und Margaret sind ein englisches Ehepaar, das an einem Städteaustausch teilnimmt. Sie werden ein deutsches Ehepaar Günther und Anke Reizmann, in ihrer Partnerstadt besuchen. Die beiden Deutschen haben gerade die Adresse der Engländer erhalten, und schreiben jetzt einen Willkommensbrief an sie. Lesen Sie sich den Brief durch, und ersetzen Sie dann alle Formen von **Sie** mit **du** bzw. **ihr**. Natürlich müssen Sie auch die entsprechenden Vornamen verwenden und die Verbformen angleichen!

Liebe Frau Fisher, lieber Herr Fisher!

Wir haben gerade Ihre Adresse erhalten, und freuen uns, Ihnen beiden jetzt zum ersten Mal schreiben zu können.

Wir möchten uns Ihnen ganz kurz vorstellen: mein Mann und ich arbeiten wie Sie als Gymnasiallehrer. Mein Mann Günther hat dasselbe Hobby wie Sie, Frau Fisher: moderne Kunst. Ich selbst interessiere mich ebenso wie Sie, Herr Fisher, für die Naturwissenschaften. Außerdem machen wir beide gerne Fahrradtouren und lange Wanderungen, was Sie beide ja auch gerne mögen!

Für die Dauer Ihres Aufenthaltes hier haben wir uns folgendes Programm überlegt: montags würden wir Ihnen beiden gerne die Sehenswürdigkeiten unserer Stadt zeigen. Am Dienstag möchte mein Mann Sie, Frau Fisher, in die Galerie für moderne Kunst führen. Ich selbst würde gerne mit Ihnen, Herr Fisher, das Naturwissenschaftliche Museum besuchen. Anschließend möchten wir Sie beide in ein gutbürgerliches Restaurant einladen.

Mittwochs und donnerstags würden wir gerne mit Ihnen beiden eine Fahrradtour in die nähere Umgebung unternehmen – da gibt es einiges zu erforschen! Zum Abschluß haben wir einen Theaterbesuch geplant, da wir wissen, daß Sie beide sich auch für Brecht interessieren!

Wir hoffen, daß Ihnen unsere Pläne zusagen, und freuen uns auf Ihre baldige Antwort.

Viele Grüße,

Anke und Günther Reizmann

7 And now for something different. What follows is a series of questions designed to reveal your state of health. Needless to say, answers cannot be given in the back of the book, since everybody will respond differently. Work out your score and read the analysis (**Auswertung**) to see how you are faring! You will find some vocabulary to help you on page 167.

Der große BUNTE-Test. Läuft Ihr Kreislauf rund?

Beim gesunden Menschen funktioniert das Bluttransportsystem ein Leben lang wartungsfrei. Aber fließt der Treibstoff nicht richtig, gerät auch der Motor Herz in Gefahr. Lassen Sie es gar nicht erst dazu kommen.

PUNKTE

1 Haben Sie mehr als 5 kg Übergewicht?

- Nein. Ich halte schon lange mein Normalgewicht 0
- Ja, bis zu 10 kg 2
- Ja, und zwar mehr als 10 kg 4

2 Haben Sie zu hohe Blutfettwerte? (Unbedingt ärztlich prüfen lassen!)

- Nein, ganz bestimmt nicht 0
- Die Blutfettwerte sind leicht erhöht 2
- Ja, besonders das Gesamtcholesterin hat einen Wert über 250 mg 4

3 Haben Sie Bluthochdruck? (Unbedingt in der Apotheke prüfen lassen!)

- Nein, mein Blutdruck liegt nicht über 130:90 bei Sitzruhe 0
- Ja, aber nicht mehr als 150:100 3
- Ja, und zwar über 150:100 6

4 Haben Sie Diabetes? (Unbedingt ärztlich prüfen lassen!)

- Nein 0
- Der Arzt sagt, ich liege im Grenzbereich 2
- Ja, ich bin zuckerkrank 6

5 Essen Sie viel Fett, Fleisch, Wurst, Kuchen und Naschwerk?
- Nein, ganz bestimmt nicht 0
- Ich weiß nicht, ob das, was ich esse, schon »viel« ist 2
- Ja, ich esse gern und oft reichlich davon 4

6 Rauchen Sie?
- Höchstens gelegentlich und immer wenig 0
- Nicht massenhaft, aber doch ca. 10 Zigaretten täglich 4
- Ja, ich rauche mehr als 10 Zigaretten pro Tag, komme vom Rauchen nicht weg 6

7 Sind Sie heute vergeßlicher als früher
- Nein, ich bin mir dessen nicht bewußt 0
- Na ja, manchmal ärgere ich mich über Vergeßlichkeiten, die mir früher nicht passiert wären 2
- Ja, ich vergesse viel. Und vieles von einem Moment zum anderen 3

8 Sind Sie geistig oder körperlich oft abgespannt?
- Nein, höchstens mal nach extremer Anstrengung 0
- Ja, mir ist öfter alles zuviel 2
- Ja, und zwar so sehr, daß es mich deprimiert und ängstlich macht 4

9 Sind Sie innerlich aufgewühlt, ruhelos, nervös?
- Nein, von seltenen Ausnahmen abgesehen 0
- Das kommt leider oft vor 2
- Ja, ständig, und ich weiß nicht mal, warum das so ist 4

10 Haben Sie reichlich Bewegung und strengen sich körperlich auch wirklich an?
- Ja, ich bin meinem Alter entsprechend ein körperlich aktiver Typ 0
- Ich glaube, daß ich mehr körperliche Aktivitäten brauche 2
- Nein, ich bin körperlich wirklich nicht aktiv 4

11 Haben Sie Hör-, Seh- oder Gefühlsstörungen (z.B. Ohrensausen, Schwarzvoraugen, Schwindelgefühl, Torkeln, Kribbeln, einschlafende Beine oder Arme, Muskelkrämpfe, kalte Gliedmaßen, sexuelle Empfindungsstörungen)?

- Nein, nichts von alledem 0
- Ja, und zwar oft und/ oder stark 2
- Ja, mehreres zusammen 6

12 Leiden/litten Eltern an Verkalkung?

- Nein, jedenfalls nicht, daß ich wüßte 0
- Ja, ein Elternteil 2
- Ja, beide Elternteile, wenn auch unterschiedlich stark 4

13 Trinken Sie Alkohol?

- Nie bzw. nur gelegentlich und auch nur sehr wenig 0
- Zwar mehrmals in der Woche, aber in Maßen 2
- Ja, täglich und manchmal auch reichlich, sogar zuviel 4

14 Haben Sie öfter als einmal monatlich Kopfweh?

- Nein, im allgemeinen nicht 0
- Ja, das kommt sicherlich wöchentlich mindestens einmal vor 2
- Ich leide mehrmals in der Woche an starken Kopfschmerzen 4

15 Müssen Sie beim Laufen öfter Pausen einlegen, weil Ihnen die Waden oder Schenkel schmerzen?

- Nein, das hatte ich noch nie; ich kann laufen und rennen, soviel ich will 0
- Wenn ich stramm laufe, kommt es schon mal vor 2
- Ja, ich bekomme nach einer gewissen Laufstrecke Muskeschmerzen in den Beinen, muß länger Pausen machen 4

rundlaufen (äu, ie, au) (sep.) *to circulate*
wartungsfrei *without check-ups*
der Treibstoff *fuel*
das Gewicht *weight*
der Blutfettwert (-e) *blood cholesterol level*
unbedingt *by any means*
ärztlich *medical*
erhöht *above average, somewhat high*
das Cholesterin *cholesterol*
die Apotheke *pharmacy*
bei Sitzruhe *when sitting still*
der Grenzbereich *limit*
zuckerkrank *diabetic*
das Naschwerk *sweets*
reichlich *plenty*
massenhaft *in large quantities*
vergeßlich *forgetful*
bewußt (+ Gen.) *conscious*
sich ärgern über (+ Acc.) *to be annoyed about*
abgespannt *weary, exhausted*
die Anstrengung *effort, strain*
deprimiert *depressed*
innerlich *inside, internal*
aufgewühlt *agitated*
ruhelos *restless*
abgesehen von (+ Dat.) *apart from*
die Ausnahme (-n) *exception*
die Bewegung *exercise*
entsprechend (+ Dat.) *corresponding to*
das Gefühl (-e) *feeling*
das Ohrensausen *ringing in the ears*
torkeln *to stagger*
kribbeln *to have pins and needles*
die Gliedmaße (-n) *limb*
die Empfindung (-en) *sensation*
leiden (ei, i, i) *to suffer*
die Verkalkung *senility*
unterschiedlich *different, varying*
in Maßen *in moderation*
die Pause (-n) *break*
einlegen (sep.) here: *to take (a break)*
die Wade (-n) *calf*
der Schenkel (-) *thigh*
stramm *firm*

AUSWERTUNG

So kämpfen Sie gegen Minuspunkte

Bis zu 12 Punkte: Ihr Risiko, frühzeitig unter Arteriosklerose zu leiden, ist gering. Eß-, Trink- und Alkoholgewohnheiten lassen sich allemal einschränken.

13 bis 24 Punkte: Sie liegen zwar im Bevölkerungsdurchschnitt, aber der Durchschnitt verkalkt ja leider auch früher als nötig. Sie sollten Risiken abbauen. Wenn Sie das allein nicht schaffen, probieren Sie es auf einer Kur anstelle des nächsten Urlaubs. Was Sie dafür an Geld bezahlen, gewinnen Sie an Lebensqualität. Falls Sie weitermachen wie bisher, müssen Sie in nicht ferner Zukunft mit Durchblutungsstörungen und Sklerose rechnen.

25 bis 36 Punkte: Sie leben mit hohen Risiken, und die ersten Anzeichen von Durchblutungsstörungen sind unverkennbar. Gehen Sie zu einem vorsorgebewußten Arzt Ihres Vertrauens und befolgen Sie seine Ratschläge. Bewegen Sie sich viel, üben Sie Körperanstrengungen. Befolgen Sie die Ratschläge auf den nächsten Seiten. Dann können sich sogar Anfangsbeschwerden bessern, die Sie vielleicht schon haben.

37 Punkte und mehr: Arztbesuch, „große Inspektion" und intensive Behandlung sind dringend erforderlich. Wenn Sie nicht unverzüglich alle Register ziehen, müssen Sie schon bald mit ernsten Durchblutungsstörungen und arteriosklerotischen Beschwerden rechnen.

(*Bunte*)

How did you do? Do take the advice seriously. Note how concerned with health matters ordinary German magazines like *Bunte* are.

Höraufgabe

Kontakt- Muß- und Genußraucher

Psychologen behaupten, daß es drei Arten von Rauchern gibt: den »Mußraucher«, den »Genußraucher« und den »Kontaktraucher«. In einer Umfrage wurden Raucher nach den Umständen gefragt, unter denen sie gerne rauchen.

1 Hören Sie sich die Aufnahme auf der Kassette an, und entscheiden Sie, ob die Befragten Mußraucher, Genußraucher oder Kontaktraucher sind.

(*a*) Renate Schliermann, 38, Kauffrau.
(*b*) Rainer Schneider, 46, Journalist.
(*c*) Bettina Gruber, 23, Studentin.

2 Schreiben Sie außerdem jeweils drei Gründe auf, warum (*a*) der Kontaktraucher, (*b*) der Mußraucher und (*c*) der Genußraucher zur Zigarette greifen.

Lesetexte

1 Raucher oder Nichtraucher?

Here is an advertisement for a service offered by a car rental firm. Read the text to see what is on offer, paying special attention to the following points:

- Where the service can be offered.
- What is now available for the benefit of non-smokers.
- Whether smokers will be disadvantaged as a result.

Ein netter Zug von Deutschlands Nummer 1:

„Raucher" oder „Nichtraucher" – ganz wie Sie wollen

Als einzige Autovermietung bietet Ihnen interRent Europcar an fast allen Verkehrsflughäfen einen ganz besonderen Service: Neben vielen Fahrzeugen, in denen Sie rauchen können, haben wir auch ein Modell für Nichtraucher reserviert. Wenn Sie also einen Mietwagen wünschen, in dem garantiert nicht geraucht wurde, kommen Sie zu Deutschlands Autovermietung Nummer 1 und fragen nach dem Nichtraucher-Service. Reservierungen an einer unserer über 400 Stationen, im Reisebüro oder rund um die Uhr zum Nulltarif unter 0130/2211.

(*Der Spiegel*)

Deutschlands Autovermietung Nummer 1

Notizen

der Zug **Zug** has many different meanings in German, from *train* to *draught*. Here the meaning is *move*, as in a board game, but there is also a hint of yet another meaning – a *drag* on a cigarette. (Consult a good dictionary for other meanings of **Zug**)
die Autovermietung car rental (firm)
der Verkehrsflughafen (¨) commercial airport
neben (+ Dat.) here the meaning is *in addition to* rather than the usual *next to* or *near*
das Fahrzeug (**-e**) vehicle
einen Mietwagen, . . . in dem . . . nicht geraucht wurde Lit. a hire car in which has not been smoked i.e. *a hire car in which nobody has smoked*) Note the use of the passive here
die Station (**-en**) here: *office*, *outlet*
zum Nulltarif *free of charge*

1 Beantworten Sie:
(*a*) Auf welchen Flughäfen findet man den hier von interRent angebotenen Service?
(*b*) Findet man diesen Service auch bei anderen Autovermietungen?
(*c*) Wieviel Modelle bietet man dem Nichtraucher an?
(*d*) Was garantiert die interRent-Autovermietung von ihrem Nichtraucher-Modell?
(*e*) Kann man so etwas eigentlich garantieren?
(*f*) Wann kann man einen interRent Mietwagen reservieren?
(*g*) Wie sagt man mit anderen Worten *kostenlos*?

2 Nennen Sie mindestens sechs Beispiele für den Gebrauch des Dativs in diesem Text.

3 Nennen Sie drei Wörter für *car* or *vehicle*, die in der Anzeige vorkommen. Zwei davon sind in einem zusammengesetzten Wort enthalten!

2 Hilfe für Raucher

1 See if you can work out the point of the advertisement opposite. In particular try to determine the following:
(*a*) In what context the World Health Organisation is mentioned.
(*b*) Who one should turn to for support and assistance.

Als Raucher haben Sie das Recht auf Ihrer Seite!

"Jeder Raucher hat das Recht, Unterstützung und Hilfe zu erhalten, sich das Rauchen abzugewöhnen" - das hat die Weltgesundheitsorganisation bereits 1988 erklärt. Nutzen Sie Ihr Recht!

Suchen Sie Unterstützung und Hilfe bei einem kompetenten Partner: Ihrem Arzt. Er weiß, mit welchen Maßnahmen Ihnen der Verzicht auf das Rauchen erleichtert werden kann, zum Beispiel mit Verhaltenstherapie und medikamentöser Behandlung.

Fordern Sie Unterstützung bei der Tabakentwöhnung. Als Raucher haben Sie das Recht dazu!

WISSENSCHAFTLICHER AKTIONSKREIS TABAKENTWÖHNUNG (WAI) e.V.

Walter-Kolb Straße 1-3 • 60594 Frankfurt am Main 70

(*Der Spiegel*)

Notizen

das Recht note the play on **Recht**, meaning both *right* (i.e. *justification*), *just cause* and ***the*** *right* (*to do something*)
die Unterstützung *support*

sich (Dat.) **etwas abgewöhnen** (sep.) *to give something up, stop (doing) something*
nutzen *to use*
erleichtern *to make easier*
der Verzicht (auf + Acc.) *giving up (of)*
die Verhaltenstherapie *behavioural therapy*
medikamentös *with drugs*
die Behandlung *treatment*
fordern *to demand*
die Entwöhnung *weaning off, curing of an addiction to*

2 Welches Wort paßt? Versuchen Sie die Lücken auszufüllen, ohne den Text anzuschauen.

(*a*) Als Raucher haben Sie das (i) ..... auf Ihrer Seite!
(*b*) Jeder Raucher hat das Recht, Unterstützung und Hilfe zu (ii) ....
(*c*) (iii) ...... Sie Ihr Recht!
(*d*) (iv) ...... Sie Unterstützung und (v) ..... bei einem kompetenten Partner: Ihrem Arzt.
(*e*) (vi) .... Sie Unterstützung bei der (vii) ....

Setzen Sie jetzt die fehlenden Wörter in das Gitter ein. Senkrecht erscheint dann ein relevantes Verb/Substantiv (viii).

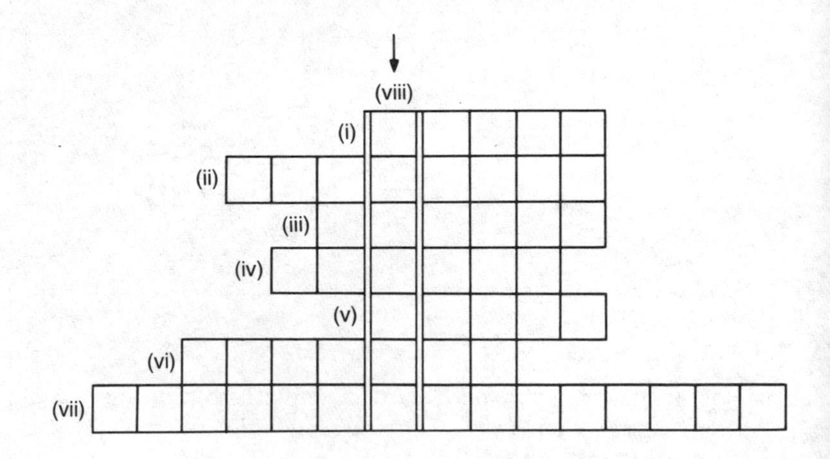

3 Gesundheits-Tips

Look at the four health tips, below and overleaf. Work out what advice or information they offer and answer these questions:

1 What is honey good for?
2 What should be kept out of the reach of children?
3 What bad news is there for people who have just given up smoking?
4 What is the moderate intake of red wine claimed to affect?

Alkoholkater – Honig vor dem Schlafengehen

Wer abends oder nachts zu viel Alkohol getrunken hat, sollte vor dem Schlafengehen einen Teelöffel Bienenhonig zu sich nehmen – empfehlen Mediziner der Universität New York. Am nächsten Morgen hat man dann weder Kopfschmerzen noch Schwindelgefühle. Wer beim Trinken auch noch raucht, sollte den Honig mit dem Saft einer Zitrone mischen und mit etwas Mineralwasser aufgießen.

(*Bunte*)

Nikotinkaugummi – Gift für kleine Kinder

Nikotinkaugummi, mit dem Erwachsene sich das Rauchen abgewöhnen, kann Kleinkindern den Tod bringen – warnt der Berliner Toxikologe Dr Reinhard Bunjes. Die Kaugummis sollen immer dort aufbewahrt werden, wo Kinder sie nicht erreichen können. Jeder dieser Kaugummis enthält 4 Milligramm Nikotin. Eine Menge, die beim Baby tödlich sein kann.

(*Bunte*)

Nikotin-Entwöhnung – 15 Jahre lang Herzgefahr

Raucher haben ein doppelt so hohes Infarktrisiko wie Nichtraucher. Auch wenn man sich Zigaretten abgewöhnt hat, hält die Anfälligkeit für Durchblutungsstörungen in den Kranzarterien noch mindestens 15 Jahre lange an – berichten irische Mediziner im »British Heart Journal«.

(*Bunte*)

Cholesterin – jeden Tag 2 Gläschen Rotwein

Menschen mit einem hohen Cholesterinspiegel sollten jeden Tag zwei Gläschen Rotwein trinken – empfehlen amerikanische Wissenschaftler der Cornell-Universität in Ithaca. Sie entdeckten im Rotwein einen Stoff (Resveratol), der Cholesterin bindet. Am meisten davon ist im roten Bordeaux enthalten.

(*Bunte*)

der Kater *hangover*
der Honig *honey*
der Teelöffel (-) *teaspoon*
die Biene (-n) *bee*
weder . . . noch . . . *neither . . . nor . . .*
das Schwindelgefühl (-e) *feeling of dizziness*
(mit Mineralwasser) aufgießen *to pour (mineral water) on*
der Kaugummi *chewing gum*
der Erwachsene *adult.* (See **Grammatische Hinweise**, page 188)
der Toxikologe *toxicologist.* Like other nouns ending in **-loge** this is a 'weak noun', i.e. it takes an **-n** in all cases except the nominative singular: **Werner Bosch ist Toxikologe** but **Kennst du den neuen Toxikologen?** (See **Lektion 7** for more about weak nouns)
aufbewahren (sep.) *to store, keep*
enthalten (ä, ie, a) *to contain*
die Menge Lit. quantity, crowd; here: *a lot*
tödlich *fatal*
der Infarkt (-e) *heart attack, coronary (infarction)*
anhalten (ä, ie, a) (sep.) *to last, go on*
die Anfälligkeit für *susceptibility to*
die Durchblutungstörung (-en) *disturbance of the blood supply, circulatory problems*
die Kranzarterie (-n) *coronary artery*
berichten *to report*
der Cholesterinspiegel *cholesterol level*
der/die Mediziner/-in (-/-nen) *medical expert*
der/die Wissenschaftler/-in (-/-nen) *scientist, scholar*
entdecken *to discover*
der Stoff (-e) *substance*
binden here: *to take up*

4 Teletext

P513 513 SAT.1-text Fr 10.09 14:16:46

Gesundheit

Glimmstengel lassen die Haut altern

Wer viel raucht, hat eine weniger elastische Haut als ein Nicht au- cher. Zu diesem Ergebnis kam eine Studie der Uni Witten-Herdecke.
Bei chronischem Nikotingebrauch (in diesem Fall etwa 30 Zigaretten am Tag) ist die Haut etwa zehn Jah- re älter als die nicht davon bela- stete. dp

100< übersicht >510

Attraktive Angebote
Das Reise-Magazin... ab 400

What information is given about skin on this Teletext page?

Testen Sie Ihr Wissen

Richtig oder falsch?

Bei Rauchern hält der Alkoholgehalt im Blut länger an als bei Nichtrauchern.

7
MÜLL UND RECYCLING

Lernziele

In this unit you will learn how to

- conduct an altercation
- challenge and answer back, call names
- form and use adjective endings, adjectival nouns, weak nouns, the imperative

Aufnahmen

1 Deutschland und England im Vergleich

Auf der Straße in Canterbury äußert sich ein junger deutscher Tourist zum Problem Müll.

Interviewer Waren Sie hier in Canterbury mal im Supermarkt?
Bodo Oh ja.
Interviewer Haben Sie irgendwelche Unterschiede bemerkt zwi-

schen einem deutschen und einem englischen Supermarkt?

Bodo Ja, in 'nem deutschen Supermarkt, da ist jetzt auf fast allen Produkten so'n grüner Punkt drauf, das heißt, daß es in die Abfalltonne geht, hier bei uns in die grüne Tonne, zum Beispiel. Und auch, daß man in deutschen Supermärkten, da kann man die Verpackung . . . man kann das Produkt auspacken und die Verpackung in einen Pappcontainer oder Blechcontainer, oder so, schon im Geschäft reinschmeißen, und man nimmt dann eigentlich sozusagen nur das Produkt, das gewünschte Produkt, mit nach Hause . . . und so was habe ich in England noch nicht gesehen.

Interviewer Nein, ich auch nicht. Und das ist in Deutschland sogar gesetzlich vorgeschrieben, jetzt, ja?

Bodo Stimmt.

Interviewer Ja, das ist schon ein großer Unterschied. Und auch mit Joghurtbechern und so weiter . . .

Bodo Ja, die werden ausgewaschen, und dann kommen die in den Plastiksack für Hartplastik.

Interviewer Wieviel verschiedene Tonnen gibt es eigentlich?

Bodo Also, das ist im Moment regional noch unterschiedlich geregelt . . . wir haben zu Hause die schwarze Tonne für allen . . . so . . . Hausrat. Dann gibt es die grüne Tonne für Papier, die gelbe Tonne für Verpackungen, und die braune Tonne für Kompost und Biomüll, und so was.

Interviewer Aha. Gibt es auch eine blaue Tonne?

Bodo Die gibt es . . . die werden, glaube ich, nicht an die Häuser geliefert, die gibt es nur auf Sammelplätzen . . . und die haben da jetzt Glascontainer, Weißblechcontainer . . .

Interviewer Und machen die meisten Leute mit? Oder gibt es auch Leute, die nicht mitmachen?

Bodo Also, es gibt natürlich immer 'n paar Leute, die nicht mitmachen, aber die meisten in unserer Nachbarschaft, würde ich sagen, sind dabei, die haben alle so um die vier Tonnen.

Interviewer Und sie verstehen auch, warum sie das machen?

Bodo Oh, ja, ja, da gibt es immer so . . . von so Initiativen, so Aufklärungsblätter, und Fernsehsendungen, und so was alles . . . und da wird die Bevölkerung aufgeklärt, und sieht das dann auch ein, weswegen Materialien eingespart werden müssen, recycelt werden müssen, und so weiter.

Interviewer Gut. Da bleibt nur zu hoffen, daß in England in dieser Hinsicht auch bald Fortschritte gemacht werden!

Bemerkungen

Note the colloquial manner in which Bodo speaks.
sich äußern zu (+ Dat.) *to make a statement about*
der Supermarkt (¨e) *the supermarket*
der Unterschied (-e) (**zwischen** + Dat.) *difference (between)*
reinschmeißen (ei, i, i) (sep.) *to throw in* (colloquial)
gesetzlich vorgeschrieben *regulated by law*
auswaschen (ä, u, a) (sep.) *to wash out*
das Hartplastik *hard plastic* (cracks when you squeeze it)
der Hausrat *household goods*
regional unterschiedlich geregelt Lit. regulated differently in different regions. The pace at which these regulations are implemented varies from region to region, and even from town to town
mitmachen (sep.) **bei** (+ Dat.) *to take part in*
die Nachbarschaft *neighbourhood*
das Aufklärungsblatt (¨**er**) *information leaflet*
die Initiative (-n) *initiative*; here: *citizens' action group*
aufklären (sep.) *to inform*

Welche Antwort paßt?

1 Gibt es eigentlich große Unterschiede zwischen einem englischen und einem deutschen Supermarkt?
(*a*) Ich gehe immer samstags einkaufen.
(*b*) In deutschen Supermärkten ist jetzt auf fast allen Produkten ein grüner Punkt.
(*c*) Supermärkte sind billiger als kleine Geschäfte.

2 Kann man in englischen Supermärkten die Verpackung dort zurücklassen?

(*a*) In englischen Supermärkten sind die meisten Produkte in Plastik verpackt.
(*b*) Nein, das gibt es bis jetzt noch nicht.
(*c*) Das Warenangebot in englischen Supermärkten ist anders.

3 Wird in Deutschland auch Plastik wiederverwertet?
(*a*) Wiederverwertung ist gesetzlich geregelt.
(*b*) Ich kaufe keine Produkte in Plastikverpackung.
(*c*) Ja, es wird im Plastiksack gesammelt.

4 Wieviel verschiedene Sammeltonnen gibt es eigentlich?
(*a*) Das Müllproblem wird immer größer.
(*b*) Es gibt im Moment vier verschiedene Tonnen.
(*c*) Meine Familie macht beim Recycling nicht mit.

5 Machen die Leute eigentlich bei diesen Sammelaktionen mit?
(*a*) Die Leute verstehen nicht, warum sie das machen sollen.
(*b*) Immer mehr Leute machen jetzt mit.
(*c*) Ich habe kein Interesse an Recycling.

6 Wie wird die Bevölkerung denn über diese Aktionen informiert?
(*a*) Ich informiere mich niemals darüber.
(*b*) Durch Fernsehsendungen, Aufklärungsblätter und andere Informationsquellen.
(*c*) Die Deutschen sind sehr umweltbewußt.

2 Roland – der Umweltflegel

Ein junger Mann, Roland, der mit seinen Freunden im Park zusammensitzt, wirft achtlos eine Bierdose auf die Wiese, und wird daraufhin von einer älteren umweltbewußten Bürgerin angesprochen.

Bürgerin Entschuldigung, aber warum werfen Sie denn ihre leere Bierdose auf die Wiese? Da vorne ist doch ein Abfalleimer!

Roland Häh? Was geht Sie das denn an? Und außerdem, die Parkarbeiter, die sollen auch mal was arbeiten, dafür werden sie ja schließlich bezahlt, von meinen Steuern!

Bürgerin Also, Sie haben vielleicht eine Auffassung – wenn jeder so denken würde wie Sie, dann würden wir bald im Müll ersticken, und der Park wäre eine Müllhalde.

Roland Ach, sind Sie etwa auch so eine, die dauernd von Umwelt und Recycling schwafelt? Davon habe ich die Nase schon lange voll. Wem nützt das denn überhaupt? Ist doch sowieso alles schon zu spät. Und dieser ganze Quatsch mit dieser Müllsortierung – da habe ich in meiner Freizeit ehrlich besseres zu tun als daran zu denken, was in welche Tonne kommt.

Bürgerin Recycling ist eine sehr sinnvolle Sache – wenn wir jetzt nichts für die Umwelt tun, wie sieht denn dann das Leben für unsere Kinder aus? Und wenn wir schon von Recycling reden: Dosen werden jetzt auch getrennt gesammelt!

Roland Wollen Sie mich auf den Arm nehmen? Soll ich jetzt etwa zum Container rennen, nur um eine einzige Blechdose wegzuwerfen? Das können Sie ja machen, wenn Sie wollen!

Bürgerin Sie könnten die Dose ja in ihre Tasche packen, und später entsorgen. Damit hätten Sie zum einen die Wiese saubergehalten, und zum anderen was für die Umwelt getan.

Roland Wenn Sie glauben, daß Sie mich bekehren können, haben Sie sich getäuscht. Das Leben ist kurz genug, und ich will mich amüsieren. Für Ihre Moralpredigten habe ich keine Zeit. Und jetzt lassen Sie mich in Ruhe!

Bürgerin Ich sehe schon, Sie sind einer von denen, die erst saftige Geldstrafen zahlen müssen, bevor sie irgendetwas tun! Und das ist dann zum Glück wirklich nicht meine Sache!

Bemerkungen

achtlos *heedless(ly)*
ansprechen (i, a, o) (sep.) *to address (someone)*
da vorne *further ahead, over there*
die Auffassung (-en) *attitude*
ersticken *to suffocate*
die Müllhalde (-n) *rubbish tip*
schwafeln *to waffle*
die Nase voll haben *to have had enough*
der Quatsch *nonsense*

jemanden auf den Arm nehmen *to pull someone's leg*
entsorgen *to dispose of*
jemanden bekehren *to convert someone*
sich täuschen *to be wrong about something*
die Moralpredigt (**-en**) (*moralizing*) *lecture*
saftig here: *hefty*, *big* (Lit. juicy)

Richtig oder falsch?

Korrigieren Sie die falschen Aussagen

1 Eine Bürgerin fragt Roland, warum er seine Bierdosen in den Container wirft.
2 Roland ist der Meinung, daß er genug für die Umwelt tut, wenn er Steuern zahlt.
3 Die Bürgerin warnt Roland davor, daß der Park eine Müllhalde werden könnte.
4 Roland glaubt, daß Recyling und Umweltschutz sehr sinnvoll sind.
5 In seiner Freizeit macht er viel für die Umwelt.
6 Die Bürgerin glaubt, daß Umweltschutz und Recycling für die nächste Generation wichtig sind.
7 Blechdosen werden jetzt auch recycelt.
8 Die Bürgerin steckt die Dose in ihre Tasche und entsorgt sie zu Hause.
9 Die Bürgerin kann Roland davon überzeugen, daß Umweltschutz und Recycling wichtig sind.
10 Manchmal kann man die Leute nur mit Geldstrafen davon überzeugen, daß sie etwas tun sollen.

Sagen Sie's auf Deutsch!

1 What business is that of yours?
2 I've long since had enough of that.
3 It's too late anyway.
4 What will life be like for our children?
5 All that nonsense about . . .
6 And talking about recycling, . . .
7 Are you pulling my leg?
8 I have no time for your lectures.
9 Leave me alone now!

3 Andere Länder, andere Sitten

Frau Müller hat einen neuen Untermieter, der seit längerer Zeit nicht mehr in Deutschland war, und daher mit dem neuen Prinzip der Müllentsorgung noch nicht vertraut ist.

Frau Müller Und mit der Müllsortierung wissen Sie ja Bescheid, Herr Schmitt, oder?

Herr Schmitt Ich habe schon darüber gelesen – es hört sich aber komisch an. Vielleicht habe ich es ja auch falsch verstanden? Wie Sie sich vorstellen können, hat man in Südamerika andere Sorgen, als sich um den Müll zu kümmern.

Frau Müller Ja, also hier sieht das ganz anders aus. Kommen Sie mal mit! (*Führt ihn zur Garage, wo drei verschiedene Tonnen stehen.*)

Herr Schmitt Machen Sie Witze? Wozu braucht man denn drei Tonnen? Das erscheint mir aber alles sehr merkwürdig.

Frau Müller Gar nicht! In Deutschland wird jetzt alles getrennt gesammelt, und dann wiederverwertet, oder umweltfreundlich entsorgt.

Herr Schmitt Das kann ich mir aber überhaupt nicht vorstellen. Wie soll denn das funktionieren?

Frau Müller Ganz einfach, Herr Schmitt. Die blaue Tonne hier ist für Papier. Die braune Tonne ist für Biomüll, und der Sack ist für alle Verpackungen, die den Grünen Punkt aufweisen. Alles wird im Wechsel vierzehntägig abgeholt.

Herr Schmitt Ist das denn nicht ungeheuer zeitaufwendig?

Frau Müller Eigentlich nicht. Sie werden sich schon schnell daran gewöhnen. Auf jeden Fall kann jetzt jeder was für die Umwelt tun – auch Sie!

Herr Schmitt Aber wäre es denn nicht besser, Müll erst gar nicht zu produzieren, als ihn dann hinterher zu sammeln und nicht zu wissen, wohin damit?

Frau Müller Naja, natürlich. Aber mit diesem System ist zumindest mal ein Anfang gemacht. Und mitmachen müssen Sie auf jeden Fall – es kostet nämlich eine schöne Stange Geld, wenn man den Müll nicht sortiert!

Herr Schmitt Und was ist denn eigentlich das da drüben?

Frau Müller Ach ja, das sind die Container für Blechdosen, Glas und Altbatterien. Wenn sie außerdem Sondermüll wie Farben oder Lacke haben, müssen Sie zur Sammelstelle fahren.

Herr Schmitt Na, das kann ja heiter werden!

Bemerkungen

andere Länder, andere Sitten *when in Rome, do as the Romans do* (Lit. different countries, different customs)
der Untermieter (-) *lodger*

Bescheid wissen (**mit** + Dat./ **über** + Acc.) *to know about*
das hört sich komisch an *that sounds strange*
Machen Sie Witze? *Are you joking?*
das erscheint mir merkwürdig *that seems strange to me*
gar nicht *not at all*
sich etwas vorstellen *to imagine something*
ganz einfach *very simple*
im Wechsel *alternately*
vierzehntägig *fortnightly*
zeitaufwendig *time-consuming*
hinterher *afterwards*
wohin damit (colloquial) here: *where to put it*
eine schöne Stange Geld *a small fortune*
das kann ja heiter werden (ironical) *that will be fun*

Welche Antwort paßt?

1 Und mit der Müllsortierung wissen Sie ja Bescheid, oder?
(*a*) Ich produziere keinen Müll.
(*b*) In Südamerika wird das auch so gemacht.
(*c*) Ich habe schon davon gehört, aber ich finde es komisch.

2 Wozu braucht man denn drei Tonnen?
(*a*) Vielleicht habe ich es falsch verstanden.
(*b*) Weil in Deutschland jetzt alles getrennt gesammelt wird.
(*c*) Das erscheint mir alles sehr merkwürdig.

3 Wie soll denn diese Müllsortierung funktionieren?
(*a*) In Deutschland wird viel für die Umwelt getan.
(*b*) Man muß jetzt umweltfreundlicher denken.
(*c*) Es ist ganz einfach. Alles wird im Wechsel vierzehntägig abgeholt.

4 Ist das denn nicht ungeheuer zeitaufwendig?
(*a*) Eigentlich nicht. Man gewöhnt sich daran.
(*b*) Ich brauche morgens immer besonders lang.
(*c*) Zeit ist nicht so wichtig.

5 Wäre es denn nicht besser, Müll erst gar nicht zu produzieren?
(*a*) Na, das kann ja heiter werden!
(*b*) Ja, aber es ist zumindest ein Anfang gemacht.
(*c*) Es kostet eine schöne Stange Geld, wenn man den Müll nicht sortiert.

Redewendungen

- Challenging someone

Entschuldigen Sie, aber warum . . .?
Was machen Sie denn da?
Was fällt Ihnen denn ein?
Haben Sie denn gar keinen Anstand?
Wofür halten Sie sich denn eigentlich?
Also hören Sie mal, wie benehmen Sie sich denn?
Hören Sie sofort mit dem Unsinn auf!
Verschwinden Sie!
Lassen Sie sich hier nicht mehr blicken!
Wenn Sie nicht augenblicklich verschwinden, rufe ich die Polizei!

- Answering back

Was geht Sie das denn an?
Kümmern Sie sich um Ihre eigenen Angelegenheiten!
Lassen Sie mich gefälligst in Ruhe!
Wollen Sie mich auf den Arm nehmen?
Sie haben vielleicht eine Auffassung!
Ich habe Ihnen jetzt aber wirklich lange genug zugehört!
Ich habe jetzt langsam die Nase voll von Ihnen!
Soll das ein Witz sein?
Machen Sie Witze?
Soll ich etwa . . .?
Wenn Sie glauben, daß . . ., dann haben Sie sich getäuscht!
Das fällt mir ja überhaupt nicht ein!
Sie können mir mal den Buckel 'runterrutschen!
Halten Sie doch Ihren Mund!/ Halt den Mund!

- Calling someone names. (Be careful with these. They are included more to inform you about what others may be saying to you!)

Sie/Du Dummkopf!
Sie/Du Esel!
Sie haben/ Du hast ja nicht mehr alle Tassen im Schrank!
Sie sind/ Du bist ja nicht ganz dicht!
Idiot!
Sie/Du Depp!

Grammatische Hinweise

1 *Adjectival endings*

An area of German grammar which English-speaking people often find difficult to master is that of adjectival endings. If you want to be a competent user of German, it is important to get the endings right! This takes time and a lot of practice, but eventually you will get a feel for what is correct.

When adjectives stand on their own rather than in front of a noun, they are said to be predicative. When adjectives are used predicatively they do not take an ending:

Kegeln ist immer **lustig**. (**Lektion 5**, **Aufnahme 2**)
Das ist ja sehr **nett** von dir. (**Lektion 5**, **Aufnahme 3**)
Einige Menschen sind **allergisch** gegen Zigarettenrauch. (**Lektion 6**, **Aufnahme 2**)

An adjective which stands in front of a noun which it qualifies is called an attributive adjective. Attributive adjectives take endings:

Kann mann wirklich ein **totales** Rauchverbot verhängen? (**Lektion 6**, **Aufnahme 2**)
. . . als ich wegen **ständiger** Kopfschmerzen beim Arzt war . . . (**Lektion 6**, **Aufnahme 3**)
. . . bei jedem **neuen** Versuch (**Lektion 6**, **Aufnahme 3**)

There are three sorts of adjectival endings which are normally referred to as strong, weak and mixed.

Strong endings are found on those attributive adjectives which are not preceded by such words as **ein**, **kein**, **mein**, **der**, **dieser**, etc. They are also used after numbers (except after **ein**-):
Deutsch**en** Weißwein trinke ich gerne. (*Acc. / m. / sing.*)
Giftig**e** Autoabgase müssen reduziert werden. (*Nom. / n. / pl.*)

Weak endings are found on those attributive adjectives which follow the definite article (**der**, **die**, **das**) or such words as **dies**-, **jed**-, **jen**-:
Ich versuche diesen gut**en** Vorsatz durchzuhalten. (*Acc. / m. / sing.*)
Ich muß die ganz**en** Abgase von den viel**en** Autos einatmen. (*Acc. / n. / pl.* and *Dat. / n. / pl.*)

Mixed endings are found on those attributive adjectives which follow the indefinite article (**ein**-), the possessive adjectives (**mein**-, **Ihr**-, **ihr**-, **sein**-, **unser**-, etc.) and after **kein**-:

Du bist mit deinen neurotisch**en** Forderungen zu weit gegangen. (*Dat./f./pl.*)
Warum hast du eine derart drastisch**e** Maßnahme ergriffen? (*Acc./f./sing.*)

Here is a summary of the three sets of endings:

Strong endings

	Masculine singular	Feminine singular	Neuter singular	All genders plural
Nom.	-er	-e	-es	-e
Acc.	-en	-e	-es	-e
Gen.	-en	-er	-en	-er
Dat.	-em	-er	-em	-en

Weak endings

	Masculine singular	Feminine singular	Neuter singular	All genders plural
Nom.	-e	-e	-e	-en
Acc.	-en	-e	-e	-en
Gen.	-en	-en	-en	-en
Dat.	-en	-en	-en	-en

Mixed endings

	Masculine singular	Feminine singular	Neuter singular	All genders plural
Nom.	-er	-e	-es	-en
Acc.	-en	-e	-es	-en
Gen.	-en	-en	-en	-en
Dat.	-en	-en	-en	-en

Note that while weak endings are used after **alle** in the plural, strong endings are used after **viele**, **einige** and **wenige**:

Nicht alle deutsch**en** Dörfer sind schön.
Viele deutsch**e** Dörfer sind aber sehr schön.

Einige deutsch**e** Dörfer sind wunderschön.
Wenig**e** deutsch**e** Dörfer sind unschön.

2 Adjectival nouns

In German, many adjectives can be converted into nouns. They take the initial capital letter typical of nouns but add the adjectival endings as indicated in the previous section:

Ein Deutsch**er** (*Nom. / m. / str.*) möchte uns heute abend besuchen.

Kennt ihr diesen Deutsch**en**? (*Acc. / m. / wk.*)
Ich bin Deutsch**e**. (*Nom. / f. / str.*)
Kevin ist mit einer Deutsch**en** (*Dat. / f. / mixed*) verheiratet.
Ich kenne viele Deutsch**e**. (*pl. / str.*)

These examples are typical of a large category of adjectival nouns which refer to people. Other such nouns include:

der Abgeordnete/ die Abgeordnete *MP, deputy*
der Angestellte/ die Angestellte *employee, white-collar worker*
der Beamte/ die Beamtin *civil servant*
der Bekannte/ die Bekannte *acquaintance*
der Erwachsene/ die Erwachsene *adult, grown-up*
der Fremde/ die Fremde *stranger, foreigner*
der Kranke/ die Kranke *sick person, patient*
der Reisende/ die Reisende *traveller*
der Tote/ die Tote *dead person*
der Verlobte/ die Verlobte *fiancé/ fiancée*
der Vorsitzende/ die Vorsitzende *chairman/chairwoman*

Now turn back to **Lektion 6, Aufnahme 4** and find three examples of adjectival nouns. What cases are they in and what kind of endings do they bear? The answers are given in the **Lösungsteil**.

3 Weak nouns

There is quite a large group of masculine nouns which add -(**e**)**n** in all cases except the nominative singular. These nouns are known as weak nouns or **schwache Substantive**. **Der Abiturient** and **der Präsident** are two such nouns that you have met in earlier units.

Other common examples include:

der Abiturient someone who has their **Abitur**
der Architekt *architect*
der Assistent *assistant*
der Automat *vending machine*
der Bär *bear*
der Bauer *peasant, farmer*
der Bayer *Bavarian*
der Bulle *bull* (slang *policeman*)
der Demonstrant *demonstrator*
der Direktor *director, head teacher*
der Fotograf *photographer*
der Franzose *Frenchman*
der Fürst *prince*
der Graf *count*
der Herr *gentleman*
der Hirt *shepherd*
der Journalist *journalist*
der Junge *boy*
der Kandidat *candidate*
der Kollege *colleague*
der Kunde *customer, client*
der Mensch *person, human being*
der Musikant *musician*
der Nachbar *neighbour*
der Präsident *president*
der Prinz *prince*
der Riese *giant*
der Russe *Russian*
der Schwede *Swede*
der Soldat *soldier*
der Student *student*
der Tourist *tourist*
der Zeuge *witness*

Here are some examples of weak nouns in use:

Helga ist mit einem Franzosen verheiratet.
Kennst du den neuen Assistenten des Bundespräsidenten?
Kannst du bitte diesem Touristen helfen?
Hat der Präsident den Vertrag unterschrieben?
Haben diese Touristen mit unserem Fotografen gesprochen?

Note that **der Herr** is slightly irregular in that it takes **-n** in the singular, but **-en** in the plural.

Kennen Sie Herr**n** Breitling?
Die Herr**en** von der Firma Hartmann warten in Ihrem Büro.
Wer empfängt die Herr**en** aus Dresden?

A few weak nouns, in addition to adding **-n** in all cases except the nominative singular, also add an **-s** in the genitive singular.

der Buchstabe *letter* (of the alphabet)
der Friede/Frieden *peace*
der Gedanke *thought*
der Glaube *belief, faith*
der Name *name*
der Wille *will, wish*

One neuter noun, **das Herz**, also behaves in this way. Examples of this category include:

Im Namen des Friedens.
Im Grunde ihres Herzens dachte sie anders.
Er ist voll guten Willens.

4 Compound nouns

The ability of German to join nouns together to form compound nouns is enormous. Note that the gender of such nouns is always taken from the last component in the noun:

das Auto + die Bahn = die Autobahn
die Woche + das Ende = das Wochenende

Here are a few examples from the last three units:

Lektion 5: die Freizeitbeschäftigung, der Schwimmunterricht, das Fußballspiel, das Reisebügeleisen, das Bundesjugendministerium.
Lektion 6: der Antiraucherfanatiker, das Rauchverbot, die Krebserkrankungen (pl.), die Folgeschäden (pl.), der Alkoholmißbrauch, die Krankenversicherung, die Blutfettwerte (pl.).
Lektion 7: die Abfalltonne, der Weißblechcontainer, das Aufklärungsblatt, die Informationsquelle, die Müllhalde.

In these examples, the compound nouns consist of two or three components. It is not unusual in German to find nouns with three or four components. Even five or six components are possible:
die Arbeitsunfähigkeitsbescheinigung *certificate of unfitness to work*
der Kriegsdienstverweigerer *conscientious objector*
das Bundesausbildungsförderungsgesetz (BAFöG) *Federal Education and Training Assistance Act*
die Rheindampfschiffahrtsgesellschaft *Rhine Steamship Company*. Presumably the personnel management of this company might be referred to as **die Rheindampfschiffahrtsgesellschafts-personalleitung**. It is even possible to refer to the office in which the personnel management is situated as **das Rheindampfschiffahrtsgesellschaftspersonalleitungs-büro**, though this is a bit long even by German standards and it would probably be preferable to say **das Personalleitungsbüro der Rheindampfschiffahrtsgesellschaft**

5 The imperative

The imperative or command form is not difficult to learn, but you do have to remember whether you are using the **Sie**, **du** or the **ihr** form.

It is often advisable to tone down a command by adding **bitte** or by using a more polite turn of phrase:

Bringen Sie mir bitte ein Glas Weißwein!
Könnten Sie mir helfen?
Würden Sie bitte einen Moment draußen warten?

The *Sie* form

To give a command in the **Sie** form all that is required is to reverse the subject and verb of the present tense form:

Kommen Sie mit!
Lassen Sie mich in Ruhe!
Vergessen Sie nicht, Brot zu kaufen!
Fangen Sie ohne mich an!
Fahren Sie doch nicht so schnell!
Laufen Sie mir nicht weg!

As might be expected, the separable particle of separable verbs goes to the end of the sentence or clause. The examples above include **mitkommen**, **anfangen** and **weglaufen**.

The exclamation mark tends to be used more often for the imperative in German than it is in English, although it is not obligatory.

The *du* form

The **du** form is also relatively straightforward. Just omit the **-st** and the **du** of the present tense form. Hence **du kommst** becomes **komm!**:

Komm mit!
Vergiß nicht, Brot zu kaufen!

Exceptions to this rule are certain verbs like **lassen**, **anfangen** and **fahren**, which do modify the middle vowel in the present tense form (**du läßt**, **du fängst an**, **du fährst**), but which do not modify this vowel in the imperative. These verbs tend to have the middle vowel

a or **au**:

Laß mich in Ruhe!
Fang ohne mich an!
Fahr doch nicht so schnell!
Lauf mir nicht weg!

The *ihr* form

For the **ihr** form of the imperative take the present tense form and omit the **ihr**:

Kommt mit!
Laßt mich in Ruhe!
Vergeßt nicht, Brot zu kaufen!
Fangt ohne mich an!
Fahrt doch nicht so schnell!
Lauft mir nicht weg!

Sein in the imperative

The imperative forms of **sein** are:

Seien Sie nicht so unfreundlich!
Sei ruhig!
Seid pünktlich!

Übungen

1 Lesen Sie diese Bunte-Umfrage und beantworten Sie anschließend die Fragen.

BUNTE FRAGT: TUN WIR GENUG FÜR DIE KINDER?

Was würden Sie eher kaufen?

1.	(*a*)	ein edel verpacktes Parfüm	6%
	(*b*)	das gleiche Parfüm in einer schlichten Glasampulle	91%
2.	(*a*)	einen schrumpligen, ungespritzten Apfel	72%
	(*b*)	einen großen, knackigen, gespritzten Apfel	22%

Wären Sie dazu bereit?	Ja	Nein
3. künftig 1 Mark mehr für den Liter Benzin zu zahlen	38%	50%
4. 5% Ihres Einkommens als Umweltsteuer abzuführen	48%	46%
5. für Temperaturen über 15 Grad in Ihrer Wohnung zusätzliche Heizkosten zu entrichten	40%	57%
6. einmal pro Jahr 100 DM für die Aufforstung geschädigter Wälder zu bezahlen	77%	21%
7. höhere Preise für Wasser zu bezahlen, wenn Ihr privater Verbrauch überdurchschnittlich steigt	75%	21%
8. 50% mehr für Elektrogeräte zu bezahlen, mit denen Sie nur halb so viel Energie verbrauchen	78%	19%
9. an Sonn- und Feiertagen Ihr Auto stehenzulassen	70%	18%
(*Bunte*)		

Beantworten Sie die folgenden Fragen mit vollständigen Sätzen:

(*a*) Wozu wären 57 Prozent der Befragten nicht bereit?
(*b*) Welche Bedeutung haben die Zahlen 6 Prozent und 91 Prozent?
(*c*) Wie ist die Reaktion der Befragten auf den Vorschlag, man soll den Literpreis für Benzin um 1 DM erhöhen?
(*d*) Welche Bedeutung hat die Zahl 78 Prozent?
(*e*) Wie lautet das Urteil der Befragten über gespritzte und ungespritzte Äpfel?
(*f*) Unter welchen Umständen wären 75 Prozent der Befragten bereit, höhere Preise für Wasser zu bezahlen?
(*g*) Wozu wären 21 Prozent der Befragten nicht bereit? (Zwei Antworten)

(*h*) Wozu wären 70 Prozent der Befragten bereit?
(*i*) Wofür würden 77 Prozent der Befragten pro Jahr 100 DM bezahlen?

2 A German friend, Helga, who has been living in Britain for 15 years, wants to know more about the new environmental measures taken in Germany. Complete the dialogue, playing the part of Helga by asking the questions. You will find possible solutions in the **Lösungsteil**.

Helga (*a*)
Anne Ja, das stimmt. In Deutschland wird jetzt alles getrennt gesammelt, und dann wiederverwertet oder umweltfreundlich entsorgt.
Helga (*b*)
Anne Es ist eigentlich ganz einfach. Die blaue Tonne ist für Papier, die braune Tonne für Biomüll, und der Plastiksack ist für alle Verpackungen mit dem Grünen Punkt.
Helga (*c*)
Anne Ja, die meisten Leute machen mit, und sind auch ganz begeistert. Wenn man nicht mitmacht, muß man saftige Strafen zahlen!
Helga (*d*)
Anne Durch Aufklärungsblätter, Initiativen und Fernsehsendungen.

3 Setzen Sie die folgenden Sätze in den Imperativ. Verwenden Sie einmal die **Sie**-Form und einmal die **ihr**-Form.

Beispiel
Das Papier muß in die blaue Tonne gegeben werden.
Geben Sie/ Gebt das Papier in die blaue Tonne.
(*a*) Verpackungen sollen im Supermarkt zurückgelassen werden.
(*b*) Anstatt Plastikbechern sollen Glasbehälter gekauft werden.
(*c*) Biomüll muß in der braunen Tonne gesammelt werden.
(*d*) Sondermüll muß auf den Sammelplatz gebracht werden.
(*e*) Die neuen Bestimmungen bezüglich der Müllsortierung müssen befolgt werden.
(*f*) Die Bevölkerung muß über die neuen Bestimmungen aufgeklärt werden.
(*g*) Joghurtbecher müssen ausgewaschen werden.

(*h*) Anstatt Plastiktüten sollen Jutesäckchen oder Einkaufskörbe verwendet werden.
(*i*) Dosen müssen in den Weißblechcontainer geworfen werden.
(*j*) Giftmüll muß besonders vorsichtig entsorgt werden.

4 Bilden Sie Sätze aus den vorgegebenen Satzteilen.

Beispiel
Materialien – einsparen
Materialien müssen eingespart werden.

(*a*) Papier – recyceln (note that **recyceln** does not form its past participle with **ge**-)
(*b*) Die Bevölkerung – informieren
(*c*) Aufklärungsblätter – verteilen
(*d*) Müllsortierung – gesetzlich regeln
(*e*) Umwelt – schützen
(*f*) Die Kinder – in der Schule aufklären
(*g*) Parks – sauberhalten
(*h*) Für Umweltsünden – saftige Geldstrafen zahlen
(*i*) Müll – getrennt sammeln
(*j*) Die Mülltonnen – im Wechsel vierzehntägig abholen

5 Bilden Sie Sätze aus den folgenden Satzteilen. Verwenden Sie dazu die passenden Wörter im richtigen Fall.

Beispiele

Der Lehrer berät	Fotograf
Der Assistent hilft	Bundespräsident
Die Königin empfängt	Junge

Lösungen
Der Lehrer berät den Jungen.
Der Assistent hilft dem Fotografen.
Die Königin empfängt den Bundespräsidenten.

Man hätte natürlich auch schreiben können: »Der Lehrer berät den Bundespräsidenten« und »Der Assistent hilft dem Jungen« usw., aber diese Lösungen sind weniger gut.

Zu beachten: die Substantive in der zweiten Spalte stehen alle im Singular. Vorsicht: zwei von den Substantiven in der rechten Spalte sind nicht schwach!

(*a*)	David besiegt	Amerikanerin
(*b*)	Der Bulle verletzt	Puppe
(*c*)	Der Richter glaubt	Demonstrant
(*d*)	Der Verkäufer widerspricht	Riese
(*e*)	Die Schafe folgen	Bauer
(*f*)	Der Reiseleiter hilft	Kunde
(*g*)	Die Polizisten verhaften	Hirt
(*h*)	Das Mädchen liebt	Zeuge

6 Ergänzen Sie die Sätze mit den Vokabeln, die in dieser Lektion vorgekommen sind.

Es gibt noch große (*a*) (*differences*) zwischen den Ländern der EG auf dem Gebiet des Umweltschutzes. In Deutschland ist die Müllsortierung zwar noch (*b*) (*regulated differently in different regions*), aber auf jeden Fall (*c*) (*regulated by law*). Die Bevölkerung wird durch (*d*) (*information leaflets and initiatives*) aufgeklärt, und (*e*) (*takes part*) bei dieser Aktion.

Es ist klar, daß etwas getan werden muß, damit die (*f*) (*rubbish tips*) nicht weiterwachsen, und wir nicht im Müll (*g*) (*suffocate*). Dosen, Plastik, Aluminium, Hausrat . . . alles wird jetzt umweltfreundlich (*h*) (*disposed of*) bzw. recycelt. Wer neu nach Deutschland kommt, ist wahrscheinlich nicht mit diesem System (*i*) (*familiar*), und kann sich das gar nicht (*j*) (*imagine*). Aber es ist eigentlich ganz einfach: der Müll, den man sammelt, wird (*k*) (*alternately*) (*l*) (*fortnightly*) abgeholt.

7 John, a British student who has just arrived in Germany, talks to Volker, a German student, about the newly introduced recycling system. You play the role of Volker and complete the dialogue with the help of the prompts in English.

John Du, wie funktioniert eigentlich diese Müllsortierung?

Volker *Tell him that there is a brown bin for organic waste, a blue one for paper, and a plastic bag for all packages which bear the 'Green Point', and that they are collected fortnightly.*

John Funktioniert das denn? Das kann ich mir gar nicht vorstellen. Macht denn da jeder mit?

Volker *Tell him yes, most people do join in; you pay heavy fines if you don't; and there are information leaflets, etc. available to inform the population. Ask him if there are* *many differences between Germany and England.*

John Oh ja, in England wird zwar auch etwas für die Umwelt getan, aber nicht so viel wie hier. Aber hat das alles denn überhaupt einen Sinn, oder ist es nicht schon zu spät für die Erde?

Volker *Tell him that you believe recycling is a very useful measure because, if nothing is done for the environment now, what will the earth be like for our children?*

John Aber ist es denn nicht besser, Müll zu vermeiden, anstatt ihn hinterher zu entsorgen?

Volker *You say yes, but at least it's a start.*

8 Bilden Sie das **sein**-Passiv mit den vorgegeben Satzteilen.

Beispiele
in Deutschland – gesetzlich vorschreiben
Das ist in Deutschland gesetzlich vorgeschrieben.

der Müll – im Wechsel vierzehntägig – abholen
Der Müll ist im Wechsel vierzehntägig abgeholt.

(*a*) regional unterschiedlich – regeln
(*b*) die Bestimmungen – vom Staat – festlegen
(*c*) die deutschen Wälder – schon seit langem – schädigen
(*d*) die Umweltverschmutzung – gesetzlich – untersagen
(*e*) das Betreten der Baustelle – strengstens – verbieten
(*f*) das Verschmutzen der Meere – nicht mehr – erlauben
(*g*) einige Umweltschutzmaßnahmen – in England – noch nicht – einführen
(*h*) das Autofahren – bis jetzt noch – gestatten
(*i*) die Gefahren der Luftverschmutzung – heute weitgehend – erforschen

Höraufgabe

Umweltschutz in Deutschland und England

1 Beantworten Sie die folgenden Fragen.

(*a*) Wie beurteilt Renate die Umweltschutzmaßnahmen in Canterbury?

(*b*) Was zeigt der Blaue Engel auf Produkten an?
(*c*) Gibt es dieses Zeichen auch auf Produkten in Großbritannien?
(*d*) Warum wird in Deutschland mehr für die Umwelt getan als in Großbritannien?
(*e*) Wie beschreibt Renate die Umweltschutzmaßnahmen in Hamburg?
(*f*) Glaubt Renate, daß der Staat verantwortlich für solche Maßnahmen ist, oder die Bürger?
(*g*) Denkt Renate gut oder schlecht über die Einstellung der Engländer zum Umweltschutz?
(*h*) Was passiert in Deutschland mit alten Kleidern und Möbeln?
(*i*) Werden Aludosen besser in Deutschland oder in England entsorgt?

2 Was müßte in England für den Umweltschutz getan werden? In der Höraufgabe sagt Renate einmal: »Eigentlich müßte eine

Strafe ausgeschrieben werden.« (*Really a fine ought to be imposed.*) Folgen Sie diesem Beispiel, und schreiben Sie Sätze im **werden**-Passiv. Verwenden Sie die folgenden Stichpunkte:

(*a*) mehr machen
(*b*) alles getrennt sammeln
(*c*) so viel wie möglich wiederverwerten
(*d*) Einkaufskörbe verwenden
(*e*) Gläser statt Plastikbecher kaufen
(*f*) mehr mit dem Fahrrad fahren
(*g*) mehr zu Fuß gehen
(*h*) auf das Autofahren verzichten

IM ZEICHEN DER NATUR

Ob diese Symbole der Umwelt helfen, ist sehr umstritten. Trotzdem sollten Sie wissen, was sie bedeuten

Der grüne Punkt sagt über die Verpackung, auf der er klebt, wenig aus. Er weist nur darauf hin, daß sie einmal wiederverwertet werden soll. Der grüne Punkt ist Teil des dualen Systems. Wenn Ihr Haushalt schon daran angeschlossen ist, bekommen Sie gelbe Müllsäcke und/oder eine gelbe Tonne, in der Sie Punkt-Verpackungen sammeln sollten. Außerdem gibt es Container als zentrale Sammelstellen.

Der blaue Umweltengel verleiht keinem Produkt einen Heiligenschein in Sachen Umweltschutz. Er will nur auf Produkte hinweisen, die nicht gar so schädlich sind wie vergleichbare Produkte der Konkurrenz. So prangt der Engel zum Beispiel auf einem Schuhspray nur dann, wenn es andere Schuhsprays gibt, die weniger umweltfreundlich sind. Damit sollen diejenigen Hersteller angespornt werden, deren Waren nach Gesichtspunkten der Naturfreundlichkeit zu wünschen übriglassen.

(*Bunte*)

Lesetexte

1 Der Umweltschutz

WIE IHRE MÜLLTONNE SCHLANKER WIRD

Umweltschutz heißt umdenken und natürliche Reserven sparen. Auch im Haushalt. Verzichten Sie beim Einkauf auf Plastiktüten. Die fressen schon bei der Herstellung wertvolle Rohstoffe und landen allzuschnell auf der Mülldeponie. Beim Verbrennen verpesten sie die Atmosphäre und sorgen so für dicke Luft.

Tip: Beim Einkauf Jutesäckchen oder Einkaufskorb verwenden. Kunststoffverpackungen, wie Joghurt im Becher, lassen Sie besser in den Regalen stehen. Es gibt viele Sorten in Gläsern. Kaufen Sie Getränke nur noch in Pfandflaschen, Flüssigreiniger in Nachfüllpacks und alles, was Fluorchlorkohlenwasserstoffe (FCKW) und Phosphate enthält, überhaupt nicht. Der »blaue Umweltengel« ist dabei hilfreicher Wegweiser durch den Warendschungel.

Recycling hält Ihre Mülltonne schlank: Papier und Kartons gehören in die Papiertonne, Flaschen in den Glascontainer. Weißblech und Aluminium werden Sie bei den Sammelstellen los. Problemmüll wie Batterien, Farbreste oder Arzneimittel nimmt das Giftmobil ihrer Stadt an. Küchenabfälle gehören auf den Kompost (hat nicht jeder) oder in die Biotonne.

Wer konsequent recycelt, kann zu Hause immerhin bis zu 80 Prozent Müll einsparen. Noch etwas: kaputte Elektrogeräte gehören nicht in die Mülltonnen, sondern sind Sondermüll.

(*Bunte*)

die Mülltonne (-n) *bin*
schlank(er) werden *to slim down*
der Umweltschutz *environmental protection*
umdenken (e, a, a) (sep.) *to rethink*
natürlich *natural*
die Reserve (-n) *reserve*
der Haushalt (-e) *household*
verzichten auf (+ Acc.) *to do without*
der Einkauf (¨e) *shopping*
fressen (i, a, e) *to eat* (of animals), *to swallow up*
die Herstellung (-en) *production*
wertvoll *valuable, precious*
der Rohstoff (-e) *raw material*
die Mülldeponie (-n) *rubbish tip*
das Verbrennen *burning*
die Atmosphäre *atmosphere*
sorgen für (+ Acc.) here: *to cause*
dicke Luft *polluted air* (Lit. thick air)
die Luft (¨e) *air*
das Jutesäckchen *small jute sack*
der Einkaufskorb (¨e) *shopping basket*
die Kunststoffverpackung (-en) *plastic wrapping*
die Verpackung (-en) *wrapping*
der Becher (-) *(plastic) cup*
die Sorte (-n) *brand*
die Pfandflasche (-n) *returnable bottle* (on which a deposit is payable)
der Flüssigreiniger (-) *liquid detergent*
der Nachfüllpack (-s) *refill pack*
der Fluorchlorkohlenwasserstoff (-e) (FCKW) *chlorofluorocarbon (CFC)*
das Phosphat (-e) *phosphate*
der Blaue Umweltengel Lit. blue environment angel; recently introduced label on products to indicate whether they are environmentally friendly
der Wegweiser (-) *signpost*
der Warendschungel (-) *mass of products* (Lit. jungle of products)
schlank halten *to keep slim;* here: *to keep low*
die Papiertonne (-) *waste-paper bin*
der Glascontainer (-) *glass container*
das Weißblech *tin plate*
das Aluminium *aluminium*
die Sammelstelle (-) *collecting point*
der Problemmüll *waste which is difficult to dispose of*
die Batterie (-n) *battery*
der Farbrest (-e) *left-over paint*
das Arzneimittel (-) *medicine*
annehmen (e, a, o) (sep.) *to accept*
das Giftmobil (-e) *van for toxic waste*
der Küchenabfall (¨e) *organic waste* (Lit. kitchen waste)
der Kompost(haufen) (-) *compost (heap)*
die Biotonne (-n) *bin for organic waste*
einsparen (sep.) *to save, cut down*
der Sondermüll *hazardous waste*

Questions for you to answer on the text are overleaf.

1 Was passiert mit dem Müll? Ordnen Sie zu.

(a)	Papier, Kartons	(i)	Sondermüll
(b)	Flaschen	(ii)	Giftmobil
(c)	Weißblech, Aluminium	(iii)	Kompost/Biotonne
(d)	Batterien, Farbreste, Arzneimittel	(iv)	Sammelstellen
(e)	Küchenabfälle	(v)	Papiertonne
(f)	kaputte Elektrogeräte	(vi)	Glascontainer

2 Fragen zum Müll:

(*a*) Was bedeutet eigentlich »Umweltschutz«?
(*b*) Warum sind Plastiktüten so schlecht für die Umwelt?
(*c*) Was soll man statt dessen beim Einkauf verwenden?
(*d*) Welche Verpackungen soll man kaufen, welche nicht?
(*e*) Wieviel Müll kann man einsparen, wenn man konsequent recycelt?

2 Wertstoffsammlung

Verpackungen
Gehören in die Werstoffsammlung

Nach der Verpackungsverordnung gehören ab 1. Januar 1993 alle gebrauchten Verpackungen in die Wertstoffsammlung. Zu diesem Termin ist die Wertstoffsammlung mit dem »Grünen Punkt« fast überall in Deutschland präsent – bei Ihnen zu Hause oder ganz in Ihrer Nähe.

Geben Sie also

- Glasflaschen und Gläser in die Glascontainer.
- Papier- und Kartonverpackungen in die Altpapiersammlung oder in den Altpapiercontainer.
- alle übrigen Verpackungen (Kunststoff, Milch- und Safttüten, Weißblech und Aluminium) in die Wertstofftonne oder den Wertstoffsack, oder nutzen Sie – soweit in Ihrer Region eingerichtet – die Wertstoffhöfe.

Für diese Wertstofferfassung brauchen Sie keine Gebühren bezahlen. Alle Kosten für die Sammlung und Verwertung sind bei Verpackungen mit dem »Grünen Punkt« bereits im Kaufpreis enthalten.

Sollten Sie noch nicht an die Wertstoffsammlung angeschlossen sein, fragen Sie Ihre Kommunalverwaltung oder Ihr Entsorgungsunternehmen, was Sie tun können, um beim Recycling mitzumachen. Dort können Sie auch noch genauer erfahren, wie das Duale System bei Ihnen funktioniert.

Achten Sie beim Einkauf darauf, überflüssige Verpackungen zu vermeiden. Wählen Sie – wo sinnvoll – Mehrwegverpackungen.

FAKTEN ZUM DUALEN SYSTEM:

- *In den angeschlossenen Regionen ist die Menge des Hausmülls teilweise schon jetzt um mehr als 15 Prozent zurückgegangen.*
- *Die Verwertung der gesammelten Verpackungen nach den Vorschriften der Verpackungsverordnung ist gesichert. Künftig dürfen nur Recyclingunternehmen, die vom Technischen Überwachungsverein (TÜV) kontrolliert werden, Verpackungen verwerten.*
- *Viele Unternehmen, die den »Grünen Punkt« nutzen, setzen heute weniger und besser recycelfähiges Material ein als in der Vergangenheit.*

Haben Sie Fragen? Schreiben Sie uns. Wir antworten gern.

Notizen

gehören *to belong*
die Wertstoffsammlung (**-en**) *collection of re-usable material*
die Verpackungsverordnung (**-en**) *regulation for dealing with packaging material*
gebraucht *used*
der Grüne Punkt Lit. the green dot; sign indicating that a piece of wrapping can be re-used
der Wertstoffhof (**¨e**) *collection point for re-usable material*
die Wertstofferfassung *registration of re-usable material*
die Verwertung (**-en**) *recycling*
angeschlossen *connected to*
die Kommunalverwaltung (**-en**) *local administration*
das Entsorgungsunternehmen (-) *company concerned with the disposal of waste*
das Recycling *recycling*
das Duale System system by which re-usable material is separated into two categories: the first includes glass and paper, the second all other material put together which bears the **Blaue Umweltengel**
achten auf (+ Acc.) *to pay attention to*
überflüssig *superfluous*
vermeiden (**ei, ie, ie**) *to avoid*
Mehrwegverpackung (**-en**) *re-usable packaging*
der Hausmüll *household waste*
die Vorschrift (**-en**) *regulation*
gesichert *secured*
der Technische Überwachungsverein (**TÜV**) organisation which controls the implementation of standards; in the case of cars, it is often compared with the MOT in Britain

1 Beantworten Sie die folgenden Fragen.

(*a*) Wie erkennt man, was in die Wertstoffsammlung gehört?
(*b*) Wie teuer ist die Wertstofferfassung?
(*c*) Wo kann man Informationen über das Recycling und das Duale System bekommen?
(*d*) Worauf soll man beim Einkauf achten?
(*e*) Ist die Menge des Hausmülls schon zurückgegangen?
(*f*) Welche Unternehmen dürfen in Zukunft Verpackungen verwerten?

(g) Wie haben die Unternehmen auf die neue Verordnung reagiert?

2 Was geschieht mit den Verpackungen? Ordnen Sie zu.

(a)	Glasflaschen, Gläser	(i)	Altpapiercontainer, Altpapiersammlung
(b)	Papier-/ Kartonverpackungen	(ii)	Wertstoffsack, Wertstofftonne, Wertstoffhöfe
(c)	Kunststoff, Milch- und Safttüten, Weißblech und Aluminium	(iii)	Glascontainer

3 Teletext

P417 417 3sat Mo 13.09.93 13:24:18

3sat Magazin Deutschland
Umwelt

RÜCKNAHMEPFLICHT FÜR ELEKTROGERÄTE

Die Hersteller von Elektrogeräten wie Fernsehern, Computern und Kühlschränken sollen künftig zur Rücknahme ihrer Geräte verpflichtet werden.

Eine entsprechende Verordnung kündigte der Vorsitzende des Bundestagsumweltausschusses, von Geldern (CDU), gegenüber der "Bild"-Zeitung an. Der Elektronik-Schrott solle "weitgehend wiederverwertet" werden. Die Geräte würden durch die Verordnung "etwa zwei bis drei Prozent" teurer.

Das Umweltministerium erklärte, bislang gebe es noch keinen Termin für die Verordnung. Klar sei, daß es für die Händler keine "Zwangsabgabe" geben werde.

Beantworten Sie die folgenden Fragen auf Englisch.

1 What are manufacturers of electrical goods going to be obliged to do?
2 Who made this announcement?
3 What effect will this regulation have on the price of electrical goods?
4 What date has been given for the introduction of the regulation?
5 What will dealers not be forced to do?

Testen Sie Ihr Wissen

Jahr für Jahr landen etwa 20 000 Tonnen Plastikmüll in der Nordsee. Heimlich von Schiffen über Bord gekippt oder achtlos von Urlaubern ins Meer geworfen. Wie lange dauert es wohl, bis sich eine Plastikflasche im Meerwasser auflöst?

- 4,5 Jahre
- 45 Jahre
- 450 Jahre

Im Recycling ist Deutschland Weltspitze: Papier und Glasabfall wird zu 40% wiederverwertet. Seit der Einführung des Dualen Systems (»Grüner Punkt«) wird der Müllberg nicht mehr größer. Besser machen es nur die Japaner. Ist ihre Recycling-Quote:

- 45%
- 50% +
- 70% ?

Ökologisch im Rückstand: die USA. Dort wird Papier nur zu

- 10%
- 25%
- 5% recycelt.

(*Bunte*)

8
TYPISCH DEUTSCH?

Lernziele

In this unit you will learn how to

- ask and express opinions
- report statements, opinions, claims
- form and use the subjunctive mood, reported speech

Aufnahmen

1 Typisch deutsche Eigenschaften

Darren Wright arbeitet für eine deutsche Firma, die eine Zweigstelle in England hat. Sein Vater ist Engländer, seine Mutter Deutsche, und er spricht fließend Deutsch. Seit kurzem ist er in der Hauptniederlassung der Firma in Frankfurt beschäftigt. In der Mittagspause unterhält er sich mit einem deutschen Arbeitskollegen über typisch deutsche Eigenschaften.

Martin Ich habe gehört, deine Mutter ist Deutsche. Hast du denn schon früher mal in Deutschland gelebt?

Darren Nein, ich bin zum ersten Mal hier in Deutschland. Meine Mutter hat aber meistens Deutsch mit mir gesprochen, und mir auch viel über deutsche Geschichte, Kultur und das tägliche Leben erzählt, worüber ich natürlich sehr froh bin. Aber weißt du, besonders neugierig war ich darauf, diese sogenannten typisch deutschen Eigenschaften zu entdecken.

Martin Welche Eigenschaften meinst du denn damit?

Darren Naja, zum Beispiel hat meine Mutter immer gesagt, daß kein Volk so fleißig sei wie die Deutschen, das würde man ja schon daran sehen, daß sie so früh morgens aufstehen. Und natürlich wäre das Wirtschaftswunder nie möglich gewesen, wenn die Deutschen nicht so arbeitsam wären!

Martin Sicher ist da 'was Wahres dran. Aber ich glaube, man sollte das nicht übertreiben. Das Wirtschaftswunder war das Ergebnis vieler Faktoren, und was die Arbeitswut der Deutschen heutzutage angeht – ich persönlich schätze meine Freizeit ganz besonders!

Darren Ich habe auch festgestellt, daß man hier nicht ganz so früh aufsteht, wie meine Mutter das immer erzählt hat. Aber immerhin, alles fängt hier schon um 8.00 Uhr an, wohingegen in England die Schule zum Beispiel erst um 9.00 Uhr beginnt, und auch die Arbeitszeit geht zumeist von neun bis fünf, oder fängt gar noch später an. Daran habe ich mich hier erst mal gewöhnen müssen!

Martin Das glaube ich dir gern. Ja, und hat dir deine Mutter auch erzählt, daß die Deutschen so ordnungsliebend und sauber sind?

Darren Genau! Aber da muß ich dir sagen, das habe ich auch festgestellt. Ich finde, die Häuser und Straßen in Deutschland sehen viel sauberer und gepflegter aus als in England. Und ich habe auch schon gemerkt, daß die Leute hier extrem viel Wert auf Hygiene legen, zum Beispiel zuhause oder beim Arzt – was natürlich nicht heißen soll, daß die Engländer dreckig sind! Aber ich finde doch, daß das hier ausgeprägter ist.

Martin Ja, manchmal habe ich das Gefühl, daß wir es ein bißchen übertreiben . . . hast du denn sonst noch Unterschiede bemerkt?

Darren Mir ist besonders aufgefallen, daß man hier in

Deutschland viel mehr Aufwand betreibt, wenn es um gewisse Anlässe geht, wie zum Beispiel Weihnachten, Ostern und so weiter. Die Leute hier machen sich so viel Arbeit, mit den ganzen Vorbereitungen für das Fest, wie Dekoration, Essen kochen, Kuchen und Plätzchen backen . . . und auch bei Geburtstagen wird viel mehr gefeiert, und die Leute schicken sich Karten, auch wenn sie nicht zusammen feiern. Das ist in England weniger der Fall.

Martin Ach ja, wirklich? Das finde ich ja alles sehr interessant. Ich glaube, wir müssen uns darüber später noch mal unterhalten.

Darren Auf jeden Fall! Ich sehe dich ja morgen bei Ullas Party!

Bemerkungen

die Hauptniederlassung (**-en**) *main branch, headquarters*
typisch *typical(ly)*
die Eigenschaft (**-en**) *characteristic*
arbeitsam *hard-working*
das Wirtschaftswunder (-) *the economic miracle*. Many Germans, especially those who took part in the reconstruction of Germany after the war, firmly believe that the economic miracle was entirely due to their hard-working attitude, and are immensely proud of it. Many fail to acknowledge the circumstances in which this economic boom took place. Nevertheless, since no other country experienced a boom of this scale, it could be argued that 'German industriousness' did indeed play a part in the success of the economic reconstruction programme carried out by the allied powers.
da ist 'was Wahres dran *there is a grain of truth in that*
die Arbeitswut *work mania*
schätzen *to appreciate*
wohingegen *whereas*
gar *even*
ordnungsliebend *liking to see things neat and tidy*
sauber *clean*
gepflegt *well-kept*
ausgeprägt *pronounced*
übertreiben (**ei, ie, ie**) *to exaggerate*
der Aufwand *expenditure* (in time/money)
der Anlaß (**¨sse**) *occasion*

der Fall sein *to be the case*

Richtig oder falsch?

Korrigieren Sie die falschen Aussagen!

1 Darrens Vater ist Deutscher.
2 Darren ist bei einer deutschen Firma beschäftigt, die eine Zweigstelle in England hat.
3 Darrens Mutter hat ihm viel über Deutschland erzählt, und auch immer Deutsch mit ihm gesprochen.
4 Sie hat ihm aber nichts über die typisch deutschen Eigenschaften erzählt.
5 Martin ist sich nicht sicher, ob die Deutschen wirklich so früh aufstehen und so fleißig sind, wie manche Leute glauben.
6 Darren hat festgestellt, daß seine Mutter recht hatte, als sie ihm über die typisch deutschen Eigenschaften erzählt hat.
7 In England fängt man den Tag nicht so früh an wie in Deutschland.
8 Darren findet, daß die Deutschen wirklich so sauber und ordnungsliebend sind, wie seine Mutter gesagt hat.
9 Martin glaubt, daß die Deutschen nicht besonders sauber und ordentlich sind.
10 In Deutschland betreibt man viel mehr Aufwand bei gewissen Anlässen, wie zum Beispiel Weihnachten oder Ostern.

2 Die deutsche Gründlichkeit

Darren und Martin treffen sich am nächsten Abend auf der Party einer Arbeitskollegin, und setzen ihre Unterhaltung vom Vortag fort.

Martin Ja, was die typisch deutschen Eigenschaften angeht, glaubst du, daß die Engländer wirklich so verschieden von den Deutschen sind?

Darren Wahrscheinlich nicht. Aber die Kultur und die Mentalität sind irgendwie doch unterschiedlich. Ich finde, zum Beispiel, daß dieses Klischee von der deutschen Gründlichkeit gar nicht so falsch ist.

Martin Tatsächlich? Das mußt du mir aber näher erläutern!

Darren Naja, nimm doch nur mal die Ausbildung hier in Deutschland: man muß in diesem Land nicht unbedingt

Abitur gemacht haben, um eine gute Stellung zu bekommen. Wer Hauptschulabschluß oder Mittlere Reife gemacht hat, bekommt in der Lehre eine gründliche Ausbildung, sowohl praktisch als auch theoretisch, und macht eine richtige Abschlußprüfung, die ihm einen guten Start ins Berufsleben gibt.

Martin Aber ist das in England nicht genauso?

Darren Es ist weniger streng geregelt. Natürlich, wenn man A-Levels oder einen Universitätsabschluß hat, macht man zumeist ein gutes Training, aber ansonsten haben die Leute nicht so eine gründliche Ausbildung. Ich meine, in Deutschland macht man ja sogar als Verkäufer in einer Bäckerei oder Metzgerei eine dreijährige Ausbildung! Das gibt es in England kaum.

Martin Und wie sieht es mit der Schulbildung in England aus?

Darren Ja, die ist schon sehr gut. Aber zum Beispiel habe ich festgestellt, daß man in Deutschland Fremdsprachen viel mehr fördert, was ja heutzutage ungeheuer wichtig ist. Und dann finde ich auch, daß hier soviel Wert auf Qualifikationen gelegt wird. Es genügt nicht, wenn man zum Beispiel eine Fremdsprache spricht, um einen Job zu bekommen. Nein, man muß gleich einen entsprechenden Nachweis erbringen, daß man eine Prüfung oder Ausbildung in diesem Fach gemacht hat.

Martin Da hast du allerdings recht! Es ist dir wahrscheinlich auch schon aufgefallen, daß man hier ungeheuer viel Wert auf Titel legt, zum Beispiel auf den Doktortitel! Früher war das selbstverständlich noch extremer. Die Kehrseite der Medaille ist allerdings, daß die Leistungsanforderungen und der Leistungsdruck schon in den Schulen so hoch sind, und in der Arbeitswelt noch viel höher. Man weiß gar nicht, wohin das noch führen soll!

Darren Aber die Gründlichkeit erstreckt sich nicht nur auf den Arbeitsbereich. Ich finde, daß die Deutschen im allgemeinen ihre Freizeitaktivitäten viel systematischer angehen als die Engländer. Sehr viele Leute betreiben ihr Hobby in einem Club, und Talente werden sofort gefördert. Daran liegt es wahrscheinlich auch, daß Deutschland im Moment so gut im Tennis ist – in England wird einfach nicht genug dafür getan!

Martin Mmmh . . . ich weiß nicht so recht. Das ist zwar alles nicht ganz falsch, was du da festgestellt hast. Aber ich bin doch sehr skeptisch, was diese typisch deutschen Eigenschaften angeht. Sicherlich ist da ein Körnchen Wahrheit dran, aber ich glaube, man kann all diese Eigenschaften auch bei Menschen anderer Nationalität feststellen.

Darren Na, ich bin nicht so sicher! Du erscheinst mir zwar auch nicht wie der typische Deutsche. Aber du weißt ja: Ausnahmen bestätigen die Regel!

Bemerkungen

das Klischee (**-s**) *cliché, stereotype*
die Gründlichkeit *thoroughness*
nimm doch nur mal . . . *just take . . .*
gründlich *thorough(ly)*
die Abschlußprüfung (**-en**) *final exam*. Both practical and theoretical knowledge acquired at the workplace and at school is tested. It is possible to resit the exam, which people do tend to do in order to improve their chances in the job market
einen guten/schlechten Start geben (+ Dat.) *to give a good / bad start*
regeln *to regulate, settle*
streng *strict(ly)*
fördern *to promote, support, foster*
Wert legen auf (+ Acc.) *to attach importance to (something)*
der Nachweis (**-e**) *proof, evidence*
erbringen (**i, a, a**) *to give, produce*
die Kehrseite der Medaille *the other side of the coin*
die Leistungsanforderung (**-en**) *demands on performance*
der Leistungsdruck *pressure to perform, work harder*. Note that **Leistung** is used in German more than *achievement* or *performance* is used in England. German society is often referred to as **eine Leistungsgesellschaft** (*a performance-related society*)
sich erstrecken auf (+ Acc.) *to stretch to*
der Arbeitsbereich (**-e**) *area of work*
angehen* (**e, i, a**) (sep.) *to tackle*
systematisch *systematical(ly)*
ein Körnchen Wahrheit *a grain of truth*
Ausnahmen bestätigen die Regel *the exception proves the rule*

Welche Antwort paßt?

1 Glaubst du, daß die Engländer wirklich so verschieden von den Deutschen sind?
(*a*) Ich bin aber kein Engländer.
(*b*) Die Engländer und die Deutschen verstehen sich meistens sehr gut.
(*c*) Wahrscheinlich nicht.

2 Was meinst du denn, wenn du von der deutschen Gründlichkeit sprichst?
(*a*) Meine Mutter hat mir immer davon erzählt.
(*b*) Ich spreche zum Beispiel von der Ausbildung hier.
(*c*) Die Engländer sind im allgemeinen gründlicher als die Deutschen.

3 Ist die Ausbildung in England denn anders als die in Deutschland?
(*a*) Ich bin in Deutschland zur Schule gegangen.
(*b*) Wir schicken unsere Kinder nach England zur Schule.
(*c*) Es ist alles weniger streng geregelt.

4 Hast du schon festgestellt, daß man in Deutschland immer gleich eine entsprechende Qualifikation vorweisen muß?
(*a*) Ich habe Fremdsprachen gelernt, aber ich habe keinen Nachweis dafür.
(*b*) Ja, ich habe das auch schon gemerkt.
(*c*) Nein, das stimmt überhaupt nicht.

5 Ist der Leistungsdruck in England auch so hoch wie in Deutschland?
(*a*) Ich weiß nicht, wohin das noch führen soll.
(b) Das ist eben die Kehrseite der Medaille.
(c) Ich habe das Gefühl, daß er in Deutschland höher ist, aber vielleicht täusche ich mich auch.

6 Sind die Deutschen auch bei ihren Freizeitaktivitäten so gründlich?
(*a*) Die Deutschen treiben weniger Sport als die Engländer.
(*b*) Ich finde, daß die Deutschen ihre Freizeitaktivitäten viel systematischer angehen als die Engländer.
(*c*) Ich habe eigentlich keine besonderen Freizeitaktivitäten.

7 Bist du nicht sehr skeptisch, was diese typisch deutschen

Eigenschaften angeht?
(*a*) Nein, ich glaube, da ist schon ein Körnchen Wahrheit dran.
(*b*) Ich finde, die Ausnahme bestätigt die Regel.
(*c*) Du erscheinst mir eigentlich nicht wie der typische Deutsche.

Sagen Sie's auf Deutsch!

1 Just take as an example training in Germany.
2 So much emphasis is put on qualifications.
3 The other side of the coin is, however, the pressure to work harder.
4 I don't know where this will lead to.
5 I think that the Germans in general tackle their leisure activities much more systematically.
6 There is certainly a grain of truth in that.
7 You don't strike me as the typical German.
8 The exception proves the rule.

3 Deutschland – der Bösewicht?

Helmut Richter ist ein Deutscher, der seit 26 Jahren in seiner Wahlheimat England lebt. Er unterhält sich mit einem deutschen Freund über die Vorurteile, die immer noch gegen Deutsche bestehen, und die er auch am eigenen Leib erfährt.

Jens Helmut, du bist jetzt schon so lange in England – fühlst du dich eigentlich mehr als Engländer oder als Deutscher?

Helmut Das kann ich so gar nicht sagen. Ich fühle mich hier natürlich sehr wohl, und habe mich auch weitgehend an die englische Lebensart angepaßt. Meine Frau ist Engländerin, und meine Kinder wachsen hier auf. Andrerseits habe ich mich auch bemüht, meine deutsche Kultur und Sprache nicht zu vergessen, und auch meinen Kindern nahezubringen.

Jens Und würdest du sagen, daß du von den Engländern akzeptiert wirst, oder hast du auch gegen Vorurteile anzukämpfen?

Helmut Im großen und ganzen sind die Leute hier sehr freundlich, und meine Familie und ich haben selten Vorurteile zu spüren bekommen. Aber natürlich sind sie vorhanden, und es tut schon weh, wenn man direkt oder indirekt als Deutscher angegriffen wird.

Jens Wie äußert sich das denn zum Beispiel?

Helmut Meine Kinder sind in der Schule schon mal von den anderen Mitschülern gehänselt worden, weil sie eben zur Hälfte Deutsche sind, obwohl sie hier aufwachsen und auch die englische Sprache völlig beherrschen. Daraufhin habe ich mit der Lehrerin gesprochen, und sie hat mit den Kindern das Thema behandelt. Seitdem ist das Problem eigentlich beseitigt. Aber ich finde, daß gerade in den Schulen solche Vorurteile von vornherein bekämpft werden sollten.

Jens Da stimme ich dir voll und ganz zu. Aber von zu Hause kommen natürlich auch Meinungen und Vorurteile, die die Kinder übernehmen. Und du selbst, hast du auch solche negativen Erfahrungen gemacht?

Helmut Leider ja. Ich erinnere mich an einen Fall, wo ich mich bei einem Handwerker beschwert habe, weil er nicht ordentlich gearbeitet hat und ständig unpünktlich war. Daraufhin hat er mich angeschrien, ich solle doch nach Deutschland zurückgehen, wenn es mir in England nicht paßt, und England müßte es den Scheißdeutschen erst mal wieder zeigen, damit sie nicht so großspurig würden, und so weiter . . . es war sehr unangenehm, und hat mich auch sehr getroffen. Aber ich muß sagen, daß solche Zwischenfälle zum Glück mehr die Ausnahme als die Regel sind.

Jens Und was hältst du von der Haltung der Presse gegenüber Deutschland und den Deutschen?

Helmut Ja, da hast du einen wunden Punkt angesprochen! Sowohl meine Frau als auch ich sind der Meinung, daß die englische Presse immer wieder Hetzkampagnen gegen Deutschland und die Deutschen führt. Besonders der Krieg und Hitler werden gerne benutzt, um antideutsche Ressentiments zu schüren. Selbstverständlich sollen die Greueltaten der Deutschen im Zweiten Weltkrieg nicht vergessen und vergeben werden, aber ich bin der Meinung, daß man dies nicht auf die heutige Generation übertragen sollte.

Jens Da denkst du wahrscheinlich besonders an die neo-nazistischen Gruppen, die im Moment soviel Krawall in Deutschland machen.

Helmut Zum Beispiel! Ich würde meine Hand dafür ins Feuer legen, daß die überwältigende Mehrheit der Deutschen solche Gruppierungen niemals mehr unterstützen würde, und daß sie keine Chance haben, politische Macht zu erlangen. Aber die Presse hier möchte die Leute glauben machen, daß alle Deutschen Nazis sind, und gefährlich, und daß man sie kontrollieren muß, damit sie keinen Dritten Weltkrieg anfangen! Das ist doch völlig lächerlich.

Jens Ich glaube auch, daß sowohl Presse als auch Politiker die Deutschen für das verantwortlich machen wollen, was in England im Argen ist.

Helmut Da hast du höchstwahrscheinlich recht. Und natürlich dienen die Kriegserinnerungen dazu, die Nation an ihre Stärke und Größe zu erinnern. Ich glaube aber, daß die meisten Engländer heute den Deutschen gegenüber positiv eingestellt sind. Diese negative Haltung wird von der Presse hochgespielt.

Jens Der Meinung bin ich auch. Ich wünsche mir nur, daß diese dummen Vorurteile einmal aus der Welt geschafft werden könnten.

Helmut Ich glaube, da können wir lange warten. Leider wird es immer wieder Vorurteile gegen alles mögliche geben!

Bemerkungen

der Bösewicht (**-e**) *the bad person, villain*
das Vorurteil (**-e**) *prejudice*
am eigenen Leib erfahren *to experience something first hand*
erfahren (ä, u, a) *to experience, learn*
weitgehend *mostly*
die Lebensart *way of life*
anpassen (sep.) *to adapt*
sich bemühen *to make an effort*
nahebringen (i, a, a) (sep.) (+ Dat.) *to make accessible to*
ankämpfen gegen (sep.) (+ Acc.) *to fight against something*
im großen und ganzen *by and large*
zu spüren bekommen *to feel the effects of*
hänseln *to tease*
das Thema (**-en**) *the subject*
behandeln here: *to deal with*

beseitigen *to remove*
von vornherein *from the start*
der/die Scheißdeutsche (-n) *bloody German* (vulgar)
es jemandem zeigen *to show someone*
großspurig *big-headed*
es hat mich getroffen *it hurt me* (Lit. it hit me)
mehr die Ausnahme als die Regel *more the exception than the rule*
der wunde Punkt *sore spot*
die Hetzkampagne (-n) *smear campaign*
das Ressentiment (-s) *antipathy, (negative) feeling*
die Greueltat (-en) *atrocity*
vergessen (i, a, e) *to forget*
vergeben (i, a, e) *to forgive*
der Krawall (-e) *riot, row*
seine Hand für etwas (+ Acc.) **ins Feuer legen** *to swear to something* (Lit. to be willing to put one's hand in the fire for something)
überwältigend *overwhelming*
die Gruppierung (-en) *group, faction*
die Macht (¨e) *power*
erlangen *to gain, obtain*
jemanden (+ Acc.) **etwas** (+ Acc.) **glauben machen** *to have someone believe something*
im Argen sein/liegen *to be in a sorry state*
hochspielen (sep.) *to blow up, exaggerate*
etwas (+ Acc.) **aus der Welt schaffen** *to eliminate*

Richtig oder falsch?

Korrigieren Sie die falschen Aussagen!

1 Helmut lebt schon seit zehn Jahren in England.
2 England ist seine Wahlheimat.
3 Er hat alles über deutsche Kultur und Sprache vergessen.
4 Er und seine Familie bekommen oft Vorurteile zu spüren.
5 Für seine Kinder ist es schwer, sich in der Schule zu integrieren.
6 Kinder übernehmen oft Vorurteile und Meinungen von ihren Eltern.
7 Helmut hat sehr oft Probleme mit englischen Handwerkern.
8 Helmut ist der Meinung, daß die englische Presse immer wieder Hetzkampagnen gegen Deutschland und die Deutschen führt.

9 Man sollte die Erfahrungen des Zweiten Weltkrieges auf die heutige Generation der Deutschen übertragen.
10 Die große Mehrheit der Deutschen lehnt die rechtsextremen Gruppierungen in Deutschland ab.
11 Jens glaubt, daß die Presse und die Politiker in England die Deutschen dafür verantwortlich machen wollen, wenn es in England Probleme gibt.
12 Die meisten Engländer sind den Deutschen gegenüber freundlich eingestellt.

Redewendungen

- Asking and expressing opinions
  Glaubst du, daß . . .?
  Manchmal habe ich das Gefühl, daß . . .
  Ich glaube, . . .
  Ich finde, . . .
  Was sagst du denn dazu?
  Meiner Meinung nach . . .
  Mich würde auch mal deine Meinung dazu interessieren!
  Wenn du mich fragst, . . .
  Wenn du meine Meinung hören willst, . . .
  Ich bin der Auffassung, daß . . .
  Ehrlich gesagt . . .

- Reporting other people's opinions/statements/claims
  Meine Mutter hat immer gesagt, . . .
  Wie schon Bundeskanzler Kohl sagte, . . .
  Wenn ich an dieser Stelle Goethe zitieren darf, . . .
  Herr Meier hat behauptet, . . .
  Frau Markwart meinte neulich, . . .
  Wie es so schön heißt, . . .
  Laut Angaben der lokalen Presse . . .
  Ich habe gehört, daß . . .
  Ich habe gelesen, daß . . .
  Man hört ja immer wieder, daß . . .
  Es wird allgemein gesagt, daß . . .
  Haben Sie schon gehört, was der Außenminister gesagt hat?

Vokabeln

Useful words for expressing/countering an opinion

wohingegen *whereas*
immerhin *nevertheless*
allerdings *though* (concession)
natürlich *of course*
grundsätzlich *basically*
wahrscheinlich *probably*
zwar *admittedly*
sicher(lich) *certainly, no doubt*
doch *all the same, still, after all; yes* (contradicting a negative)
einerseits *on the one hand*
andrerseits *on the other hand*
im großen und ganzen *on the whole*
obwohl *although*
trotzdem *nevertheless*

Adjectives for positive attributes

sauber *clean*
gepflegt *(well) cared for*
pünktlich *punctual*
ordnungsliebend *liking things neat and tidy*
fleißig *hard-working, industrious*
arbeitsam *hard-working*
korrekt *correct*
gründlich *thorough*
systematisch *systematic*
freundlich *friendly*
höflich *polite*

Adjectives for negative attributes

dreckig *dirty*
schlampig *scruffy*
unpünktlich *unpunctual*
großspurig *big-headed, arrogant*
unordentlich *untidy*
faul *lazy*
arbeitsscheu *work-shy*
unfreundlich *unfriendly*
unhöflich *impolite*
nachlässig *careless, lax*

Grammatische Hinweise

1 The subjunctive mood

The grammatical category 'subjunctive' is referred to as a 'mood' because it reflects the speaker's attitude to what is being said. The indicative mood tends to present states, events and actions as facts, whereas the subjunctive mood tends to introduce an element of doubt or possibility.

In English, the subjunctive has more or less died out except in fixed expressions (such as the conditional *If I **were** you*), and English speakers have to resort to various devices such as using adverbs (e.g. *possibly*, *probably*, *presumably*) to indicate their attitudes.

You only have to listen to a newscast or read a newspaper report to ascertain that the subjunctive is alive and well in German. It is, however, difficult to lay down clear-cut rules for the use of the subjunctive, since in practice there is a considerable degree of variation and flexibility. So, where in formal German the report of someone's account of an event (which cannot as yet be vouched for as 100 per cent correct) will undoubtedly contain examples of the subjunctive, a similar account in conversational German may well employ the indicative.

In the past, the forms of the German subjunctive were referred to in English by the names of the various tenses (e.g. present subjunctive, past subjunctive, etc.). Because, however, the use of the subjunctive forms does not correspond anywhere near as consistently as the indicative forms with differences in time, it is nowadays common practice to divide the subjunctive forms into major groups using the German terms **Konjunktiv I** and **Konjunktiv II**:

Konjunktiv I **geben**	**Former English name**
es gebe	*present subjunctive*
es habe gegeben	*perfect subjunctive*
es werde geben	*future subjunctive*
Konjunktiv II	
es gäbe	*past subjunctive*
es hätte gegeben	*pluperfect subjunctive*
es würde geben	*conditional*

Forms of *Konjunktiv I*

The basic form of **Konjunktiv I** (or the present subjunctive) is entirely straightforward since it is regular for all verbs except **sein**. The strong and irregular verbs do not undergo vowel changes. Merely take the stem of the infinitive and add the appropriate endings as indicated below:

	spiel-en	**komm-en**	**woll-en**	**werd-en**	**hab-en**	**sein**
ich	spiel-**e**	komm-**e**	woll-**e**	werd-**e**	hab-**e**	sei
du	spiel-**est**	komm-**est**	woll-**est**	werd-**est**	hab-**est**	sei(e)st
er/sie/es	spiel-**e**	komm-**e**	woll-**e**	werd-**e**	hab-**e**	sei
wir	spiel-**en**	komm-**en**	woll-**en**	werd-**en**	hab-**en**	seien
ihr	spiel-**et**	komm-**et**	woll-**et**	werd-**et**	hab-**et**	seiet
sie/Sie	spiel-**en**	komm-**en**	woll-**en**	werd-**en**	hab-**en**	seien

The compound forms of **Konjunktiv I** are also straightforward. You merely need to know the **Konjunktiv I** forms of the auxiliary verbs **haben**, **sein** and **werden** and use these in conjunction with the past participle or infinitive of the verb concerned:

Er habe gespielt. (*perfect with* **haben**)
Er sei gekommen. (*perfect with* **sein**)
Er werde spielen. (*future using* **werden**)
Er werde gesehen. (*present passive*)
Er sei gesehen worden. (*perfect passive*)
Er werde gesehen werden. (*future passive*)

Forms of *Konjunktiv II*

For weak verbs, the basic form of **Konjunktiv II** (past or imperfect subjunctive) is the same as the past indicative (e.g. **ich spielte, du spieltest, er/sie/es spielte**, etc.).

For most strong verbs, you take the past indicative form, add an Umlaut to the vowel wherever possible, and then add the appropriate endings, as indicated below:

Infinitive	fahren	kommen	geben	gehen	fliegen	bleiben
Past indicative	fuhr	kam	gab	ging	flog	blieb
ich	führ-**e**	käm-**e**	gäb-**e**	ging-**e**	flög-**e**	blieb-**e**
du	führ-**est**	käm-**est**	gäb-**est**	ging-**est**	flög-**est**	blieb-**est**
er/sie/es	führ-**e**	käm-**e**	gäb-**e**	ging-**e**	flög-**e**	blieb-**e**
wir	führ-**en**	käm-**en**	gäb-**en**	ging-**en**	flög-**en**	blieb-**en**
ihr	führ-**et**	käm-**et**	gäb-**et**	ging-**et**	flög-**et**	blieb-**et**
sie/Sie	führ-**en**	käm-**en**	gäb-**en**	ging-**en**	flög-**en**	blieb-**en**

Irregular verbs, whether strong or weak, also often add an umlaut, or undergo a vowel change in the basic form of **Konjunktiv II**:

Infinitive	sein	haben	werden	können	bringen	wissen
Past indicative (ich form)	war	hatte	wurde	konnte	brachte	wußte
Konjunktiv II (ich form)	wäre	hätte	würde	könnte	brächte	wüßte

Although the **Konjunktiv II** forms of **helfen** and **stehen** can be expressed in the regular way (**ich hälfe** and **ich stände**), what one finds in practice are the forms **ich hülfe** and **ich stünde**.

The compound forms of **Konjunktiv II** (often referred to as the conditional or **würde** form) is created by taking the **Konjunktiv II** form of the auxiliary verb **werden** and adding the infinitive of the verb:

ich würde spielen	wir würden spielen
du würdest spielen	ihr würdet spielen
er/sie/es würde spielen	sie/Sie würden spielen

2 Reported speech

One of the main uses of the subjunctive, particularly of **Konjunktiv I**, is in what is known as reported speech or indirect speech. When we want to report what someone has said, claimed, asserted, and so on, we can do so in two ways:

directly
The old woman said (claimed, declared, etc.), 'I am ill'.

indirectly
The old woman said (that) she was ill.

Note that there has been a switch from the present tense in the direct report to the past tense in the indirect report.

In German, the indirect report can be marked by the subjunctive:

direct speech
Die alte Frau sagte (behauptete, erklärte), »Ich bin krank.«

indirect speech

Die alte Frau sagte, daß sie krank **sei**. Die alte Frau sagte, sie **sei** krank.

There are, however, several ways of marking indirect speech in modern German, although they are not all entirely interchangeable. Here are the main possibilities when the verb in question is in the third person singular:

direct speech

Frau Werner sagte, »Mein Sohn fliegt bald nach Italien.«

indirect speech

Frau Werner sagte, . . .

1 ihr Sohn fliege bald nach Italien. (**Konjunktiv I**)
  daß ihr Sohn bald nach Italien fliege. (**Konjunktiv I**)
2 ihr Sohn flöge bald nach Italien. (**Konjunktiv II**)
  daß ihr Sohn bald nach Italien flöge. (**Konjunktiv II**)
3 ihr Sohn würde bald nach Italien fliegen. (**Konjunktiv II**, **würde**-*form*)
  daß ihr Sohn bald nach Italien fliegen würde. (**Konjunktiv II**, **würde**-*form*)
4 ihr Sohn fliegt bald nach Italien. (*present indicative*)
  daß ihr Sohn bald nach Italien fliegt. (*present indicative*)

Form 1 is typical of formal written German, especially if the **daß** is omitted. It is also often used in language that has been written to be spoken, for instance in newscasts. It is not used in colloquial German.

Form 2 is typical of spoken German in cases where the basic form of **Konjunktiv II** is still in current use and differs from the past indicative form. It can also be found in written German.

Form 3 is typical of spoken German in cases where the basic form of **Konjunktiv II** is not in current use or is the same as the past indicative form. In practice, it is also used by many speakers instead of the basic form of **Konjunktiv II**, even when this does differ from the past indicative form. It is not good style in written German.

Form 4 is the most frequently found form in normal spoken German. When this form is used in the written language, it is usual for the **daß** to be included.

When the verb in question is in the third person plural, there is a need to distinguish Form 1 (**Konjunktiv I**) from Form 4 (present indicative) in formal written German. In such cases, Form 2 (**Konjunktiv II**) is used:

Frau Werner sagte, . . .
ihre Söhne flögen bald nach Italien.
daß ihre Söhne bald nach Italien flögen.

rather than:

Frau Werner sagte, . . .
ihre Söhne fliegen bald nach Italien.
daß ihre Söhne bald nach Italien fliegen.

The latter version would be typical of spoken German.

Guidelines for indirect speech in formal German

Despite all the variations mentioned above for marking indirect speech, there are certain guidelines which all grammar books tend to prescribe for use in formal German:

- Use the **Konjunktiv I** form unless this is indistinguishable from the indicative form. The indicative tenses used in the direct speech versions are converted into **Konjunktiv I** forms in the indirect speech versions, as follows:

Direct speech

present indicative
Er sagte, »Ich halte einen Vortrag.« — *He said, 'I am giving a lecture.'*

future indicative
»Ich werde einen Vortrag halten.« — *'I shall give a lecture.'*

past indicative
»Ich hielt einen Vortrag.« — *'I gave a lecture.'*

perfect indicative
»Ich habe einen Vortrag gehalten.« — *'I have given a lecture.'*

pluperfect indicative
»Ich hatte einen Vortrag gehalten.« — *'I had given a lecture.'*

Indirect speech

Konjunktiv I (*present subjunctive*)

Er sagte, er halte einen Vortrag. — *He said he was giving a lecture.*

Konjunktiv I (*future subjunctive*)

Er sagte, er werde einen Vortrag halten. — *He said he would give a lecture.*

Konjunktiv I (*perfect subjunctive*)

Er sagte, er habe einen Vortrag gehalten. — *He said he had given a lecture.*

Konjunktiv I (*perfect subjunctive*)

Er sagte, er habe einen Vortrag gehalten. — *He said he had given a lecture.*

Konjunktiv I (*perfect subjunctive*)

Er sagte, er habe einen Vortrag gehalten. — *He said he had given a lecture.*

(In practice, the most likely version in the last instance would be: **Er sagte, er hätte einen Vortrag gehalten**.)

- When the **Konjunktiv I** form is the same as the indicative form, then use the **Konjunktiv II** form. In practice, the only distinct **Konjunktiv I** forms of most verbs (except for **sein**) are those of the third person singular. In the following examples, the **Konjunktiv I** forms would be **sie halten**, **sie werden halten** and **sie haben gehalten**. Because these are no different from the indicative forms, the **Konjunktiv II** forms are used:

Direct speech

present indicative

Sie sagten, »Wir halten einen Vortrag.« — *They said, 'We are giving a lecture.'*

future indicative

»Wir werden einen Vortrag halten.« — *'We shall give a lecture.'*

past indicative

»Wir hielten einen Vortrag.« — *'We gave a lecture.'*

perfect indicative

»Wir haben einen Vortrag gehalten.« — *'We have given a lecture.'*

pluperfect indicative

»Wir hatten einen Vortrag gehalten.« — *'We had given a lecture.'*

Indirect speech

Konjunktiv II (*past subjunctive*)

Sie sagten, sie hielten einen Vortrag. — *They said they were giving a lecture.*

Konjunktiv II (**würde** *form, conditional*)

Sie sagten, sie würden einen Vortrag halten. — *They said they would give a lecture.*

Konjunktiv II (*pluperfect subjunctive*)

Sie sagten, sie hätten einen Vortrag gehalten. — *They said they had given a lecture.*

Konjunktiv II (*pluperfect subjunctive*)

Sie sagten, sie hätten einen Vortrag gehalten. — *They said they had given a lecture.*

Konjunktiv II (*pluperfect subjunctive*)

Sie sagten, sie hätten einen Vortrag gehalten. — *They said they had given a lecture.*

Using the above guidelines in reported speech does not necessarily cast doubt on the truth of the claims made, but it does mean that no guarantees are provided. For this reason, you will find the guidelines most widely in evidence in newspaper reports and newscasts.

The use of **Konjunktiv I** often extends beyond the sentence in which an indication of the source is given:

Im Fernsehen hieß es, Tschernobyl-Gesetze des Parlaments in Kiew seien von der Exekutive auf allen Ebenen »offen sabotiert« worden. Die Regierung habe nichts getan, um den Opfern zu helfen.

(*Frankfurter Rundschau*)

(*It was claimed on television that the Kiev parliament's Chernobyl laws had been 'openly sabotaged' by the executive at all levels. The government had [further claimed] done nothing to help the victims.*)

Übungen

1 Stellen Sie im folgenden Text jedes Vorkommen des Konjunktivs fest.

ZU VIEL WASSER GETRUNKEN

Mit reinem Wasser hat sich ein 31jähriger Brite zu Tode getrunken. Das erklärte jedenfalls der Leichenbeschauer nach einer Autopsie des ungewöhnlichen Trinkers. Der Brite habe übermäßig viel Wasser im Gehirngewebe, in Magen und Lunge gehabt. Er sei damit Opfer einer »Wasservergiftung« geworden, wie sie weltweit etwa 100 Mal pro Jahr registriert werde. Einmal sei der Brite dabei beobachtet worden, wie er 13 Half-Pint-Gläser (etwa 3,2 Liter) Wasser hintereinander getrunken habe. Wenn Wasser ins Gehirn eindringt, führe dies – so der Leichenbeschauer – zu ähnlichen Trunkenheitssymptomen wie Alkoholgenuß. Der Mensch verliere dann die Orientierung und beginne zu lallen. Dieser Tod sei ein Mißgeschick.

(Nach einem Artikel im *Schwarzwälder Bote*)

2

Ein Australier erzählt Ihnen über sein Bild von den Deutschen, bevor er nach Deutschland kam. Sie erzählen jetzt das Gesagte einem Freund oder einer Freundin. Weil Sie mit Ihrem Freund oder Ihrer Freundin ganz familiär reden, ist es angebracht, die einfache **Konjunktiv II**-Form (oder auch die **würde**-Form) zu verwenden. Beginnen Sie die Sätze mit »Er glaubte, er dachte, er meinte, er war der Meinung«, usw.

Beispiele
»Alle Deutschen sind reich.«
Der Australier glaubte, **daß** alle Deutschen reich **wären**.
»In Deutschland gibt es komische Sachen zu essen.«

Er dachte, **daß** es in Deutschland komische Sachen zu essen **gäbe/geben würde**.

(*a*) »Alle Deutschen sind besonders fleißig und arbeitsam.«
(*b*) »In Deutschland steht man jeden Tag um 6.00 Uhr auf.«
(*c*) »Alle Deutschen haben blonde Haare und blaue Augen.«
(*d*) »In Deutschland fängt die Schule um 7.00 Uhr morgens an.«
(*e*) »Alle Deutschen sind ordnungsliebend und sauber.«
(*f*) »In Deutschland sehen die Straßen und Häuser immer viel gepflegter aus.«
(*g*) »Die Deutschen betreiben bei gewissen Anlässen immer viel größeren Aufwand als die Engländer.«
(*h*) »In Deutschland geht man alles viel systematischer an als in England.«
(*i*) »Die Deutschen trinken viel Bier.«
(*j*) »Die Deutschen sind arrogant.«

3 Petra, eine deutsche Studentin, unterhält sich mit Clare, einer englischen Austauschstudentin, über Klischees und Vorurteile. Setzen Sie die Sätze in die richtige Reihenfolge.

(*a*) Und findest du, daß das stimmt?
(*b*) Vorurteile eigentlich nicht. Aber ich hatte natürlich manche Klischeevorstellungen über Deutschland und die Deutschen.
(*c*) Naja, außerdem hatte ich natürlich noch gedacht, daß alle Deutschen so sauber, fleißig, gründlich und pünktlich seien.
(*d*) Sag' mal, Clare, bevor du nach Deutschland gekommen bist, hattest du da gewisse Vorurteile den Deutschen gegenüber?
(*e*) Vielleicht ein bißchen! Aber ich finde, man kann diese Eigenschaften auch bei Menschen anderer Nationalität feststellen.
(*f*) Nein, natürlich nicht! Die deutsche Küche ist sehr gesund, schmackhaft und abwechslungsreich.
(*g*) Welche Vorstellungen hattest du denn noch?
(*h*) Und würdest du jetzt sagen, daß das ein korrektes Bild ist?
(*i*) Welche Klischees denn zum Beispiel?
(*j*) Naja, zum Beispiel hatte ich gedacht, daß alle Deutschen sich von Bratwürsten mit Sauerkraut oder Schweinebraten mit Klößen ernähren würden.

4 Was heißt das heute: deutsch? Die *Bunte* hat prominente

Deutsche gefragt:

(*a*) Wer oder was ist für Sie typisch deutsch?
(*b*) Haben Sie Freunde in den neuen Bundesländern?
Lesen Sie ihre Antworten. Hilfe mit den Vokabeln finden Sie im **Glossar**.

Gabriele Henkel, Kunstmäzenin, geboren in Düsseldorf:

(*a*) Der deutsche Schäferhund: stolz auf Gehorsam. Mein Name ist typisch deutsch. Wenn ich die deutsche Nationalhymne höre, bin ich froh, daß nicht mehr die erste Strophe gesungen wird.
(*b*) Absurd ist, daß wir in allen Ländern mehr Freunde haben, als in den neuen Bundesländern. Aber das wird sich ändern.

Dr. Peter Gauweiler, 43, bayerischer Staatsminister, geboren in München:

(*a*) Typisch deutsch ist, schlecht über den typisch Deutschen zu reden. Ich rede manchmal auch schlecht über uns.
(*b*) Freunde, Bekannte und Kollegen aus diesem Teil Deutschlands sehe ich jeden Monat. Nach wie vor sind ihr Auftreten und ihre Formulierungen gepflegter, ordentlicher und gesetzter und damit im guten Sinne des Wortes deutscher als bei uns.

Fürstin Gloria, 32, Chefin des Hauses Thurn & Taxis, geboren in Stuttgart:

(*a*) Ein korrekter und pünktlicher Mensch. Ich selbst liebe auch die Ordnung und Genauigkeit. Die Deutschen sind das selbstkritischste Volk der Welt. Wegen ihrer Vergangenheit trauen sie sich nicht, Nationalstolz zu zeigen. In jedem anderen Land wäre dies absurd.
(*b*) Ja. Vor einem Jahr lernte ich sie kennen. Sie sind gestreßter.

Peter Hoffmann, 47, Opernsänger aus Bayreuth, geboren in Böhmen:

(*a*) Helmut Kohl. Kümmert sich um deutsche Angelegenheiten. Ein Hang zur Perfektion. Typisch deutsch an den Deutschen ist, daß sie meistens über sich selbst meckern. Ich meckere nie. Ich kann auch die Furcht der Deutschen vor Ausländern nicht verstehen. Ich habe keine schlechten Erfahrungen mit Ausländern gemacht.
(*b*) Ich habe noch keine Freunde dort.

(*Bunte*)

Lesen Sie sich die Aussagen der vier Prominenten nochmals durch, und setzen Sie sie dann in die indirekte Rede/Konjunktiv I.

Beispiel
Gabriele Henkel sagt, der deutsche Schäferhund **sei** typisch deutsch.

oder:

Gabriel Henkel sagt, **daß** der deutsche Schäferhund typisch deutsch **sei**.

Verwenden Sie bei manchen Aussagen die erste Variante, bei anderen die zweite. Es erscheint jeweils nur eine Lösung im **Lösungsteil**. Ihnen ist aber bekannt, daß sich das Verb bei der **daß**-Variante am Ende des Satzes befinden muß.

5 Ersetzen Sie die englischen Worte in Klammern mit den entsprechenden Vokabeln aus **Lektion 8**.

Die Deutschen werden im allgemeinen als (*a*) (*hard-working*), (*b*) (*industrious*), (*c*) (*clean*) und (*d*) (*thorough*) angesehen. Man weiß natürlich, daß diese sogenannten typischen deutschen (*e*) (*characteristics*) oft nur (*f*) (*stereotypes*) sind, denn man kann sie auch bei Menschen anderer (*g*) (*nationality*) feststellen. Besonders berühmt ist die deutsche (*h*) (*thoroughness*). Es stimmt aber, daß in Deutschland vieles (*i*) (*more strictly regulated*) ist als in anderen Ländern. Die Deutschen gehen außerdem ihre Arbeit und ihre Freizeit oftmals (*j*) (*more systematically*) an. Ein anderes Problem jedoch sind die (*k*) (*prejudices*), gegen die Deutsche im Ausland oft (*l*) (*to fight against*) müssen. Besonders der Krieg und Hitler werden von der ausländischen Presse gerne benutzt, um (*m*) (*anti-German feelings*) zu schüren. Selbstverständlich sollten diese (*n*) (*atrocities*), die im Zweiten Weltkrieg geschehen sind, nicht (*o*) (*forgotten*) werden, aber man sollte sie nicht auf die (*p*) (*present generation*) übertragen. Die meisten Deutschen heute würden (*q*) (*to swear to it*), daß neonazistische (*r*) (*factions*) nie wieder politische Macht (*s*) (*to gain*) können.

6 Setzen Sie die Endungen in den folgenden Text ein!

Genießen, was die Natur uns schenkt: Emmentaler SWITZERLAND

Wann genießen auch Sie das ehrlich- (*a*) Geschenk Schweizer Natur? Den Emmentaler SWITZERLAND aus d- (*b*) Schweizer Emmental. Rein und ursprünglich.

Aus naturbelassen- (*c*) Rohmilch. Vom Käsermeister geschaffen nach alt- (*d*) Rezepturen. Sorgsam gepflegt in klein- (*e*) Dorfkäsereien läßt man jed- (*f*) Laib Zeit, viel Zeit, natürlich zu reifen, bis sich sein zart- (*g*) Nußgeschmack voll entfaltet. Genießen Sie deshalb d- (*h*) einzigartig- (*i*) Emmentaler SWITZERLAND. Genießen Sie dies- (*j*) ehrlich- (*k*) Stück, das die Schweizer Natur uns schenkt.

(*Der Spiegel*)

7 Setzen Sie den folgenden Text in die indirekte Rede. Sie schreiben den Bericht als Zeitungsartikel. Fangen Sie mit dem Satz »Es wurde gestern berichtet, daß . . .« an.

JÜDISCHE BÜRGER ZU GAST

Die Stadt Freiburg hat 50 Jahre nach Kriegsende ehemalige jüdische Mitbürger zu einem Treffen in der alten Heimat eingeladen. Ein Sprecher der Stadtverwaltung äußerte die Erwartung, daß mindestens 50 Personen der Einladung folgen werden. Das für Mitte Juni geplante

Wiedersehen mit den ehemaligen Freiburgern will die Stadt zugleich zum Anlaß nehmen, daß der Grundstein für eine neue Synagoge gelegt werde.

(Nach einem Artikel im *Schwarzwälder Bote*)

8 Ergänzen Sie den Dialog mit Hilfe der englischen Sätze!

Holger und Stefanie sind zwei Deutsche, die schon lange in England leben. Oftmals begegnen sie Vorurteilen oder Klischees bezüglich Deutschlands und der Deutschen. Gerade sprechen sie über ihre Erfahrungen.

Holger Sag mal, Stefanie, fühlst du dich eigentlich mehr als Engländerin oder als Deutsche?

Stefanie *Tell him that you have adapted largely to the English way of life, although you have made an effort not to forget your German culture and language.*

Holger Und wirst du von den Engländern akzeptiert, oder hast du auch gegen Vorurteile und Klischees anzukämpfen?

Stefanie *Tell him that you know they exist, but that luckily, you find they are more the exception than the rule. Tell him that sometimes people ask you about the typical German characteristics such as German thoroughness, or whether the Germans really get up so early in the morning and work so hard.*

Holger Und was antwortest du auf solche Fragen?

Stefanie *Tell him that mostly you laugh and say that you are very sceptical as far as these typical German characteristics are concerned, and that you think that one can find them in people of other nationalities as well.*

Holger Bist du der Meinung, daß die Presse in England eine negative Haltung gegen Deutschland und die Deutschen einnimmt?

Stefanie *Tell him that you think that some newspapers do indeed conduct smear campaigns against Germany and the Germans in order to put the blame for things that go wrong on others.*

Holger Glaubst du, daß die Engländer im allgemeinen so denken?

Stefanie *Tell him that you think that in general the English have a positive attitude towards the Germans, and that negative attitudes are exaggerated by the press.*

Höraufgabe

Vergleiche zwischen Engländern und Deutschen

Helga ist gerade von einem Urlaub in England zurückgekommen. Sie spricht mit ihrer Freundin Karin über die Vorstellungen, die sie vor ihrem Auslandsaufenthalt von England und den Engländern hatte, und auch davon, welche Vorstellungen sich die Engländer von den Deutschen und Deutschland machen.

1 Hören Sie sich den Dialog genau an, und versuchen Sie, die Eigenschaften, die den Deutschen/Deutschland beziehungsweise den Engländern/England zugeordnet werden, herauszuschreiben.

2 Hören Sie sich den Dialog noch einmal an, und schreiben Sie die Sätze heraus, die in der indirekten Rede sind. Es sind insgesamt elf Beispiele im Dialog vorhanden.

Lesetext

Teil 1

VORSICHT BEI WITZEN UND ZEBRASTREIFEN

Trotz der Millionen, die das Bonner Außenministerium ausgibt, um die deutsche Kultur im Ausland zu verbreiten, bleibt das Bild, das man sich dort von den Deutschen macht, erstaunlich unergiebig. Um die Deutschen von ihrer besten Seite kennenzulernen, mag daher der folgende kleine Leitfaden von Nutzen sein:

1. Vergessen Sie nie, die Hand zu geben. Dies gilt besonders für Partys und Empfänge, wenn Sie Hunderte von zusammengepreßten Fingern zugleich schütteln müssen.

2. Wenn Sie sich vorstellen, denken Sie immer daran, Ihren Nachnamen möglichst unverständlich auszusprechen. Vor allem am Telephon haben die Deutschen das instinktive Bedürfnis, ihren Nachnamen anzugeben.

3. Seien Sie nett zu den Kellnerinnen. Deutsche Kellnerinnen, besonders die in Rüschenblüschen, die in Cafés Buttercremekuchen servieren, gehören zu den liebenswürdigsten der Welt.

4. Reden Sie Menschen, die Sie gerade kennengelernt haben (einschließlich der in Regel 3 genannten), nie mit Vornamen an. Es sei denn, Sie sind Mitglied desselben Sport-/Hobby-/Gärtner-Clubs.

5. Machen Sie keine Witze über die folgenden Themen: das Ozonloch, die Lance-Raketen, den Autotyp Ihres Gastes/Gastgebers/Taxifahrers, Michael Gorbatschow, das Baumsterben, Professoren, das Sozialversicherungssystem und die Grünen. Empfehlenswert dagegen sind unverfängliche Themen, die fast jeder amüsant findet, wie zum Beispiel Helmut Kohl.

6. Bemühen Sie sich, Gespräche auf deutsch zu führen. Es gibt so viele Fremdworte in der deutschen Sprache, daß Sie mit etwas Glück alles Wesentliche verstehen werden, besonders, wenn Ihr Gesprächspartner Diplomat, Computerprogrammierer oder Spiegel-Leser ist.

7. Entschuldigen Sie sich nicht für Ihr schlechtes Deutsch. Die Deutschen wissen, daß Sie ihre Sprache nie beherrschen werden. Sofern Sie nicht ein Fußball-Hooligan oder Flüchtling sind, finden die Deutschen Engländer eigentlich ganz nett; sie gelten als harmlos.

8. Vergessen Sie nicht, daß nur Engländer gern übers Wetter reden. Die Deutschen sprechen dagegen lieber über ihre Gesundheit. Schauen Sie also nicht gelangweilt drein, wenn Ihnen jemand erzählt, daß er so viel arbeiten müsse und warum er urlaubsreif sei.

9. Beachten Sie unbedingt die Fußgängerregeln. Die Versicherungsvorschriften besagen, daß ein Busfahrer Sie nur einsteigen lassen darf, wenn Sie nicht weiter als einen Meter von der Bushaltestelle entfernt stehen. Meiden Sie auf öffentlichen Fußwegen die Pfade der Radfahrer. Die Radfahrer halten nicht an – Sie müssen es tun.

10. Versuchen Sie, einigermaßen pünktlich zu sein. Wenn Sie nicht gerade Franzose sind, deren Unpünklichtkeit als charmant gilt, wird sie in Deutschland weniger als Unhöflichkeit, sondern als Zeichen für mangelnde Selbstdisziplin gewertet. [. . .]

(Fortsetzung folgt in **Teil 2**)

trotz (+ Gen.) *despite*
verbreiten *to spread*
unergiebig *unrewarding, unproductive*
der Leitfaden (¨) *textbook, basic introduction*
zusammengepreßt *squeezed*
unverständlich *unclear*
das Bedürfnis (-se) *need*
die Rüschenbluse (-n) *blouse with frills*
der Buttercremekuchen (-) *butter-cream cake*
liebenswürdig *kind, charming*
das Mitglied (-er) *member*
das Sozialversicherungssystem (-e) *social security system*
empfehlenswert *advisable*
das Wesentliche *the essential(s)*
beherrschen *to master*
der Flüchtling (-e) *refugee*
urlaubsreif *ready for/in need of a holiday*
die Fußgängerregel (-n) *rule for pedestrians*
die Versicherungsvorschrift (-en) *insurance regulation*
die Bushaltestelle (-n) *bus stop*
meiden (ei, ie, ie) *to avoid*
einigermaßen *more or less, to some extent*
pünktlich *punctual, on time*
werten *to judge, assess*

1 Ist das deutsche Außenministerium erfolgreich damit, die deutsche Kultur im Ausland zu verbreiten?
2 Wie sollte man sich auf Partys verhalten?
3 Was sollte man beachten, wenn man jemanden kennenlernt, oder am Telefon mit jemandem spricht, den man nicht kennt?
4 Was kann man in deutschen Cafés essen?
5 Wie sollte man Menschen, die man gerade kennengelernt hat, ansprechen?

6 Worüber sollte man mit den Deutschen sprechen, und worüber nicht?
7 Warum ist es möglich, in der deutschen Sprache fast alles zu verstehen?
8 Welche Haltung haben die Deutschen den Engländern gegenüber?
9 Was ist ein Lieblingsthema der Deutschen?
10 Was sollte man beachten, wenn man in Deutschland am Verkehr teilnimmt?
11 Warum sollte man in Deutschland immer pünktlich sein?
12 Meint der Autor des Textes wirklich, was er sagt, oder macht er Spaß?
13 Glauben Sie, daß Stereotypen immer falsch sind, oder kann es sein, daß sie ein Körnchen Wahrheit enthalten?

Teil 2

11. Beim Schlangestehen ist Vorsicht angeraten. Die Deutschen neigen dazu, an Bus- und Straßenbahnhaltestellen oder an Zeitungskiosken in Haufen zu stehen, anstatt sich richtig anzustellen. Dies mag Ihnen ein falsches Gefühl von Freiheit vermitteln: Versuchen Sie nie, sich an einem Wurstwarenstand im Supermarkt vorzudrängeln, vor allem dann nicht, wenn ältere Damen dahinter stehen. Die Folgen könnten unerfreulich für Sie sein.

12. Fahren Sie unbedingt mit der Bahn. Die Bundesbahn-Schaffner sind im allgemeinen äußerst zuvorkommend und erzählen manchmal sogar Witze (beachten Sie aber Regel 5). Vergessen Sie nicht, Ihren Mitreisenden „Auf Wiedersehen" zu sagen, wenn Sie das Abteil verlassen.

13. Halten Sie Ihre Kinder von Kränen, Bulldozern oder Baustellen fern, es sei denn, Sie haben eine Versicherungspolice von einer renommierten deutschen Versicherung, die für alle eventuell entstehenden Schäden aufkommt.

14. Pfeifen Sie nicht im Bus, auf der Straße oder in Geschäften. Dadurch fühlen sich die Leute gestört, vor allem die älteren, von denen es erstaunlich viele gibt.

15. Wenn Sie ein britisches Auto fahren, überholen Sie auf keinen Fall einen Mercedes oder BMW auf der Autobahn.

16. Halten Sie nie am Zebrastreifen, um Fußgänger passieren zu lassen, es sei denn, die Ampel steht auf rot, ein Polizist befiehlt es Ihnen oder ein Mensch liegt auf dem Zebrastreifen und bewegt sich nicht.

17. Werfen Sie Batterien, Papier und Glas in die von der Stadtverwaltung dafür vorgesehenen Müllbehälter. Tun Sie dies aber nicht nach 22 oder vor 7 Uhr, wenn Sie nicht wegen Ruhestörung Strafe zahlen wollen.

18. Wenn Sie zum Mittagessen, Tee, Abendessen oder Cocktail eingeladen sind, bringen Sie Blumen mit. Bitten Sie die Verkäuferin, sie in umweltfreundliches Papier einzuwickeln.

19. Zögern Sie nicht, Hitler und den Krieg anzusprechen. Viele Deutsche reden gern über dieses Thema mit Ausländern. Ihre Auffassungen darüber sind eindeutig und können innerhalb weniger Stunden dargelegt werden.

20. Vergessen Sie nie, daß Deutschland ein traditionsreiches Land ist. Besuchen Sie unbedingt einen lokalen Jahrmarkt, eine Karnevalsveranstaltung, einen Umzug, ein Bier- oder Weinfest. Beachten Sie dabei, daß bei diesen Gelegenheiten die Regeln 1, 2, 4, 5, 9, 10, 11 und 14 zeitweise außer Kraft gesetzt werden können, ohne daß die Voraussetzungen dafür Ihnen auch nur im entferntesten einsichtig wären.

(David Marsh, *Die Zeit*)

das Schlangestehen *queueing up, standing in line*
es ist Vorsicht angeraten *one should be on one's guard*
neigen zu (+ Dat.) *to tend to*
der Haufen here: *crowd* (Lit. heap)
sich anstellen (sep.) *to queue up, stand in line*
vermitteln *to give, provide*
der Wurstwarenstand (¨e) *sausage counter*
sich vordrängeln (sep.) *to jump the queue, push one's way forward*
unerfreulich *unpleasant*
die Bundesbahn (-en) *German railway* (Lit. federal railway)

der Schaffner (-) *conductor*
zuvorkommend *obliging, courteous*
fernhalten (ä, i, a) (sep.) *to keep away*
der Kran (¨e) *crane*
der Bulldozer (-) *bulldozer*
die Baustelle (-n) *building site*
die Versicherungspolice (-n) *insurance policy*
renommiert *renowned*
eventuell *possibly*
entstehen* (e, a, a) *to occur*
aufkommen (sep.) here: *to pay (for damage)*
pfeifen (ei, i, i) *to whistle*
stören *to disturb*
passieren lassen *let cross*
die Ampel (-n) *traffic lights*
die Ampel steht auf rot *the traffic lights are red.* (Note that in German the word for traffic lights is singular, and also that the verb **stehen** (*to stand*) is used with this noun
befehlen (ie, a, o) *to order*
die Ruhestörung (-en) *disturbance (of the peace)*
einwickeln (sep.) *to wrap*
traditionsreich *rich in tradition*
beachten *to note*
zeitweise *from time to time*
außer Kraft setzen *to countermand, repeal*
auch nur im entferntesten *not in the least*
einsichtig *understandable*

1 Welche Situationen beschreibt der Autor in **Teil 2**? Ordnen sie die folgenden Überbegriffe den entsprechenden Paragraphen zu.

11.	(*a*)	Müllentsorgung
12.	(*b*)	Zweiter Weltkrieg
13.	(*c*)	Baustellen
14.	(*d*)	Schlangestehen
15.	(*e*)	Verhalten in der Öffentlichkeit
16.	(*f*)	Veranstaltungen
17.	(*g*)	Einladungen
18.	(*h*)	Verkehr
19.	(*i*)	Bahnfahren
20.	(*j*)	Autobahnfahren

2 Überlegen Sie, wie sich die Engländer in diesen Situationen verhalten würden – im allgemeinen! – und vergleichen Sie es mit dem Verhalten der Deutschen. Nehmen Sie den Inhalt dieser Übung nicht gar so ernst! Eine mögliche Lösung finden Sie im **Lösungsteil**.

Beispiel
Die Engländer stellen sich immer in einer ordentlichen Schlange an, wohingegen die Deutschen sich in Haufen anstellen.

(*a*) Müllentsorgung (*b*) Zweiter Weltkrieg

(*c*) Baustellen
(*d*) Verhalten in der Öffentlichkeit
(*e*) Veranstaltungen
(*f*) Einladungen
(*g*) Verkehr
(*h*) Bahnfahren
(*i*) Autobahnfahren

GUTE NOTEN FÜR KULTUR UND WIRTSCHAFT

Wie bewerten Sie die Fähigkeiten und Leistungen der Deutschen auf folgenden Gebieten?

Schulnoten von 1 bis 6

Gesamterscheinungsbild und Ansehen	*noch gut*	2,5
Auftreten und Selbstdarstellung	*befriedigend*	2,8
Weltpolitischer Einfluß	*gut*	1,9
weltwirtschaftliche Bedeutung	*sehr gut*	1,3
kulturelle Bedeutung	*noch sehr gut*	1,5
Innovationsleistung/ Forschungsstandard	*sehr gut*	1,3
Politische Kultur und Bewußtsein	*gut*	2,3
Soziales Engagement und Völkerbeziehung	*gut*	2,1

FOCUS-Magazin/M. Zang

9
ENERGIE

Lernziele

In this unit you will learn how to

- express commitment to a cause or idea
- distance yourself from a cause or idea
- express the need for change
- form and use the conditional, the pluperfect, correct word order and extended participial phrases

Aufnahmen

1 Jugendliche als umweltbewußte Bürger

Schüler sprechen sich in einer Diskussion für Energiesparen und Umweltschutz aus.

Lehrer Glaubt ihr, daß Umweltschutz und Energiesparen Sache der Regierung ist, oder daß die Bürger auch etwas dafür tun müssen?

Sascha Es langt nicht, wenn ich allein etwas tue, auch die Politiker und die Industrie müßten mehr unternehmen. Man sollte mehr Geld für die Erforschung und Nutzung alternativer Energiequellen ausgeben. Außerdem wünsche ich mir mehr Informationen, wo und an welcher Stelle ich Energie noch aktiver einsparen könnte.

Lehrer Was könnte man denn zum Beispiel tun, um mehr Strom zu sparen?

Ela Das mit dem Strom ist so eine Sache. Von Atomkraft sollte man auf Dauer ganz wegkommen. Biomasse könnte doch mehr genutzt werden. Erneuerbare Energien sind meiner Meinung nach langfristig sowieso viel sinnvoller. Abgesehen davon müßte die Sonnenenergie stärker genutzt werden – das wäre vielleicht auch eine ganz gute Alternative.

Andreas Ich denke auch, daß wir allgemein einfach mehr mit Solarenergie oder anderen Energiequellen arbeiten sollten, die viel umweltfreundlicher sind.

Lehrer Wie spart ihr denn zuhause Energie?

Sascha Wenn ich aus meinem Zimmer gehe, mache ich den Computer und das Licht aus. In der Küche haben wir nur wenige automatische Geräte; wir machen das meiste mit der Hand. Das Radio machen wir auch immer aus, wenn wir es nicht mehr brauchen.

Ela Wir haben einen speziellen Zähler an der Heizung, der uns anzeigt, wieviel Energie wir verbrauchen. Außerdem haben wir Solarzellen auf dem Dach und Energiesparlampen im Haus. Ich glaube aber, daß allgemein noch zu wenig getan wird.

Lehrer Denkt ihr auch daran, zuhause Wasser zu sparen?

Sascha Ich dusche, statt zu baden – so spart man einiges an Wasser. Außerdem trage ich meine Klamotten nicht bloß einen Tag, sondern lege sie zurück in den Schrank, wenn sie noch nicht stinken.

Andreas Zum Zähneputzen nehme ich ein Glas Wasser – das Wasser muß ja nicht die ganze Zeit laufen. Und wenn sich morgens meine Mutter zuerst wäscht, läßt sie das Wasser in der Wanne, das geht ja auch. Und das Geschirr spülen wir mit der Hand ab. Nur bei sehr viel Geschirr machen wir auch mal die Spülmaschine an.

Lehrer Und was haltet ihr davon, auf das Autofahren zu verzichten, um Energie zu sparen?

Andreas Ich finde, man kann einiges an Energie sparen, wenn man mit dem Bus fährt, anstatt jeder für sich mit dem eigenen Auto. Außerdem gibt es inzwischen auch spezielles Pflanzenöl, mit dem man die Autos betreiben könnte.

Ela Die Autos könnte man auch abschaffen. Was man da an Sprit sparen würde – das wäre eine tolle Maßnahme! Oder vielleicht Solarautos – das wäre auch super.

(*Izze-Blitz*)

Bemerkungen

das Energiesparen *saving of energy*
langen *to be sufficient*
jemandes Sache sein (+ Gen.) *to be of someone's concern*
unternehmen (i, a, o) *to do something*
die Erforschung *research*
die Nutzung *use*
die Energiequelle (-n) *source of energy*
alternativ *alternative*
der Strom *electricity*
wegkommen* (sep.) *to get away from*
die Biomasse *biomass*
erneuerbar *renewable*
langfristig *in the long run*
sinnvoll *sensible*
die Sonnenenergie *solar energy* (Lit. energy of the sun)
die Solarenergie *solar energy*
ausmachen (sep.) *to switch off, turn off*
elektrische Geräte (n. pl.) *electrical appliances*
speziell *special*
der Zähler (-) *meter*
die Heizung *heating*
anzeigen (sep.) *to indicate*
die Solarzelle (-n) *solar cell*
die Energiesparlampe (-n) *energy-saving light bulb*
einiges *a considerable amount*
das Zähneputzen *brushing / cleaning one's teeth*
abspülen (sep.) *to wash (the dishes)*
das Geschirr *the dishes*
das Autofahren *car driving*

das Pflanzenöl *vegetable oil*
abschaffen (sep.) *to abolish*
der Sprit *petrol* (colloquial)
toll *fantastic*

Richtig oder falsch?

Korrigieren Sie die falschen Aussagen!

1 Wenn jeder Bürger etwas für die Umwelt tun würde, dann müßte die Regierung nichts mehr unternehmen.
2 Die Regierung sollte mehr Geld für Energiesparen und Umweltschutz ausgeben.
3 Die Bürger informieren sich nicht genug darüber, wie sie besser Energie einsparen können.
4 Ela glaubt, daß man in Zukunft nur noch mit Atomkraft arbeiten sollte.
5 Erneuerbare Energien, Sonnenenergie oder andere Energiequellen sind langfristig umweltfreundlicher und energiesparender.
6 Zuhause kann man fast keine Energie sparen.
7 Die Jugendlichen kennen verschiedene Methoden, wie man zuhause Wasser sparen kann.
8 Auf das Autofahren wollen die Jugendlichen aber nicht verzichten.
9 Wenn man Autos abschaffen würde, könnte man viel Energie sparen.

2 Kernenergie: Pro und Contra

Horst und Rainer diskutieren über Vor- und Nachteile der Kernenergie.

Rainer Bist du für oder gegen die Kernenergie?
Horst Also, ich bin grundsätzlich dafür. Den größten Vorteil sehe ich darin, daß das Uran so billig ist, und die Vorkommen auch relativ groß sind, so daß man nicht von anderen Ländern abhängig ist.
Rainer Sicherlich, das hört sich sehr positiv an. Aber andrerseits ist die Entsorgung oder Wiederaufbereitung des Atommülls auch mit ungeheuren Kosten verbunden. Außerdem habe

ich immer das Gefühl, daß diese atomaren Abfälle eine Zeitbombe sind – wer weiß, was da alles passieren kann!

Horst Also, ich bin der Meinung, daß die Sorgen um die Sicherheit der Atomkraft weitaus übertrieben sind. Was die Sicherheitsvorkehrungen anbelangt, so werden sie ständig verbessert. Und in Bezug auf das Personal – Arbeiter in einem Atomkraftwerk haben erwiesenermaßen keine Berufskrankheiten wie zum Beispiel die Bergwerkarbeiter. Auch gibt es weniger tödliche Arbeitsunfälle als zum Beispiel in der Erdölindustrie.

Rainer Das mag schon sein. Aber du mußt doch zugeben, daß ein Unfall wie der in Tschernobyl Ausmaße hat, die viel größere Probleme aufwerfen als in den herkömmlichen Industrien. Und man kann eben noch so sichere Technologien entwerfen, aber wenn menschliches Fehlverhalten und Versagen ins Spiel kommen, nützt das alles nichts mehr.

Horst Aber so ein Unfall wie in Tschernobyl ist bis jetzt doch erst einmal vorgekommen, und die Internationale Atomenergiebehörde hat ja schon verbesserte Sicherheitsvorschriften international gefordert.

Rainer Na und? Ob das was nützt, bleibt noch abzuwarten. Und Experten sind sich klar darüber, daß so ein GAU immer wieder passieren könnte.

Horst Aber dafür ist die Kernkraft wesentlich umweltfreundlicher und gesünder als fossile Brennstoffe. Kohle zum Beispiel trägt durch die enorme Luftverschmutzung zum Sauren Regen bei, und wenn man an die Erdölkatastrophen denkt, die die Meere verseuchen!

Rainer Das sind natürlich die üblichen Argumente derer, die nicht zugeben wollen, wie umweltschädlich und gesundheitsschädlich Kernenergie ist. Man weiß doch, daß immer wieder Lecks an den Kernkraftwerken auftreten, die Strahlung an die Umwelt abgeben. Das Krebsrisiko erhöht sich außerdem auch wesentlich durch radioaktive Strahlung. Man hat schon festgestellt, daß Kleinkinder, die in der Nähe eines Atomkraftwerkes leben, immer öfter schwere Krankheiten, wie zum Beispiel Leukämie, bekommen. Abgesehen davon: es ist heutzutage möglich, die

Umweltrisiken durch Erdöl und Kohle einzudämmen, und Langzeitschäden zu verringern, aber wenn ein größerer Atomunfall passiert, so verseucht das ganze Gebiete auf unabsehbare Zeit hinaus.

Horst Sicher, es gibt Nachteile. Aber ich bin dennoch der Meinung, daß wir auf Kernkraft nicht mehr vezichten können. Es gibt einfach keine Alternative!

Rainer Vielleicht keine billigere Alternative. Aber bestimmt eine, mit der die Menschen besser leben können!

Bemerkungen

das Uran *uranium*
das Vorkommen (-) *deposit*
abhängig von (+ Dat.) *dependent on*
die Entsorgung *disposal*
die Wiederaufbereitung (**-en**) *reprocessing*
die Wiederaufbereitungsanlage (**-n**) *reprocessing plant*
der Atommüll *atomic waste*
verbunden sein mit *to be linked with*; here: *to cause*
der atomare Abfall (**¨e**) *atomic waste*
die Zeitbombe (**-n**) *time bomb*
die Sicherheit (**-en**) *security*
die Atomkraft *nuclear power*
die Sicherheitsvorkehrung (**-en**) *security precaution*
anbelangen (sep.) *to concern*
das Atomkraftwerk (**-e**) *nuclear power station*
erwiesenermaßen *as has been proved*
die Berufskrankheit (**-en**) *occupational disease*
der Bergwerkarbeiter (-) *miner*
das Bergwerk (**-e**) *mine*
tödlich *fatal*
der Arbeitsunfall (**¨e**) *industrial accident, accident at work*
die Erdölindustrie (**-n**) *oil industry*
das Ausmaß (**-e**) *scope*
aufwerfen (**i, a, o**) (sep.) *to raise*
entwerfen (**i, a, o**) *to design*
menschlich *human*
das Fehlverhalten (-) *incorrect conduct*
das Versagen *error, failure*

ins Spiel kommen *to come into play, come into it*
die Internationale Atomenergiebehörde *International Atomic Energy Agency*
die Sicherheitsvorschrift (**-en**) *security regulation*
der GAU (**größter anzunehmender Unfall**) *greatest imaginable accident*
die Kohle *coal*
das Erdöl *oil*
üblich *usual*
die Kernenergie (**-n**) *atomic energy*
das Leck (**-s**) *leak*
das Kernkraftwerk (**-e**) *nuclear power station*
die Strahlung (**-en**) *radiation*
abgeben (**i, a, e**) (sep.) *to release*
das Krebsrisiko (**-risiken**) *cancer risk*
das Risiko (**die Risiken**) *risk*
die Leukämie *leukaemia*
das Umweltrisiko (**-en**) *environmental risk*
der Langzeitschaden (¨) *long-term damage*

Richtig oder falsch?

Korrigieren Sie die falschen Aussagen!

1 Horst ist für die Kernenergie, weil das Uran so leicht zu verarbeiten ist.
2 Viele Länder haben Uranvorkommen.
3 Es ist relativ billig, Atommüll wiederaufzubereiten oder zu entsorgen.
4 Rainer glaubt, daß atomare Abfälle eine Zeitbombe sind.
5 Die Sicherheitsvorkehrungen in Kernkraftwerken werden ständig verbessert.
6 Horst ist der Meinung, daß Atomkraft nicht so sicher ist wie andere Energiequellen.
7 Wenn ein atomarer Unfall passiert, sind die Ausmaße viel größer, als wenn ein Unfall in der Kohle- oder Erdölindustrie passiert.
8 Neue Technologien sind in der Lage, menschliches Fehlverhalten und Versagen auszuschließen.
9 Verbesserte Sicherheitsvorschriften können Unfälle wie Tschernobyl verhindern.
10 Ein GAU kann immer wieder passieren.

11 Kohle und Erdöl tragen viel zur Umweltverschmutzung bei.
12 Kernenergie ist sehr umweltfreundlich.
13 Radioaktive Strahlung erhöht das Krebsrisiko.
14 Menschen, die in der Nähe von Atomkraftwerken leben, haben ein höheres Risiko.
15 Ein großer atomarer Unfall verursacht Langzeitschäden.

Sagen Sie's auf Deutsch!

1 That sounds very positive.
2 And as far as the personnel are concerned . . .
3 That may well be the case.
4 All of that will be useless.
5 It is known for a fact that . . .
6 . . . and apart from that . . .
7 Certainly there are disadvantages.

3 Erneuerbare Energien – unsere Zukunft?

Zwei befreundete Ehepaare, Marianne/Walter und Eva/Dieter, haben gegensätzliche Ansichten über die Energieformen der Zukunft. Marianne und Walter haben vor kurzem einen Sonnenkollektor auf ihrem Dach installieren lassen, und versuchen, ihre Freunde von den Vorteilen alternativer Energiequellen zu überzeugen.

Eva Sagt mal, ihr beiden, ist denn euer Solarzellenpanel schon in Betrieb?

Walter Seit drei Wochen etwa. Wir sind wirklich froh, diesen Schritt getan zu haben, obwohl es natürlich wesentlich teurer gekommen ist, als wir gedacht hatten. Aber wir haben jetzt wenigstens das beruhigende Gefühl, einen großen Schritt in Richtung Umweltschutz getan zu haben.

Marianne Habt ihr denn schon mal daran gedacht, auf Solarenergie umzusteigen?

Dieter Also, ehrlich gesagt, wir halten beide nicht soviel von diesen sogenannten erneuerbaren Energien. Das hört sich zwar alles recht gut an, aber langfristig gesehen ist es erstens zu kostspielig, und zweitens nicht ausreichend, um den Energiebedarf der gesamten Bevölkerung zu decken.

Marianne Es gehören natürlich zwei Seiten dazu: zum einen muß jeder Verbraucher konsequent Energie einsparen, und zum anderen müssen diese Möglichkeiten ja noch viel stärker ausgeschöpft werden.

Walter Nehmt doch als Beispiel die Solarenergie. Ich habe gestern gelesen, daß die Kosten für Strom aus Solarzellen unter bestimmten Voraussetzungen von heute 2 DM/kWh bis auf 70 Pf/kWh im Jahr 2010 zurückgehen werden. Und wenn die Nachfrage nach Solarzellen steigt, können natürlich auch die Herstellungskosten gesenkt werden.

Eva Aber trotzdem wird Solarenergie niemals so billig und konkurrenzfähig sein wie zum Beispiel Energie aus Kohlekraftwerken.

Dieter Und dabei hat man auf dem Gebiet der Solarenergie noch relative Erfolge zu verzeichnen. Windenergie zum Beispiel ist schon viel komplizierter. Wo soll man denn diese riesigen Windpark-Komplexe errichten? Das mag ja vielleicht noch in der Wüste Kaliforniens möglich sein, aber bestimmt nicht im dichtbesiedelten Europa! Und ihr müßt auch bedenken, daß derartige Projekte ungeheurer stark subventioniert werden, da sie ansonsten gar nicht wirtschaftlich wären.

Marianne Sicherlich habt ihr da recht. Aber man muß ja nicht unbedingt davon ausgehen, daß diese erneuerbaren Energien den gesamten Energiebedarf abdecken werden. Zumindest wäre jedoch ein Anfang gemacht, und man könnte dann die Nutzung von Kohle, Erdöl und Kernkraft immer stärker einschränken.

Walter Außerdem gibt es ja nicht nur Solarenergie und Windenergie – denkt doch nur mal an die Energie, die man aus Wasser und den Gezeiten gewinnen könnte!

Eva Natürlich ist da ein Potential vorhanden, und es sind ja auch schon Anfänge gemacht worden. Aber die Probleme, die gerade Wasser- und Gezeitenenergie hervorrufen können, solltet ihr auch nicht unterschätzen. Der Assuan-Staudamm zum Beispiel hat große Umweltprobleme mit sich gebracht, und Gezeitenkraftwerke können die natürlichen Lebensräume der dort lebenden Tierarten verändern oder gar zerstören!

Marianne Aber ihr glaubt doch nicht im Ernst, daß diese Nachteile, die wir ja gar nicht abstreiten wollen, schwerer wiegen als die Vorteile, die solche Energieformen mit sich bringen?

Dieter Natürlich nicht. Wir bezweifeln ja bloß, daß man in der Lage sein wird, ganz ohne herkömmliche Energieformen auszukommen.

Bermerkungen

die Energie (**-n**) *energy*
erneuern *to renew*
die Energieform (**-en**) *form of energy*
installieren *to install*
der Sonnenkollektor (**-en**) *solar panel* (Lit. sun collector)
das Solarzellenpanel (**-e**) *solar panel*
wesentlich *essential*
teuer kommen *to turn out to be expensive*
wenigstens *at least*
kostspielig *expensive*
decken *to cover, meet*
die Kosten *the cost*
kWh. Kilowattstunde *kilowatt hour*
zurückgehen* (**e, i, a**) (sep.) *to go down, become less*
senken *to lower*
steigen (**ei, ie, ie**) *to rise*
der Windpark (**-s**) *wind park*
dichtbesiedelt *densely populated*
subventionieren *subsidise*
wirtschaftlich *economically viable*
davon ausgehen, daß *to assume that*
der Energiebedarf *energy requirements*
abdecken (sep.) *to meet, cover*
die Gezeiten (pl.) *tides*
vorhanden sein *to exist*
hervorrufen (**u, ie, u**) (sep.) *to cause*
unterschätzen *to underestimate*

mit sich bringen *to entail*
das Gezeitenkraftwerk *tidal power station*
die Gezeitenenergie (-**n**) *tidal energy*
der Lebensraum (¨**e**) *habitat*
die Tierart (-**en**) *species*
der Nachteil (-**e**) *disadvantage*
schwer wiegen *carry weight* (figurative)
herkömmlich *traditional*
auskommen* (**o**, **a**, **o**) (sep.) (**mit** + Dat.) *to make do with, manage with*

Welche Antwort paßt?

1 Ist denn euer neuer Sonnenkollektor schon in Betrieb?
(*a*) Ja, wir lassen jetzt einen Sonnenkollektor installieren.
(*b*) Ja, wir sind auch für Solarenergie.
(*c*) Ja, seit einigen Wochen schon, und mit Erfolg.

2 Habt ihr auch schon mal daran gedacht, auf Solarenergie umzusteigen?
(*a*) Kernenergie ist schädlicher als Solarenergie.
(*b*) Eigentlich halten wir nicht soviel von diesen erneuerbaren Energien.
(*c*) Jeder muß mitmachen, wenn Energie gespart werden soll.

3 Was haltet ihr eigentlich von diesen erneuerbaren Energien?
(*a*) Wir sind der Meinung, daß diese Energien keine Zukunft haben.
(*b*) Erneuerbare Energien werden von immer mehr Menschen genutzt.
(*c*) Diese Energien sind zwar teurer, aber auch umweltfreundlicher.

4 Kann denn Solarenergie in der Zukunft konkurrenzfähig werden?
(*a*) Solarenergie ist weitaus umweltfreundlicher als Kernenergie.
(*b*) Sie wird zwar billiger werden, aber immer teurer bleiben als herkömmliche Energiequellen.
(*c*) Jeder sollte Solarenergie nutzen.

5 Wo könnte man einen Windpark-Komplex errichten?

(*a*) Die Menschen müssen auch darauf achten, weniger Energie zu verbrauchen.
(*b*) In Europa gibt es bis jetzt noch nicht so viele Windpark-Komplexe.
(*c*) Das ist nur möglich in einem Gebiet, das nicht so dichtbesiedelt ist.

6 Sind Wasserkraftwerke und Gezeitenkraftwerke auch eine gute Möglichkeit der Energiegewinnung?
(*a*) Ja, aber sie sind noch nicht genügend ausgeschöpft worden.
(*b*) Wasserkraftwerke und Gezeitenkraftwerke bringen mehr Probleme mit sich als Kohlekraftwerke.
(*c*) Es wird in Zukunft nur noch Wasserkraftwerke und Gezeitenkraftwerke geben.

Redewendungen

- Expressing commitment to a cause/idea

An der Lösung dieses Problems **ist mir wirklich sehr gelegen**.
Es würde mir sehr viel bedeuten, wenn diese Umweltmaßnahmen eingeführt würden.
Das Problem der Müllentsorgung **liegt mir sehr am Herzen**.
Ich stehe voll hinter der Idee, die Autos abzuschaffen.
Die Forderung, eine Umweltsteuer einzuführen, **hat meine volle Unterstützung**.
Ich bin voll und ganz dafür, die Kernkraft durch erneuerbare Energien zu ersetzen.
Mit der Umweltpolitik dieser Partei **kann ich mich voll und ganz identifizieren**.
Ich bin schon seit langem **ein großer Anhänger dieser Idee**.
Ich trete schon seit mehreren Jahren **für** die Rechte der Frau **ein**.
Ich bin eine große Verfechterin der Frauenbewegung.
Dieser Sache **messe ich größte Bedeutung bei**.

- Distancing oneself from a cause/idea

Mit diesen Demonstranten gegen die Atomkraft **kann ich leider nicht sympathisieren**.

Mit dieser Sache **möchte ich nichts zu tun haben**.

Mit dieser Politik **kann ich mich überhaupt nicht identifizieren**.

Von diesen radikalen Forderungen **muß ich mich distanzieren**.

Ich werde diese Forderungen **nicht unterstützen**.

Ich kann mich für diese neue Idee **nicht im geringsten begeistern**.

Wie dieser Streit um Umweltmaßnahmen ausgeht, **ist mir unwichtig**.

Die Probleme der Dritten Welt **berühren mich eigentlich wenig**.

Für diese Aktion gegen Tierversuche **werde ich mich nicht engagieren**.

Dieser Idee **messe ich keinerlei Bedeutung bei**.

Für die Forderung nach einem neuen Abtreibungsgesetz **kann ich nicht eintreten**.

- Expressing the need for change

Es ist unbedingt notwendig, daß die Partei einen Kurswechsel vornimmt.

Man sollte wirklich langsam **etwas** gegen das Waldsterben **unternehmen**.

Es sollte meiner Meinung nach viel **mehr** für die Umwelt **getan werden**.

Wenn nicht bald etwas für die Umwelt **getan wird**, werden die langfristigen Konsequenzen verheerend sein.

Es ist (höchste) Zeit, daß die Bürger sich um diese Umweltprobleme kümmern.

Die Politiker müssen auch dafür eintreten, **daß entsprechende Maßnahmen ergriffen werden**.

Man müßte in dieser Angelegenheit **mehr/äußerste Entschlossenheit zeigen**.

Es ist dringend notwendig, daß sich die Meinung der Bürger in dieser Angelegenheit ändert.

Es ist höchst wünschenswert, daß alle Mitgleider der Partei **eine reformierte Haltung** zu dieser Frage **einnehmen**.

Was das Ozonloch angeht, **so ist es fünf Minuten vor zwölf**.

In Bezug auf Umweltschutz **müssen einschneidende Veränderungen vorgenommen werden**.

Vokabeln

Fossile Energiequellen

das Mineralöl *mineral oil*
die Steinkohle *(hard) coal*
die Braunkohle *lignite*
das Uran *uranium*

Erneuerbare Energiequellen

die Sonne *sun*
das Wasser *water*
die Gezeiten (pl.) *tides*
der Wind *wind*
das Erdgas *natural gas*
der Müll *rubbish, garbage*
das Holz *wood*
die Holzabfälle *wood waste*
das Stroh *straw*

Kraftwerke

das Kohlekraftwerk *coal-fired power station*
das Kernkraftwerk/Atomkraftwerk *nuclear power station*
die Windkraftanlage *wind power plant*
das Wasserkraftwerk *hydro-electric power station*
das Sonnenkraftwerk/die Photovoltaïkanlage *solar power plant*
das Gezeitenkraftwerk *tidal power plant*
die Anlage zur Verbrennung von Stroh/Holz/Holzabfällen *plant for the burning of straw/wood/waste wood*

Grammatische Hinweise

1 Conditional sentences

One way of expressing a condition is to use a **wenn** clause with a verb in the present tense and a main clause with the verb in either the present or the future tense:

Wenn ich Zeit habe, gehe ich mit meinen Freunden ins Kino.

Wenn ich Zeit habe, werde ich mit meinen Freunden ins Kino gehen.

In this case, I may or may not go to the cinema with my friends; I'm just not sure yet.

If, however, the condition is subject to a greater degree of improbability or uncertainty than in these two examples, then **Konjunktiv II** is called for. Either the straightforward **Konjunktiv II** form or the **würde(n)** + infinitive form can be used in both the **wenn** clause and the main clause. When you use which form is very much a matter of register and of which particular verb is being used:

Wenn ich Zeit **hätte**, **würde** ich mit meinen Freunden ins Kino gehen.
(i.e. *I haven't got time, so I am **not** going to the cinema with my friends.*)

Wenn ich jünger **wäre**, **würde** ich Drachenfliegen gehen.
(i.e. *I am **not** so young, so I won't be going hang-gliding.*)

Wenn ich nicht arbeiten **müßte**, **wäre** alles viel leichter.
(i.e. *I **do** have to work, so things are going to go on being difficult!*)

Wenn ich die Prüfung bestehen **würde**, so **würden** sich meine Eltern riesig freuen.
(i.e. *The likelihood of my passing my exam and of my parents then being enormously pleased is not too great, but it **could** happen.*)

Note that in the last example the word **so** has been slipped in between the **wenn** clause and the main clause. **So** or **dann** are often inserted in this way.

Konjunktiv II forms of modal verbs

Since the **Konjunktiv II** forms of modal verbs are used particularly frequently, they are listed below for your attention:

	können	**müssen**	**dürfen**	**sollen**	**wollen**	**mögen**
ich	könnte	müßte	dürfte	sollte	wollte	möchte
du	könntest	müßtest	dürftest	solltest	wolltest	möchtest
er/sie/es	könnte	müßte	dürfte	sollte	wollte	möchte
wir	könnten	müßten	dürften	sollten	wollten	möchten
ihr	könntet	müßtet	dürftet	solltet	wolltet	möchtet
sie/Sie	könnten	müßten	dürften	sollten	wollten	möchten

These forms of the modal verbs are also often used when no **wenn** clause is present:

Könntest du mir helfen?	*Could you help me?*
Ich müßte jetzt eigentlich gehen.	*I actually ought to be going now.*
Dürfte ich mitkommen?	*Might I come too?*
Ich sollte heute zu Hause bleiben.	*I ought to stay at home today.*
Wir möchten einen Sprachkurs machen.	*We should like to take a language course.*

Omission of *wenn*

It is possible to omit the **wenn** from a **wenn** clause. The verb then moves to the initial position:

Hätte ich eine eigene Wohnung, so würde ich dich einladen.	*If I had my own apartment, I would invite you (round).*
Könnte ich ihn nur sehen, so wäre ich dann zufrieden.	*If only I could see him, I would be content.*

Pluperfect of *Konjunktiv II*

To express a hypothetical possibility in the past, the pluperfect form of **Konjunktiv II** is used. For more information on the pluperfect, see below.

Wenn wir schneller gelaufen wären, hätten wir den Bus noch erreicht.	*If we had run faster, we would have caught the bus.*
Hätte ich Zeit gehabt, so wäre ich nach Potsdam gefahren.	*If I had had the time, I would have gone to Potsdam.*

Note that the pluperfect form of **Konjunktiv II** is used in both the **wenn** clause and the main clause.

2 *Pluperfect tense*

The pluperfect tense was already mentioned in passing in **Lektionen 6** and **8**. It is formed in German by using the past tense of the appropriate auxiliary verb, **haben** or **sein**, together with the past participle of the verb in question:

spielen	gehen
ich hatte gespielt	ich war gegangen
du hattest gespielt	du warst gegangen
er/sie/es hatte gespielt	er/sie/es war gegangen
wir hatten gespielt	wir waren gegangen
ihr hattet gespielt	ihr wart gegangen
sie/Sie hatten gespielt	sie/Sie waren gegangen

The use of the pluperfect in German is very similar to that in English:

Als ich aufstand, **hatten** meine Freunde schon **gefrühstückt**.
Nachdem ich die Zeitung **gelesen hatte**, spielte ich Karten.
Ich wollte Karin besuchen, aber sie **war** schon in Urlaub **gefahren**.

For examples of the pluperfect passive see **Lektion 6**, page 154.

The pluperfect is also sometimes used in colloquial German where the simple past is being referred to:

Hattest du das gelesen? *Did you read that?*
Der Jürgen war auch gekommen. *Jürgen came too.*

3 Sequencing of sentence elements

As you will no doubt already be aware, the sequencing of sentence elements is considerably more flexible in German than it is in English. In fact it is usually possible for any sentence element to appear in initial position (except of course the verb, which has to occupy second position in the declarative sentence):

Der Bundespräsident ist gestern mit seiner Gattin zu einem offiziellen Besuch nach Kanada gefahren.
Gestern ist der Bundespräsident mit seiner Gattin zu einem offiziellen Besuch nach Kanada gefahren.
Mit seiner Gattin ist der Bundespräsident gestern zu einem offiziellen Besuch nach Kanada gefahren.
Zu einem offiziellen Besuch ist der Bundespräsident gestern mit seiner Gattin nach Kanada gefahren.
Nach Kanada gefahren ist gestern der Bundespräsident mit seiner Gattin zu einem offiziellen Besuch.

Generally speaking, the initial position is occupied by information taken for granted by both the speaker and the listener(s). This is the standard (or 'unmarked') word order:

Klaus hat mir ein Paket gegeben. **Das Paket** soll ein Geschenk sein für seine Mutter. **Seine Mutter** wohnt in Dresden und ist zur Zeit krank.

The most important, and usually, new information is found towards the end of the sentence, where the main stress falls.

However, it is possible to opt for a 'marked' word order, and the initial position can then be used to highlight and give emphasis to certain information:

Herrn Fink kenne ich überhaupt nicht. **Mit seiner Frau Anke** arbeite ich aber seit zwei Jahren.

Almost any sentence element may be highlighted in this way, including the past participle:

Gesagt hat sie nichts. **Nur geweint** hat sie.

4 Extended participial phrases

A construction which is practically unknown in English, but which is very common in formal written German is what is known as the extended participial phrase, or extended adjectival attribute. This phrase occupies the slot in the sentence normally occupied by an attributive adjective and contains either a present participle or a past participle:

Present participle

(*a*) Die **/in der Bundesrepublik ständig zunehmende/** Anzahl von Gewalttaten gegen Ausländer erweckt im vernünftigen Bürger nichts als Entsetzen.
(*The number of acts of violence against foreigners, **which is constantly on the increase in the Federal Republic**, evokes nothing but horror in the rational citizen.*)

(*b*) Dem **/wegen Verfolgung in der Heimat seit mehreren Jahren im Exil lebenden/** Dichter wird jetzt die Möglichkeit angeboten, zurückzukehren.
(*The writer, **who has been living in exile for several years***

because of persecution at home*, is now being given the opportunity to return.*)

Past participle

(*c*) Die **/von der Telekom angebotenen/** Geräte umfassen Telefon, Decoder, Farbbildschirm und Bedienungstastatur.
(*The appliances* ***offered by Telekom*** *comprise a telephone, decoder, colour screen and keyboard.*)

(*d*) Die **/von den EG-Staaten mit Ausnahme Großbritanniens 1989 verabschiedete/** Urkunde über die sozialen Grundrechte der Arbeitnehmer bildete 1993 die Grundlage für die Festlegung europaweiter sozialer Mindeststandards.
(*The document concerning the basic social rights of employees,* ***accepted in 1989 by the Community States with the exception of Great Britain****, in 1993 formed the basis for the establishing of Europe-wide minimum standards.*)

To unravel an extended participial phrase, you need to decide where it begins and where it ends. There is often, though not always, a determiner (such as **ein**, **der**, **dieser**, etc.) at the beginning, and of course the participle at the end, usually just before the noun which it qualifies. In order to obtain an acceptable English version you then need to create a relative clause out of the extended phrase and move it all to the right of the noun (as in examples (*a*) and (*b*) above). Sometimes the relative clause can be reduced – that is, the relative pronoun and auxiliary verb can be omitted, as in examples (*c*) and (*d*) above. Unfortunately, moving the participial phrase to the right of the noun sometimes brings problems with it since it cannot always be placed directly after the noun. Example (*a*) above is a case in point. There can then be difficulties in avoiding ambiguities, since it may not be clear to which noun the relative clause is referring. In (*a*) above, the use of *which is* rather than *who are* does make it clear that it is the number of acts of violence that is on the increase and not the foreigners. But there are often cases where the possible ambiguity is difficult to avoid.

In English, there are admittedly a few more or less fixed expressions such as *a never-to-be-forgotten evening* or *a never-again-to-be-repeated experience* in which the extended adjective tends to be made into a single unit by the use of hyphens. But, generally speaking, the construction is alien to English and therefore tends to present problems for the English speaker of German. For this reason it requires a certain amount of attention and practice. A glance at the quality German press should provide you with plenty of opportunity to practise!

Übungen

Fahrverbot für Autos bei Sommer-Smog?

JA

HARALD B. SCHÄFER

Der Pädagoge und SPD-Politiker, 54, ist seit 1992 Landesumweltminister in Baden-Württemberg. Schäfer plant mit einem viertägigen Fahrverbot in Heilbronn einen Großversuch im Kampf gegen das Sommer-Ozon.

Jährlich nehmen die Ozonwerte um 8 Prozent zu, 10 Prozent der Menschen sind durch Ozon gesundheitlich beeinträchtigt. Der Verkehr ist unbestritten Hauptverursacher des Ozons.

Deswegen: Nicht die Kinder ins Kinderzimmer, sondern die Autos ohne G-Kat in die Garage! Hauptalibi fürs Nichtstun war bisher das Ozon selbst: Weil es angeblich nur weiträumig herantrans-

NEIN

KLAUS TÖPFER

Der 54jährige Volkswirtschaftsprofessor ist seit 1987 Bundesumweltminister. Der CDU-Politiker entwarf 1991 die Verpackungsverordnung, um den Einstieg in die ökologische Marktwirtschaft zu wagen.

Kind spielt in Garage, Auto fährt spazieren – ein mögliches Szenario dank der Untätigkeit des Umweltministers? Eindeutig nein!

Bereits in den 70er Jahren wurden weitaus höhere Ozonspitzenwerte als heute gemessen. Ozon entsteht aus Stickstoffoxiden und flüchtigen Kohlenwasserstoffen in Verbindung mit Sonneneinstrahlung – europaweit. Die Stickstoffoxide kommen zu

JA

portiert und gerade in Schadstoffgebieten nachts schnell abgebaut wird, hieß es: „Nicht lokale, nur globale Maßnahmen sind wirksam."

Kenner ahnen: Das Ozon steigt, und der Bundesumweltminister kündigt jährlich (die gleichen) Maßnahmen an, ohne Taten folgen zu lassen. Natürlich müssen wir die Vorläufersubstanzen vor allem weiträumig bekämpfen. Tempolimits, Verbot von nicht schadstoffarmen Autos, Vermeidungsstrategien – die Wege sind da, es fehlt am politischen Willen.

Wenn uns jetzt aber der Nachweis gelingt, daß lokale Verkehrsbeschränkungen lokale Ozonspitzen merklich senken, haben wir den Hebel für eine Sommer-Smog-Verordnung. Eine solche wäre Ouvertüre für das ohnehin nötige Hauptstück: ein strenges Gesetzespaket gegen Sommer-Smog.

Lokale Verbote erzeugen

NEIN

70 Prozent und die Kohlenwasserstoffe zu etwa 50 Prozent aus dem Verkehr. Die weiteren Verursacher sind Kraftwerke, Hausbrand und lösungsmittelhaltige Farben sowie Reinigungsmittel.

Ozon baut sich langfristig und großräumig auf. So wurden die „Ozonspitzen" nicht in innerstädtischen, sondern in Reinluftgebieten gemessen. Gerade hier zeigt sich, daß es unmöglich ist, mit kurzzeitigen lokalen Fahrverboten in Ballungsräumen direkten Einfluß auf die erhöhten Ozonwerte in Reinluftgebieten zu nehmen. Dies ist nicht der geeignete Weg.

Wir müssen im Kampf gegen den Sommer-Smog weiter an den Ursachen ansetzen. Wir haben mit umfangreichen Maßnahmen die Luftbelastung vermindert: durch die Kat-Pflicht für alle Autos, durch die Nachrüstung von Kraftwerken und die Abgasrückführung an Tankstellen.

JA	NEIN
erst den nötigen Druck für globale Maßnahmen. Die Angst vor dem möglichen Aufschrei der Wirtschaft berührt die Bonner Koalitionäre erfahrungsgemäß mehr als der Aufschrei besorgter Mütter. Es wird Zeit, riesige Anstrengungen nicht nur für den Schutz des werdenden, sondern auch des geborenen Lebens zu unternehmen.	So werden heute 600 000 Tonnen Stickstoffoxide und 200 000 Tonnen flüchtige organische Verbindungen pro Jahr weniger emittiert. Wir werden aber noch mehr tun, wie etwa schärfere Abgasnormen für alle Kfz EG-weit einführen und den Spritverbrauch für neue Pkw auf rund 7,7 Liter senken. (*Focus*)

1 Pro und Contra – wer sagt was? Ordnen Sie die Sätze Schäfer oder Töpfer zu.

(*a*) Die Ozonwerte steigen ständig.
(*b*) Schon vor 20 Jahren gab es weitaus höhere Ozonspitzenwerte als heute.
(*c*) Kraftwerke, Heizungen in privaten Haushalten, Verkehr, gewisse Farben und Reinigungsmittel sind auch für die Erzeugung von Ozon verantwortlich.
(*d*) Hauptschuldiger für die Zunahme des Ozons ist der Verkehr.
(*e*) Durch lokale Fahrverbote kann man am besten die öffentliche Meinung dazu bewegen, globale Maßnahmen zu unterstützen.
(*f*) Es ist nicht möglich, Ozonwerte durch lokale Fahrverbote zu beeinflussen.
(*g*) Weitreichende Maßnahmen gegen die Luftbelastung sind schon unternommen worden.
(*h*) Die Emissionen von Stickstoffoxiden und organischen Verbindungen haben abgenommen.
(*i*) Zehn Prozent der Menschen sind durch Ozon gesundheitlich gefährdet.

(*j*) Es fehlt am politischen Willen, Maßnahmen gegen das Ozon zu ergreifen.

2 Walter und Harald besprechen die verschiedenen Energiequellen und wie man an Energie sparen könnte. Vervollständigen Sie den Dialog, indem Sie die Rolle von Walter spielen. Mögliche Lösungen finden Sie im **Lösungsteil**.

Walter (*a*)

Harald Also, ich bin grundsätzlich gegen Atomkraft, aber ich glaube, im Moment gibt es keine bessere Alternative.

Walter (*b*)

Harald Ich finde diese Möglichkeiten sehr gut. Besonders Wasserenergie und Solarenergie. Aber die Regierung müßte noch mehr Geld für die Erforschung und Nutzung solcher alternativer Energiequellen ausgeben.

Walter (*c*)

Harald Wenn ich aus dem Zimmer gehe, mache ich das Licht aus. Außerdem achte ich darauf, elektrische Geräte so wenig wie möglich zu benutzen.

Walter (*d*)

Harald Ich dusche, statt zu baden, und zum Zähneputzen nehme ich immer ein Glas Wasser, anstatt das Wasser laufen zu lassen.

Walter (*e*)

Harald Ich halte sogar sehr viel davon. Denk doch nur mal, wieviel Energie man sparen könnte, wenn man die meiste Zeit mit dem Bus fahren würde! Oder besser noch: man sollte die Autos ganz abschaffen.

3 Sagen Sie es anders. Formen Sie die folgenden Satzpaare wie in den Beispielen angegeben um.

Beispiele

Ich kann heute abend deswegen nicht ausgehen, weil ich morgen arbeiten muß.

Wenn ich morgen nicht arbeiten müßte, könnte ich heute abend ausgehen/ würde ich . . . ausgehen können.

Ich kann mich deswegen nicht freuen, weil die Regierung keine neuen Umweltmaßnahmen einführt.

Wenn die Regierung neue Umweltmaßnahmen einführte/ einführen würde, könnte ich mich freuen/ würde ich mich freuen können.

(*a*) Ich will deswegen nicht ins Kino gehen, weil ich erkältet bin.
(*b*) Ich fahre im Sommer deswegen nicht nach Ägypten, weil es mir dann zu heiß ist.
(*c*) Ich wohne deswegen nicht im Stadtzentrum, weil es mir zu teuer ist.
(*d*) Mit der Politik dieser Partei kann ich mich deswegen nicht identifizieren, weil sie sich nicht um die Dritte Welt kümmert.
(*e*) Ich engagiere mich deswegen nicht für die Aktion gegen Tierversuche, weil sie von Extremisten organisiert wird.
(*f*) Die Regierung nimmt deswegen keine einschneidenden Veränderungen vor, weil die Bevölkerung keine radikalen Forderungen stellt.
(*g*) Mit diesen Demonstranten kann ich deswegen nicht sympathisieren, weil sie nicht für einen Kurswechsel eintreten.
(*h*) Ich bin für die Idee von erneuerbarer Wasser- und Gezeitenenergie deswegen nicht zu begeistern, weil diese Methoden die natürlichen Lebensräume verschiedener Tierarten zerstören.

4 Formen Sie aus den vorgegeben Satzteilen **wenn . . . dann** - Sätze wie im Beispiel angegeben.

Beispiel

Politiker/ nichts unternehmen – keine Änderungen eintreten/ können

(i) Wenn die Politiker nichts unternehmen, dann können keine Änderungen eintreten.
(ii) Wenn die Politiker nichts unternehmen würden, dann könnten keine Änderungen eintreten.
(iii) Wenn die Politiker nichts unternommen hätten, dann hätten keine Änderungen eintreten können.

(*a*) Bürger/ aufgeklärt werden – sie/ mehr für die Umwelt tun/ können
(*b*) Leute/ nicht demonstrieren – Regierung nichts tun/ können
(*c*) alle Menschen/ mitmachen – man/ viel erreichen/ können
(*d*) man/ erneuerbare Energien/ nutzen – man/ langfristig auf Kernenergie verzichten/ können
(*e*) man/ Vorsichtsmaßnahmen/ treffen – man/ Unglücksfälle

verhindern/ können

(*f*) die Regierung/ mehr für Forschung ausgeben – man/ erneuerbare Energien besser nutzen/ können

5 Translate the following text into English, paying special attention to the extended participial phrases. You will find one possible English version in the **Lösungsteil**.

UNTERSTÜTZUNG FÜR DEN EG-STAHL

BRÜSSEL, 24 November. Die EG-Mitglieder wollen sich zügig über ein Konzept zur Gesundung der Stahlindustrie verständigen. Bei den Beratungen der für die krisengeschüttelte Branche zuständigen Minister und Staatssekretäre herrschte am Dienstag Einvernehmen darüber, bis zum kommenden Februar Klarheit über das von der EG-Kommission in der vergangenen Woche vorgelegte Hilfsprogramm zu erzielen. Keine Bedenken gab es gegen die Absicht, die für soziale Hilfen vorgesehenen EG-Mittel um rund 475 auf 900 Millionen DM aufzustocken. Die Diskussion wurde durch den spanischen Antrag zur Billigung von Subventionen in Höhe von fast neun Milliarden DM für zwei Stahlkocher des Landes überlagert.

Am Dienstag unterstützte nur der italienische Vertreter das spanische Anliegen. Italien hat in der Vergangenheit bereits mehrfach ungeachtet des in der EG seit 1986 wieder uneingeschränkt geltenden Beihilfenverbots die Zustimmung zu Subventionen für die staatliche Stahlindustrie erbeten.

(*Frankfurter Allgemeine Zeitung*)

6 Ergänzen Sie den Dialog mit Hilfe der englischen Sätze. Sie diskutieren mit einer Arbeitskollegin, Ute, über das Thema Energie.

Ute Was hältst du eigentlich von diesen sogenannten erneuerbaren Energien?

Sie *Tell her that you are very much in favour of them. Say that you are already doing a lot to save energy, and that you plan to have a solar panel installed in the near future.*

Ute Was tust du denn, um Energie zu sparen?

Sie *Tell her that you do most things in the kitchen by hand, and that you have very few electrical appliances. Also, you take showers rather than baths to save water, and you use the dishwasher only when you have guests.*

Ute Aber glaubst du denn, es hat einen Sinn, wenn nur die Bürger etwas tun – ich finde, der Staat sollte noch viel mehr machen.

Sie *Tell her that you agree, but that you think it is important that the citizens do something as well. Also, you say that more money should be spent on the research and use of alternative energy sources.*

Ute Wahrscheinlich bist du auch gegen die Nutzung von Kernkraft, oder?

Sie *Tell her that you think it's very dangerous, but that it must be difficult to do without it at the moment. However, you are in favour of it being abolished in the future.*

7 Ergänzen Sie die Sätze mit Vokabeln aus **Lektion 9**, und setzen Sie sie horizontal in das Kreuzworträtsel ein (see page 266). Vertikal ergibt sich dann das Lösungswort (*k*).

(*a*) Eine wichtige ...., um Energie zu sparen und die Umwelt zu schützen, ist die Erforschung neuer Energiequellen.

(*b*) Diese erneuerbaren Energien, wie zum Beispiel Solarenergie, Windenergie, Wasserenergie und Gezeitenenergie, sind zwar im Moment noch sehr ....., aber auf lange Sicht umweltfreundlicher als traditionelle Energiequellen.

(*c*) Die .... von Kernenergie ist sehr umstritten, hat aber auch Vorteile.

(*d*) Ein großer Vorteil ist der, daß die ...... relativ niedrig sind, weil das Uran so billig ist.

(*e*) Hinzu kommt, daß die .... nach alternativen Energieformen noch nicht sehr groß ist, weil die Leute noch sehr skeptisch sind.

(*f*) Allerdings lassen sich immer mehr Leute jetzt .....zellen auf ihrem Dach installieren, um einen Schritt in Richtung Umweltschutz zu tun.

(*g*) Diese erneuerbaren Energien haben jedoch noch einen anderen ....: es kann sein, daß sie die Lebensräume gewisser Tierarten verändern oder gar zerstören, wie im Fall der Gezeitenenergie.

(*h*) Auf jeden Fall bringt die .... jedoch wesentlich mehr Probleme als alle anderen Energiequellen, denn ein GAU kann fatale Folgen für weite Regionen haben.

(*i*) Es ist daher sehr wichtig, daß jeder Bürger .... spart.

(*j*) Wenn das getan wird, kann man den gesamten Energieverbrauch ......, und somit die Umwelt schützen.

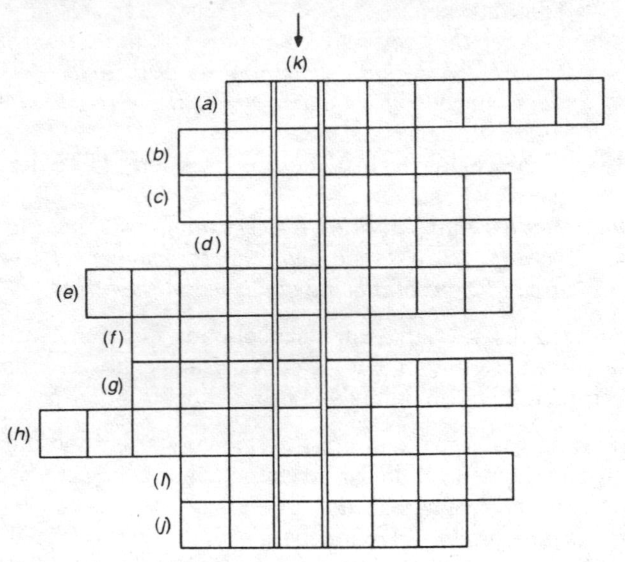

Höraufgabe

Lassen Sie Ihr Auto stehen!

Rainer, ein deutscher Student und Martin, ein englischer Austauschstudent, diskutieren darüber, wie man im Bereich Transport und Verkehr mehr für Umweltschutz und Energiesparen tun könnte.

1 Hören Sie sich den Dialog genau an, und notieren Sie dann, was die Bürger tun können bzw. was der Staat tun kann, um im Bereich Transport und Verkehr Energie zu sparen und die Umwelt zu schützen. Schreiben Sie keine ganzen Sätze, sondern nur Stichpunkte, wie in den Beispielen angegeben.

Was die Bürger tun können:
(*a*) weniger mit dem Auto fahren
(*b*) (usw. bis (*h*))

Was der Staat tun kann:
(*a*) das Bewußtsein der Bürger schärfen
(*b*) (usw. bis (*f*))

2 **Diktat**: Hören Sie sich den Dialog genau an und schreiben Sie mit: von »Ich bin nur erstaunt, daß . . .« bis ». . . besser ausgenutzt würden.« (Ende des Dialogs.) Die korrekte Version des Diktats finden Sie fettgedruckt im Transkriptionssteil.

Lesetexte

1 Phantasie oder Wirklichkeit?

HOHER BESUCH AUF DER HARDTHÖHE

Was heute noch der Höhepunkt eines Zoobesuchs ist, könnte in nicht allzuferner Zukunft zu einem eintrittsfreien *Ereignis* werden: grasende Giraffen in den Rheinauen, suhlende Flußpferde im Isarschlamm, Raubtiere auf Beutegang in der Lüneburger Heide.

Heute vielleicht noch eine *Vorstellung* für Phantasiebegabte. Aber wenn sich unser Planet noch weiter aufheizt, kommen nicht nur die Polkappen ins *Schwitzen*, vielleicht gerät sogar das gesamte Weltklima ins *Wanken*. Und unsere Breiten könnten ein tierischer Ort zum *Leben* werden.

Damit die Welt nicht entgültig zu einem Toll- und Treibhaus wird, müssen wir den *Ausstoß* von Kohlendioxid verringern. Eine Aufgabe, an der die deutschen Stromerzeuger mit Erfolg arbeiten: zum einen durch die verantwortungsvolle *Nutzung* von Kernkraft zum *Schutz* unserer Umwelt. Das erhitzt zwar die Gemüter, erwärmt aber nicht die Atmosphäre. Denn die Energieversorgung durch Kernkraft erzeugt keine Treibhausgase.

Zum anderen durch modernste Technologien, mit denen heute aus Steinkohle doppelt soviel Energie gewonnen werden kann wie noch vor einigen Jahrzehnten. Entsprechend geringer sind die Emissionen pro Kilowattstunde Strom. Und wenn Sie persönlich bereit sind, bei energiesparenden Maßnahmen mitzumachen, können Sie sich der *Unterstützung* Ihres Energieversorgungsunternehmens sicher sein.

Hohe Tiere sind uns zwar immer willkommen. Aber lieber im Zoo oder auf Staatsbesuch . . .

(*Focus*)

nicht allzufern *not too distant*
eintrittsfrei *free of charge on entry*
grasen *to graze*
die Giraffe (-n) *giraffe*
die Rheinauen *meadows along the River Rhine* (poetic)
sich suhlen *to wallow*
das Flußpferd (-e) *hippopotamus*
der Isarschlamm (no. pl.) *the mud of the River Isar*
das Raubtier (-e) *predator, beast of prey*
der Beutegang *hunt*
die Lüneburger Heide *the Luneburg Heath*
die Vorstellung (-en) *the idea*
der/die Phantasiebegabte (-n) *person gifted with a lively imagination*
sich aufheizen (sep.) *to heat up*
ins Schwitzen kommen *to start sweating*
die Polkappe (-n) *the polar cap*
ins Wanken geraten (ä, i, a) *to become shaky, begin to totter*
gesamt *total*
die Breiten *latitude*
tierisch *beastly* (in both meanings of the word)
das Tollhaus (¨er) *madhouse*
das Treibhaus (¨er) *greenhouse*
der Ausstoß *output*
das Kohlendioxid *carbon dioxide*
verringern *to reduce*
der Stromerzeuger (-) *generating station*
mit Erfolg *successfully*
zum einen . . . zum anderen *on the one hand . . . on the other hand*
verantwortungsvoll *responsible*
das erhitzt die Gemüter *that makes feelings run high*
erwärmen *to warm up*
erzeugen *to generate, produce*
das Treibhausgas (-e) *greenhouse gas*

doppelt soviel . . . wie *twice as much as*	**mir** (Dat.) **dessen** (Gen.) **sicher** *to be sure of something/ I am sure of it*
entsprechend geringer *respectively lower*	**das Energieversorgungsunternehmen** *electricity station*
die Emission (-en) *emission*	**das hohe Tier (-e)** *big shot* (slang)
bereit sein *to be prepared*	**der Staatsbesuch (e)** *state visit*
sich sicher sein (+ Gen.)/ **ich bin**	

1 Beantworten Sie die folgenden Fragen.

(*a*) Was könnte passieren, wenn sich die Erde noch weiter aufheizt?
(*b*) Was muß getan werden, um die Erwärmung unseres Planeten zu verhindern?
(*c*) Welchen Vorteil hat Kernkraft im Vergleich zu anderen Energieformen?
(*d*) Was tun die Stromerzeuger, um Steinkohle als Energiequelle zu verbessern?
(*e*) Kann der Verbraucher auch etwas dazu tun?

2 Finden Sie zu den kursiv gedruckten Substantiven im Text das jeweils passende Verb. Geben Sie auch die Artikel der Substantive an.

Beispiel
das Ereignis – ereignen

2 Erdgas als relativ umweltfreundliche Energiequelle

Ruhrgas macht Erdgas intelligent

Wir stehen für Erdgas

Erdgas hat natürliche Talente, im Pflichtfach Umweltschutz gute *Noten* zu *bekommen*: Dennoch setzen wir Erdgas auf die Schulbank *und bringen ihm bei,* noch weniger Schadstoffe und CO_2 (Kohlendioxid) *freizusetzen*. Und wir verbessern die Gastechnik, um durch Energiesparen und bessere Verbrennung die Umwelt zu *schonen*.

Erdgas verbrennt in unseren neuentwickelten Brennern noch emissionsärmer. Mit Brennwertgeräten, Blockheizkraftwerken oder Gasturbinen machten unsere Beratungsingenieure schon viele Kunden zu Energiesparern.

Wir werden weiter daran arbeiten, daß unser Erdgas beim Umweltschutz Bestnoten erhält.

Wir *beziehen* Erdgas aus Deutschland, Holland, Rußland, aus der norwegischen und dänischen Nordsee. *Wegen* der hohen Produktions- und Transportkosten müssen wir das Erdgas gleichmäßig über das ganze Jahr beziehen.

Unseren Kunden liefern wir das Erdgas, wie es von ihnen *benötigt* wird, *vor allem* im Winter für die Heizung. Wir machen das Erdgas mit Hilfe unserer technischen *Anlagen* und gaswirtschaftlichen Möglichkeiten für unsere Kunden verbrauchsgerecht und sicher. Dabei kümmern wir uns intensiv um Energieeinsparungs- und Umweltschutzlösungen. So machen wir Erdgas zur Dienstleistung.

Ruhrgas AG – Postfach – 4300 Essen 1

(*Focus*)

das Talent (-e) *talent*
das Pflichtfach (¨er) *compulsory subject*
gute Noten bekommen *to get good marks*
auf die Schulbank setzen *to put back to school*
beibringen (i, a, a) (sep.)(+ Dat.) *to teach*
freisetzen (sep.) *to release, emit*
schonen *to treat with care, protect, conserve*
der Brenner (-) *burner*
das Brennwertgerät (-e) *meter measuring calorific value*
das Blockheizkraftwerk (-e) *central plant for district heating*
die Gasturbine (-n) *gas turbine*

der Beratungsingenieur (-e) *consultant engineer*	**gaswirtschaftlich** *pertaining to the gas industry*
die Bestnote (-n) *best mark*	**verbrauchsgerecht** *favourable to consumers*
erhalten (ä, ie, a) *to receive*	**sicher** *safe*
beziehen (ie, o, o) *to receive, obtain*	**die Dienstleistung (-en)** *service*
gleichmäßig *regular(ly), equal(ly)*	

1 Beantworten Sie die folgenden Fragen.

(*a*) Ist Erdgas eine gute Energiequelle?
(*b*) Was tut Ruhrgas, um Erdgas noch weiter zu verbessern?
(*c*) Wie können die Kunden mit Erdgas Energie sparen?
(*d*) Woher bezieht Ruhrgas sein Erdgas?
(*e*) Warum muß Ruhrgas das Erdgas gleichmäßig über das ganze Jahr beziehen?
(*f*) Müssen die Kunden das Erdgas auch das ganze Jahr über kaufen?
(*g*) Wie macht Ruhrgas die Nutzung von Erdgas verbrauchsgerecht und sicher?
(*h*) Wodurch wird Erdgas zur Dienstleistung?

2 Welches Wort paßt? Ersetzen Sie die kursiv gedruckten Wörter im Text mit dem jeweils passenden Wort aus der angegebenen Liste.

(*a*) auf Grund
(*b*) Einrichtungen
(*c*) bekommen
(*d*) besonders
(*e*) auszustoßen
(*f*) gebraucht
(*g*) lehren es
(*h*) erhalten
(*i*) Zensuren
(*j*) schützen

3 Anzeige

BESUCH ERWÜNSCHT

Sind Deutschlands Kernkraftwerke wirklich sichere Stromlieferanten? Haben die Betreiber tatsächlich Vorkehrungen gegen jede denkbare Gefahr für Menschen und Umwelt getroffen?

Überzeugen Sie sich bitte selbst! Für unsere Anlagen gilt: Besuch erwünscht. Wenn Sie uns die Karte schicken, nennen wir Ihnen das nächstgelegene Informationszentrum. Und die Besuchszeiten, zu denen Sie dort willkommen sind.

Fehlt die Antwortkarte? Dann schreiben Sie bitte an den Info-Service STROM, Postfach 19 05 45 20, 5308 Rheinbach.

Ihre Stromversorger

(*Bunte*)

Beantworten Sie die folgenden Fragen auf Englisch.

1. What two questions introduce this advertisement?
2. How can these questions best be answered, according to the advertisement?
3. What information will you receive if you send off the reply card?
4. What are you supposed to do, if the reply card is missing?

10
REAKTIONEN — ZUR DEUTSCHEN — EINHEIT

Lernziele

In this unit you will learn how to

- express positive and negative reactions
- express sympathy
- attempt to calm someone down
- improve your essay technique

Aufnahmen

1 Eine Stimme gegen die Einheit

»Ich war stolz auf dieses Land«

The following people are being interviewed about their views against unity:

Claudia Benndorf, 19, hat eine Ausbildung als Reiseverkehrskauffrau begonnen;

Robert Handrow, 18, will im kommenden Frühjahr die Abschlußprüfung seiner Drucker-Ausbildung mit Abitur ablegen;

Katharina Door, 19, studiert im ersten Semester Wirtschaftsmathematik;

Franka Jentzsch, 18, besucht die Abiturklasse eines Gymnasiums.

Teil 1

Interviewer Ihr seid in der DDR geboren und aufgewachsen. Nun seid ihr Bundesbürger. Wie fühlt ihr euch dabei?

Claudia Ich bin Ossi. Ich will meine Vergangenheit nicht verstecken. Die hat mich geprägt, die macht mich aus. Wenn mich jemand fragt, wo ich herkomme, sag' ich »ex-DDR«. Nicht Deutschland.

Katharina Ich kann nicht sagen »Bundesbürger«, denn es ist ja nicht wahr, daß wir die gleichen Rechte haben. Wir verdienen weniger, wir kriegen fremde Gesetze übergestülpt.

Franka Ich fühle mich als Leipziger, das war schon immer so. Verstecken kann man das sowieso nicht, die Sachsen hört man ja überall raus.

Robert Ich fühle mich als Leipzig-Connewitzer. Deutschland ist mir egal.

Interviewer Was habt ihr dagegen, Deutsche zu sein? Ihr seid die FDJ und die SED los, ihr habt neue Freiheiten . . .

Franka Was habe ich denn davon? Meinen Ausbildungsgang, Berufsausbildung mit Abitur, schaffen sie ab. Und meine Lehrstelle haben sie mir eh' gekündigt. Jetzt kann ich froh sein, daß ich noch einen Platz auf dem Gymnasium bekommen habe, und ich muß ein ganzes Schuljahr doppelt machen.

Claudia Ich wollte eigentlich Sport studieren – ich bin Leistungsschwimmerin – und das lasse ich jetzt bleiben. Denn etwas hab' ich schon gelernt über den Kapitalismus: Entweder du willst eine Familie und ein ordentliches Heim und ein geregeltes Leben – oder die Karriere. Beides kannst du dir gleich abschminken als Frau. Sehe ich doch an meiner Mutter: Die hat in ihrer neuen Arbeit nicht mal Zeit fürs Mittagessen.

Interviewer Wo arbeitet sie?

Claudia Auf dem Arbeitsamt. Krisenfester Job.

Bemerkungen

ich bin in . . . geboren *I was born in . . .*
aufwachsen (a, u, a) (sep.) *to grow up*
sich fühlen *to feel*
die Vergangenheit (no pl.) *past*
verstecken *to hide*
prägen *to shape*
ausmachen (sep.) (+ Acc.) here: *to constitute*
das Gesetz (-e) *law*
überstülpen (sep.) (+ Dat.) here: *to impose* (on top of what existed previously)
(he)raushören *to hear, detect*
egal sein (+ Dat.) *to be all the same* (*to*)
etwas dagegen haben *to mind*
der Ausbildungsgang (¨e) *training syllabus*
kündigen *to hand one's notice in*; when used with the dative: *to dismiss someone*
das Gymnasium (Gymnasien) (West German) *grammar school*. Note that there were considerable differences between the East and West German school systems and that these had to undergo a difficult process of harmonisation
der/die Leistungsschwimmer/in (-)/(**-nen**) *competitive swimmer*
etwas bleibenlassen (sep.) *to drop something, not to do something*
sich etwas abschminken (sep.) *to forget about* (colloquial), *to drop*
krisenfest *unaffected by crises*

Richtig oder falsch?

Korrigieren Sie die falschen Aussagen!

1. Claudia schämt sich, weil sie eine ehemalige DDR-Bürgerin ist.
2. Katharina ist der Meinung, daß Ost- und Westdeutsche nicht gleich behandelt werden.
3. Franka will die Tatsache verstecken, daß sie aus Leipzig kommt.
4. Robert ist froh, daß es jetzt endlich ein einheitliches Deutschland gibt.
5. Die jungen Leute haben durch die Wiedervereinigung große Probleme bekommen.

6 Claudia ist der Meinung, daß man in einem kapitalistischen System als Frau Nachteile hat.
7 Claudias Mutter ist arbeitslos.

Teil 2

Robert Ich bin einer der letzten, die noch gleichzeitig Abi und Lehre machen können, meinen Job als Drucker habe ich noch. Und ich finde vieles ziemlich mies, was zur Zeit in der Schule passiert. Zum Beispiel sagte der Gesellschaftskundelehrer neulich, daß wir jetzt nicht mehr Ethik und Philosophie haben. Was soll das? Spielt das alles denn keine Rolle mehr?

Interviewer Immerhin geht es in der Schule viel freier und lockerer zu. Oder hättet ihr gern die strammen alten Zeiten zurück?

Katharina Sicher, es war vieles ziemlich übel. Aber vieles war eben auch gar nicht so schlecht.

Interviewer Was denn?

Franka Man wußte, wo es langgeht. Und einen sicheren Job hatte man auch.

Interviewer Habt ihr früher an die DDR geglaubt?

Katharina Mir hat die DDR damals nur Gutes gegeben. Negative Seiten? Die habe ich nicht bemerkt. Ich hatte ja ein klares Ziel, ich wollte Mathematik studieren. Meine Eltern haben gut verdient. Das Leben war schön.

Claudia Ich habe richtig von der DDR profitiert. Also, damals mit 14 fühlte ich mich voll als DDR-Bürger. Ich war sogar stolz auf dieses Land und war fest überzeugt, daß die Staatsführung alles richtig macht. Daß das alles so den Berg runtergeht . . .

Robert . . . das war ein ziemlicher Schock.

Bemerkungen

das Abi (no pl.) see **das Abitur** in **Lektion 3**, page 57. Note that the school and professional training systems of the former two German states differed considerably; East Germans often complained after unification that their system was simply overridden by that of West Germany

der Drucker (-) *print worker*
mies *rotten, lousy*
der/die Gesellschaftskundelehrer/in (-)/(-**nen**) *teacher of social studies*
neulich *recently*
die Ethik (no pl.) *ethics*
Was soll das? *What is all that about?*
(k)eine Rolle spielen *to be (un-)important*
immerhin *at least*
locker *casual*
zugehen* (sep.) *to go on*
übel *bad*
man wußte, wo es langgeht *you knew the rules*
glauben an (+ Acc.) *to believe in*
bemerken *to realise, notice*
klar *concrete, clear*
das Ziel (-**e**) *goal*
verdienen *to earn*
profitieren von (+ Dat.) *to profit from*
stolz sein auf (+ Acc.) *to be proud of*
überzeugt sein von (+ Dat.) *to be convinced of*
die Staatsführung (-**en**) *the government* (Lit. state leadership – East German expression)
den Berg runtergehen *to go downhill* (colloquial)
ziemlich here: *considerable*
der Schock (-s) *shock*

Fragen zum Text

1 Welche besondere Ausbildung macht Robert?
2 Welche Veränderungen in der Schule kritisiert Robert?
3 Was hat Franka am alten System gefallen?
4 Haben die jungen Leute an die DDR geglaubt?
5 Wie war ihre Reaktion, als sie gemerkt haben, daß die DDR zusammenbricht?

Teil 3

Interviewer Und was hättet ihr geändert am DDR-Staat?
Claudia Also, wir hätten schnellstens das Leistungsprinzip

	eingeführt. Wir haben doch gesehen, was in der Wirtschaft los war. Die Leute haben gearbeitet, wann Sie Lust hatten – keiner hat sich für irgendetwas verantwortlich gefühlt. Und um die DDR wieder richtig aufzubauen, mußte erst mal was mit der Wirtschaft passieren, das war klar. Es muß schließlich jeder an seiner Lohntüte merken, wenn er Mist gebaut hat.
Robert	Wir haben ja schon einen Vorgeschmack davon bekommen, wie das Leben eines Werktätigen ablief. »Praktische Arbeit« hieß das, da sollten sie uns im »Lehrkabinett« einige Grundlagen der Technik beibringen. Das ging voll in die Hose. Wir haben nur Gammeln gelernt. Das war völlig lächerlich – es war einfach keine Arbeit da.
Interviewer	Und die Werktätigen?
Robert	Die fanden das völlig normal! Da hab' ich zum erstenmal gesehen, wie man als DDR-Bürger in den Trott reingerät, in diese Selbstgefälligkeit, aus der man nicht mehr rauskommt. Man findet sich ab. Man sitzt in der Wohnstube und diskutiert Politik, man guckt Westfernsehen und denkt, daß die das besser haben, aber daß man sich mal zusammengetan hätte, gemeinsam, um aus der Misere rauszukommen – das gab's nicht.

(Nach einem *Spiegel*-Interview mit Leipziger Abiturienten über ihr Leben in Ostdeutschland vor und nach der Wende, *Der Spiegel*)

Bemerkungen

ändern an (+ Dat.) *to change about*
das Leistungsprinzip (**-ien**) *achievement principle, competitive principle*
lossein (sep.) *to be going on* (colloquial)
Lust haben *to be in the mood*
verantwortlich *responsible*
aufbauen (sep.) *to build up*
schließlich *finally, in the end, after all*
die Lohntüte (**-n**) *wage packet*

Mist bauen *to mess things up* (colloquial)
der Vorgeschmack (no pl.) *first taste*
der/die Werktätige (**-n**) *the working man/woman*
ablaufen (sep.) *to pass*
das Lehrkabinett (**-e**) *training workshop*. Note that this is an East German expression, and once more reflects the differences that had developed between East and West Germany over the 40 years of division
die Grundlage (**-n**) *basis, foundation*
voll in die Hose gehen *to be a complete flop* (colloquial)
das Gammeln (no pl.) *loafing around*
lächerlich *ridiculous*
in den Trott reingeraten (**a, ie, a**) *to be dragged into a routine*
die Selbstgefälligkeit (**-en**) *complacency*
rauskommen *to get out* (short for **herauskommen**)
sich abfinden mit (+ Dat.) *to come to terms with*
die Wohnstube (**-n**) *living-room*
gucken *to watch*
sich zusammentun *to get together*
die Misere (**-n**) *wretched, dreadful state*

Fragen zum Text

1. Was hätten die jungen Leute am alten System geändert?
2. Was war das Hauptproblem in der Wirtschaft?
3. Welche Erfahrungen hat Robert im Lehrkabinett gemacht?
4. Was kritisiert Robert an den ehemaligen DDR-Bürgern?

Sagen Sie's auf Deutsch!

Schauen Sie sich die drei Teile des Dialogs noch einmal an und versuchen Sie, die entsprechenden Ausdrücke/Sätze zu finden.

1. What is all that about?
2. Has all of that suddenly become unimportant?
3. You knew the rules.
4. Everyone should realise . . . when they have messed things up.
5. That was a complete flop.
6. Messing about was the only thing that we learned.
7. You learn to accept things.
8. Why do you mind being German?

 2 Deutsche Einheit – warum?

Thomas Trebling, 24, Student an der Universität Marburg, äußert sich zur Frage der deutschen Einheit.

Paul Was hältst du von der deutschen Einheit?

Thomas Also, ich war schon von Anfang an dagegen.

Paul Wieso? Hast du dich nicht gefreut, als die Mauer runtergekommen ist?

Thomas Natürlich, es war schon irgendwie bewegend, die Gesichter der Leute zu sehen, wie sie sich gefreut haben, und wie sich wildfremde Menschen in die Arme gefallen sind an der Mauer. Aber rational betrachtet habe ich noch nie einen Grund gehabt, mir eine Wiedervereinigung der beiden Staaten zu wünschen.

Paul Aber glaubst du nicht, daß Ost- und Westdeutschland historisch zusammengehören?

Thomas Warum denn? Dieses Argument regt mich schon lange auf. Schließlich gab es ein einheitliches Deutschland erst seit 1871, seit Bismarck diese Idee in die Tat umgesetzt hat . . . Da könnte man ja genauso gut die Bundesrepublik und Österreich zusammenschließen – da ist eine gemeinsame Sprache vorhanden, eine gemeinsame Geschichte und eine gemeinsame wirtschaftliche Struktur. Und wenn man an Belgien denkt, oder die Schweiz – Teile davon sprechen ja auch Deutsch, also warum nicht diese Länder zusammenfassen?

Paul Ich glaube, das ist doch zu weit hergeholt. Ich meine, das wäre ja dasselbe, wie wenn man heute Amerika oder Australien wieder zu Teilen von Großbritannien machen wollte, bloß weil sie dieselbe Sprache haben, und geschichtliche Verbindungen. Aber das liegt doch so weit zurück – wohingegen die Bundesrepublik und die DDR ja eigentlich durch unglückselige Umstände getrennt wurden. Und die kulturellen Gemeinsamkeiten sind in diesem Fall ja viel stärker . . . bist du vielleicht nicht eher gegen die Einheit, weil sie finanzielle Probleme und Belastungen für die Westdeutschen bedeutet, und auch gesellschaftliche Spannungen entstehen?

Thomas Sicher, das sind auch Gründe, die gegen die

Wiedervereinigung sprechen. Ich verstehe einfach nicht, warum man unbedingt eine Einheit wollte. Konnte denn die DDR nicht einfach weiterexistieren, als ein separater Staat? Schließlich hatte sich dieser Staat ja auch unabhängig von der Bundesrepublik entwickelt. Also, ich sehe da ganz große Widersprüche.

Paul Hast du denn auch persönlich Nachteile erfahren durch diese Entwicklung?

Thomas Sicherlich, in Marburg ist es zum Beispiel jetzt noch schwieriger, ein Zimmer zu bekommen, und die Mietspreise sind ungeheuer angestiegen, seit viel mehr Ossis rübergekommen sind . . .

Paul Naja, vielleicht wirst du ja in 20 Jahren anders über alles denken.

Bemerkungen

von Anfang an *from the start*
runterkommen *to come down* (short for **herunterkommen**)
dagegen sein *to be against it*
bewegend *moving*
wildfremde Menschen *total strangers*
sich in die Armen fallen *to embrace, hug*
rational betrachtet *from a rational point of view*
historisch *historical(ly)*
zusammengehören (sep.) *to belong together*
aufregen (sep.) *to irritate, excite*
in die Tat umsetzen *to realise, make come true*
genauso gut *just as well*
zusammenschließen (ie, o, o) (sep.) *to unite*
zusammenfassen (sep.) *to put together*
zu weit hergeholt *too far-fetched*
die Verbindung (**-en**) *link*
zurückliegen (ie, a, e) (sep.) *to be in the past*
unglückselig *unfortunate*
der Umstand (**¨e**) *circumstance*
trennen *to separate*
die Gemeinsamkeit (**-en**) *common feature*
eher *rather*
gesellschaftlich *social(ly)*
die Spannung (**-en**) *tension*
bedeuten *to mean*

gegen etwas sprechen *to weigh against something*
einfach here: *simply, just*
sich entwickeln *to develop*
der Widerspruch (¨e) *contradiction*

Richtig oder falsch?

Korrigieren Sie die falschen Aussagen

1 Thomas wollte schon immer eine Wiedervereinigung Deutschlands.
2 Er war der Meinung, daß es sehr bewegend war, als die Mauer gefallen ist.
3 Er glaubt, daß es viele Gründe für eine Wiedervereinigung gab.
4 Historisch gesehen gibt es Deutschland erst seit 1871.
5 Paul glaubt, daß West- und Ostdeutschland historisch gesehen zusammengehören.
6 Thomas glaubt, daß man die Bundesrepublik und Österriech vereinigen sollte.
7 Thomas findet, daß es absurd ist, zwei Länder zu vereinigen, weil sie dieselbe Sprache sprechen.
8 Die Wiedervereinigung hat vor allem finanzielle und soziale Probleme gebracht.
9 Thomas hätte lieber zwei deutsche Staaten gehabt als ein wiedervereinigtes Deutschland.
10 Er persönlich hat keine Nachteile durch die Wiedervereinigung erfahren.

Redewendungen

- Expressing positive reactions

Das finde ich gut.
Das finde ich ganz normal.
Das ist gar nicht so schlecht.
Das ist aber schön!
Das ist ja toll/super!
Ich bin ganz begeistert.
Das hat mich sehr beeindruckt.
Das erstaunt mich aber sehr.

Das gibt mir wenigstens wieder Hoffnung.

- Expressing negative reactions

Das finde ich nicht so gut.
Das finde ich ziemlich schlecht.
Das ist aber zu weit hergeholt.
Das ist ja lächerlich/unerhört/unverschämt/unglaublich.
Das ist/war ein ziemlicher Schock.
Das hat mich vollkommen unerwartet getroffen.
Ich bin entsetzt!
Das enttäuscht mich aber sehr.
Das beängstigt mich aber sehr.
Das macht mir Angst.

- Expressing sympathy

Das tut mir aber leid.
Ich verstehe das sehr gut.
Ich kann dir das nachfühlen.
Ich kann dich gut verstehen.
Du tust mir wirklich leid.
Darf ich Ihnen mein Beileid/aufrichtiges Bedauern aussprechen?
Das muß wirklich schrecklich für Sie/dich sein.

- Attempting to calm someone down

Das darfst du nicht so ernst nehmen.
Nimm das doch nicht so schwer.
Mach' dir doch nichts daraus!
Das wird schon wieder werden!
Das ist doch alles halb so schlimm!
Beruhige dich/ Beruhigen Sie sich doch.
Regen Sie sich/ Rege dich doch nicht so auf.

Guide to essay writing

As in English, essay writing in German requires a relatively formal style. There are also many formal set phrases which people tend to use in essays. Here are a few hints as to how to make your own essays read better in German.

1 Einleitung (*Introduction*)

Possible introductions

- Comparison of the present situation (in relation to the question) with the past

Im Vergleich zu früher haben sich die Arbeitsbedingungen wesentlich verbessert.
Wenn man die heutigen Umweltprobleme **mit denen vor** 50 Jahren **vergleicht**, so kann man sagen, daß . . .
Um die heutigen Probleme des Landes **besser verstehen zu können, muß man zuerst** seine Rolle in der Geschichte Europas **betrachten/untersuchen**.
Die Geschichte hat uns gezeigt, daß . . .

- General statement relating to the specific essay topic

Allgemein betrachtet ist dieses Problem etwas, das die gesamte Bevölkerung betrifft.
Bevor ich mich mit dem spezifischen Problem der Jugendarbeitslosigkeit befasse, **möchte ich kurz** die Auswirkungen **beschreiben**, die die Arbeitslosigkeit **im allgemeinen** auf die Menschen und ihre Familie hat.
Das Problem der Kindesmißhandlung **ist weit verbreitet**, und kommt in der Tat in allen Schichten der Bevölkerung vor.
In der heutigen Zeit ist Prüfungsangst ein Problem, das alle Altersstufen betrifft.

- Telling a short anecdote relating to the specific topic

Vor kurzem konnte man in der Zeitung lesen, daß . . .
Erst gestern hat sich wieder ein Zwischenfall ereignet, **der die Wichtigkeit** der Frage **deutlich macht**.
Die Geschichte der Helga R. zeigt uns, wohin ein derartiges Verhalten führen kann.
Einleitend möchte ich ein Beispiel anführen, das das Ausmaß der Kriminalität **verdeutlicht**.

2 Hauptteil (*Main part*)

- Discussing the pros and cons of a particular issue

  Ein wichtiger Grund, der für eine solche Maßnahme spricht, ist . . .
  Dagegen spricht, daß . . .
  Ein weiterer Vorteil dieser Maßnahme wäre . . .
  Jedoch muß man beachten, daß . . .
  Zusätzlich würde durch eine solche Maßnahme . . . drastisch verbessert.
  Man sollte dennoch nicht vergessen, daß . . .
  Es gibt einen weiteren Punkt, der diese Maßnahme als vorteilhaft erscheinen läßt.
  Trotzdem darf man nicht außer acht lassen, daß . . .
  Für diese Maßnahme spricht, daß . . .
  Auf der anderen Seite muß man sagen, daß . . .

- Arguing in favour of one particular idea, linking various arguments

  Wenn man dieses Problem **genauer untersucht**, so **lassen sich** vier **Hauptbereiche/Hauptpunkte unterscheiden**.
  Ich möchte zuerst auf die Frage der hohen Jugendarbeitslosigkeit **eingehen**.
  Dies ist ein Aspekt der Kriminalität, **den man nicht unterbewerten sollte**.
  Es ist offensichtlich, daß in diesem Bereich ein Zusammenhang besteht.
  Bei näherer Betrachtung wird klar, daß darin eine der Hauptursachen für die steigende Kriminalität in Großstädten zu finden ist.
  Dabei muß man bedenken, daß die Dunkelziffer wahrscheinlich um vieles höher liegt.
  Ein zweiter wichtiger Gesichtspunkt ist die hohe Zahl der Drogentoten.
  Natürlich kann man über diesen Standpunkt diskutieren, aber . . .
  Wie schon vorher gesagt, ist dies ein Problem, das uns alle betrifft.
  Man darf auch nicht vergessen, daß dieses Problem immer größere Ausmaße annimmt.
  Dies hängt natürlich davon ab, was sich in den nächsten Monaten ereignet.

Wie schon erwähnt, ist es unmöglich, dies zu übersehen.
Zum dritten muß der Einfluß des Elternhauses **näher untersucht werden.**
Obwohl es richtig ist, daß . . ., **sollte man nicht vergessen**, daß . . .
Außerdem muß man in Betracht ziehen, daß die Zahl der Opfer ständig steigt.
Es kommt natürlich darauf an, ob man gewillt ist, dieses Problem anzugehen.
Leider kann man immer wieder feststellen, daß die Mehrzahl der Bürger kein Interesse zeigt.
Es wird wohl nicht mehr lange dauern, bis ein Zustand erreicht ist, der ein rasches Handeln verlangt.
Der letzte, und wichtigste, Aspekt dieser Frage ist die Auswirkung der Massenmedien auf Teenager.
Zum einen ist dies unbedingt erforderlich, **zum anderen** leider schwer in die Tat umzusetzen.
Einerseits wollen die Bürger, daß etwas getan wird, **andrerseits** tun sie selbst nicht genug dafür.
Man sollte sich fragen, ob es nicht wichtiger wäre, die Ursachen dieses Problems herauszufinden, anstatt immer nur die Folgen zu behandeln.
Es ist dringend erforderlich, daß schnell etwas geschieht.
Neuesten Erkenntnissen zufolge kann man sagen, daß diese Methode die erfolgreichste ist.

3 Schluß (*Conclusion*)

- Summing up and offering a concluding idea

Zusammenfassend kann man sagen, daß . . .
Abschließend kann man sagen, daß . . .
Wenn man alle Punkte in Betracht zieht, muß man eine eindeutige Schlußfolgerung ziehen.
Aus der obigen Diskussion ergibt sich eine eindeutige Lösungsmöglichkeit dieses Problems.

- Taking up the idea of the introduction and completing it

Um nun zum Ausgangspunkt der Diskussion zurückzukehren . . .

Zu Beginn dieses Artikels/Aufsatzes habe ich ein Beispiel angeführt . . .
Es ist also doch nicht alles so düster, **wie die obengenannte Prognose** glauben läßt.
Seit diese Frage zum ersten Mal in den Medien aufgetaucht ist, sind also, wie man sieht, fundamentale Änderungen eingetreten . . .

- Giving future prospects/ pointing to potential problems

Allerdings darf man **mögliche Gefahren** dieser Maßnahme nicht außer acht lassen.
Man sollte sich schon jetzt darauf vorbereiten, daß diese Probleme immer weiter zunehmen werden.
Es bleibt nichts anderes übrig als abzuwarten.
Wenn diese Maßnahmen befolgt werden, dann wird in einigen Jahren ein deutlicher Erfolg zu verzeichnen sein.

- Giving one's own opinion on the matter

Meiner Meinung nach kann man nur eines tun . . .
Meines Erachtens sollte man möglichst schnell . . .
Ich bin zu dem Schluß gekommen, daß diese Lösung die beste ist.
Ich persönlich würde folgendes vorschlagen . . .
Aus meiner Perspektive ist dieser Fall eindeutig . . .

Choose a topic of current interest and write an essay in German of about 500–600 words. Follow the guidelines given above and include some of the typical German phrases which have been introduced.

Because you will be concentrating on the structure and content of your essay, you may find that a number of grammatical errors creep into your German. It is therefore important to go back and check your work for gender, case, verb forms, word order, and so on.

Grammatische Hinweise

The essay writing has replaced this unit's grammar section. As usual, the exercises offer practice and, this time, revision.

Übungen

1 Bilden Sie Fragen im Präsens und Antworten im Perfekt nach den folgenden Beispielen. Benutzen Sie in jedem Paar **erst morgen/ schon gestern**:

Beispiele
Maria/ die untrennbaren Verben/ wiederholen.
Wiederholt Maria erst morgen die untrennbaren Verben?
Nein, sie hat sie schon gestern wiederholt.

Der Architekt/ den Bauplan/ entwerfen.
Entwirft der Architekt erst morgen den Bauplan?
Nein, er hat ihn schon gestern entworfen.

Zu beachten ist, daß das Perfekt hier manchmal mit **haben** und manchmal mit **sein** gebildet wird!

(*a*) Professor Schmidt/ den Präsidenten empfangen.
(*b*) Hans/ um 5.00 Uhr losfahren.
(*c*) Franziska/ am Kongreß teilnehmen.
(*d*) Bernd/ den Benzinverbrauch messen.
(*e*) Der Direktor/ den Vertrag unterschreiben.
(*f*) Herr Göller/ aus der Partei austreten.
(*g*) Unsere Studenten/ den neuen Text übersetzen.
(*h*) Heike und Werner/ ihren Eltern/ nach Spanien folgen.

2 Schreiben Sie die fehlenden Präpositionen und Pronominaladverbien (**darum**, **darauf**, **darüber**, usw.) auf.

Beispiel
Ich muß . . . (*x*) . . . nachdenken, ob ich . . . (*y*) . . . diesem Kursus teilnehme oder nicht.
(*x*) = darüber (*y*) = an

(*a*) Erinnerst du dich . . . (i) . . ., wann ich . . . (ii) . . . dir . . . (iii) . . . dieses Thema gesprochen habe?
(*b*) Ich werde mich . . . (iv) . . . Ihrem Chef . . . (v) . . . beklagen, daß Sie sich gar nicht . . . (vi) . . . mich gekümmert haben.
(*c*) Hörst du jetzt . . . (vii) . . . dem Unsinn auf? Oder möchtest du vielleicht . . . (viii) . . . dein Taschengeld verzichten?
(*d*) Ich möchte mich . . . (ix) . . . erkundigen, ob ich mich . . . (x)

... verlassen kann, daß dieser Zug rechtzeitig ankommt.

(*e*) Antje unterhielt sich ... (xi) ... ihrem Freund, während Florian sich ... (xii) ... vorbereitete, sich ... (xiii) ... seiner Freundin ... (xiv) ... sein schlechtes Verhalten zu entschuldigen.

3 Sebastian, ein Student aus Ostdeutschland, und David, ein englischer Austauschstudent, unterhalten sich über die Wiedervereinigung. Bringen Sie die Sätze in die richtige Reihenfolge.

(*a*) Zum anderen war ich der Meinung, daß durch die Wiedervereinigung die wirtschaftliche Lage in Ostdeutschland schnell besser werden würde.
(*b*) Ich war uneingeschränkt dafür.
(*c*) Einerseits die wirtschaftlichen Probleme: man hatte geglaubt, daß die wirtschaftliche Umstrukturierung einfacher und schneller sein würde. Das hat sich leider als Irrtum erwiesen.
(*d*) Und was denkst du jetzt darüber, nachdem ja einige Zeit vergangen ist?
(*e*) Du, Sebastian, warst du eigentlich für oder gegen eine Wiedervereinigung?
(*f*) Zum einen hatte ich das Gefühl, daß die beiden Staaten historisch gesehen zusammengehören, und daß die Gelegenheit für eine Wiedervereinigung einmalig sei.
(*g*) Und warum warst du dafür?
(*h*) Welche Nachteile meinst du denn zum Beispiel?
(*i*) Andrerseits natürlich die starken gesellschaftlichen Spannungen, die aus der Unzufriedenheit der Bevölkerung entstanden sind, auf beiden Seiten. Die Westdeutschen glauben, daß sie nichts gewonnen haben außer Schulden, und die Ostdeutschen fühlen sich als Bürger zweiter Klasse.
(*j*) Ich bin immer noch der Meinung, daß es ein guter Schritt war. Aber natürlich sehe ich auch die großen Probleme, die die Wiedervereinigung gebracht hat.

4 Fangen Sie jeden (overleaf) Satz mit **Ich weiß, daß ...** an.

Beispiele
Klaus hat gestern sein Auto von Mario waschen lassen.
Ich weiß, daß er gestern sein Auto von Mario hat waschen lassen.

Bernd kann seine Tochter nicht weinen sehen.
Ich weiß, daß er seine Tochter nicht weinen sehen kann.

(*a*) Werner hat vor dem eigenen Haus nicht parken dürfen.
(*b*) Tante Gerda mußte nach ihrem Unfall wieder laufen lernen.
(*c*) Harald hat sich im Oktober scheiden lassen.
(*d*) Der Mathias hat eigentlich mit uns essen gehen wollen.
(*e*) Der Soldat wollte sich nicht die Haare schneiden lassen.

5 Translate the following text into English. Pay special attention to the extended participial phrases.

TÜRKISCHER ARBEITER DARF BLEIBEN

KARLSRUHE. Ein wegen zweifachen Trunkenheitsdelikts im Straßenverkehr von der Ausweisung bedrohter Türke hat jetzt vor dem Bundesverfassungsgericht einen Teilerfolg errungen. Auf die Verfassungsbeschwerde des 38jährigen Türken hin hoben die Karlsruher Richter Beschlüsse des Verwaltungsgerichts Neustadt/Weinstraße sowie des Oberverwaltungsgerichts Rheinland-Pfalz auf, die eine von der Kreisverwaltung ausgesprochene »sofortige Ausweisungsverfügung« bestätigt hatten.

Der jeweils wegen eines Blutalkoholgehaltes von 1,64 bzw. 1,47 Promille zu einer Geldstrafe und Führerscheinentzug verurteilte Arbeiter in einer Autofabrik hatte nach eigenen Angaben rund 10 000 Mark aufgewendet, um seine Familie in die Bundesrepublik zu holen.

Das Verfassungsgericht entschied, daß die Verpflichtung zur umgehenden Ausreise den Beschwerdeführer in seinem grundgesetzlichen Anspruch auf »wirkungsvollen Rechtsschutz« verletze.

(Nach einem Artikel im *Schwarzwälder Bote*)

6 Setzen Sie den folgenden Text in die indirekte Rede. Fangen Sie mit dem Satz »Professor Meier ist der Meinung, daß . . .« an.

Setzen sie die Verben nach den in **Lektion 8** gegebenen Regeln in den Konjunktiv.

DEUTSCHLAND – ENDLICH EINE ERFREULICHE PROGNOSE

Neben all den schlechten läßt sich heute eine gute Prognose stellen: Wenn nicht alle Zeichen trügen, wird es mit der Integration zwischen Ost- und Westdeutschen in absehbarer Zeit rasch vorangehen.

Nicht mehr lange wird es verkennbar sein, daß die Probleme des Landes künftig ebensosehr im Westen wie im Osten liegen. Das zeigen Umfrageergebnisse, wonach der Anteil der Optimisten im Osten höher ist als im Westen.

Längst ist deutlich geworden, daß man auch im Westen – übrigens mit sehr unreinem – Wasser kocht und daß den Ostdeutschen manches beigebracht wird, was auch im Westen im Grunde schon überholt ist. So wird auch bald offenkundig werden, daß beide Seiten voneinander zu lernen haben.

So werden viele Barrieren abgebaut und abgeschmolzen, die zur Zeit noch im Wege stehen. So werden die Ostdeutschen im gemeinsamen Staat, in der gemeinsamen Gesellschaft viel rascher Fuß fassen, als man letzthin noch gedacht hat.

(Nach einem Artikel von Professor Christian Meier, Historiker, im *Focus*)

7 Ergänzen Sie den Text mit den angegebenen Vokabeln aus **Lektion 10**.

Viele junge Leute, die in der DDR geboren und aufgewachsen sind, (*a*) (*feel*) auch nach der (*b*) (*unification*) nicht als richtige Deutsche. Ihre (*c*) (*past*) hat sie geprägt und macht sie aus. Ein anderes Problem ist, daß viele Ostdeutsche glauben, sie hätten nicht die (*d*) (*same rights*) wie die Westdeutschen, und sie bekämen (*e*) (*foreign laws*) übergestülpt. In der Tat wurde und wird vieles in Ostdeutschland nach westdeutschem Muster umstrukturiert: (*f*) (*the training syllabuses*), (*g*) (*the grammar schools*) und (*h*) (*the economy*). Viele Menschen in der ehemaligen DDR hatten (*i*) (*believed in the GDR*), und hatten nicht bemerkt, daß vieles im Argen war. Sie waren (*j*) (*convinced of the fact*), daß (*k*) (*the state leadership*) alles richtig macht, und waren sogar (*l*) (*proud of*) ihren Staat. In der Wirtschaft wurde vieles (*m*) (*changed*): das Leistungsprinzip (*n*) (*was introduced*), es wurde rationalisiert, und die Arbeitslosigkeit nahm zu. Dies war (*o*) (*a shock*) für viele Ostdeutsche, denn in der DDR hatte jeder (*p*) (*a secure job*), obwohl oftmals überhaupt keine Arbeit da war.

8 Katrin, eine westdeutsche Studentin, und Regina, eine ostdeutsche Studentin, unterhalten sich über die Wiedervereinigung. Vervollständigen Sie den Dialog mit Hilfe der englischen Anregungen.

Katrin Du, Regina, wie fühlst du dich denn jetzt eigentlich nach der Wiedervereinigung?

Regina *Tell her that you feel rather bad. You think that as an East German you have not got the same rights as the West Germans. You earn less, and you are forced to adopt foreign laws. Really, you do not feel as a German; you do not care about Germany.*

Katrin Aber du hast doch jetzt viel mehr Freiheiten, es ist alles freier und lockerer.

Regina *Tell her that you don't know what is in it for you. You think that a lot of things about the GDR had not been so bad, that you knew the rules and had a secure job.*

Katrin Warst du etwa nicht für die Wiedervereinigung?

Regina *Tell her that you were against it from the start. You did not know why people wanted unification, and why the GDR could not just continue to exist as a separate state. After all, that state had developed independently from West Germany for 40 years. And you don't think that the common language is an argument for unification.*

Katrin Aber so, wie er war, hätte der DDR-Staat doch nicht weiterexistieren können. Was hättest du denn geändert?

Regina *Tell her that you agree. You would have changed the economic system and introduced the achievement principle first of all. But you think that the current economic and social problems brought about by unification could have been avoided if the GDR had continued to* *exist, and there would have been friendly relations and co-operation between the two states.*

Höraufgaben

1 Professor Dr. Rolf Herwig: die Wiedervereinigung

1 Professor Dr. Rolf Herwig – Angaben zur Person. Finden Sie folgendes heraus:

(*a*) Alter
(*b*) Familienstand
(*c*) Beruf
(*d*) Nationalität
(*e*) Wohnort

2 Beantworten Sie die folgenden Fragen.

(*a*) Was dachten Professor Herwig und seine Frau über die Wiedervereinigung Deutschlands vor 1989?
(*b*) Waren sie dafür oder dagegen, als es endlich soweit war?
(*c*) Was haben sie gemacht, als die Grenze im Herbst 1989 geöffnet wurde?
(*d*) Wo war Professor Herwig am 3. Oktober 1990?
(*e*) Welcher Tag war das?
(*f*) Was passierte während der Veranstaltung in Marburg?
(*g*) Welche Auswirkung hat die Wiedervereinigung auf die Arbeitslosenzahl in Ostdeutschland gehabt?
(*h*) Wie hat sich die Wiedervereinigung auf die soziale und politische Situation in Deutschland ausgewirkt?
(*i*) Was denken die meisten Menschen in Deutschland heute über die Wiedervereinigung?
(*j*) Was denkt Professor Herwig über die Wiedervereinigung?

2 Eine Abiturientin aus Ostdeutschland zur Wiedervereinigung

Beantworten Sie die folgenden Fragen:

1 Wie hat sich Damaris gefühlt, als die Mauer im November 1989 geöffnet wurde?
2 Welche positiven Seiten der Wiedervereinigung nennt sie?
3 Welche Nachteile glaubt sie, daß die Wiedervereinigung hat?
4 Glaubt sie, daß auch das DDR-System Nachteile gehabt hat?
5 Wie hat ihr das Leben in der DDR gefallen?
6 Was hat sie gedacht, wenn sie Westfernsehen geschaut hat?
7 Was vermißt sie an der Gesellschaft im Westen?
8 War Damaris für oder gegen die Einigung?
9 Warum, glaubt sie, ist die Einigung so schnell vollzogen worden?
10 Ist sie der Meinung, daß eine reformierte DDR eine bessere Lösung gewesen wäre?
11 Was kritisiert sie besonders an der Wiedervereinigung?

Lesetexte

1 Die deutsche Währungsunion

Die Mark allein löste die Probleme nicht

BERLIN. *Der Jubel* ist schon lange verhallt. Als am 1. Juli 1990 die deutsche Währungsunion vollzogen wurde, waren die Hoffnungen der *DDR-Bürger* noch groß. Eine historisch beispielslose Aktion, der größte währungspolitische Schnitt seit der Währungsreform 1948, war *geglückt*, das Ende der DDR eingeleitet und der Weg zur Wiedervereinigung geebnet. Doch wirklich geeint hat die D-Mark das dann am 3. Oktober 1990 auch politisch vereinigte Land nicht.

Der Stunde Null fieberten in der Sommernacht zum 1. Juli 1990 tausende Ostberliner entgegen. Vor den Schaltern der Deutschen Bank am Alexanderplatz, die Punkt 0 Uhr *öffneten*, kam es zu *tumultartigen* Szenen. *Bereits* in den ersten Stunden der Währungsunion gingen etwa 2,6 Milliarden DM über die Tresen von Banken und Sparkassen; 25 Milliarden DM hatte die Bundesbank in den Osten *gekarrt*, um den ersten Hunger nach Westgeld zu stillen.

Mit dem »richtigen« Geld ausgestattet erfüllten sich die DDR-Deutschen lange unerfüllbare Konsumwünsche: Autos und HiFi-Anlagen, Kleidung und Kosmetik, Haushaltsgeräte und Möbel – und Reisen gen Westen. Die Sucht nach Westwaren hatte für viele Ostfirmen *fatale* Folgen: Umsatzstarke westliche Handelsketten und Kaufhauskonzerne drängten ins Land. Fast über Nacht verschwanden die Ostwaren aus den Regalen. Auf den Kaufrausch folgte die Ernüchterung. Bald zeigte sich, daß das neue Geld allein die Probleme der maroden DDR-Wirtschaft nicht *lösen* konnte. Denn D-Mark und westliche Marktwirtschaft brachten auch Arbeitslosigkeit, steigende Preise, höhere Mieten und soziale Unsicherheit.

Heute ist zwar die politische *Teilung* Vergangenheit, die soziale und ökonomische Teilung aber noch längst nicht überwunden.

(*Süddeutsche Zeitung*)

der Jubel *enthusiasm*
verhallen *to wane, faint away*
die Währungsunion *monetary union*
beispielslos *unprecedented*
der währungspolitische Schnitt *drastic change in monetary policy*
die Währungsreform (-en) *currency reform*
die Wiedervereinigung *re-unification*
einleiten *to start, introduce*
einen *to unite*
entgegenfiebern (sep.) (+ Dat.) *to look forward to an event with nervous anticipation*
der Schalter (-) *cashpoint, window at a bank counter*
tumultartig *turbulent, tumultuous*
der Tresen (-) *counter*
karren *to cart*

1 Beantworten Sie:

(*a*) Was fühlten die DDR-Bürger, als am 1. Juli 1990 die Währungsunion vollzogen wurde?
(*b*) Was waren die Intentionen dieser Maßnahme?
(*c*) Was geschah in der Nacht zum 1. Juli 1990?
(*d*) Was machten die DDR-Deutschen mit dem Geld, das sie umgetauscht hatten?
(*e*) Was waren die Folgen dieser Reaktion?
(*f*) Hat die Währungsunion die Probleme der DDR-Wirtschaft lösen können?
(*g*) Welche negativen Folgen hatte die Währungsunion in Ostdeutschland?
(*h*) Sind die beiden Teile Deutschlands heute wirklich geeint?

2 Welches Wort paßt? Ersetzen Sie die kursiv gedruckten Wörter im Text mit dem jeweils passenden Wort aus der nachfolgenden Liste.

(*a*) transportiert
(*b*) schwerwiegende
(*c*) beseitigen
(*d*) schon
(*e*) Spaltung
(*f*) gelungen
(*g*) Ostdeutschen
(*h*) aufmachten
(*i*) die große Freude
(*j*) chaotischen

LÖSUNGSTEIL
(*Key to the Exercises*)

Lektion 1

Aufnahmen

1 Richtig oder falsch? (R. = Richtig; F. = Falsch) 1 R. 2 F. Sie will alleine fahren. 3 R. 4 F. Man nimmt die A30 in Richtung Bad Oeynhausen. 5 F. Man kommt bei Bad Oeynhausen auf die A2. 6 R. 7 F. Sie hat eine Ente. 8 R. 9 R. 10 F. Sie wird sich nach den Flügen erkundigen.

2 Welche Antwort paßt? 1 (*a*) 2 (*b*) 3 (*c*) 4 (*a*) 5 (*c*) 6 (*c*)

3 Richtig oder falsch? 1 R.
2 F. Sie fährt mit der 109. 3 F. Die Taxifahrt würde sie ungefähr das Zehnfache kosten. 4 R. 5 F. Sie hat nicht viel Gepäck. 6 F. Es ist drei U-Bahn-Stationen vom Bahnhof Zoo entfernt.
7 F. Es sind drei U-Bahn-Stationen bis zum Hotel. 8 R.

4 Rätsel: 1 Bundesallee 2 Entschuldigen 3 Richtung 4 schönen 5 U-Bahn 6 Danckelmann 7 Fuß 8 umsteigen 9 Oslauer 10 Stadtplan 11 Schönefeld

Übungen

1 (*a*) mit dem Wagen = Dat. (*b*) für die ganze Fahrt = Akk. (*c*) nach den Flügen = Dat. (*d*) ohne dich = Akk. (*e*) seit einer Stunde = Dat. (*f*) einen Stadtplan = Akk. (*g*) einen Kaffee = Akk. (*h*) mir = Dat./ den Koffer = Akk. (*i*) dir = Dat./ alles Gute = Akk. (*j*) auf unserer Reise = Dat./ so viel Spaß = Akk.

2 (*a*) Ihnen (*b*) einen (*c*) den (*d*) einem/Ihrem (*e*) Ihrem (*f*) den (*g*) einer (*h*) einen (*i*) Ihren (*j*) den

3 (*a*) Die erste Maschine startet um 6.35. (*b*) Nein, das ist mit BA. (*c*) Doch, um 6.40 geht die erste Maschine mit Lufthansa. (*d*) Um 8.00 Uhr. (*e*) Um 20.35 Uhr. (*f*) 21.55 Uhr.

4 A: Wann startet am Mittwoch die erste Maschine nach München, bitte? **B**: Um 6.35 Uhr. **A**: Welche Fluglinie ist das denn? **B**: Das ist British Airways. **A**: Wann kommt die Maschine in München an? **B**: Um 7.50 Uhr. **A**: Wann startet die letzte Maschine zurück nach Berlin? **B**: Um 20.35 Uhr. **A**: Und wann kommt die Maschine in Berlin an? **B**: Um 21.55 Uhr.

5 (*a*) Wegen des dichten Verkehrs müssen wir eine halbe Stunde früher abfahren. (*b*) Trotz dieses guten Stadtplans finden wir den Weg nicht. (*c*) Trotz der billigen Busfahrt nach Berlin möchte ich lieber fliegen. (*d*) Wegen des kalten Wetters wollen wir heute nicht spazieren gehen. (*e*) Trotz der neuen Maschine war der Flug sehr unbequem. (*f*) Trotz des späten Rückflugs nach Münster möchte ich lieber dann als Montag früh zurückfliegen. (*g*) Wegen unserer schwierigen finanziellen Probleme können wir dieses Jahr nicht in Urlaub fahren. (*h*) Trotz der modernen Unterkunft finden die Touristen diese Preise zu hoch.

6 Wir sind hier in der Brandenburgischen Straße. Sehen Sie die Ampel an der nächsten Kreuzung?
Dort biegen Sie nach rechts in die

Düsseldorfer Straße. Nach ungefähr 300 Metern kommen Sie zur Konstanzer Straße. Gehen Sie über die Konstanzer Straße, ungefähr 300 Meter geradeaus, bis Sie zur Bayerischen Straße kommen. Biegen Sie an dieser Kreuzung links in die Bayerische Straße.

Nein, nicht rechts, sondern links in die Bayerische Straße. Dann ungefähr einen Kilometer weiter bis zur Pariser Straße.

Bitte schön.

Höraufgabe
1 (*a*) good (*b*) a good journey **2** (*a*) A3 (*b*) Richtung Frankfurt (*c*) 6 km (*d*) A5 (*e*) Richtung Karlsruhe (*f*) 4 km (*g*) A7 (*h*) Richtung Würzburg (*i*) 4 km

Lesetexte
1 Kurzreise nach Berlin: 1 They will be arranged. (b) Breakfast. Distribution of rooms. Short tour of city with first important information given. Afternoon free. Dinner with the group. 3 For Monday and Tuesday. 4 On Wednesday. 5 Visit of Charlottenburg Castle and East Berlin. 6 Free day. Visit of Potsdam, lunch with the group. 7 Return journey, 3 x bed and breakfast, 1 x breakfast buffet, 3 cooked meals, guided tours and visits, guide throughout the journey, de luxe travelling coach. 8 They should be booked well in advance. 9 A minimum number of people taking part. 10 From the Otfried Laur agency or the tourist office in Berlin.

2 Eine Fahrt durch Berlin: 1 Mit dem Auto. 2 Hauptsächlich hintere Stoßstangen. 3 Vom Oberdeck des Busses. 4 Beim U-Bahn-Fahren. 5 Mit der S-Bahn. 6 Die Berliner Hinterhöfe. 7 Weil er so viel vom Berliner-Berlin gesehen hat. 8 Mit dem BVG-24-Stunden-Ticket.

Testen Sie Ihr Wissen: Es sind 8959 in den alten und 1917 in den neuen Bundesländern, zusammen also insgesamt 10 876 Kilometer.

Lektion 2

Aufnahmen
1 Richtig oder falsch?
1 R. 2 F. Er hat noch keine Kinder. 3 R. 4 F. Es ist im Süden der ehemaligen DDR. 5 R. 6 R. 7 R. 8 F. Er steht um halb acht auf. 9 R. 10 F. Er trinkt eine Tasse Kaffee, türkisch. 11 R. 12 F. Am Vormittag bereitet er Seminare vor oder liest. 13 R. 14 F. Er ißt mittags in der Mensa. 15 F. Er liest ausgiebig die Zeitung. 16 F. Er schaut die Nachrichten im Fernsehen an. 17 R. 18 R.

2 Welche Antwort paßt? 1 (*b*) 2 (*c*) 3 (*a*) 4 (*c*) 5 (*b*) 6 (*a*) **Sagen Sie's auf Deutsch!** 1 Es kommt darauf an . . . 2 gegen eins 3 Ich stelle mich dann schnell unter die Dusche. 4 eine Scheibe Toast 5 ab und zu 6 höchstens viermal im Jahr 7 zu Weihnachten 8 bei Geburtstagen

3 Complete the sentences:
1 langweilig 2 um 7.00 Uhr auf 3 auf meinem Balkon 4 für Politik 5 zu Mittag 6 in die Umgebung 7 zu stricken 8 gar kein Interesse

Übungen
1 (*a*) Ihnen (*b*) einen (*c*) mir (*d*) Ihnen (*e*) mir (*f*) mir (oder: viel) (*g*) Sie (*h*) einen (*i*) den (*j*) Ihnen
2 (a) Fährst du oft . . .? (*b*) Läufst du oft . . .? (*c*) Siehst du oft fern? (*d*) Gibst du oft . . .? (*e*) Nimmst du oft an einem Kongreß teil? (*f*) Ißt du oft . . .? (*g*) Sprichst du oft . . .? (*h*) Triffst du ihn oft . . .?
3 (*f*) (*b*) (*h*) (*g*) (*j*) (*a*) (*c*) (*e*) (*i*) (*d*)
4 (*a*) In der Stadtbücherei. (*b*) Auf dem Tennisplatz. (*c*) Im Restaurant »La Taverna«. (*d*) Auf der Dresdner Bank. (*e*) In der Kunst-Galerie.
5 (*a*) Aufs/Auf das Arbeitsamt./ Zum Arbeitsamt. (*b*) Auf den Bahnhof./ Zum Bahnhof. (*c*) In die Metzgerei./ Zur Metzgerei. (*d*) In die Alpen. (*e*) In die Diskothek »Hot Live«./ Zur Diskothek . . .

6 (*a*) Für Gedichte und Frauenliteratur interessiere ich mich besonders. (*b*) Mein Tagesablauf beginnt morgens um halb acht. (*c*) Meistens gehe ich aber erst gegen Mittag in die Stadt. (*d*) Manchmal laufe ich auch in die Stadt. (*e*) Am Wochenende besuchen wir öfters Freunde oder gehen essen. (*f*) Zum Frühstück trinke ich ein Glas Orangensaft, oder eine Tasse Kaffee, und esse ein Brötchen mit Marmalade (*g*) Zum Windsurfen fahren mein Freund und ich am Wochenende an den Starnberger See. (*h*) In meinem Zimmer habe ich nur eine Kochnische mit einer Heizplatte und einem kleinen Kühlschrank. (*i*) Im Sommer sitze ich in der Morgensonne auf meinem Balkon. (*j*) Während des Tages gehe ich öfters meine Freunde besuchen.
7 (*a*) Gedichte (*b*) Kaffee (*c*) Saft (*d*) Witwe (*e*) besuchen (*f*) mittags (*g*) Wäsche (*h*) öfters (*i*) stricken (*j*) Kellnerin (*k*) Gaststätte
8 Es kommt darauf an, ob ich arbeite oder Freizeit habe. Während der Woche stehe ich meistens gegen sieben Uhr auf, am Wochenende meistens gegen zehn.

Zum Frühstück trinke ich normalerweise eine Tasse Kaffee, und esse Brötchen mit Marmelade und Butter, außerdem ein Glas Saft. Dabei lese ich die Zeitung.

Gewöhnlich schaue ich Nachrichten im Fernsehen, lese ein Buch oder stricke.

Manchmal besuche ich Freunde oder meine Eltern, gelegentlich gehe ich spazieren, oder ich mache die Arbeit, die während der Woche liegengeblieben ist.

Leider sehe ich sie höchstens dreimal im Jahr.

Höraufgabe
1 (*a*) 29 (*b*) married (*c*) one (*d*) five years old (*e*) Jena, Thüringen (*f*) German (*g*) assistant lecturer (*h*) teacher **2** (*a*) Er ist flexibler. (*b*) Der Vater. (*c*) Normalerweise mit dem Fahrrad. Bei schlechtem Wetter aber mit dem Bus oder der Straßenbahn. (*d*) In Semester. (*e*) Manchmal muß er spät abends noch arbeiten. (*f*) Es ist ihm egal. (*g*) Er arbeitet oft auch nachmittags. (*h*) Er arbeitet im Garten. (*i*) Er arbeitet an seiner Promotion. (*j*) Zum Beispiel Leichtathletik.

Lesetexte:
1 (*a*) (iii) (*b*) (i) (*c*) (ii) **2** (*a*) (v) (*b*) (iii) (*c*) (i) (*d*) (iv) (*e*) (ii) **3** (*a*) draußen (*b*) streßfrei (*c*) mit eigenen PS zur Arbeit zu reiten (*d*) Erwerbstätigen (*e*) im Laden (*f*) alle übrigen (*g*) zu diesem Zweck (*h*) allmorgendlich (*i*) öffnen (*j*) vor allem

Lektion 3

Aufnahmen
1 Richtig oder falsch? 1 F. Sie macht eine Lehre bei der Deutschen Bank. 2 R. 3 R. 4 F. Sie kennt sehr viele, die keine Arbeit gefunden haben. 5 R. 6 F. Die Wirtschaft kann so viele akademisch qualifizierte Leute nicht aufnehmen. 7 F. Sie macht jeden Tag von ihren Englischkenntnissen Gebrauch. 8 R. 9 R. 10 F. Sie bereut es ein bißchen.

2 Welche Antwort paßt? 1 (*b*) 2 (*c*) 3 (*a*) 4 (*b*) 5 (*b*) **Sagen Sie's auf Deutsch!** 1 Ist hier noch frei? 2 Ich studiere Anglistik im vierten Semester. 3 Du hast aber Glück! 4 Ende nächsten Semesters will ich das Staatsexamen ablegen. 5 Und was möchtest du dann werden? 6 Und du, was hast du vor? 7 Ich möchte Gymnasiallehrerin für Englisch werden. 8 . . . wird hoffentlich wieder Nachfrage nach Lehrern für Englisch bestehen. 9 Es hat ungeheuer viel Spaß gemacht.

3 Richtig oder falsch? 1 F. Sie hat noch keine Lehrstelle gefunden. 2 F. Sie hat erst zwei Vorstellungsgespräche gehabt. 3 R. 4 F. Sie will lieber etwas Kreatives machen. 5 F. Er will eine Lehre als Industriekaufmann machen. 6 R. 7 R. 8 F. Er hat eine gute Chance, weil seine Zensuren gut sind, und weil er schon ein Praktikum bei dieser Firma gemacht hat. 9 R. 10 F. Dann will er die

Mittlere Reife machen. 11 F. Sie wollen, daß er die Mittlere Reife macht.
Vervollständigen Sie die Sätze! 1 . . . in Aussicht nach dem Quali? 2 . . . mir überhaupt nicht. 3 . . . bei dir aus? 4 . . . einen Ausbildungsplatz als Industriekaufmann . . . 5 . . . gegen die Leute mit Mittlerer Reife? 6 . . . ein Praktikum bei eben diesem Unternehmen gemacht. 7 . . . es nicht klappt?

Übungen

1 (*a*) abgeholt (*b*) geparkt (*c*) besichtigt (*d*) renoviert (*e*) bestellt (*f*) ausgeruht (*g*) gekostet (*h*) besucht (*i*) geschenkt (*j*) gefreut (*k*) gehört (*l*) gespielt
2 (i)(*i*) (ii)(*e*) (iii)(*o*) (iv)(*b*) (v)(*h*) (vi)(*p*) (vii)(*r*) (viii)(*a*) (ix)(*g*) (x)(*c*) (xi)(*a*) (xii)(*j*)/(*k*)/(*l*)
3 (*a*) Peter ist Englischlehrer an einer deutschen Universität, die sehr alt ist. (*b*) Birgits Tochter geht in einen Kindergarten, der ganz in der Nähe ist. (*c*) Am Wochenende machen wir die Hausarbeiten, die während der Woche liegengeblieben sind. (*d*) Corinna arbeitet als Kellnerin in einem Restaurant, das bis um Mitternacht durchgehend geöffnet ist. (*e*)Corinna besucht nur selten ihre Eltern, die sehr weit von ihr entfernt wohnen. (*f*) Abends geht sie ab und zu mit ihrem Freund ins Kino, das ein gutes Programm bietet. (*g*) Frau Beitz denkt oft an ihren Mann, der vor einigen Jahren verstorben ist. (*h*) Im Sommer frühstückt sie auf ihrem Balkon, der in der Morgensonne liegt. (*i*) Am Wochenende kommt sie ihr Sohn Helmut besuchen, der mit seiner Frau in Hamburg wohnt. (*j*) Frau Beitz strickt gerade einen Pullover für ihre Urenkelin, die in Osnabrück wohnt.
4 (*a*) Ich habe fünf Jahre lang bei Freunden in der Schellingstraße gewohnt. (*b*) Ich bin meistens zu Fuß zur Uni gegangen. (*c*) Mittags habe ich in der Mensa gegessen. (*d*) Oft habe ich in der Bibliothek gearbeitet. (*e*) Das Leben in München hat mir sehr gut gefallen. (*f*) Ein Auslandsjahr habe ich in England verbracht. (*g*) Dort habe ich viele britische Studenten kennengelernt. (*h*) Ich habe meine Englischkenntnisse natürlich auch enorm verbessert. (*i*) Eigentlich habe ich in England bleiben wollen. (*j*) Ich bin aber zurückgekommen und habe das Staatsexamen abgelegt. (*k*) In den Sommerferien habe ich immer Freunde in England besucht. (*l*) Vor drei Jahren habe ich mich um eine Stelle als Englischlehrerin beworben.
5 (*a*) Ich wohnte . . . (*b*) Ich ging . . . (*c*) Mittags aß ich . . . (*d*) Oft arbeitete ich . . . (*e*) Das Leben in München gefiel mir . . . (*f*) Ein Auslandsjahr verbrachte ich . . . (*g*) Dort lernte ich . . . kennen. (*h*) Ich verbesserte . . . (*i*) Eigentlich wollte ich (*j*) Ich kam aber zurück und legte das Staatsexamen ab. (*k*) In den Sommerferien besuchte ich immer . . . (*l*) Vor drei Jahren bewarb ich mich um . . .
6 (*a*) Sonntag nachmittag ist er mit seiner Familie spazieren gegangen. (*b*) Montag abend hat er bei Freunden ferngesehen. (*c*) Dienstag hat er acht Stunden in der Bibliothek gearbeitet. (*d*) Dienstag abend hat er in der Stadt zu viel getrunken. (*e*) Mittwoch ist er sehr spät aufgestanden. (f) Mittwoch nachmittag hat er Briefe geschrieben. (*g*) Donnerstag früh ist er nach Berlin gefahren. (*h*) In Berlin hat er viele Studienbücher gekauft. (*i*) Bis 4.00 Uhr morgens hat er in der Diskothek getanzt. (*j*) Von fünf bis neun hat er bei einem Freund auf der Couch geschlafen.
7 (*a*) Banklehre (*b*) Studium (*c*) besteht (*d*) Abitur (*e*) Mittlere (*f*) Glück (*g*) Industrie (*h*) Hauptschul (*i*) Zensuren (*j*) ungeheuer (*k*) Ausbildung
8 (*a*) Hast du denn schon eine Lehrstelle in Aussicht? (*b*) Wofür hast du dich denn eigentlich beworben? (*c*) Hast du denn da überhaupt Chancen? (*d*) Und was machst du, wenn es nicht klappt?
9 Ich wollte eigentlich studieren, aber ich wollte auf keinen Fall arbeitslos werden. Deshalb will ich eine Lehre machen.

Ich möchte unbedingt eine Schreinerlehre machen, aber die Leute mit Hauptschulabschluß oder Mittlerer Reife haben da größere Chancen.

Ich weiß, daß sich immer mehr Leute mit Abitur um diese Stellen bewerben, aber ich möchte lieber kreativ arbeiten als einen Bürojob machen.

Dann möchte ich Biologie studieren und Lehrer werden. Hoffentlich wird dann wieder Nachfrage nach Lehrern bestehen, wenn ich mit dem Staatsexamen fertig bin.

Höraufgaben
1 Auslandsstudium 1 In Canterbury, England. 2 Betriebswirtschaft. 3 Im achten Semester. 4 Weil das Studium im Ausland kürzer ist als in Deutschland. 5 Ja. 6 Nein, viel größer. 7 Fast gar nicht. 8 Weil er seine Freunde und seinen Freizeitclub nicht aufgeben will. 9 Nein. 10 Ja.
2 Studienkosten: ein Ost–West-Vergleich 1 Noch fünf Jahre. 2 Sie bekommt BaföG. 3 Sie muß mindestens die Hälfte davon zurückzahlen. 4 Es hängt davon ab, wie lange man braucht, und wie gut man ist. 5 Nein. 6 Die ostdeutschen Studenten bekommen weniger BaföG als die westdeutschen Studenten. 7 Weil es angeblich im Ostteil Deutschlands billiger ist. 8 Es gleicht sich sehr schnell an, und oft sind die Preise schon gleich. 9 Sie sind höher in Westdeutschland. 10 Nein, sie sind niedriger als in Westdeutschland, ungefähr nur 80 Prozent der Löhne in Westdeutschland.

Lesetexte
1 Studienzeiten: 1 (*a*)(iii) (*b*)(v) (*c*)(ii) (*d*)(i) (*e*)(vi) (*f*)(iv) **2** Vier bis fünf Jahre. **3** (*a*) im Durchschnitt (*b*) weniger als (*c*) erfolgreich (*d*) am längsten (*e*) benötigt (*f*) brauchen (*g*) vorgesehen (*h*) schaffen (*i*) genau (*j*) nicht viel schneller
2 Anzeige: das Arbeitsamt: 1 (*a*) Sie beweisen, daß die Schulleistung und die Lebensleistung nicht immer miteinander zu tun haben. (*b*) Schwächeren Schulabgängern, ausländischen Jugendlichen und Körperbehinderten. (*c*) Wegen der niedrigen Geburtenrate in den siebziger Jahren. (*d*) Marktwirtschaftlich. (*e*) Sie sollen überzeugende Ausbildungskonzepte bieten, und zu Schnupperlehre, Ferienjobs und Betriebsführungen einladen. (*f*) Das Arbeitsamt. **2** (*a*) die Tat (*b*) einstellen (*c*) das Bedenken (*d*) das Vertrauen (*e*) anbieten (*f*) das Verhalten (*g*) sich bemühen (*h*) die Unterstützung (*i*) der Anruf (*j*) beraten

Lektion 4

Aufnahmen
1 Richtig oder falsch? 1 F. Er fliegt nach Budapest. 2 F. Sie hat geschäftlich in Wien zu tun. 3 R. 4 R. 5 F. Frauen sind in diesem Beruf immer noch eine Minderheit. 6 R. 7 F. Er ist leitender Angestellter. 8 F. Er ist sehr zufrieden mit seinem Beruf. 9 R. 10 R.
2 Richtig oder falsch? 1 F. Er unterrichtet zur Zeit Deutsch als Fremdsprache am Sprachinstitut in der Herder Straße. 2 F. Die Bezahlung gefällt ihm nicht so gut. 3 R. 4 F. Er muß noch so lange warten, weil es so viele Anwärter gibt. 5 R. 6 F. Er arbeitet in einem Heim für körperlich und geistig behinderte Kinder. 7 F. Die Arbeit gefällt ihm sehr gut. 8 R. 9 F. Er weiß, daß Zivildienst schwerer und anstrengender ist als Militärdienst. 10 R. 11 F. Es gibt zur Zeit recht viele Stellen für Sozialarbeiter. **Sagen Sie's auf Deutsch! 1** Lange nicht gesehen. 2 Und was machst du jetzt für eine Arbeit? 3 im allgemeinen 4 sie haben es nötig 5 wenn das so ist 6 wie du weißt 7 Wie kommst du denn zurecht? 8 Es gefällt mir sehr gut. 9 Ich komme mir jedenfalls nützlicher vor, als . . . 10 es werden viele Stellen angeboten
3 Richtig oder falsch? 1 F. Er ist seit sechs Monaten arbeitslos. 2 R. 3 R. 4 F. Es besteht kaum eine Chance, eine neue

Stellung zu finden. 5 F. Er will auf jeden Fall im Osten bleiben. 6 F. Sie will eine Stellung im Westen suchen. 7 R. 8 F. Klaus möchte ein paar Computer-Kurse machen. 9 F. Er hat alle seine Freunde im Osten. 10 R.

Übungen

1 (*a*) Morgen besuchen wir unsere Eltern. (*b*) Am Dienstag arbeite ich im Garten. (*c*) Demnächst lassen wir das Haus renovieren. (*d*) Ich fange bald mit meinem Englischkurs an. (*e*) Im Oktober fahren wir nach England. (*f*) Im September kommt Martin in die Schule. (*g*) In zwei Wochen fange ich meinen Job als Bedienung an. (*h*) Übermorgen gehe ich zum Friseur. (*i*) Am Wochenende gehen wir zum Windsurfen. (*j*) Übrigens, das Abendessen ist gleich fertig!

2 (*a*) Frau Kubig wird am Dienstag zu einem Ingenieurskongreß gehen. (*b*) Herr Krause wird dort Verhandlungen mit einer ungarischen Firma führen./ Herr Krause wird dort mit einer ungarischen Firma Verhandlungen führen. (*c*) Ich werde ab September Deutschunterricht in einem Sprachinstitut geben./ Ich werde ab September in einem Sprachinstitut Deutschunterricht geben. (*d*) Ich werde nächstes Jahr Zivildienst machen. (*e*) Heiko wird nach seinem Studium als Lehrer arbeiten. (*f*) Danach wird er als Sozialpädagoge arbeiten. (*g*) Wir werden im Oktober arbeitslos werden. (*h*) Ihr werdet in Zukunft auf dem Arbeitsmarkt kämpfen müssen. (*i*) Wir werden uns morgen nach Computer-Kursen erkundigen. (*j*) Renate wird bald in den Westen gehen.

3 (*d*) (*j*) (*e*) (*a*) (*c*) (*g*) (*b*) (*i*) (*f*) (*h*) oder (*d*) (*b*) (*i*) (*f*) (*h*) (*g*) (*j*) (*e*) (*a*) (*c*)

4 (*a*) Herr Krause wird wohl zu Verhandlungen nach Budapest fliegen. (*b*) Frau Kubig wird wohl zu einem Ingenieurkongreß gehen. (*c*) Roland und Birgit werden wohl auch nächstes Jahr nach Ungarn in den Urlaub fahren. (*d*) Herr Falke wird wohl eine sehr wichtige Stellung in der Firma haben. (*e*) Dadurch wird er wohl so wenig Zeit für seine Familie haben. (*f*) Für viele Leute wird Reisen wohl einer der attraktivsten Aspekte ihres Berufs sein. (*g*) Jochen wird wohl aus Ostdeutschland kommen. (*h*) Du wirst Hans wohl nicht verstehen können. (*i*) Ihr werdet wohl müde von der langen Fahrt sein. (*j*) Man wird hier wohl nicht parken dürfen.

5 (*a*) Er fliegt oft nach Budapest, weil/da/seit(dem) er dort geschäftlich zu tun hat. (*b*) Herr Krause ist erstaunt, weil/da Frau Kubig Bauingenieurin ist. (*c*) Er ist erstaunt, weil/da er sich Bauingenieur immer als Männerberuf vorgestellt hat. (*d*) Herr Krause bringt seinen Kindern und seiner Frau immer etwas mit, wenn er auf Geschäftsreisen geht. (*e*) Frau Kubig mag ihren Beruf, weil/da sie viel reisen kann. (*f*) Gerd will Sozialarbeiter werden, wenn er in zwei Monaten mit seinem Zivildienst fertig ist. (*g*) Heiko unterrichtet an einem Sprachinstitut, seit(dem) er mit seinem Studium fertig ist. (*h*) Klaus ist arbeitslos, seit(dem) seine Firma vor sechs Monaten stillgelegt worden ist. (*i*) Sie ist einsam, seit(dem)/da/weil ihr Mann vor einiger Zeit gestorben ist.

6 Order of vocabulary: Wirtschaftsklima, Arbeitslosigkeit, berufstätig, beschäftigt, Geschäftsreise, Bezahlung, Betrieben, Kurzarbeit, Stillegung, Stellung suchen, Arbeitsamt.

7 (*a*) Frau Kubig fliegt nach Budapest, um an einem Ingenieurskongreß teilzunehmen. (*b*) Wir fahren nach Deutschland, um Verwandte zu besuchen. (*c*) Heiko arbeitet in einem Sprachinstitut, um Geld zu verdienen. (*d*) Gerd studiert Sozialpädagogik, um Sozialarbeiter zu werden. (*e*) Renate geht zum Arbeitsamt, um sich nach freien Stellen zu erkundigen. (*f*) Klaus macht einen Computer-Kurs, um mehr Chancen zu haben. (*g*) Renate geht nach Westdeutschland, um eine Stellung zu finden.

8 Ich bin Bauingenieurin, und bin im allgemeinen mit meinem Beruf zufrieden. Mir gefällt besonders, daß ich soviel reisen kann. Aber natürlich ist Zeitmangel eines meiner größten Probleme. Und was machst du jetzt?

Das stelle ich mir aber sehr schwierig vor. Wie kommst du denn zurecht, und was hast du außerdem vor?

Gute Idee! Zur Zeit werden ja viele Stellen angeboten, die auf diesem Gebiet Kenntnisse verlangen. Ich wünsche dir viel Glück dabei!

Höraufgabe
1 (*a*) Seit sechs Monaten. (*b*) Er hat Fernsehapparate hergestellt. (*c*) Sie konnte nicht mit den westlichen Firmen konkurrieren. (*d*) Weil es zu teuer war. (*e*) Dreiundzwanzig Jahre lang. (*f*) Er ist jetzt 46 Jahre alt. (*g*) Ja. (*h*) Er will sich an einem Fortbildungskurs beteiligen.

Lesetexte
1 Ein Traumjob: 1 (*a*) Three days work per week, and full salary, sometimes even above the agreed rate of pay. (*b*) The police force in Hesse. (*c*) For working too little while being paid too much. (*d*) No. (*e*) Too high salaries, uneconomical system, too many employees. (*f*) No, it often differs considerably. (*g*) A mechanic employed with the police needs a month for the work that a mechanic employed in industry does in three days. (*h*) He wants to raise the number of cars to be maintained from 14 to 15. **2** (*a*) besitzen (*b*) schafft (*c*) volles Gehalt (*d*) künftig (*e*) geschehen (*f*) absolut (*g*) schieben schon seit Jahrzehnten eine ruhige Kugel (*h*) moniert (*i*) zuständig ist (*j*) betreuen
2 Statistik Europas Frauen im Beruf: 1 Spanien hat den niedrigsten Prozentsatz berufstätiger Frauen. 2 Dänemark hat den höchsten Prozentsatz berufstätiger Frauen. 3 In der Dienstleistung.

Lektion 5

Aufnahmen
1 Richtig oder falsch? 1 F. Ihre Eltern haben sie schon mit fünf Jahren zum Schwimmunterricht geschickt. 2 R. 3 F. Sie schwimmt für diesen Club schon seit zehn Jahren. 4 R. 5 R. 6 F. Es ist ihr überhaupt nicht langweilig. 7 R. 8 F. Sie ist daran gewöhnt. 9 R. 10 F. Beim Schwimmen ist man mit Leuten zusammen, und man hat eine sinnvolle Freizeitbeschäftigung. 11 R. 12 F. Man kann es bis ins hohe Alter betreiben.

2 Richtig oder falsch? 1 F. Sie geben nächstes Wochende eine Party. 2 F. Sie sind mit dem Kegelclub in England. 3 R. 4 F. Es sagt ihnen nicht immer zu. 5 R. 6 F. Das wäre ganz und gar nicht nach ihrem Geschmack. 7 F. Sie hat den Französischkurs aufgegeben. 8 R. 9 F. Kegeln ist eine Betätigung, die man bis ins hohe Alter ausüben kann. 10 R.
Sagen Sie's auf Deutsch! 1 Habt ihr nächstes Wochenende schon was vor? 2 Toll, da kommen wir gern. 3 Könnt ihr das nicht mal ausfallen lassen? 4 So ein Pech! 5 Das sagt uns auch nicht immer zu. 6 Also ich hätte davon schon längst genug. 7 Das wäre ganz und gar nicht nach meinem Geschmack. 8 Da hast du schon recht. 9 Aber du darfst auch nicht vergessen . . . 10 Denk doch nur mal . . . 11 Naja, jeder nach seinem Geschmack!

3 Welche Antwort paßt? 1 (*c*) 2 (*a*) 3 (*c*) 4 (*b*) 5 (*b*) 6 (*b*)

Vokabeln
(*a*) 20 (*b*) 15 (*c*) 35 (*d*) 39 (*e*) 37 (*f*) 30 (*g*) 22 (*h*) 29 (*i*) 27 (*j*) 4 (*k*) 26 (*l*) 7 (*m*) 9 (*n*) 31 (*o*) 10 (*p*) 8 (*q*) 2 (*r*) 23 (*s*) 6 (*t*) 25 (*u*) 18 (*v*) 28 (*w*) 33 (*x*) 3

Übungen
1 (*a*) Um sich die Haare zu trocknen. (*b*) Um schwimmen zu gehen. (*c*) Um sich vor der Sonne zu schützen. (*d*) Um Wörter nachzuschlagen. (*e*) Um die Schuhe zu putzen. (*f*) Damit man

morgens rechtzeitig aufsteht. (*g*) Um zu lesen. (*h*) Um die Kleider zu bügeln. (*i*) Um die Wanderwege zu finden. (*j*) Damit man Benzin nachfüllen kann, wenn der Tank plötzlich leer ist.
2 (*a*) Hast du Lust, mit mir zu einem Fußballspiel zu gehen? (*b*) Interessierst du dich denn nicht für Sport? (*c*) Bist du da denn nicht oftmals ziemlich ausgepumpt? (*d*) Hast du jemals daran gedacht, aufzuhören? (*e*) Interessierst du dich auch für Kultur?
3 (*a*) Von wem laßt ihr denn euren Garten herrichten? (*b*) Von wem laßt ihr denn euren Hund impfen? (*c*) Von wem läßt du dir denn einen neuen Hausschlüssel machen? (*d*) Von wem läßt du dir denn deine Anzüge reinigen? (*e*) Von wem laßt ihr denn eure Versicherungspolice verlängern? (*f*) Von wem laßt ihr denn euer Dach reparieren? (*g*) Von wem läßt du dir denn den neuen Modekatalog schicken? (*h*) Von wem läßt du dir denn deine Augen untersuchen? (*i*) Von wem laßt ihr denn eure Stereoanlage überprüfen? (*j*) Von wem läßt du denn deine Mitgliedskarte im Fitneßverein erneuern?
4 (*a*)(vi) (*b*)(v) (*c*)(iv) (*d*)(iii) (*e*)(ix) (*f*)(viii) (*g*)(x) (*h*)(vii) (*i*)(i) (*j*)(ii)
5 (*a*) gestalten (*b*) spontan (*c*) Sport (*d*) Turnier (*e*) steigern (*f*) verplanen (*g*) Vorliebe (*h*) Karte (*i*) bieten (*j*) vorziehen (*k*) Sportplatz

6 (*a*) Wir freuen uns darauf, daß ihr uns besucht. (*b*) Er beschwert sich darüber, daß die Kinder so viel Lärm machen. (*c*) Sie dankte ihm dafür, daß er sich bemüht hatte. (*d*) Ich habe mich darüber aufgeregt, daß mein Nachbar so unverschämt war. (*e*) Er bestand darauf, daß sein Geburtstag groß gefeiert würde. (*f*) Ich warte immer noch darauf, daß er sich entschuldigt. (*g*) Sie war sehr traurig darüber, daß sie ihre Eltern verloren hatte. (*h*) Wir rechnen schon seit langem damit, daß ihr uns einladet. (*i*) Ich habe ihn davon überzeugt, daß meine Aussage richtig war. (*j*) Wir glauben leider nicht mehr daran, daß wir uns mit unseren Freunden versöhnen werden.
7 Ich schwimme seit acht Jahren für einen Club, und bin auch Mitglied in einem Kegelclub.
Manchmal denke ich ja auch, daß es ein bißchen zuviel ist. Aber es hat auch eine Menge Vorteile.
Man trifft viele Leute, hält sich fit, und sieht viele neue Orte, wenn man mit den Clubs auf Turnier geht.
Doch, ich interessiere mich für Kultur, aber ich mag Sport lieber.
Ehrlich gesagt ziehe ich moderne Musik vor, und ich gehe auch gerne ins Kino.

Höraufgabe
1 (*a*) In zwei Tagen. (*b*) Er will den Führerschein machen. (*c*) Man kann die Fahrerlaubnis entzogen bekommen. (*d*) Zwanzig. (*e*) Er will einen Tanzkurs machen. (*f*) Ja. (*g*) Zwei. (*h*) Er will in einen Tanzclub eintreten. (*i*) Er schwimmt für einen Club. (*j*) Er interessiert sich für Kultur. **2** In meinen Ferien werde ich . . . (*a*) ins Schwimmbad gehen (*b*) ins Kino gehen (*c*) einen Tanzkurs machen (*d*) in die Disco gehen (*e*) Tennis spielen (*f*) ein Konzert besuchen/ in ein Konzert gehen (*g*) meine Eltern besuchen (*h*) den Führerschein machen (*i*) Französisch lernen (*j*) einen Kochkurs machen

Lesetexte
1 Was Kinder wirklich sehen: 1 (*a*) In the evening programme. (*b*) Comedies, football, fantasy films, game shows. (*c*) Criticism and worry. (*d*) Yes, they are more relaxed about it. (*e*) She suggests establishing a separate channel for children. (*f*) They ridiculed it. (*g*) 'Sesamstraße', 'Sendung mit der Maus', 'Siebenstein', 'Löwenzahn', 'Logo'. (*h*) She argues that the state channels neglect their duty to educate the children. (*i*) They want to change the times at which the children's programmes are broadcast.

(*j*) He thinks that the term children's programmes is defined by the children's own wishes, not by what adults consider appropriate for children. **2** (*a*) Die CDU-Politikerin Yzer glaubt dagegen, daß die Öffentlich-Rechtlichen ihren speziellen Erziehungs- und Bildungsauftrag hier »nicht erfüllen«.
(*b*) Kinderprogramm ist, was Kinder sehen. (*c*) Den Vorschlag der parlamentarischen Staatssekretärin im Bundesjugendministerium, Cornelia Yzer (31, ledig), einen eigenen Kinderkanal einzurichten, werteten deshalb ARD und ZDF als Botschaft aus dem Tal der Ahnungslosen. (*d*) Kinder gucken nun mal nicht in erster Linie das, was speziell für sie erdacht wurde. (*e*) Das ZDF überlegt unterdessen, wie es die jungen Zuschauer am Sonntag besser erreichen kann. (*f*) Die beliebtesten Kindersendungen laufen im Abendprogramm, meist nach acht. (*g*) Beim ZDF verweist Redaktionsleiter Michael Albus nicht ohne Stolz auf Sendungen wie »Siebenstein«, »Löwenzahn« oder die werktäglichen Nachrichten für Kinder namens »Logo«.

2 Teletext: Drivers must expect damp or wet roads, possibly storms and – on the N2 motorway from Bellinzona South to Rivera – fog with a visibility of 50 metres.

Lektion 6

Aufnahmen
1 Richtig oder falsch? 1R. 2 F. Jochen ist Raucher. 3 F. Sie findet, daß jeder das Recht haben sollte, reine Luft zu atmen. 4 F. Er glaubt, daß beide Unrecht/Recht haben. 5 F. Es ist ihm egal. 6 F. Er will das Rauchen nicht aufgeben. 7 Es ist ihm egal, ob er ein paar Jahre früher stirbt. 8 R. **Sagen Sie's auf Deutsch!** 1 Ganz und gar nicht! 2 Das ist ja ein Witz! 3 Da ist bestimmt was dran. 4 Das ist mir egal. 5 Mir macht das Rauchen unheimlich viel Spaß. 6 Es ist mir schon recht so.

2 Richtig oder falsch? 1 F. Sie findet, daß Rauchen im Restaurant rücksichtslos ist. 2 F. Sie ist der Meinung, daß es beim Essen besonders störend ist. 3 R. 4 R. 5 R. 6 R. 7 F. Aber die Zahl wächst. 8 F. Es wird noch lange dauern, bis die Mehrheit der Leute das akzeptiert.

3 Welche Antwort paßt? 1 (*b*) 2 (*b*) 3 (*a*) 4 (*c*) 5 (*b*)

4 Richtig oder falsch? 1 F. Er hat vor den Gefahren des Alkoholismus gewarnt. 2 F. Die Öffentlichkeit weiß es oftmals nicht. 3 R. 4 F. In Deutschland gibt es etwa anderthalb bis zwei Millionen Alkoholkranke. 5 R. 6 R. 7 F. Aber sie geben einen Betrag aus, der 70 Prozent der Krankenversicherungssumme entspricht. **The genitive:** des Alkoholismus; der deutschen Ärztekammer; des stark zunehmenden Alkoholismus; der Alkoholtoten; der Drogentoten; jahrelangen Alkoholmißbrauchs; der Ärztekammer; alkoholischer Getränke; der Beträge.

Vokabeln
Kollokationen:
1(*o*) 2(*i*) 3(*d*) 4(*s*) 5(*k*) 6(*a*) 7(*p*) 8(*x*) 9(*w*) 10(*c*) 11(*j*) 12(*r*) 13(*l*) 14(*f*) 15(*q*) 16(*h*) 17(*b*) 18(*z*) 19(*v*) 20(*t*) 21(*m*) 22(*y*) 23(*n*) 24(*g*) 25(*u*) 26(*e*)

Übungen
1 (*b*) (*d*) (*f*) (*h*) (*a*) (*i*) (*j*) (*e*) (*g*) (*c*)
2 (*a*) so lautet die Argumentation (*b*) starke Raucher (*c*) der Allgemeinheit (*d*) Raucher (*e*) Sonderabgaben (*f*) Genußmittel (*g*) Alkoholkonsumenten (*h*) Rauchen gefährdet die Gesundheit (*i*) beim Alkoholgenuß
3 (*a*) Das Rauchen in Lokalen wird von vielen Leuten als eine Belästigung empfunden. (*b*) Das Rauchen nach einer Mahlzeit wird von manchen Menschen genossen. (*c*) In allen Restaurants sollte ein totales Rauchverbot verhängt werden. (*d*) Diese Idee wird von der Mehrheit der Leute akzeptiert. (*e*) Es sollten noch viel drastischere

Maßnahmen gegen das Rauchen ergriffen werden. (*f*) Ein Zusammenhang zwischen dem Rauchen und Bluthochdruck kann nicht ausgeschlossen werden. (*g*) Gegen das Rauchen in der eigenen Wohnung kann man aber nichts einwenden. (*h*) Die Gefahren des Alkoholismus werden von den meisten Menschen verkannt. (*i*) Jährlich wird von den Deutschen eine ungeheure Summe für Alkohol und Zigaretten ausgegeben. (*j*) Der Alkoholkonsum sollte aus Gesundheitsgründen verringert werden.

4 (*a*) Bei uns zu Hause trinkt man öfters mal ein Glas Wein zum Essen. (*b*) Deshalb ist man aber noch lange nicht alkoholabhängig. (*c*) Man verkennt allerdings oftmals die Gefahren des Alkohols. (*d*) In Deutschland gibt man viel zu viel Geld für Alkohol und Zigaretten aus. (*e*) Man sollte sich mehr um seine Gesundheit kümmern. (*f*) In Deutschland raucht man auch oft zu viele Zigaretten. (*g*) Man sollte das Rauchen in den Restaurants verbieten. (*h*) Man sollte auch viel mehr Rücksicht auf Nichtraucher nehmen. (*i*) Man sollte Gesetze gegen das Rauchen erlassen. (*j*) Man sollte sein Geld für sinnvollere Dinge ausgeben.

5 Ich habe mir Sorgen um meine Gesundheit gemacht. Ich hatte Bluthochdruck, und als ich beim Arzt war, sagte er, er könne einen Zusammenhang zwischen dem Bluthochdruck und dem Rauchen nicht ausschließen. Außerdem ist mein Mann allergisch gegen Rauch.

Ja, sehr sogar. Ich bin der Meinung, daß das Rauchen in der Öffentlichkeit verboten werden sollte, besonders in Restaurants, wenn Leute essen.

Oh ja, ich bin sogar zwei- oder dreimal rückfällig geworden, aber dann ist in mir die Entschlossenheit gewachsen, das Rauchen aufzugeben. Hast du eigentlich deinen Alkoholkonsum gedrosselt?

War das, weil du dir Sorgen um die Folgeschäden des Alkoholmißbrauches gemacht hast?

6 Liebe Margaret, lieber Charles!; Eure; Euch beiden; Euch; Günther; Ihr; omit **mein Mann**; Du; Margaret; Du; Charles; Ihr beide; mögt; Eures; Euch beiden; Günther; Dich; Margaret; Dir; Charles; Euch beide; Euch beiden; Ihr beide Euch; interessiert; Euch; Eure; Viele Grüße; omit **Reizmann**.

Höraufgabe

1 (*a*) Genußraucherin (*b*) Mußraucher (*c*) Kontaktraucherin **2** (*a*) Wenn er/sie mit Rauchern zusammen ist./ Wenn er/sie seine/ihre Verlegenheit überspielen will./ Wenn er/sie mit Leuten in Kontakt kommen will. (*b*) Wenn er/sie reizbar, nervös oder innerlich unruhig ist./ Wenn er/sie nicht an eine Arbeit herangehen will/ Wenn er/sie den Hunger überbrücken will. (*c*) Zwischen und nach dem Essen. Wenn er/sie ein Hobby betreibt./ Wenn er/sie im Urlaub ist.

Lesetexte

1 Raucher oder Nichtraucher: 1 (*a*) Auf fast allen Verkehrsflughäfen. (*b*) Nein. (c) Ein Modell. (*d*) Daß darin nie geraucht wurde. (*e*) Nein. (*f*) Rund um die Uhr. (*g*) Zum Nulltarif. **2** bietet Ihnen; an fast allen Verkehrsflughäfen; neben vielen Fahrzeugen; in dem garantiert nicht geraucht wurde; kommen Sie zu Deutschlands Autovermietung; fragen Sie nach dem Nichtraucher-Service; an einer unserer über 400 Stationen; im Reisebüro; zum Nulltarif. 3 das Fahrzeug; der Mietwagen; das Auto.

2 Hilfe für Raucher: 1 (*a*) The WHO is quoted to support the advertisement's claim that smoking is a health risk. (*b*) One should seek the assistance of a doctor. **2** (i) Recht (ii) erhalten (iii) nutzen (iv) suchen (v) Hilfe (vi) fordern (vii) Tabakentwöhnung (vii) rauchen

3 Gesundheits-Tips: 1 Honey helps to prevent a headache after too much alcohol. 2 Chewing gum containing nicotine. 3 Even after giving up smoking, the risk of circulatory problems remains for another 15 years at least. 4 It is supposed to reduce the level of cholesterol.

4 Teletext: A smoker's skin is less elastic than a non-smoker's. If you smoke 30 cigarettes a day your skin looks approximately 10 years older than that of someone who doesn't smoke.

Testen Sie Ihr Wissen: R.

Lektion 7

Aufnahmen
1 Welche Antwort paßt? 1(*b*) 2(*b*) 3(*c*) 4(*b*) 5(*b*) 6(*b*)

2 Richtig oder falsch? 1 F. Sie fragt ihn, warum er seine Bierdose auf die Wiese wirft. 2 R. 3 R. 4 F. Er glaubt, daß es sinnlos ist, und zu spät. 5 F. Er will sich in seiner Freizcit amüsieren, und sich nicht auch noch um die Umwelt kümmern. 6 R. 7 R. 8 F. Sie schlägt Roland vor, das zu tun. 9 F. Sie kann ihn nicht davon überzeugen. 10 R.
Sagen Sie's auf Deutsch! 1 Was geht Sie das denn an? 2 Davon habe ich die Nase schon lange voll. 3 Ist doch sowieso alles schon zu spät. 4 Wie sieht denn dann das Leben für unsere Kinder aus? 5 Dieser ganze Quatsch mit . . . 6 Und wenn wir schon von Recycling reden, . . . 7 Wollen Sie mich auf den Arm nehmen? 8 Für Ihre Moralpredigten habe ich keine Zeit. 9 Und jetzt lassen Sie mich in Ruhe!

3 Welche Antwort paßt? 1(*c*) 2(*b*) 3(*c*) 4(*a*) 5(*b*)

Grammatische Hinweise: Die Zahl der Alkoholtoten (Gen./pl/wk); die der Drogentoten (Gen./pl./wk); anderthalb bis zwei Millionen Alkoholkranke (Acc./pl./str.)

Übungen
1 (*a*) Sie wären nicht bereit, mehr Geld für mehr Heizung auszugeben. (*b*) Die Leute möchten zwar Qualität kaufen, sind aber bereit, auf teure Verpackungen zu verzichten, um der Umwelt zu helfen. (*c*) Die Hälfte der Befragten ist nicht bereit, auf den Luxus des Autofahrens zu verzichten. (*d*) Die Leute sind anscheinend umweltbewußter geworden, und sind auch bereit, dafür mehr Geld zu bezahlen. (*e*) Die Befragten sind bereit, auf chemische Mittel zu verzichten, obwohl das Produkt dann nicht so attraktiv aussieht wie eines, das gespritzt ist. (*f*) Sie wären dazu bereit, wenn ihr Wasserverbrauch überdurchschnittlich steigen würde. (*g*) (i) 21 Prozent wären nicht bereit, mehr für überdurchschnittlichen Wasserverbrauch zu bezahlen. (ii) 21 Prozent wären nicht bereit, einmal pro Jahr DM 100 für die Aufforstung geschädigter Wälder zu bezahlen. (*h*) 70 Prozent der Befragten wären bereit, an Sonn- und Feiertagen ihr Auto stehenzulassen. (*i*) 77 Prozent der Befragten würden einmal pro Jahr 100 DM für die Aufforstung geschädigter Wälder bezahlen.
2 (*a*) Stimmt es, daß in Deutschland jetzt das Recycling ganz streng geregelt ist? (*b*) Das kann ich mir aber überhaupt nicht vorstellen. Wie soll denn das funktionieren? (*c*) Und machen denn die Leute auch mit? (*d*) Und wie wird denn die Bevölkerung über diese neuen Maßnahmen informiert?
3 (*a*) Lassen Sie/ Laßt Verpackungen im Supermarkt zurück. (*b*) Kaufen Sie/ Kauft Glasbehälter statt Plastikbecher. (*c*) Sammeln Sie/ Sammelt Biomüll in der braunen Tonne. (*d*) Bringen Sie/ Bringt Sondermüll auf den Sammelplatz. (*e*) Befolgen Sie/ Befolgt die neuen Bestimmungen bezüglich der Müllsortierung. (*f*) Klären Sie/ Klärt die Bevölkerung über die neuen Bestimmungen auf. (*g*) Waschen Sie/ Wascht Joghurtbecher aus. (*h*) Verwenden Sie/ Verwendet Jutesäckchen oder Einkaufskörbe anstatt Plastiktüten. (*i*) Werfen Sie/ Werft Dosen in den

Weißblechcontainer. (*j*) Entsorgen Sie/ Entsorgt Giftmüll besonders vorsichtig.
4 (*a*) Papier muß recycelt werden. (*b*) Die Bevölkerung muß informiert werden. (*c*) Aufklärungsblätter müssen verteilt werden. (*d*) Die Müllsortierung muß gesetzlich geregelt werden. (*e*) Die Umwelt muß geschützt werden. (*f*) Die Kinder müssen in der Schule aufgeklärt werden. (*g*) Die Parks müssen saubergehalten werden. (*h*) Für Umweltsünden müssen saftige Geldstrafen gezahlt werden. (*i*) Der Müll muß getrennt gesammelt werden. (*j*) Die Mülltonnen müssen im Wechsel vierzehntägig abgeholt werden.
5 (*a*) David besiegt den Riesen. (*b*) Der Bulle verletzt den Bauern. (*c*) Der Richter glaubt dem Zeugen. (*d*) Der Verkäufer widerspricht dem Kunden. (*e*) Die Schafe folgen dem Hirten. (*f*) Der Reiseleiter hilft der Amerikanerin. (*g*) Die Polizisten verhaften den Demonstranten. (*h*) Das Mädchen liebt die Puppe.
6 (*a*) Unterschiede (*b*) regional unterschiedlich geregelt (*c*) gesetzlich geregelt (*d*) Aufklärungsblätter und Initiativen (*e*) macht mit (*f*) Müllhalden (*g*) ersticken (*h*) entsorgt (*i*) vertraut (*j*) vorstellen (*k*) im Wechsel (*l*) vierzehntägig
7 Also, es gibt eine braune Tonne für Biomüll, eine blaue für Papier, und einen Plastiksack für alle Verpackungen, die den Grünen Punkt haben. Alles wird im Wechsel vierzehntägig abgeholt.

Ja, die meisten Leute machen mit. Wenn man nicht mitmacht, muß man saftige Strafen zahlen. Es gibt ja auch Aufklärungsblätter und so weiter, um die Bürger zu informieren. Gibt es eigentlich große Unterschiede zwischen Deutschland und England?

Ich glaube, daß Recycling eine sehr sinnvolle Sache ist – denn wenn wir jetzt nichts für die Umwelt tun, wie sieht dann die Welt für unsere Kinder aus?

Natürlich, aber es ist zumindest ein Anfang gemacht.
8 (*a*) Das ist regional unterschiedlich geregelt. (*b*) Die Bestimmungen sind vom Staat festgelegt. (*c*) Die deutschen Wälder sind schon seit langem geschädigt. (*d*) Die Umweltverschmutzung ist gesetzlich untersagt. (*e*) Das Betreten der Baustelle ist strengstens verboten. (*f*) Das Verschmutzen der Meere ist nicht mehr erlaubt. (*g*) Einige Umweltschutzmaßnahmen sind in England noch nicht eingeführt. (*h*) Das Autofahren ist bis jetzt noch gestattet. (*i*) Die Gefahren der Luftverschmutzung sind heute weitgehend erforscht.

Höraufgabe
1 (*a*) Sie findet, daß in Canterbury zu wenig für die Umwelt getan wird, obwohl es dringend notwendig ist. (*b*) Er zeigt an, daß die Verpackung des Produkts/ das Produkt selbst wiederverwertbar, beziehungsweise verbrennbar ist, ohne schädliche Stoffe abzugeben. (*c*) Renate hat es noch nie gesehen. (*d*) Renate glaubt, daß Deutschland mehr für die Umwelt tun kann, weil es reicher ist als England. (*e*) Sie sagt, daß in Hamburg besonders viel für die Umwelt getan wird: es gibt Sammelstellen für Altglas, Altpapier, Altbatterien; außerdem wird Müll getrennt, und es gibt Biotonnen. (*f*) Sie glaubt, daß der Staat mehr tun muß, um die Bürger zum Umweltschutz zu erziehen. (*g*) Sie findet, daß die Engländer viel zu wenig an die Umwelt denken. (*h*) Sie werden auch gesammelt, aber die Leute haben die Möglichkeit, sich alte Sachen kostenlos zu holen. (*i*) Sie werden bis jetzt besser in England entsorgt. **2** (*a*) Eigentlich müßte mehr gemacht werden. (*b*) Eigentlich müßte alles getrennt gesammelt werden. (*c*) Eigentlich müßte so viel wie möglich wiederverwertet werden. (*d*) Eigentlich müßten Einkaufskörbe verwendet werden. (*e*) Eigentlich müßten Gläser statt Plastikbecher gekauft werden. (*f*) Eigentlich müßte mehr mit dem Fahrrad

gefahren werden. (*g*) Eigentlich müßte mehr zu Fuß gegangen werden. (*h*) Eigentlich müßte auf das Autofahren verzichtet werden.

Lesetexte

1 Der Umweltschutz: 1 (*a*)(v) (*b*)(vi) (*c*)(iv) (*d*)(ii) (*e*)(iii) (*f*)(i) **2** (*a*) Umweltschutz heißt umdenken und natürliche Reserven sparen. (*b*) Sie sind so schädlich, weil sie schon bei der Herstellung wertvolle Rohstoffe verbrauchen, und zu schnell weggeworfen werden. (*c*) Man soll Jutesäckchen oder einen Einkaufskorb verwenden. (*d*) Man soll die Verpackungen kaufen, die unschädlich oder wiederverwertbar sind. (*e*) Wenn man konsequent recycelt, kann man bis zu 80 Prozent Müll einsparen.

2 Wertstoffsammlung: 1 (*a*) Man erkennt es am Grünen Punkt auf den Verpackungen. (*b*) Sie ist umsonst. (*c*) Man kann sich bei der Kommunalverwaltung oder bei einem Entsorgungsunternehmen informieren. (*d*) Man soll überflüssige Verpackungen vermeiden, oder Mehrwegverpackungen wählen. (*e*) Ja, sie ist teilweise schon um 15 Prozent zurückgegangen. (*f*) Das dürfen in Zukunft nur Recyclingunternehmen, die vom Technischen Überwachungsverein kontrolliert werden, machen. (*g*) Viele Unternehmen setzen jetzt schon weniger und besser recycelfähiges Material ein. **2** (*a*)(iii) (*b*)(i) (*c*)(ii)

3 Teletext: 1 To take back goods such as televisions, computers and refrigerators. 2 The chairman of the Federal Committee for the Environment, von Geldern. 3 It will make them 2–3 per cent dearer. 4 None as yet. 5 To return goods (to the manufacturers).

Testen Sie Ihr Wissen: 450 Jahre; 50%+; 25%.

Lektion 8

Aufnahmen

1 Richtig oder falsch? 1 F. Sein Vater ist Engländer. 2 R. 3 R. 4 F. Sie hat ihm viel über die typisch deutschen Eigenschaften erzählt. 5 R. 6 F. Er hat gemerkt, daß vieles nicht ganz so ist, wie seine Mutter gesagt hat. 7 R. 8 R. 9 F. Er glaubt, daß sie manchmal zu ordentlich und sauber sind. 10 R.

2 Welche Antwort paßt? 1(*c*) 2(*b*) 3(*c*) 4(*b*) 5(*c*) 6(*b*) 7(*a*)

Sagen Sie's auf Deutsch! 1 Nimm doch nur mal die Ausbildung in Deutschland. 2 Soviel Wert wird auf Qualifikationen gelegt. 3 Die Kehrseite der Medaille ist allerdings der Leistungsdruck. 4 Ich weiß nicht, wohin das noch führen soll. 5 Ich glaube, daß die Deutschen im allgemeinen ihre Freizeitaktivitäten viel systematischer angehen. 6 Da ist sicher ein Körnchen Wahrheit dran. 7 Du erscheinst mir nicht wie der typische Deutsche. 8 Die Ausnahme/Ausnahmen bestätigt/bestätigen die Regel.

3 Richtig oder falsch? 1 F. Er lebt schon seit 26 Jahren in England. 2 R. 3 F. Er bemüht sich, seine deutsche Sprache und Kultur zu bewahren, und auch seinen Kindern nahezubringen. 4 F. Es passiert nur manchmal. 5 F. Sie haben nur einmal Probleme gehabt. 6 R. 7 F. Er hat nur einmal Probleme gehabt. 8 R. 9 F. Man sollte die Erfahrungen zwar nicht vergessen, aber auch nicht auf die heutige Generation übertragen. 10 R. 11 R. 12 R.

Übungen

1 habe gehabt; sei geworden; registriert werde; sei beobachtet worden; getrunken habe; führe; verliere; beginne; sei.

2 Er glaubte/ meinte/ dachte/ war der Meinung, . . . (*a*) daß alle Deutschen besonders fleißig und arbeitsam wären. (*b*) daß man in Deutschland jeden Tag um 6.00 Uhr aufstünde/aufstehen würde. (*c*) daß alle Deutschen blonde Haare und blaue Augen hätten/haben würden. (*d*) daß in Deutschland die Schule um 7.00 Uhr anfinge/anfangen würde. (*e*) daß alle

Deutschen ordnungsliebend und sauber wären. (*f*) daß in Deutschland die Straßen und Häuser immer viel gepflegter aussähen/aussehen würden. (*g*) daß die Deutschen bei gewissen Anlässen immer viel größeren Aufwand betrieben/betreiben würden als die Engländer. (*h*) daß man in Deutschland alles viel systematischer anginge/angehen würde als in England. (*i*) daß die Deutschen viel Bier tränken/trinken würden. (*j*) daß die Deutschen arrogant wären.

3 (*d*) (*b*) (*i*) (*j*) (*a*) (*f*) (*g*) (*c*) (*h*) (*e*)

4 Gabriele Henkel sagt, (*a*) ihr Name sei typisch deutsch. (Sie sagt,) Wenn sie die deutsche Nationalhymne höre, sei sie froh, daß nicht mehr die erste Strophe gesungen werde. (*b*) . . . daß es absurd sei, daß sie in allen Ländern mehr Freunde hätten als in den neuen Bundesländern, aber daß sich das ändern werde./ Dr P. Gauweiler sagt, (*a*) es sei typisch deutsch, schlecht über den Deutschen zu reden. (Er sagt,) Er rede auch manchmal schlecht über sie. (*b*) . . . daß er Freunde, Bekannte und Kollegen aus jenem Teil Deutschlands jeden Monat sehe, daß ihr Auftreten und ihre Formulierungen nach wie vor gepflegter, ordentlicher und gesetzter und damit im guten Sinne des Wortes deutscher seien als bei ihnen./ Gloria von Thurn & Taxis sagt, (*a*) typisch deutsch sei für sie ein korrekter und pünktlicher Mensch. (Sie sagt), Sie selbst liebe auch die Ordnung und Genauigkeit. (Sie sagt), Die Deutschen seien das selbstkritischste Volk der Welt. (Sie sagt,) Wegen ihrer Vergangenheit trauten sie sich nicht, Nationalstolz zu zeigen, und in jedem anderen Land sei dies absurd. (*b*) . . . daß sie sie vor einem Jahr kennengelernt habe, und daß sie gestreßter seien./ Peter Hoffmann sagt, (*a*) für ihn sei Helmut Kohl typisch deutsch. Er kümmere sich um deutsche Angelegenheiten und habe einen Hang zur Perfektion. (Er sagt,) Typisch deutsch an den Deutschen sei, daß sie meistens über sich selbst meckerten. (Er sagt,) Er meckere nie. (Er sagt,) Er verstehe die Furcht der Deutschen vor Ausländern nicht, und er habe keine schlechten Erfahrungen mit Ausländern gemacht. (*b*) . . . daß er noch keine Freunde dort habe.

5 (*a*) arbeitsam; (*b*) fleißig; (*c*) sauber; (*d*) gründlich; (*e*) Eigenschaften; (*f*) Klischees; (*g*) Nationalität; (*h*) Gründlichkeit; (*i*) viel strenger geregelt; (*j*) viel systematischer; (*k*) Vorurteile; (*l*) ankämpfen; (*m*) antideutsche Ressentiments (*n*) Greueltaten; (*o*) vergessen; (*p*) heutige Generation; (*q*) ihre Hand dafür ins Feuer legen; (*r*) Gruppierungen; (*s*) erlangen.

6 (*a*) -e (*b*) -em (*c*) -er (*d*) -en (*e*) -en (*f*) -em (*g*) -er (*h*) -en (*i*) -en (*j*) -es (*k*) -e

7 Es wurde gestern berichtet, daß die Stadt Freiburg . . . eingeladen habe; habe geäußert; folgen würden; wolle; gelegt werde.

8 Ich habe mich weitgehend an die englische Lebensart angepaßt, obwohl ich mich bemüht habe, meine deutsche Kultur und Sprache nicht zu vergessen.

Ich weiß, daß sie existieren, aber glücklicherweise sind sie mehr die Ausnahme als die Regel. Manchmal fragen mich die Leute über die typisch deutschen Eigenschaften, wie zum Beispiel die deutsche Gründlichkeit, oder ob die Deutschen wirklich so früh aufstehen und so hart arbeiten.

Meistens lache ich und sage, daß ich sehr skeptisch bin, was diese typisch deutschen Eigenschaften anbelangt. Ich glaube, man kann sie auch in Menschen anderer Nationalität entdecken.

Ich glaube, daß die englische Presse manchmal Hetzkampagnen gegen Deutschland und die Deutschen führt, um sie für das verantwortlich zu machen, was in England im Argen ist.

Ich denke, daß die Engländer im

allgemeinen den Deutschen gegenüber positiv eingestellt sind, und daß diese negative Haltung von der Presse hochgespielt wird.

Höraufgabe
1 Deutschland und die Deutschen:
1 sauber und korrekt; früh aufstehen und soviel arbeiten; deutsche Gründlichkeit; Sauerkraut und Bratwürste; Schweinebraten mit Klößen. England und die Engländer: kalt und verregnet; *steak and kidney pie*; *fish and chips*; kühl und reserviert; ihre Art von Humor.
2 . . . daß England ein so kaltes und verregnetes Land (1) **sei** und man dort nichts außer *steak and kidney pie* zu essen (2) **bekäme**./ . . . sie (3) **seien** so kühl und reserviert, daß man nie mit ihnen in Kontakt (4) **käme** . . ./ . . . daß die heutige Generation der Deutschen nicht dafür verantwortlich (5) **gemacht werden könne**, und daß (6) **sich** Deutschland **verändert hätte**./ . . . daß diese rechtsextremen Gruppen nicht nur ein deutsches Problem (7) **seien**, und daß England auch Probleme mit der Integration seiner ethnischen Minderheiten (8) **habe**./ . . . daß alle Deutschen so sauber und korrekt (9) **seien**, so früh (10) **aufstehen** und so viel **arbeiten würden**./ . . . die Deutschen (11) **würden sich** von Bratwürsten mit Sauerkraut und Schweinebraten mit Klößen **ernähren**!

Lesetext
Teil 1: 1 Nein, nicht sehr erfolgreich, trotz des vielen Geldes, was ausgegeben wird. 2 Man sollte nie vergessen, die Hand zu geben. 3 Man sollte immer seinen Nachnamen angeben. 4 Buttercremekuchen. 5 Nie mit Vornamen, immer mit Nachnamen. 6 Man sollte keine Witze über das Ozonloch, die Lance-Raketen, Autos oder Michael Gorbatschow machen. Man kann jedoch Witze über Helmut Kohl machen. 7 Weil es so viele Fremdworte in der deutschen Sprache gibt. 8 Sie halten sie für harmlos. 9 Ihre Gesundheit. 10 Die Fußgängerregeln. 11 Weil Unpünktlichkeit als Zeichen mangelnder Selbstdisziplin gewertet wird. 12 Er macht Spaß, indem er verallgemeinert. 13 [Your own opinion is asked here!]

Teil 2: 1 11.(*d*) 12.(*i*) 13.(*c*) 14.(*e*) 15.(*j*) 16.(*h*) 17.(*a*) 18.(*g*) 19.(*b*) 20.(*f*)
2 (mögliche Lösungen) (*a*) Die Engländer kümmern sich nicht so sehr um Müllentsorgung wie die Deutschen. (*b*) Die Engländer sprechen öfters über den Krieg als die Deutschen. (*c*) Die Engländer haben nicht so viele Vorschriften wie die Deutschen. (*d*) Die Engländer sind toleranter als die Deutschen. (e) Die Engländer haben nicht so viele traditionelle Veranstaltungen wie die Deutschen. (f) Bei Einladungen bringen die Engländer selten Blumen mit, wohingegen die Deutschen fast immer Blumen mitbringen. (g) Der Verkehr in England ist nicht so streng geregelt wie in Deutschland. (h) Die Bahnschaffner in England sind genauso nett wie die in Deutschland. (i) Die Deutschen fahren auf der Autobahn immer schneller als die Engländer.

Lektion 9

Aufnahmen
1 Richtig oder falsch? 1 F. Die Regierung muß viel mehr unternehmen. 2 R. 3 F. Die Regierung liefert nicht genug Informationen zum Thema Umweltschutz und Energiesparen. 4 F. Ela glaubt, daß man in Zukunft auf Atomkraft verzichten sollte, und Biomasse mehr nutzen sollte. 5 R. 6 F. Man kann zuhause sehr viel Energie sparen. 7 R 8 F. Sie sind der Meinung, daß weniger oder gar keine Autos besser für die Umwelt sind. 9 R.

2 Richtig oder falsch? 1 F. Er ist dafür, weil das Uran so billig ist. 2 R. 3

F. Es ist mit enormen Kosten verbunden. 4 R. 5 R. 6 F. Er glaubt, daß Atomkraft viel sicherer ist als andere Energiequellen. 7 R. 8 F. Sie können es nicht ausschließen. 9 F. Sie können sie nicht verhindern. 10 R. 11 R. 12 F. Sie ist zwar relativ umweltfreundlich, aber trotzdem gibt es Risiken, zum Beispiel durch Lecks. 13 R. 14 R. 15 R. **Sagen Sie's auf Deutsch!** 1 Das hört sich ja sehr positiv an. 2 Und in bezug auf das Personal . . . 3 Das mag schon sein. 4 Nützt das alles nichts mehr. 5 Man weiß doch, daß . . . 6 Und abgesehen davon . . . 7 Sicher, es gibt Nachteile.

3 Welche Antwort paßt? 1(*c*) 2(*b*) 3(*a*) 4(*b*) 5(*c*) 6(*a*)

Übungen

1 (*a*) Schäfer (S) (*b*) Töpfer (T) (*c*)T (*d*)S (*e*)S (*f*)T (*g*)T (*h*)T (*i*)S (*j*)S

2 (*a*) Bist du eigentlich für oder gegen die Kernenergie? (*b*) Und was hältst du von diesen sogenannten erneuerbaren Energien? (*c*) Wie sparst du denn zuhause Energie? (*d*) Denkst du auch daran, Wasser zu sparen? (*e*) Und was hältst du davon, auf das Autofahren zu verzichten, um Energie zu sparen?

3 Die am häufigsten vorkommenden Versionen sind: (*a*) Wenn ich nicht erkältet wäre, würde ich ins Kino gehen wollen. (*b*) Wenn es mir dann nicht zu heiß wäre, würde ich im Sommer nach Ägypten fahren. (*c*) Wenn es mir nicht zu teuer wäre, würde ich im Stadtzentrum wohnen. (*d*) Wenn sie sich um die Dritte Welt kümmerte/ kümmern würde, würde ich mich mit der Politik dieser Partei identifizieren. (*e*) Wenn sie nicht von Extremisten organisiert wäre, würde ich mich für die Aktion gegen Tierversuche engagieren. (*f*) Wenn die Bevölkerung radikale Forderungen stellte/ stellen würde, würde die Regierung einschneidende Veränderungen vornehmen. (*g*) Wenn sie für einen Kurswechsel einträten/ eintreten würde, würde ich mit diesen Demonstranten sympathisieren. (*h*) Wenn sie die natürlichen Lebensräume verschiedener Tierarten nicht zerstörten/ nicht zerstören würden/ wäre ich von der Idee von erneuerbaren Wasser- und Gezeitenenergie begeistert/ würde ich . . . begeistert sein.

4 (*a*) (i) Wenn die Bürger aufgeklärt werden, dann können sie mehr für die Umwelt tun. (ii) Wenn die Bürger aufgeklärt würden, dann könnten sie mehr für die Umwelt tun. (iii) Wenn die Bürger aufgeklärt worden wären, dann hätten sie mehr für die Umwelt tun können. (*b*) (i) Wenn die Leute nicht demonstrieren, dann kann die Regierung nichts tun. (ii) Wenn die Leute nicht demonstrieren würden, dann könnte die Regierung nichts tun. (iii) Wenn die Leute nicht demonstriert hätten, dann hätte die Regierung nichts tun können. (*c*) (i) Wenn alle Menschen mitmachen, dann kann man viel erreichen. (ii) Wenn alle Menschen mitmachen würden, dann könnte man viel erreichen. (iii) Wenn alle Menschen mitgemacht hätten, dann hätte man viel erreichen können. (*d*) (i) Wenn man erneuerbare Energien nutzt, kann man langfristig auf Kernenergie verzichten. (ii) Wenn man erneuerbare Energien nutzen würde, könnte man langfristig auf Kernenergie verzichten. (iii) Wenn man erneuerbare Energien genutzt hätte, hätte man langfristig auf Kernenergie verzichten können. (*e*) (i) Wenn man Vorsichtsmaßnahmen trifft, kann man Unglücksfälle verhindern. (ii) Wenn man Vorsichtsmaßnahmen treffen würde, könnte man Unglücksfälle verhindern. (iii) Wenn man Vorsichtsmaßnahmen getroffen hätte, hätte man Unglücksfälle verhindern können. (*f*) (i) Wenn die Regierung mehr für Forschung ausgibt, kann man erneuerbare Energien besser nutzen. (ii) Wenn die Regierung mehr für Forschung ausgeben würde, könnte man erneuerbare Energien besser nutzen. (iii)

Wenn die Regierung mehr für Forschung ausgegeben hätte, hätte man erneuerbare Energien besser nutzen können.

5 Support for EC Steel: The member states of the European Community are aiming to reach speedy agreement on a plan for the recovery of the steel industry. In the discussions held by the ministers and secretaries of state responsible for the crisis-ridden industry there was unanimity on Tuesday on the need to achieve by next February clarity on the aid programme presented by the EC Commission last week. There were no reservations concerning the intention to boost by around 475 million marks to 900 million marks the EC finances ear-marked for social welfare. The debate was overshadowed by Spain's application for consent to subsidies to the tune of almost nine million marks for two of its steelworks. On Tuesday, only the Italian representative supported Spain's request. Italy has in the past already on a number of occasions sought approval for subsidies to the state-owned steel industry, irrespective of the ban on intervention which has since 1986 once again been fully in force in the Community.

6 Ich bin sehr dafür. Ich mache schon eine ganze Menge, um Energie zu sparen, und ich beabsichtige jetzt, Solarzellen installieren zu lassen.

Ich mache die meisten Dinge in der Küche mit der Hand, und habe sehr wenige elektrische Geräte. Außerdem dusche ich statt zu baden, um Wasser zu sparen, und benutze die Geschirrspülmaschine nur, wenn ich Gäste habe.

Da hast du recht, aber ich finde, es ist wichtig, daß die Bürger auch etwas tun. Ich bin auch der Meinung, daß mehr Geld für die Erforschung und Nutzung alternativer Energiequellen ausgegeben werden sollte.

Ich glaube, es ist sehr gefährlich, aber auch sehr schwierig, im Moment ohne Kernkraft auszukommen. Trotzdem bin ich dafür, daß sie in Zukunft abgeschafft werden sollte.

7 (*a*) Maßnahme (*b*) teuer (*c*) Nutzung (*d*) Kosten (*e*) Nachfrage (*f*) Solar (*g*) Nachteil (*h*) Atomkraft (*i*) Energie (*j*) senken (*k*) Autofahren

Höraufgabe

1 Was die Bürger tun können: (*b*) ganz auf ein Auto verzichten (*c*) Mitfahrzentralen in Anspruch nehmen (*d*) Fahrgemeinschaften bilden (*e*) öfters auch mal zu Fuß gehen (*f*) mit dem Fahrrad fahren (*g*) öffentliche Verkehrsmittel benutzen (*h*) *Park & Ride* benutzen/ Was der Staat tun kann: (*b*) höhere Steuern erheben (*c*) Fuß- und Radfahrwege noch stärker ausbauen (*d*) die Möglichkeiten für die Bürger attraktiver machen (*e*) viel stärker subventionieren (f) viel mehr Geld investieren, um alternative Möglichkeiten weiterzuentwickeln

Lesetexte

1 Phantasie oder Wirklichkeit: 1 (*a*) Das gesamte Weltklima könnte sich ändern, und man könnte in Deutschland wilde Tiere sehen. (*b*) Der Ausstoß von Kohlendioxid muß verringert werden. (*c*) Die Kernkraft erzeugt keine Treibhausgase. (*d*) Sie verwenden modernste Technologien. (*e*) Ja. **2** die Vorstellung – vorstellen; das Schwitzen – schwitzen; das Wanken – wanken; das Leben – leben; der Ausstoß – ausstoßen; die Nutzung – nutzen; der Schutz – schützen; die Unterstützung – unterstützen.

2 Erdgas als relativ umweltfreundliche Energiequelle:
1 (*a*) Ja, weil es wenig Schadstoffe und CO_2 freisetzt. (*b*) Ruhrgas verbessert die Gastechnik. (*c*) Indem sie die neuen Brenner verwenden. (*d*) Aus Deutschland, Holland, Rußland, aus der

norwegischen und dänischen Nordsee. (*e*) Wegen der hohen Produktions- und Transportkosten. (*f*) Nein, nur wenn sie es benötigen. (*g*) Mit Hilfe von technischen Anlagen und gaswirtschaftlichen Möglichkeiten. (*h*) Dadurch, daß Ruhrgas sich um Energieeinsparungs- und Umweltschutzlösungen kümmert.
2 (*a*) wegen (*b*) Anlagen (*c*) beziehen (*d*) vor allem (*e*) freizusetzen (*f*) benötigt (*g*) bringen ihm bei (*h*) bekommen (*i*) Noten (*j*) schonen

3 Anzeige: 1 Are Germany's nuclear power stations really safe electricity producers? Have the operators really taken precautions against every conceivable danger for human beings and for the environment? 2 By convincing yourself. German nuclear power stations are looking for visitors. 3 You will be told the nearest information centre and times when you will be welcome to visit. 4 Write to the address given in the advertisement.

Lektion 10

Aufnahmen
1 Teil 1: Richtig oder falsch? 1 F. Sie will ihre Vergangenheit nicht verstecken. 2 R. 3 F. Sie fühlt sich als Leipzigerin. 4 F. Deutschland ist ihm egal. 5 R. 6 R. 7 F. Sie arbeitet auf dem Arbeitsamt. **Teil 2: Fragen zum Text** 1 Robert macht gleichzeitig Abitur und eine Lehre als Drucker. 2 Er findet es nicht gut, daß Fächer wie Ethik und Philosophie abgeschafft werden. 3 Es hat ihr gefallen, daß man ein geregeltes Leben und einen sicheren Arbeitsplatz hatte. 4 Ja, weil sie nur die guten Seiten gesehen haben. 5 Sie waren geschockt darüber, weil sie geglaubt haben, daß die Staatsführung alles richtig macht. **Teil 3: Fragen zum Text** 1 Sie hätten das Wirtschaftssystem geändert, und das Leistungsprinzip eingeführt. 2 Das Hauptproblem war, daß sich keiner für irgendetwas verantwortlich gefühlt hat. 3 Er hat gemerkt, daß keiner richtig gearbeitet hat. 4 Er kritisiert, daß jeder zwar über das System geklagt hat, aber keiner etwas getan hat, um die Situation zu ändern. **Sagen Sie's auf Deutsch!** 1 Was soll das? 2 Spielt das denn alles keine Rolle mehr? 3 Man wußte, wo es langgeht. 4 Es muß ja schließlich jeder merken . . ., wenn er Mist gebaut hat. 5 Das ging voll in die Hose. 6 Wir haben nur Gammeln gelernt. 7 Man findet sich ab. 8 Was habt ihr dagegen, Deutsche zu sein?

2 Richtig oder falsch? 1 F. Er war noch nie für eine Wiedervereinigung. 2 R. 3 F. Er glaubt, daß es gar keine Gründe dafür gibt. 4 R. 5 R. 6 F. Er nennt nur ein Beispiel, um zu zeigen, daß die beiden Teile Deutschlands nicht unbedingt zusammengehören. 7 R. 8 R. 9 R. 10 F. Er hat Nachteile dadurch gehabt, daß die Mietspreise in Marburg gestiegen sind und Zimmer schwerer zu bekommen sind.

Übungen
1 (*a*) Empfängt Professor Schmidt erst morgen den Präsidenten? Nein, er hat ihn schon gestern empfangen. (*b*) Fährt Hans erst morgen um 5.00 Uhr los? Nein, er ist schon gestern um 5.00 Uhr losgefahren. (*c*) Nimmt Franziska erst morgen am Kongreß teil? Nein sie hat schon gestern daran teilgenommen. (*d*) Mißt Bernd erst morgen den Benzinverbrauch? Nein, er hat ihn schon gestern gemessen. (*e*) Unterschreibt der Direktor erst morgen den Vertrag? Nein, er hat ihn schon gestern unterschrieben. (*f*) Tritt Herr Göller erst morgen aus der Partei aus? Nein, er ist schon gestern aus der Partei/ daraus/ ausgetreten. (*g*) Übersetzen unsere Studenten erst morgen den neuen Text? Nein, sie haben schon gestern den neuen Text übersetzt. (*h*) Folgen Heike und Werner erst morgen ihren Eltern nach Spanien? Nein, sie sind ihnen schon gestern dorthin/ nach Spanien/ gefolgt.

2 (i) daran (ii) mit (iii) über (iv) bei (v) darüber (vi) um (vii) mit (viii) auf (ix) danach (x) darauf (xi) mit (xii) darauf (xiii) bei (xiv) für

3 (*e*) (*b*) (*g*) (*f*) (*a*) (*d*) (*j*) (*h*) (*c*) (*i*)

4 (*a*) Ich weiß, daß er vor dem eigenen Haus nicht hat parken dürfen. (*b*) Ich weiß, daß sie nach ihrem Unfall wieder laufen lernen mußte. (*c*) Ich weiß, daß er sich im Oktober hat scheiden lassen. (*d*) Ich weiß, daß er eigentlich mit uns hat essen gehen wollen. (*e*) Ich weiß, daß er sich nicht die Haare schneiden lassen wollte.

5 Turkish worker allowed to stay: KARLSRUHE. A Turk, threatened with deportation on account of two drink-driving convictions, has won a partial victory from the Federal Constitutional Court. In response to the 38-year-old Turk's complaint concerning an infringement of the Constitution, the Karlsruhe (Constitutional Court) judges rescinded the decisions of the Admininstrative Court in Neustadt on the Weinstraße (Lit. wine route) and of the Higher Administrative Court of the *Land* Rhineland Palatinate which had confirmed the 'immediate deportation order' issued by the District Authority. The car-worker, who had been fined and lost his licence because of blood alcohol levels of 164 and 147 mgs (per 100 mls of blood) respectively, had according to his own information spent approximately 10 000 marks (£4,200) in bringing his family over to the Federal Republic. The Constitutional Court decided that the requirement to leave the country immediately infringed the complainant's right to 'effective legal protection' as guaranteed by the Basic Law.

6 Professor Meier ist der Meinung, daß neben all den schlechten sich heute eine gute Prognose stellen lasse. . . . trügten . . . werde . . . werde . . . lägen. . . . zeigten . . . sei . . . sei . . .koche . . . werde . . . sei . . . werde . . . hätten. . . . würden . . . stünden [ständen] . . . würden . . . habe.

7 (*a*) fühlen sich (*b*) Wiedervereinigung (*c*) Vergangenheit (*d*) gleichen Rechte (*e*) fremde Gesetze (*f*) die Ausbildungslehrgänge (*g*) die Gymnasien (*h*) die Wirtschaft (*i*) an die DDR geglaubt (*j*) überzeugt davon (*k*) die Staatsführung (*l*) stolz auf (*m*) geändert (*n*) wurde eingeführt (*o*) ein Schock (*p*) einen sicheren Job

8 Ich fühle mich eigentlich eher schlecht, weil ich glaube, daß man als Ostdeutscher nicht die gleichen Rechte hat wie die Westdeutschen. Außerdem kriegen wir fremde Gesetze übergestülpt. Eigentlich fühle ich mich nicht als Deutsche; Deutschland ist mir egal.

Und was hab' ich davon? Vieles an der DDR war gar nicht so schlecht, man wußte, wo's langgeht, und einen sicheren Job hatte man auch.

Ich war schon von Anfang an dagegen. Ich weiß nicht, warum die Leute unbedingt eine Wiedervereinigung wollten, und warum die DDR nicht einfach weiterexistieren konnte, als ein separater Staat. Schließlich hat sich dieser Staat ja auch 40 Jahre lang unabhängig von der Bundesrepublik entwickelt. Und ich glaube nicht, daß die gemeinsame Sprache ein Argument für die Wiedervereinigung ist.

Da hast du schon recht. Ich hätte zuallererst das Wirtschaftssystem geändert und das Leistungsprinzip eingeführt. Aber ich glaube auch, daß man die momentanen wirtschaftlichen und sozialen Probleme, die durch die Wiedervereinigung entstanden sind, hätte vermeiden können, wenn die DDR weiterexistiert hätte. Dann hätte man auch freundschaftliche Beziehungen und Kooperation zwischen den zwei Staaten aufbauen können.

Höraufgaben

1 Professor Dr Rolf Herwig: die Wiedervereinigung: 1 (*a*) 51 Jahre (*b*)

verheiratet (*c*) Dozent für Anglistik und Amerikanistik (*d*) deutsch (*e*) Jena
2 (*a*) Es war für sie nur ein Traum. Sie hofften, daß sie als Rentner nach Westdeutschland fahren könnten. (*b*) Sie waren uneingeschränkt dafür. (*c*) Sie sind nach Westdeutschland gefahren, nach Bayern. (*d*) Er war in Marburg, auf einer Konferenz. (*e*) Es war der Tag der Wiedervereinigung. (*f*) Es gab Kämpfe zwischen links- und rechtsradikalen Gruppen. (*g*) Die Zahl der Arbeitslosen in Ostdeutschland ist drastisch gestiegen. (*h*) Die Situation ist viel gespannter und instabiler geworden. (*i*) Die meisten Menschen haben die Wiedervereinigung schon fast vergessen oder sehen sie als ein Ereignis der Vergangenheit an. (*j*) Er sieht die Wiedervereinigung als eines der wichtigsten Ereignisse seines Lebens an.

2 Eine Abiturientin aus Ostdeutschland zur Wiedervereinigung: 1 Sie war nicht besonders glücklich, weil sie an die Probleme in der Zukunft gedacht hat. 2 Daß sie in England studieren kann; die Reisefreiheit; die starke Währung. 3 Das Überstülpen der westlichen Werte; die hohe Arbeitslosigkeit; die Schließung der Kindergärten; die Verschlechterung des Nahverkehrssystems. 4 Ja, aber sie hat das nicht so sehr bemerkt. 5 Gut, denn sie ist ja in diesem System aufgewachsen. 6 Daß es interessant und gleichzeitig erschreckend war. 7 Die Freundlichkeit zwischen den Menschen. 8 Eher dagegen; sie glaubt, daß es zu früh war. 9 Weil die Menschen dachten, daß es eine einmalige Gelegenheit sei, und weil es der leichteste Weg war. 10 Sie glaubt, daß es für die Menschen im Osten besser gewesen wäre, aber wirtschaftlich schlecht. 11 Daß alles im Osten an den Westen angepaßt wird, und auch die guten Seiten der ex-DDR einfach beiseite geschoben werden.

Lesetexte
1 (*a*) Sie hatten sehr große Hoffnungen. (*b*) Sie sollte das Ende der DDR einleiten, und die Wiedervereinigung leichter machen. (*c*) Die Banken fingen an, das Ostgeld gegen Westgeld einzutauschen. (*d*) Viele erfüllten sich Wünsche nach Konsumgütern oder Reisen. (*e*) Viele Ostfirmen machten Bankrott, weil niemand mehr ihre Waren kaufen wollte. (*f*) Nein. (*g*) Sie brachte zuerst einmal Arbeitslosigkeit, steigende Preise, höhere Mieten und soziale Unsicherheit. (*h*) Obwohl die politische Teilung überwunden ist, gibt es immer noch soziale und wirtschaftliche Barrieren.
2 (*a*) gekarrt (*b*) fatale (*c*) lösen (*d*) bereits (*e*) Teilung (*f*) geglückt (*g*) DDR-Bürger (*h*) öffneten (*i*) der Jubel (*j*) tumultartigen

TRANSKRIPTIONEN DER HÖRAUFGABEN

(*Transcriptions of the listening exercises*)

Lektion 1
Vekehrsmeldungen

1 (*Signal*) Die Verkehrsredaktion meldet keine Störungen. Weiterhin gute Fahrt! (*Signal*)

2 (*Signal*) Die Verkehrsredaktion meldet Staus oder Behinderungen auf folgenden Strecken:

Nordrhein-Westfalen: Autobahn 3 von Oberhausen in Richtung Frankfurt zwischen Kreuz Leverkusen und Köln Dellbrück 6 Kilometer.

Baden-Württemberg: Autobahn 5 Richtung Karlsruhe zwischen Appenweier und Achern 4 Kilometer.

Autobahn 7 Ulm Richtung Würzburg zwischen Giengen und Heidenheim 4 Kilometer. (*Signal*)

Lektion 2
Robert Paulsen: Tagesablauf

Mein Name ist Robert Paulsen. Ich bin verheiratet und habe eine Tochter. Sie ist fast fünf. Ich wohne in Jena, in Thüringen, eines der fünf neuen Bundesländer. Ich bin von Beruf Wissenschaftlicher Assistent und arbeite an der Uni im Institut für Anglistik und Amerikanistik in Jena. Normalerweise unterscheidet sich doch schon der Tagesablauf eines an der Uni beschäftigten Wissenschaftlers von dem zum Beispiel eines Arbeiters dahingehend, daß diejenigen, die an der Uni arbeiten, doch einen flexibleren Tagesablauf haben; das heißt, wir müssen nicht ganz so früh aufstehen. Das hat Vorteile, zum Beispiel dahingehend, daß unsere Tochter nicht so zeitig in den

Kindergarten muß. Das heißt, ich bringe sie, je nachdem wie mein Stundenplan aussieht, zwischen halb acht und acht in den Kindergarten.

Meine Frau ist meistens dann schon um diese Zeit auf Arbeit. Sie ist Lehrerin, arbeitet in einer Realschule, und die Schule fängt sehr zeitig an. Das heißt also, wenn man so eine erste Stunde hat, geht's um sieben früh los.

Normalerweise fahre ich mit dem Fahrrad zur Arbeit in die Uni, da es nicht allzu weit ist. Und, ja, bei schlechtem Wetter oder im Winter benutze ich meistens den Bus oder die Straßenbahn. Zuvor liegt aber an, daß unsere Tochter in den Kindergarten gebracht wird, und das geschieht dann auch meist mit dem Fahrrad, beziehungsweise auch gelegentlich mit dem Auto.

Normalerweise hat man bei uns im Studium die Einteilung, daß es keine Trimester sind, sondern zwei Semester, eins im Herbst/Winter, das andere eben im Frühjahr/Sommer. Momentan befinden wir uns gerade im Sommersemester, welches vom 4. März bis etwa Ende Juni gehen wird. Das heißt, es sind also Lehrveranstaltungen zu machen, und danach richtet sich auch im wesentlichen der Tagesablauf. Da es an der Universität Jena doch relativ viele Studenten und wenig Unterrichtsräume gibt, sind die Zeiten, wie sicher an jeder anderen Universität auch, von früh bis ziemlich spät in den Abend hinein ausgeplant. Das heißt, der Vorteil dieser flexibleren Arbeitszeit einer Universität kann auch mitunter zum Nachteil werden, wenn man so höchstens einmal sehr zeitig beginnt, beziehungsweise eben auch sehr spät in den Abend hinein Seminare machen muß. Mir ist es eigentlich, da ich ja mit 29 Jahren relativ jung bin, relativ egal, wann ich unterrichte.

Frühstück esse ich normalerweise zu Hause, wenn das möglich ist. Ich muß dann relativ zeitig los, und bin dann meist bis zum frühen Nachmittag an der Uni, fahre dann mit dem Rad, mit der Straßenbahn oder mit dem Auto nach Hause, hole entweder, je nachdem wir das zu Hause abgesprochen haben, meine Tochter vom Kindergarten ab, beziehungsweise das erledigt eben meine Frau. Wenn die Schule, wie ich das schon gesagt habe, schon um sieben zeitig los geht, ist sie wenigstens mittags so zu Ende, daß das Kind zum Beispiel nicht im Kindergarten schlafen muß, sondern das zu Hause machen kann, und man einen relativ freien Nachmittag zur Verfügung hat. Der geht zwar dann auch oft

für Vorbereitungen für den nächsten Tag beziehungsweise für Versammlungen und Ähnliches in der Schule drauf, aber es läßt einem dann doch eine gewisse Freiheit, die einem eine gesetzte Arbeitszeit, was auch immer in dieser Zeit - acht oder achtunddreiviertel Stunden am Tage - stattfindet, nicht läßt.

Meist bin ich also doch am späteren Nachmittag zu Hause, besonders während der Semesterzeit. Und da ich in einem Haus mit meiner Familie allein wohne, hat man doch immer relativ viel daran zu tun, dem also Garten in Ordnung halten und so weiter angeht. Das sind also Dinge, die sich natürlich im Frühjahr, Sommer und im Frühherbst konzentrieren. Und das sind Arbeiten, die mir natürlich auch Spaß machen, dahingehend weil es doch eine Abwechslung ist im Vergleich zum Sitzen am Schreibtisch und Arbeit an einer Dissertation zum Beispiel, beziehungsweise eben Arbeit an Vorbereitungen für Seminare oder das Lesen von Essays. Allerdings ist es momentan bei mir so, daß ich kaum zu solchen Nebenarbeiten komme, wie also den Garten in Ordnung halten, da ich so schnell wie möglich meine Promotion beenden muß. Das heißt also, daß ich zu meinen eigentlichen Hobbys, wie eben Leichtathletik, nur selten komme.

Lektion 3

1 Auslandsstudium

Thomas Hallo, Stefan. Dich habe ich ja schon eine Ewigkeit nicht mehr gesehen!

Stefan Mensch, Thomas! Das freut mich aber. Ich habe gehört, du hast in England studiert. Stimmt das?

Thomas Ja, in Canterbury, Betriebswirtschaft. Ich bin gerade vor einem Monat fertiggeworden. Jetzt versuche ich, hier eine Stellung zu finden.

Stefan Fertiggeworden?? Willst du mich auf den Arm nehmen? Wir haben doch gleichzeitig mit dem Studium angefangen, und ich bin jetzt gerade erst mal im achten Semester - wahrscheinlich werde ich noch mindestens vier weitere brauchen.

Thomas Genau das war ja einer der Hauptgründe, warum ich mich damals entschlossen habe, nach England zu gehen. Ein Bekannter meines Vaters hatte mir erzählt, daß die Engländer nach drei Jahren ihren ersten Studienabschluß machen – der allerdings bei uns nicht voll anerkannt wird – und nach vier Jahren den zweiten, der unserem Diplom entspricht, und auch als gleichwertig anerkannt wird. Da habe ich mir gedacht, so eine Gelegenheit, die darfst du dir nicht entgehen lassen.

Stefan Da kann man ja direkt neidisch werden. Du sprichst doch jetzt bestimmt auch fließend Englisch, oder?

Thomas Klar, das war eine angenehme Begleiterscheinung. Ich habe viele Engländer kennengelernt, und auch eine Menge anderer ausländischer Studenten. Die Atmosphäre war sehr international, und es wurde hauptsächlich Englisch gesprochen. Außerdem waren die Vorlesungen, Seminare und schriftlichen Arbeiten natürlich in englischer Sprache.

Stefan Ich habe gehört, daß die Vorlesungen und Seminare an englischen Universitäten etwas kleiner sein sollen als bei uns. Stimmt das?

Thomas Etwas kleiner ist wohl noch untertrieben. Wieviele seid ihr denn in deinen BWL-Vorlesungen?

Stefan Naja, so grob geschätzt, ungefähr 600, manchmal auch mehr. Meine Kommilitonen und ich wechseln uns natürlich ab, einer geht hin und schreibt mit, die anderen kopieren sich dann seine Notizen. Anders kannst du es auch gar nicht machen, bei diesem Andrang kannst du noch froh sein, wenn du einen Platz auf der Treppe bekommst. Und in den Seminaren sind wir meistens um die 70.

Thomas Also, in Canterbury waren wir schätzungsweise 30 bis 50 Leute in den Vorlesungen, und etwa fünf bis zehn Studenten in den Seminaren. Das hatte den Vorteil, daß man die Profs persönlich kannte, und mit eventuellen Problemen auch jederzeit zu ihnen kommen konnte.

Stefan Das gibt's ja gar nicht. Weißt du, wann ich meinen Prof zum letzten Mal gesehen habe? Ungefähr vor einem Jahr – und da hatte ich das Gefühl, er wollte mich so schnell wie möglich wieder loswerden, und als ich ihn einige Tage danach auf der Straße getroffen habe, konnte er sich schon gar nicht mehr an meinen Namen erinnern.

Thomas Wenn ich das so höre, bin ich nochmal so froh, daß ich mich für ein Auslandsstudium entschieden habe. Hast du denn schon mal an ein Auslandssemester oder Auslandsjahr gedacht, Stefan?

Stefan Naja, daran gedacht habe ich schon. Aber letztlich hat mir doch die Entschlußkraft gefehlt. Außerdem habe ich ja hier meine ganzen Freunde, und bin auch freizeitmäßig schwer engagiert. Das würde mir, glaube ich, schon fehlen.

Thomas Also, ich hatte keine Probleme, an der Uni Anschluß zu finden. Man verbringt ja die meiste Zeit auf dem Campus. Und was das Freizeitangebot anbelangt, konntest du gar nicht alles machen, was angeboten wurde! Ich habe von ein paar Leuten hier schon gehört, daß man sich ziemlich reinhängen muß, um an deutschen Universitäten einen Freundeskreis aufzubauen.

Stefan Da hast du recht. Deshalb studiere ich auch in Frankfurt, damit ich meine Freude und Freizeitclubs nicht aufgeben muß. Aber mal was anderes – stimmt es, daß die englischen Universitäten Studiengebühren verlangen?

Thomas Leider! Das war auch in meinen Augen der einzige große Nachteil. Bis zum BA wurden meine Gebühren ja von der EU übernommen. Aber für das letzte Jahr hat mein Vater ganz schön in die Tasche greifen müssen – umgerechnet circa 6600 Mark.

Stefan Wahnsinn! Da ist das ganze Schul System wohl ziemlich elitär, was?

Thomas Naja, es gab schon ein paar Reiche an der Uni. Ich bin ja auch dafür, daß das Studieren vom Staat bezahlt werden sollte. Andererseits haben die Engländer eben nicht das Problem der Überfüllung an den Hochschulen. Ich denke, beides hat wohl Vor- und Nachteile! Ich persönlich finde, daß sich der finanzielle Aufwand gelohnt hat, wenn ich bedenke, daß ich erstens so schnell fertiggeworden bin, und zweitens die Auslandserfahrung und die Sprachfertigkeit gewonnen habe.

Stefan Da magst du recht haben.

2 Studienkosten: ein Ost-West-Vergleich

Interviewer Und wie geht es jetzt weiter mit ihrem Studium?

Damaris Also, wenn ich jetzt nach Berlin zurückgehe, dann werde ich schätzungsweise noch drei Jahre studieren, und dann ans Gymnasium gehen, zwei Jahre Referendariat, und dann bin ich fertig mit meiner Ausbildung.

Interviewer Und wie läßt sich das finanzieren?

Damaris Also, bei mir finanziert sich das über das BaföG-Amt . . . Also, das ist eine bestimmte Summe, die der Student monatlich vom Staat erhält . . .

Interviewer Ein Stipendium?

Damaris Eine Art Stipendium, von dem ich die Hälfte dann am Ende der Studienzeit zurückzahlen muß.

Interviewer Ach so, das muß zurückgezahlt werden?

Damaris Wieviel man zurückzahlt, hängt davon ab, wie gut man abschließt, wie schnell man fertig ist . . .

Interviewer Und werden ex-DDR-Studenten bevorzugt?

Damaris Nein.

Interviewer Die werden nicht bevorzugt?

Damaris Nein. Es gibt sogar einen Unterschied in dem BaföG-Satz zwischen dem Ost- und Westteil Deutschlands . . .

Interviewer Ach, so . . .

Damaris . . . die Studenten im Ostteil bekommen weniger, mit der Begründung, daß es ja bei uns billiger ist – was überhaupt nicht so ist . . . wir bezahlen dieselben Preise für Produkte wie im Westteil . . .

Interviewer Aber die Mieten sind wahrscheinlich billiger, oder?

Damaris Ja. Auch die Löhne sind eben weniger, nur 80 Prozent der Löhne, die die Arbeiter im Westteil kriegen, und . . .

Lektion 4
Arbeitslosigkeit

Regina Seit wann sind Sie arbeitslos?

Gerd Seitdem meine Firma vor sechs Monaten zumachen mußte.

Regina Und warum mußte sie zumachen?

Gerd Na ja, wir hatten Fernsehapparate hergestellt. Nach der Einigung haben wir versucht, mit den westlichen Produzenten zu konkurrieren. Das ist uns aber leider nicht gelungen.

Regina Warum eigentlich nicht?

Gerd Erstens waren unsere Produktionssmethoden veraltet, und zweitens gab es keine Nachfrage mehr für unsere Produkte. Die Leute haben nur Westprodukte kaufen wollen.

Regina Und haben dann keine westdeutschen Unternehmen Interesse daran gezeigt, Ihre Firma zu übernehmen?

Gerd Doch, Übernahmeangebote gab es schon reichlich. Als aber den Interessenten klarwurde, wieviel sie investieren müßten, konnte man sie vor Staub nicht mehr sehen! Die Firma war also gar nicht konkurrenzfähig und mußte schließen. Nach 23 Jahren bei der gleichen Firma wurde ich auf einmal arbeitslos.

Regina Und wie sieht Ihre Zukunft aus?

Gerd Also, ich habe noch Hoffnungen, einen Arbeitsplatz zu finden. Ich weiß, daß die Prognose ziemlich pessimistisch ist, und in meinem Alter – ich bin ja schon 46 – wird es gar nicht leicht sein, mich den Anforderungen der Marktwirtschaft anzupassen. Ich habe vor, mich in naher Zukunft an einem Fortbildungskurs zu beteiligen. Dann werde ich potentiellen Arbeitgebern wenigstens gewisse Fachkenntnisse anbieten können.

Regina Ich wünsche Ihnen viel Erfolg bei Ihrer Suche nach einem Job.

Gerd Danke schön.

Lektion 5
Pläne für die Sommerferien

Sebastian Mensch, ich bin vielleicht froh, daß die Sommerferien übermorgen anfangen!

Jochen Und ich erst! Was hast du denn eigentlich so geplant?

Sebastian Also, ich werde meinen Führerschein anfangen. Meine Eltern haben mich endlich in der Fahrschule angemeldet, und in zwei Wochen geht's los.

Jochen Bist du denn schon vorher mal gefahren?

Sebastian Wo denkst du hin! Ich will doch nicht riskieren, daß mir die Fahrerlaubnis für zwei Jahre entzogen wird! Das ist übrigens dem Peter passiert, und jetzt hat er das neue Auto zuhause stehen, das ihm seine Eltern schon vorher gekauft hatten, und kann nicht damit fahren . . .

Jochen Wieviel Stunden glaubst du denn, daß du brauchen wirst?

Sebastian Naja, 20 ist ja so der Durchschnitt – und wenn ich nicht durchfalle, müßte ich meinen Deckel Anfang des neuen Schuljahres schon haben! Und was hast du denn eigentlich vor?

Jochen Meine Eltern haben mir versprochen, daß ich meinen dritten Tanzkurs machen kann. Da freue ich mich schon total drauf.

Sebastian Bist du da etwa immer noch dabei? Ich habe ja auch einen gemacht, vor etwa drei Jahren, aber einer hat mir gereicht. Ich gehe sowieso nur in die Disco, und da brauche ich so 'was ja nicht – höchstens mal bei meiner Hochzeit, und bis dahin habe ich wahrscheinlich schon wieder alle Schritte vergessen! Hast du denn eine Partnerin für den Kurs?

Jochen Ja, du kennst doch die Sybille, oder? Wir haben schon den ersten und zweiten Kurs zusammen gemacht, und nach dem dritten wollen wir in den Tanzclub eintreten, und auch auf Turniere gehen.

Sebastian Da muß man doch ziemlich oft trainieren, oder? Glaubst du denn nicht, daß dir das zuviel wird?

Jochen Ach, außer dem Tanzen, und dann noch meinem Schwimmtraining, mache ich eigentlich nichts weiter in meiner Freizeit. Und es ist ja eine gute Gelegenheit, neue Leute kennenzulernen und sich auch fitzuhalten.

Sebastian Sicherlich. Aber das wäre mir ehrlich gesagt zuviel. So eingebunden zu sein würde mir überhaupt nicht gefallen. Ich persönlich ziehe es vor, meine Freizeit flexibel zu gestalten. Außerdem bin ich eher kulturinteressiert – Sport hat mich eigentlich schon immer gelangweilt.

Lektion 6
Kontakt-, Muß- und Genußraucher

Interviewer Entschuldigen Sie, bitte. Ich sehe, daß Sie gerade eine Zigarette rauchen. Darf ich Sie fragen, wann Sie am liebsten rauchen?

Renate Na, wie Sie sehen, rauche ich gern zwischen den Gängen einer Mahlzeit. Auch nach dem Essen, vor allem am Feierabend und am Wochenende. Ich rauche auch dann gern, wenn ich mein Hobby betreibe, zum Beispiel beim Lesen.

Interviewer Gibt es noch andere Situationen, wo Sie das Bedürfnis nach einer Zigarette haben?

Renate Ja – zum Beispiel, wenn ich entspannt und faul in der Sonne liege, also im Urlaub sozusagen, oder auch, wenn ich erfolgreich war und so richtig zufrieden mit mir bin. Aber ich muß sagen, daß ich sehr langsam rauche, mit relativ langen Zeitabständen zwischen den einzelnen Zügen.

Interviewer Und wie ist es bei Ihnen, mein Herr? Wann rauchen Sie vor allem, wenn ich fragen darf?

Rainer Also, ich muß gestehen, daß ich vor allem dann rauche, wenn ich reizbar, nervös oder innerlich unruhig bin. Also, zum Beispiel, wenn ich auf jemanden warten muß, oder wenn ich im Straßenverkehr nicht vorwärtskomme. Auch zum Beispiel morgens, wenn ich mich unausgeschlafen und müde fühle, und mit den hohen Anforderungen des Alltags fertigwerden muß.

Interviewer Und rauchen Sie auch bei der Arbeit?

Rainer Ja, dann besonders. Ich finde, daß mir eine Zigarette besonders hilft, wenn ich an eine Aufgabe nicht herangehen mag, oder wenn mir zu einer Aufgabe oder Arbeit nichts einfällt. Natürlich rauche ich auch, um den Hunger zu überbrücken, denn sonst würde ich bei der Arbeit ständig Süßigkeiten essen!

Interviewer Und die junge Dame hier. Darf ich Sie fragen, wann Sie für gewöhnlich rauchen?

Bettina Also, ich rauche eigentlich nur, wenn ich mit Rauchern zusammen bin. Mein Partner raucht auch, und wenn wir dann mit Freunden und Bekannten zusammen sind, rauche ich auch, damit es nicht heißt, ich sei ungemütlich. Wenn ich nicht immer wieder eine Zigarette angeboten bekäme, hätte ich schon längst mit dem Rauchen aufgehört, glaube ich.

Interviewer Rauchen Sie bevorzugt in Lokalen, oder am Arbeitsplatz?

Bettina In Lokalen rauche ich ehrlich gesagt gerne eine Zigarette, weil ich mich dann irgendwie sicherer fühle, ich kann meine Verlegenheit überspielen, und kann mich mehr entspannen. Apropos Arbeitsplatz, ich bin Studentin, und in den Aufenthaltsräumen an der Uni wird ziemlich viel geraucht, und ich glaube, einer der Gründe ist, daß das Anbieten einer Zigarette den Kontakt erleichtert.

Lektion 7
Umweltschutz in Deutschland und England

Interviewer Was halten Sie vom Umweltschutz hier in Canterbury?

Renate Hier in Canterbury gibt es einfach zu viel Tourismus, und zu viele Touristen, die überhaupt nicht darauf achten, was hier überhaupt los ist, und denen die Umwelt eigentlich ziemlich egal zu sein scheint – obwohl eigentlich hier in Canterbury ziemlich viel darauf geachtet werden muß . . . vor allem wegen den vielen Abgasen, und den alten Gebäuden hier überall . . . und hier wird eigentlich kaum was gemacht, würd' ich mal sagen.

Interviewer Da muß ich leider mit Ihnen übereinstimmen! Was ist eigentlich der »Blaue Engel«?

Renate Der Blaue Engel ist ein Zeichen der Umweltbehörde, daß dieses Produkt wiederverwertbar, beziehungsweise verbrennbar ist, ohne schädliche Stoffe abzugeben.

Interviewer Haben Sie so etwas auch schon mal hier in Großbritannien gesehen? Also, ich muß zugeben, ich bin noch nicht darauf gestoßen.

Renate Ich auch nicht. Und auch den Grünen Punkt habe ich noch nicht gesehen . . . den gibt es ja in Deutschland jetzt auch. Also, ich muß sagen, in Deutschland wird ja weitaus mehr gemacht als hier in England. Es liegt eventuell auch daran, daß Deutschland etwas reicher ist . . . Also, das ist jetzt ein komisches Beispiel, aber McDonald's hat in Deutschland zum Beispiel schon Trennware, also so Essensreste, und Kunststoff, und Kartons, und das wird alles getrennt weggeschmissen . . .

Interviewer . . . in verschiedene Tonnen?

Renate Ja, während man hier noch die ganz alten Verpackungen hat, die aus Plastik. Das ist unverschämt, also . . .

Interviewer Ja, finde ich auch. Aber das Publikum muß dann was neues verlangen, denke ich, hier in Großbritannien, wenn etwas geändert werden soll. Bis wir etwas unternehmen, wird McDonald's nichts tun, oder?

Renate Ja, nun, ich kann nur sagen, ich komme aus Hamburg, und da wird ziemlich viel gemacht, da kann man an jeder Ecke 'nen Altglascontainer finden, oder Altpapiercontainer . . . Es ist gar kein Problem, Sachen wiederzuverwerten; das machen wir seit mehreren Jahren schon. Und Kompost, und Trennmüll, und . . . Also, ich meine, ich habe Freunde, die haben zu Hause fünf Mülltonnen 'rumstehen, für die ganzen verschiedenen Sachen, und so was habe ich hier noch nicht gesehen. Nicht mal bei Boots oder so steht ein Kasten für Altbatterien – was es in Deutschland seit Jahren gibt, glaube ich. Und so was gibt's hier nicht.

Interviewer Nein.

Renate Und das finde ich eigentlich unverschämt, wenn . . . vor allem weil Großbritannien ja nun ziemlich am Wasser liegt, da kommt ja auch ziemlich viel ins Wasser, und das wird dann überall anders hingespült. Ich würde sagen, die bräuchten hier mal so was, ich glaube nämlich, daß sich viele Leute darum scheren müßten, aber eigentlich müßte eine Strafe ausgeschrieben werden.

Interviewer Ja, richtig. Woher kommt das, sind die Engländer denn apathisch, oder?

Renate Also, ich kann das nicht so richtig beantworten, weil ich eben kein Engländer bin, und zu Hause auch ziemlich drauf achte. Vor allem finde ich's quatschig, daß sie hier zum Beispiel Chips verkaufen, die fünffach verpackt sind, und . . . ich weiß es nicht, die Engländer scheinen das gar nicht so richtig zu begreifen, beziehungsweise scheinen das selber gar nicht mitzukriegen, . . . also Hauptsache, die anderen Länder tun was . . . sie sollten sich lieber mal an die eigene Nase fassen, würde ich mal sagen.

Interviewer Und wie ist das mit dem Hausrat, und den Altkleidern, und so weiter?

Renate Also, in Deutschland, da stehen . . . ich kann nicht sagen, Mülltonnen, aber so Plastiksäcke rum, wo man seine alten Schuhe reinwerfen kann, oder Pullover, oder so, und die dann an arme Leute weitergegeben werden, die gewaschen werden, und die dann Obdachlose und so weiter abholen können, und tragen können. Das finde ich eine sehr gute Sache, denn, ich meine, wieviele Klamotten hat man, die man eigentlich nicht mehr trägt. Also, das fände ich schon viel besser. Und Möbel werden meistens auf den Sperrmüll geworfen, da kann jeder hingehen und sich was aussuchen, am nächsten Tag wird's von der Müllabfuhr abgeholt – kein Problem.

Interviewer Und wie ist es mit Aludosen, und so?

Renate Da . . . nee, also da ist, glaube ich, noch nicht so viel in Deutschland, also hier gibt's ja schon diesen Crusher, wo man die Dosen reintun kann, von Cola und so, so was haben wir in Deutschland nicht. Aber eigentlich gibt es gar nicht so viele Dosen, die man kauft, man kauft eigentlich ziemlich viel in Gläsern. Also, ich kann von unserem Haushalt reden, und wir kaufen ziemlich viel in Gläsern. Man kann zwar die Aludosen wiederverwerten, das ist aber viel Aufstand, und man hat noch nicht so viele Container dafür, also in Deutschland auf jeden Fall. Hier werden die eigentlich ziemlich viel gesammelt, würd' ich sagen.

Interviewer Würde ich auch sagen.

Renate Da wird hier also mehr gemacht. Naja, ein kleiner Anfang ist auch was, nicht?

Lektion 8

Vergleiche zwischen Engländern und Deutschen

Karin Und wie hat es dir in England gefallen?

Helga Also, ich muß dir sagen, es war einfach super. Ich war erst eine Woche in London, und bin dann für eine Woche nach Cornwall gefahren. London ist natürlich eine tolle Stadt, und in Cornwall ist die Landschaft einfach phantastisch.

Ich werde auf jeden Fall in meinem nächsten Urlaub wieder nach England fahren!

Karin Ach, ich kann mich aber erinnern, daß du zu Anfang recht kritisch warst, was England und die Engländer anbelangt. Erst hast du doch gemeint, daß England ein so kaltes und verregnetes Land sei, und daß man dort nichts außer *steak and kidney pie* und *fish and chips* zu essen bekäme. Und von den Engländern hast du gesagt, sie seien so kühl und reserviert, daß man nie mit ihnen in Kontakt käme, erst recht nicht, wenn man ihre Art von Humor nicht versteht!

Helga Naja, das waren halt so die typischen Vorurteile, die man irgendwann mal aufgeschnappt hat. Ehrlich gesagt, ich habe so viele nette Leute kennengelernt, mit denen ich mich großartig verstanden habe. Ein paarmal war ich zum Essen eingeladen, und es war ausgezeichnet. Was das Wetter anbelangt, so ist es eigentlich fast so wie in Deutschland – natürlich kann man nicht gerade einen Badeurlaub dort verbringen . . .

Karin Und hast du auch irgendwelche Vorurteile gegenüber den Deutschen bemerkt?

Helga Im großen und ganzen nicht. Ich habe mich mit meinen Bekannten über die Situation in Deutschland nach der Wiedervereinigung unterhalten, und die Probleme, die das mit sich gebracht hat, besonders in bezug auf neo-nazistische Tendenzen, und die Angst der anderen EU-Staaten vor einem übermächtigen Deutschland.

Karin Und was haben deine Freunde dazu gesagt?

Helga Sie waren überwiegend positiv eingestellt. Natürlich haben sie den Zweiten Weltkrieg erwähnt, aber sie waren auch der Meinung, daß die heutige Generation der Deutschen nicht dafür verantwortlich gemacht werden könne, und daß sich Deutschland verändert hätte. Außerdem haben sie auch gesagt, daß diese rechtsextremen Gruppen nicht nur ein deutsches Problem seien, und daß England auch Probleme mit der Integration seiner ethnischen Minderheiten habe.

Karin Da bin ich ja froh, daß das Bild der Deutschen nicht ganz so schlecht ist, wie man annehmen könnte!

Helga Naja, es gibt natürlich auch einige Klischees, die die Engländer über die Deutschen haben, genauso wie ich vorher über die Engländer und England!

Karin Was denn zum Beispiel?

Helga Ach, zum Beispiel die Vorstellung, daß alle Deutschen so sauber und korrekt seien, so früh aufstehen und so viel arbeiten würden. Außerdem hatten sie natürlich schon von der deutschen Gründlichkeit gehört. Aber das Beste war, daß sie gedacht haben, die Deutschen würden sich von Bratwürsten mit Sauerkraut und Schweinebraten mit Klößen ernähren!

Lektion 9
Lassen Sie Ihr Auto stehen!

Rainer Apropos Energiesparen und Umweltschutz – ich finde, daß man im Bereich Transport und Verkehr viel mehr unternehmen könnte. Ich war gerade in der Stadt, und ehrlich gesagt, ich konnte vor Autos fast nichts mehr sehen, und diese stinkenden Abgase – ich bin überzeugt, daß die Ozonwerte heute wieder besonders hoch sind!

Martin Und dabei ist ja in Deutschland schon einiges getan worden, um die Abgasemissionen zu verringern – ich war wirklich erstaunt, als ich gehört habe, daß hier so gut wie jedes Auto bleifrei fährt oder einen Katalysator hat. In Großbritannien sind wir da viel weiter zurück.

Rainer Klar, da ist schon ein großer Schritt in die richtige Richtung getan worden. Aber ich bin der Meinung, daß der Staat noch viel mehr tun müßte, um das Verkehrsaufkommen zu verringern. Zum Beispiel könnten ja noch höhere Steuern erhoben werden, um die Bürger dazu zu bringen, daß sie weniger mit dem Auto fahren, oder ganz auf das Auto verzichten.

Martin Ich glaube ehrlich gesagt nicht, daß du mit höheren Steuern allein etwas erreichen kannst. Es ist viel wichtiger, das Bewußtstein der Bürger zu schärfen, damit sie sich aus eigener Initiative um Energiesparen und Umweltschutz in diesem Bereich kümmern. Und da muß ich sagen, daß die Deutschen im allgemeinen schon sehr viel Eigeninitiative entwickelt haben, was Transport und Verkehr anbelangt.

Rainer Und woran siehst du das?

Martin Naja, nimm doch nur mal als Beispiel die

Mitfahrzentralen, die es in ganz Deutschland gibt, und die viele Leute in Anspruch nehmen. Davon habe ich in England noch nie was gehört. Zum einen kann man Geld sparen, wenn man zu zweit oder zu dritt längere Strecken fährt, und zum anderen ist die Kapazität des Autos einfach besser ausgenutzt. Man spart Energie und schont die Umwelt.

Rainer Stimmt! Und dann natürlich werden auch immer mehr Fahrgemeinschaften gebildet. Ist das in England auch weit verbreitet?

Martin Ja, das machen schon viele Leute. Aber allgemein gesagt sollte sich dieses Prinzip noch viel mehr durchsetzen. Denk doch nur mal, wieviel besser der Verkehr wäre, wenn in jedem Auto vier Personen sitzen würden – im Moment sehe ich zumeist nur eine Person in fast jedem Auto sitzen.

Rainer Da hast du allerdings recht. Außerdem könnten die Leute ja auch öfters mal zu Fuß gehen oder mit dem Fahrrad fahren. Das wäre nicht nur umweltfreundlicher, sondern auch gesünder!

Martin Das finde ich auch. Aber natürlich müssen die entsprechenden Fuß- und Radfahrwege noch viel stärker ausgebaut werden, um diese Möglichkeit attraktiver zu machen. Ich war ja schon erstaunt, wie viele Radfahrwege es hier in Münster gibt. Das ist ein wahres Paradies für Radfahrer. Wenn ich da an England denke – die wenigsten Leute würden dort mit dem Rad fahren, weil es einfach zu wenige Radfahrwege gibt, und daher zu gefährlich ist. In diesem Fall sollte der Staat wirklich dringend was unternehmen.

Rainer Dasselbe gilt eigentlich auch für öffentliche Verkehrsmittel, oder solche Angebote wie *Park and Ride* – das wird alles noch viel zu wenig genutzt. Der Staat sollte den Bürgern diese Möglichkeiten attraktiver machen als das Autofahren. Natürlich muß das alles noch viel stärker subventioniert werden, damit es auch preislich akzeptabel wird.

Martin Ich bin nur erstaunt, daß es auf den deutschen Autobahnen immer noch kein Tempolimit gibt. Dadurch könnte doch auch etwas zum Umweltschutz beigetragen werden, besonders was die Ozonwerte anbetrifft. Gerade wo das Baumsterben in Deutschland schon so fortgeschritten ist. Also, in England haben wir schon seit einiger Zeit ein Tempolimit auf den Autobahnen.

Rainer Das habe ich auch schon immer gesagt! Langfristig gesehen finde ich sowieso, daß man Autos weitgehend abschaffen sollte. Man sollte auch viel mehr Geld investieren, um solche alternativen Möglichkeiten wie Solarautos oder mit einem speziellen Pflanzenöl betriebene Autos weiterzuentwickeln.

Martin Da müßte sich das Bewußtsein der Bürger aber schon gewaltig umstellen, glaube ich. Immerhin ist für viele Leute ein Auto ein Statussymbol, und auch Inbegriff der persönlichen Freiheit . . . aber es wäre schon viel geholfen, wenn diese anderen Möglichkeiten, von denen wir gesprochen haben, besser ausgenutzt würden!

Lektion 10

1 Professor Dr. Rolf Herwig: die Wiedervereinigung

Mein Name ist Rolf Herwig. Ich bin 51 Jahre alt und verheiratet. Ich arbeite als Dozent an der Universität in Jena, in Thüringen, am Institut für Anglistik und Amerikanistik.

Wenn man mich befragt nach meiner Haltung, nach meinen Erfahrungen in bezug auf die deutsche Wiedervereinigung, so muß ich sagen, daß bis zum Herbst 1989 das für mich und meine Frau ein Thema war, das bestenfalls ein Traum war, eine Sehnsucht. Wir hatten uns im Prinzip damit abgefunden, in zwei unterschiedlichen Deutschländern zu leben. Wir in der DDR und die anderen, die wir eigentlich überhaupt nicht kannten, und bei denen wir auch gar keine Verwandten hatten, in dieser BRD.

Es war völlig unwahrscheinlich, daß wir lebend noch ein einiges Deutschland erleben würden. Was uns geblieben war, das war eine Art Sehnsucht, eine Hoffnung auf unser Rentnerdasein. Dann, wenn wir 60 sein würden, meine Frau 60 sein würde und dann, wenn ich 65 sein würde, dann wären wir beide Altersrentner gewesen. Dann hätten wir reisen dürfen, zwar finanziell sehr eingeschränkt, aber das wäre dann die einizige Möglichkeit gewesen, einmal am Rhein zu stehen oder die Alpen zu betrachten.

Als es dann so weit war, oder deutlich wurde, daß die Wiedervereinigung Deutschlands bevorstehen würde, waren wir –

das muß ich sagen – uneingeschränkt dafür. Wir waren auch, wie viele andere, wie Millionen in Deutschland begeistert, in einer Art von Rausch, sicherlich in einem sentimentalen Rausch, aber wir waren dafür. Und ich muß sagen, ich bin es auch heute noch, auch wenn sich vieles verändert hat, auch wenn dieser Rausch verflogen ist, auch wenn die ursprüngliche Begeisterung nicht mehr vorhanden ist.

Um ein Beispiel zu nennen, wie begeistert wir waren – als die Grenze geöffnet wurde im Herbst 1989, sind wir nach Bamberg gefahren, im Süden, in Bayern, und da standen wir beide auf einer Brücke, und unserc Geographie von der anderen Hälfte Deutschlands war so schlecht, daß wir gar nicht wußten, welcher Fluß das ist, der unter uns wegfloß. Und also dann, herausbekommen haben wir, das war der Main, als wir die Stadt Bamberg vor uns liegen sahen, in der Sonne mit dem Dom. Da waren wir so gerührt, daß uns beiden die Tränen gekommen sind.

Den 3. Oktober 1990, den Tag der Wiedervereinigung selbst, habe ich in Marburg erlebt. Zu einer Konferenz war ich nach Marburg gefahren, und am Abend fand auf dem Marktplatz von Marburg eine Veranstaltung statt, eine festliche, feierliche Veranstaltung des Stadtrates aus Anlaß und zu Ehren der Wiedervereinigung. Das war eine entsetzliche Sache. Es waren die Schlägertruppen von links und rechts aufgezogen, zum Teil schon betrunken. Und es wurden Losungen gebrüllt: Hoch die internationale Solidarität! Nieder mit dem Imperialismus! Deutschland verrecke! Es war so entsetzlich, daß im Prinzip überhaupt keine Feier stattfinden konnte, daß alle Vorbereitungen der Veranstalter zunichte gemacht wurden. Und als es dann um Mitternacht so weit war, daß der Bürgermeister die Wiedervereinigung Deutschlands verkünden wollte, fielen die Schlägertruppen von links und rechts aufeinander, übereinander her, und verprügelten sich, und die Polizei mußte einschreiten und zwar sehr gewaltsam einschreiten, so daß das Ganze abstoßend war.

Wir haben inzwischen noch ganz andere Erfahrungen machen können, denn der ökonomische Niedergang der DDR – auch die Betriebe, die wir für konkurrenzfähig gehalten hatten, die Großbetriebe, etwa Carl Zeiß in Jena – hat dazu geführt, daß wir eine verheerende Arbeitslosigkeit schon jetzt haben, und jedermann spricht davon, und auch Experten sprechen davon, daß es im Sommer noch anders aussehen wird. Am 30. Juni 1991 laufen eine Reihe von Schutzgarantien aus, wie Kündigungsschutz und andere

Sondermaßnahmen, die mit dem Einigungsvertrag vereinbart worden waren.

Es ist eine gefährliche Entwicklung, weil diese soziale Unsicherheit mit sich bringt eine politische Instabilisierung. Es sind vor allen Dingen jugendliche Kräfte, meist die Skinheads, die laut und aggressiv und brutal in der Öffentlichkeit auftreten, aber bis zu einem gewissen Grad eben doch Ideologieträger sind einer zumindest faschistoiden Ideologie. Es ist – das muß ich auch deutlich sagen – keine Wiederholung etwa dessen, was 1933 gewesen ist. Es ist aber ein Haß auf alles, was anders ist, und aussieht und denkt als sie, vor allem gegen die Ausländer gerichtet. Wobei es in Jena, Gott sei Dank, zu größeren Brutalitäten nicht gekommen ist. Das sind also Dinge, die uns die Wiedervereinigung auch gebracht hat, genauso wie Rauschgiftprobleme. Es ist nach wie vor – das muß ich ganz deutlich sagen – die Überzeugung der Masse, der Mehrheit aller Menschen bei uns, daß die Wiedervereinigung keinesfalls rückgängig gemacht werden sollte. So daß die Lösung der Probleme, so wie sie sich jetzt uns in solcher Dimension aufzeigen, daß die Lösung dieser Probleme innerhalb der Bundesrepublik, innerhalb der Gemeinschaft der Länder erfolgen muß, auch wenn für viele, die unmittelbar betroffen sind, von der Arbeitslosigkeit, vom sozialen Abstieg, der Weg in eine bessere Zukunft gegenwärtig noch nicht erkennbar ist.

Die deutsche Wiedervereinigung ist ein Thema, das für die meisten schon fast vergessen oder abgeschrieben ist, als politische oder kulturelle oder wie auch immer Erfahrung des Herbstes von 1990. Was sie sich gegenüberstehen sehen, das ist ein sozialer Kampf, das ist Arbeitskampf, das ist Kampf um die Erhaltung ihrer Arbeitsplätze, um die Verbesserung ihres Lebensstandards, um die Angleichung des Lebensstandards an den in der alten Bundesrepublik. Aber wenn man mich fragt, wie ich meine Meinung und meine Erfahrungen zusammenfassen würde, dann muß ich sagen, die Wiedervereinigung Deutschlands war eines der herausragendsten Erlebnisse in meinem Leben, so wichtig und so bedeutsam wie die Eheschließung, die Geburt der Kinder, und alles zusammen, das möchte ich auf gar keinen Fall vermissen.

2 Eine Abiturientin aus Ostdeutschland zur Wiedervereinigung

Interviewer Wie war Ihnen denn zur Zeit des Falls der Mauer zumute?

Damaris Ich hatte das Gefühl, daß es zu früh passiert, und daß alles eigentlich sehr chaotisch war, und daß es niemals so positiv ablaufen wird, wie sich das jeder vorgestellt hat. Ich habe immer gedacht, das kann nicht sein, die Leute wissen gar nicht, worauf sie sich einlassen – aber stehen da und sind begeistert und jubeln – und keiner sieht, was danach kommt.

Interviewer Aber Sie haben es doch gesehen?

Damaris Also, ich habe es mir irgendwo vorgestellt – ich dachte, ich wüßte es . . . und ich glaube, ich habe es auch in einigen Punkten gewußt.

Interviewer Es hat aber doch auch positive Seiten gehabt, oder?

Damaris Ja, hat es.

Interviewer Zum Beispiel?

Damaris Naja, zum Beispiel, daß ich eben hier in England sein kann, und studieren kann, und die sogenannte Reisefreiheit, die ja jeder zuerst zitiert, und die starke Deutschmark. Aber es gibt eben nicht nur Vorteile, sondern auch Nachteile.

Interviewer Und was sind die größten Nachteile?

Damaris Die größten Nachteile sind, daß . . . die meisten Leute in der ehemaligen DDR denken, daß es ein . . . Überstülpen der westlichen Gesellschaft war. Daß wir eben jetzt eine hohe Arbeitslosenrate haben, die wir vorher überhaupt nicht kannten. Daß solche Einrichtungen wie Kindergärten geschlossen werden, weil sie zu ineffektiv sind. Der Nahverkehr, das geht alles nicht mehr so gut, es werden einfach Züge und Busse eingestellt, weil sie zu wenig genutzt werden, weil es zu teuer ist für die Leute – und die ganze allgemeine soziale Unsicherheit, die wir vorher nicht kannten, die bedrückt jeden, sehr sogar.

Interviewer Aber auch das ehemalige System hatte gewisse Nachteile, oder?

Damaris Ja, das stimmt. Also . . . ich ganz persönlich kann sagen, ich habe wenig von diesen Nachteilen gespürt, weil ich in meiner Entwicklung noch nicht so weit war, um an die Grenzen zu stoßen. Das wäre sicherlich so weit gewesen, wenn ich angefangen hätte zu studieren – ganz schnell sogar. Aber so war ich eigentlich ziemlich zufrieden . . . mit diesem Leben – weil ich es ja auch gar nicht anders kannte. Ich bin in diesem System aufgewachsen.

Interviewer Aber Sie haben doch etwas anderes gekannt durch das Fernsehen.

Damaris Ja. Es war schon interessant, all das Konsumangebot im Westteil, und diese Reisefreiheit. Aber es hat mich auch immer abgeschreckt, all diese soziale Unsicherheit und dieser Machtkampf, und dieser enorme Leistungsdruck, der in der Gesellschaft herrscht, der soviel kaputtmacht . . . zum Beispiel die freundliche Beziehung der Menschen untereinander . . . das gibt es sehr viel weniger im Westteil als bei uns.

Interviewer Ja, das stimmt. Das kommt wahrscheinlich eher durch den Wohlstand, oder?

Damaris Ja, durch den Kampf nach Wohlstand. Weil jeder eben soviel haben möchte, wie er kann, und . . . dadurch Intrigen entstehen, und Kämpfe gegeneinander, Rücksichtslosigkeit . . . die sogenannte Ellenbogengesellschaft.

Interviewer Aber auch in der ehemaligen DDR hat es Konflikte gegeben zwischen den Menschen, oder?

Damaris Ja. Das läßt sich nicht vermeiden, im Arbeitsbereich, oder auch im privaten Bereich. Aber ganz allgemein, und das haben mir auch Freunde hier bestätigt, die in der ehemaligen DDR Urlaub gemacht haben – die haben gemeint, die Leute dort sind so freundlich, das kennen sie gar nicht.

Interviewer Das stimmt. Aber sie sind dann doch nicht so weit gegangen, daß sie in der DDR gezogen wären.

Damaris Nein, dafür ist ihnen der Wohlstand zu lieb, den sie in ihrem Ort genießen.

Interviewer Ja, ja, eben. Es kam also zur Einigung. Waren Sie auch gegen die Einigung?

Damaris Nicht grundsätzlich. Aber ich dachte eben, daß es zu früh ist, zu schnell. Man hätte sich das besser überlegen sollen . . . andererseits war es der leichteste Weg. Und viele Leute sagen ja, vielleicht wäre es gar nicht zur Vereinigung gekommen, wenn man noch

	länger gewartet hätte – und da hat man eben die Chance genutzt.
Interviewer	Einige meiner Bekannten in der ehemaligen DDR waren eigentlich gegen die Einigung. Sie wollten eine reformierte DDR. Wäre das auch eine Lösung gewesen?
Damaris	Tja, ich weiß nicht. Es wäre vielleicht für die Menschen im Osten, für ihre Identität und ihre Ideen besser gewesen, weil so fühlen sie sich ziemlich . . . ziemlich überrannt. Weil von der eigentlichen DDR ist nichts mehr übriggeblieben – auch nicht die guten Seiten, die es gegeben hat. Es wurde erst mal alles beiseite geschoben, und wir mußten uns eben der westlichen Gesellschaft anpassen, in jeder Beziehung. Und in dieser Hinsicht wäre es wahrscheinlich besser gewesen, einen reformierten Staat aufzubauen. Aber ob das ökonomisch überhaupt möglich gewesen wäre, das weiß ich nicht.
Interviewer	Das läßt sich doch bezweifeln.
Damaris	Ja. Das wäre wahrscheinlich sehr schwierig gewesen.

DEUTSCH-ENGLISCHES GLOSSAR

(*German–English glossary*)

The bold numbers in this glossary refer to the unit in which the word first appears in this book.

A1 die *motorway 1*
ab und zu **2** *every now and again*
abbauen (sep.) **9** *to dismantle, remove*
abdecken (sep.) **9** *to cover, to meet*
Abendprogramm das; (-e) **5** *evening programme*
Abfahrt die; (-en) **5** *departure*
Abfall der; (-e) **9** *waste, rubbish*
sich abfinden; (sep.) mit + Dat. **10** *to accept, come to terms with*
abführen (sep.) **7** *to deduct*
Abgase die (pl.) **6** *exhaust fumes*
abgeben (sep.); (i,a, e) **7** *to release, give off*
abgesehen von **6** *apart from*
abgespannt **6** *weary, exhausted*
sich etwas abgewöhnen **6** *to give something up, stop doing something*
abhängen von + Dat. **10** *to depend on*
abhängig von + Dat. **9** *dependent on*
abholen (sep.) **3** *to pick up, collect*
Abitur das **3** *school leaving examination usually sat by 18-19 year olds; equivalent of A-levels taken in England and Wales*
Abiturient der; (wk. n.) **3**
Abiturientin die; (-nen) *person leaving school with the* Abitur
ablaufen* (sep.); (äu,ie,au) **10** *to pass, to happen*
ablegen (sep.) **3** *to sit (an exam)*
absagen (sep.) **4** *to cancel*
sich abreagieren; (sep.) **5** *to work off, to calm down*
abschaffen (sep.) **9** *to abolish*
abschließen **3** *to finish (one's studies)*
abschließend **10** *in conclusion*
Abschluß der; (-schlüsse) **6** zum Abschluß *conclusion; in conclusion, finally*
Abschlußprüfung die; (-en) **8** *final examination*
abschmelzen (sep.) (i,o,o) **10** to melt; reduce
abschmettern (sep.) **5** *to turn a deaf ear*
abschminken (sep.); (refl.) **10** *to take one's makeup off;* coll: sich etwas abschminken: *to drop, to forget about something*
abschrecken (sep.) **10** *to deter, scare off*
absehbar; in absehbarer Zeit *forseeable; for the forseeable future*

Absicht die; (-en) **4** *intention*
absitzen (sep.) (i,a,e) **4** *to serve* (coll.); Lit.: *to sit through*
absprechen (sep.) **2** *to discuss*
abspülen (sep.) **9** *to wash (the dishes)*
abstoßend **10** *repulsive*
Abtreibung die **9** *abortion*
abwarten (sep.) **10** *to wait (and see)*
sich abwechseln (sep.) **3** *to take turns*
Abwechslung die; (-en) **2;** *change*
zur Abwechslung *for a change*
acht **10** *regard*
außer acht lassen (ä,ie,a) *to disregard, ignore*
achten (auf + Akk.) **7** *to pay attention to*
achtlos **7** *heedless(ly)*
ähneln (+ Dat.) **5** *to resemble*
ahnen **9** *to suspect*
ähnlich **2** *similar*
Akademiker der; (-) **3** *(M.A.) graduate*
alkoholabhängig **5** *dependent on alcohol*
Alkoholgenuß der; **6** *consumption of alcohol*
Alkoholkranke der/die (adj. n.) **6** *person who is ill from alcohol-related problems*
Alkoholmißbrauch der **6** *alcohol abuse*
Alkoholtote der/die (adj. n.) **6** *person who has died from alcohol-related problems*
allerdings *though, certainly*
allerhand **2** *all sorts (of things)*
alles andere als . . . **3** *anything but*
allgemein *general;* im allgemeinen **4** *generally, in general*
allmorgendlich **2** *every morning*
allzuviel **2** *too much*
Alpen die **2** *the Alps*
als nächstes **2** *next*
Altensilo das: (-s) **6** *derogatory for: old people's home*
Alter das **2** *age*
altern **6** *to age*
alternativ **9** *alternative*
Altersrentner der **10** *pensioner*
Altersstufe die; (-n) **10** *age group*
Aluminium das **7** *aluminium*
Amerikanistik die **3** *American Studies*
Ampel die; (Sing.) *traffic light(s)*
an der Ampel **1** *at the traffic light*
die A. steht auf rot **8** *the traffic lights are red*
Amtssprache die **7** *officialese*
anbelangen (sep.) **3**; *to concern;* Was . . . anbelangt, . . . *in so far as . . ., is concerned . . .*
anbetreffen (i,a,o) **9** *to concern*
Was . . . anbetrifft *in so far as . . . is concerned . . .*
anbieten (ie,a,o) (sep.) **4** *to offer*
andere **7**; *other; different:* andere Länder, andere Sitten *when in Rome, do as the Romans do.* (Lit.: *different countries, different customs)*
ändern **4** *to change*
sich ändern *to change, alter*
anders **4**; *different(ly);* ich habe es mir anders überlegt *I've changed my mind*
anderthalb **6** *one and a half*
Änderung die; (-en) **1** *change*
Andrang der **3** *crowd, crush, surge*
andrerseits **10** *on the other hand*
anfallen* (sep.) (ä,ie,a) **2** *to come up (of work)*
Anfälligkeit die; (für + Akk.) **6** *susceptibility to*
Anfang der (¨-e) **10**; *beginning;* von Anfang an *from the start*
Anforderung die; (-en) **4** *demand*
anführen (sep.) **10** *to adduce, quote, give (an example)*
Angabe die; (-n) **8** *information*
angeblich **9** *allegedly*
Angebot das; (-e) **9** *offer, range*
angehen (sep.); (e,i,a) **5** *to concern;* Das geht dich nichts an *That doesn't concern you*
angehen (sep.); (e,i,a) **8** *to tackle*
Angelegenheit die; (-en) **7** *matter, affair*
Angeln das; **5** *fishing*
angemessen **3** *appropriately*
angeschlossen (an + Akk.) **7** *connected to*

angesichts (+ Gen.) **1** *in view of*
Angestellte der/die; (adj. n.) **4** *employee*
angleichen (ei,i,i) (sep.) **6** *to bring into line*
Anglistik die **3** *English language and literature*
Angst die; (-¨e) **8** *fear, anxiety*
anhalten (ä,ie,a); (sep.) **6** *to last, to go on*
Anhänger der; (-) **9** *supporter*
ankämpfen (sep.); (gegen + Akk.) **8** *to fight against*
ankommen* (sep.) (o,a,o) **1** *to arrive*
ankommen((sep.) (o,a,o) (auf + Akk.) **1** *to depend on, come down to*
ankündigen (sep.) **7** *to announce*
Ankunft die **1** *arrival*
ankurbeln (sep.) **6** *to boost*
Anlage die; (-n) **9** *plant*
Anlaß der **8;** *occasion;* zum Anlaß nehmen *to use as an opportunity*
anliegen (sep.) **2**; Was liegt an? *to be done; What is to be done?*
Anliegen das **9** *request*
anmelden (sep.) **5** *to register, enrol*
annehmen (sep.) (i,a,o) **7** *to accept; to take on*
sich einer Sache anpassen (sep.); **8** *to adapt to something*
Anreise die; (-n) **5** *arrival*
sich etwas anschauen **2** *to watch, look at something*
anschließend **2** *afterwards, subsequently*
Anschluß der; an + Akk. **3** *contact*
ansetzen (sep.) an + Dat. **9** *to address*
ansonsten **1** *otherwise*
ansprechen (sep.); (i,a,o) *to address*
Anspruch der; (¨-e) (auf + Akk.) **2** *demand (for), claim (to)*
in Anspruch nehmen *to take up, take advantage of*
Anstand der (kein pl.) **7** *(sense of) decency*
anstatt (+ Gen.) **1** *instead of*
sich anstellen; (sep.) **8** *to queue up*
ansteuern (sep.) **4** *to make for, head for*
Anstrengung die; (-en) **6** *effort, strain*
Anteil der; (-e) **10** *proportion*
Antrag der; (-¨e) **9** *application*
anwachsen* (sep.); (ä,u,a) *to grow, increase*
Anwärter der; (-); die Anwärterin (-nen) **4** *candidate*
Anzahl die **9** *number*
anzeigen (sep.) **9** *to indicate*
Anzug der; (-¨e) **6** *suit*
Apfel der; (¨) 7 *apple*
Apotheke die; (-n) **6** *pharmacy*
arbeitsam **8** *hard-working*
Arbeitsamt das; (¨-er) **2** *job centre*
Arbeitsbedingungen die; (pl.) **10** *conditions of work*
Arbeitsbereich der; (-e) **8** *area of work*
Arbeitslose, der/die (adj. n.) **4** *unemployed person*
Arbeitslosenrate die **10** *rate of unemployment*
Arbeitslosigkeit die **10** *unemployment*
Arbeitsplatz der; (¨-e) **2** *work-place*
Arbeitstag der; (-e) **2** *work day*
Arbeitsunfall der; (¨-e) **9** *industrial accident, accident at work*
Arbeitsweg der; (-e) **2** *way to work*
Arbeitswut die **8** *work-mania*
Architekt der (wk. n.) **7** *architect*
Architektur die **3** *architecture*
Arg das: *malice;* im Argen liegen **8** *to be in a sorry state*
sich ärgern über + Akk. **6** *to be annoyed about*
Arm der; (-e) *arm*
jdn auf den A. nehmen **7** *to pull someone's leg (coll.)*
sich in die Arme fallen **10** *to embrace, to hug*
Artikel der; (-) **10** *article*
Arzneimittel das; (-) **7** *medicine*
Ärztekammer die **6** *chamber of doctors*
ärztlich **6** *medical*
Assistent der; (wk. n.) **7** *assistant*
atmen **6** *to breathe*
Atmosphäre die **7** *atmosphere*
atomar **9** *atomic*
Atomkraft die **9** *nuclear power, energy*
Atomkraftwerk das; (-e) **9** *nuclear*

plant, power-station
Atommüll der **9** *atomic waste*
sich aufbauen (sep.) **9** *to build up*
aufbauen (sep.) **10** *to rebuild*
aufbewahren (sep.) **6** *to store, keep*
aufbringen (sep.); (i,a,a) **6** *to raise, find (money)*
aufbürden (sep.) (+ Dat.) **6** *to load onto*
Anfenthalt der; (-e) **6** *stay*
Aufenthaltsraum der; (-¨e) **6** *common room*
Auffassung die; (-en) **7** *attitude*
Aufforstung dic **7** *afforestation*
auffrischen (sep.) **2** *to freshen up, to polish up*
Aufgabe die; (-n) **6** *task*
aufgeben (sep.); (i, a, e) **3** *to drop*
aufgewühlt **6** *agitated*
aufgießen (sep.); (ie,o,o) **6** *to fill up, to pour on*
aufheben (sep.) (e,o,o) **10** *to lift, rescind, revoke*
sich aufheizen (sep.); **9** *to heat up*
aufhören (sep.) **7** *to stop, cease*
aufklären (sep.) **7** *to inform*
Aufklärungsblatt das; (¨-er) **7** *information leaflet*
aufkommen* (sep.); (o,a,o); **8** *to come up; also: to pay (for damage)*
sich auflösen (sep.) in (+ Akk.) **4** *to dissolve into*
aufnehmen (sep.); (i,a,o) **3** *to accept, absorb*
aufpolieren (sep.) **5** *to brush up*
aufräumen (sep.) **2** *to clear up*
aufregen (sep.) **10**; es regt mich auf *to annoy; that annoys me*
aufrichtig *sincere, honest, genuine*
Aufsatz der; (-¨e) **10** *essay*
aufschnappen (sep.) **8** *to pick up, hear* (coll.)
Aufschrei der **9** *outcry*
aufsichtführend **5** *supervisory*
aufstehen* (sep.) **2** (e,a,a) *to get up*
aufstocken (sep.) **9** *to boost, increase*
auftauchen* (sep.) **10** *to crop up, appear*
auftreten* (i,a,e) (sep.) **10** *to behave, appear*
Auftreten das **8** *manner; appearance*
aufwachsen* (sep.) **10** *to grow up*
Aufwand der **3** *expense (in time / money)*
aufwenden (sep.) **10** *to spend*
aufwerfen (sep.); (i,a,o) **9** *to raise*
sich aufzeigen (sep.) **10** *to be apparent*
aufziehen* (ie,o,o) (sep.) **10** *to gather*
augenblicklich **7** *instantly*
aus (+ Dat.) **1** *out of, from*
ausbauen (sep.) **9** *to extend*
ausbilden (sep.) **3** *to train*
Ausbildung die **3** *training*
Ausbildungsgang der (¨-e) **10** *training syllabus*
Ausbildungsplatz der; (¨-e) **3** *training place*
ausfallen lassen (ä,i,a) **5** *to skip*
Ausflug der; (¨-e) **2** *excursion, trip*
Ausgang der; (¨-e) **1** *exit, way out*
Ausgangspunkt der; (-e) **10** *starting point*
ausgeben (i,a,e) (sep.) **6** *to spend (of money)*
ausgehen* (sep.) (e,i,a) **9**; davon ausgehen, daß *to conclude; to assume that*
ausgeprägt **8** *pronounced*
ausgepumpt **5** *exhausted*
ausgiebig **2** *thoroughly*
auskommen* (sep.); (o,a,o); (mit + Dat) **9** *to make do with*
Ausländer der; (-) **8** *foreigner*
Auslandserfahrung die; (-en) **3** *experience of living abroad*
Auslandsstudium das **3** *study abroad*
ausmachen (sep.) **10** *to account for, to constitute*
ausmachen (sep.) **9** *to switch / turn off*
Ausmaß das; (-e) **9** *scope, extent*
Ausnahme die; (-n) **6** *exception*
ausnutzen (sep.) **9** *to take advantage of*
Ausreise die **10** *departure (from the country)*
ausreichen (sep.) **6** *to suffice, be enough*
sich ausruhen (sep.) **3** *to rest, have a rest*

ausschließen (sep.); (ie,o,o) **6** *to exclude*
sich ausschließen (sep.); (ie,o,o) **5** *to exclude oneself*
ausschließlich (+ Gen.) **1** *exclusive of*
ausschreiben (sep.) (ei,ie,ie) **7** *to write out, impose (fine)*
Ausschuß der; (Ausschüsse) **7** *committee*
aussehen (sep.) (ie,a,e) **2** *to look (like)*
Außenminister der **8** *foreign minister*
außer (+ Dat) **1** *except (for)*
außer acht lassen (ä,ie,a) **10** *to disregard, ignore*
außerhalb (+ Gen) **1** *outside of*
äußern 8 *to express*
sich äußern zu + Dat. **7** *to make a statement about*
Aussicht die; (-en) *prospect, view;* in Aussicht haben **3** *to have the prospect of*
aussprechen (sep. (i,a,o) **10**; sich aussprechen für + Akk. (i,a,o) (sep.) **6** *to pronounce, express; to speak in favour of*
aussteigen* (ei,ie,ie) (sep.) **1** *to get off, out of (a train, a bus etc)*
Ausstellung, die; (-en) **5** *exhibition*
austauschen (sep.) **3** *to exchange*
austreten* (sep.), (i,a,e) (aus + Dat.) **5** *to leave (a club, a society, etc.)*
ausüben (sep.) **5** *to practice, to do*
auswärts **5** *away, out of town*
auswaschen (sep.), (ä, u, a) **7** *to wash out*
Ausweisung die; **10** *expulsion, deportation*
Auswertung die; (-en) **6** *analysis, evaluation, assessment*
Auswirkung die; (-en) **10** *effect*
die Autobahn; (-en) **5** *motorway*
Autofahren das **9** *motoring*
Automat der; (wk. n.) **7** *vending machine, slot machine*
Autovermietung die; (-en) **6** *car rental (firm)*
sich baden **2** *to take a bath*
Badeurlaub der **8** *swimming holiday, sunshine holiday*
Badminton das; **5** *badminton*
BAFöG das (Abkürzung für: Bundesausbildungsförderungsgesetz) **3** *German student grant / loan system*
BAFöG-Satz der **3** *grant / loan rate*
Bahn die; (-en) **2**; mit der Bahn **2** *railway; by rail*
Bahnhof der; (-¨e) **2** *station*
Bahnhof Zoo der **1** *short for* Bahnhof Zoologischer Garten; *major intersection of the mainline railway, the U-Bahn and the S-Bahn*
bald **10** *soon*
baldig **6** *speedy, quick*
Ballungsraum der; (-¨e) **9** *conurbation*
Banklehre die; (-n) **3** *banking apprenticeship*
Bankwesen das **3** *banking system*
Barriere die; (-n) **10** *barrier*
Batterie die; (-n) **7** *battery*
Bauarbeiten die **1** Lit. *building works; roadworks*
Bauer der; (wk. n.) **7** *peasant, farmer*
Bauingenieur der; (-e) **4** *civil engineer*
Bauingenieurwesen das **3** *civil engineering*
Baustelle die; (-n) **8** *building site*
Bayer der; (wk. n.) **7** *Bavarian*
bayerisch **8** *Bavarian*
beabsichtigen **4** *to intend*
beachten **8** *to note, bear in mind*
beängstigen *to worry, unsettle, alarm*
Becher der; (-) **7** *cup*
bedauern **3** *to regret*
Bedauern das; **10** *regret; sympathy*
bedenken (e,a,a) **3** *to consider, bear in mind*
Bedenken das; (-e) **9** *reservation, qualm*
bedeuten **10** *to mean, to signify*
Bedeutung die **9** *importance, significance*
Bedingung die; (-en) **1** *condition*
bedrohen **3** *to threaten*
bedrücken **10** *to depress*
Bedürfnis das; (-se) (nach + Dat.) **6** *need (for)*

beeindrucken **10** *to impress*
beeinträchtigen **9** *to impair*
Befahrbarkeit die **5** *passability (of roads)*
sich befassen mit + Dat. **10** *to concern oneself with*
befehlen (ie,a,o) (+ Dat.) **8** *to order, to command*
befolgen **10** *to follow*
befördern **3** *to promote*
befragen **10** *to question*
befriedigend **2** *satisfactory*
begegnen (+ Dat.) **8** *to encounter*
begeistern **2** *to fill with enthusiasm*
sich begeistern für + Akk. **5** *to be enthusiastic about*
begeistert **10** *enthusiastic, keen*
Begeisterung die **10** *enthusiasm*
Begleiterscheinung die; (-en) **3** *concomitant*
begreifen (ei,i,i) **7** *to grasp, understand*
Begründung die **3** *reason, explanation*
behandeln **8** *to deal with, to treat*
Behandlung die; (-en) **6** *treatment*
behaupten **8** *to claim, maintain*
beherrschen **8** *to master*
behindern **5** *to impede, hold up*
behindert **4** *handicapped*
beibringen (sep.) *to teach*
beiderseits (+ Gen.) **1** *on both sides of*
Beihilfe die **9** *assistance, aid*
Beileid das; **10** *sympathy, condolences*
beimessen (sep.) (i,a,e) (+ Dat.) **9** *to attach (importance etc)*
das Beispiel (-e) (für + Akk.) **5** *example (of)*
ein Beispiel anführen **10** *to give an example*
beispiellos **10** *unprecedented*
bekämpfen **9** *to combat*
Bekannte der/die (adj. n.) **2** *acquaintance*
bekanntlich **3** *as is well known*
bekehren **7** *to convert (someone)*
sich beklagen über + Akk. **10** *to complain (about)*
bekommen (o,a,o) **2** *to get, to receive*
belasten **5** *to strain, burden*
Belastung die; (-en) **4** *strain, burden*
belegen **1** *to occupy (a room)*
beliebt **5** *popular*
bemerken **10** *to realise, to notice*
sich bemühen **7** *to make an effort, try*
Bemühung die; (-en) **3** *effort*
sich benehmen (i,a,o) **7** *to behave*
benutzen **1** *to use*
Benutzer der; (-) **1** *user*
Benzin das **7** *petrol, gasolene*
Bequemlichkeit die; (-en) **2** *laziness, idleness; also: comfort*
beraten (ä,ie,a) **7** *to advise*
Beratung die; (-en) **9** *discussion, deliberation*
Beratungsingenieur; (-); Beratungsingenieurin; (-nen) **9** *consultant engineer*
Bereich der; (-e) **3** *area, department*
bereit sein **9** *to be ready, prepared*
Bereitschaft die; **3** *readiness*
Berg der; (-e) **2** *mountain*
bergsteigen* (ei,ie,ie) **2** *to go mountain-climbing*
Bergsteigen das; **5** *mountain-climbing*
Bergwerk das; (-e) **9** *mine*
Bergwerkarbeiter der; (-) **9** *miner*
berichten **6** *to report*
berlinern **1** *to speak Berlin dialect*
Berufsberatung die; **3** *occupational guidance*
Berufskrankheit die; (-en) **9** *occupational disease*
berufstätig **4** *(gainfully) employed*
sich beruhigen **10** *to calm down*
berühmt **3** *famous*
berühren **9** *to touch*
sich beschäftigen mit + Dat. **2** *to concern oneself with*
beschäftigen **2** *to employ*
Bescheid wissen 7 (über + Akk.) *to know about*
Beschluß der; (Beschlüsse) **10** *decision*
beschreiben (ei,ie,ie) **10** *to describe*
Beschwerde die; (-n) **10** *complaint, appeal*
Beschwerdenführer der; (-) **10** *complainant, appellant*

beseitigen **8** *to remove*
besichtigen **3** *to view, look round*
Besichtigung die (-en) **1** *sightseeing*
besiegen **7** *to defeat*
bestanden **3** *passed*
bestätigen **10** *to confirm*
bestehen (e,a,a); (auf + Dat.) *to insist on*
bestehen (e,a,a) **3** *to exist*
bestellen **3** *to order*
bestenfalls **10** *at best*
besteuern **6** *to tax*
Bestnote die; (-n) **9** *best mark*
besuchen **3** *to visit*
betonen **2** *to emphasise*
Betracht: in Betracht ziehen (ie,o,o) **10** *to take into consideration*
betrachten **1** *to look at, observe*
betrachten (von obern herab) **1** *to consider, to view; to look down on (also condescendingly)*
Betrachtung die **10**; bei näherer Betrachtung *consideration; on close consideration*
Betrag der; (¨-e) **6** *amount (of money)*
betreffen (i,a,o) **10** *to concern*
betreiben (ei,ie,ie) **5** *to pursue, to carry on, to do, to run*
Betreiber der; (-) **9** *person running, here, a nuclear power plant*
betreuen **4** *to look after*
Betrieb der; (-e) **4** *company*
Betriebsführung die; (-en) **3** *guided tour of a company / workshop*
Betriebswirtschaftslehre die; (BWL) **3** *business management science*
Beutegang der; (¨-e) **9** *hunt*
Bevölkerung die; (-en) **10** *population*
bevorstehen (e,a,a) (sep.) **10** *to be imminent*
bevorzugen **3** *to prefer, give preference to*
bewältigen **3** *to cope with*
bewegend **10** *touching, moving*
Bewegung die; (-en) **6** *movement, exercise*
beweisen (ei,ie,ie) **3** *to prove*
sich bewerben (i,a,o) um + Akk. **3** *to apply for*
Bewerber der; (-) **3**; Bewerberin die; (-nen) *applicant*
bewußt (+ Gen.) **6** *conscious*
Bewußtsein das **9** *consciousness, awareness*
Bezahlung die **4** *pay*
beziehen (ie,o,o) **9** *to obtain, receive*
Beziehung die; (-en) *respect; relationship*
beziehungsweise **2** *alternatively*
bezug: in bezug auf + Akk. **8** *concerning, regarding*
bezüglich (+ Gen.) **1** *concerning, with regard to*
bezweifeln **10** *to doubt*
Bibliothek die; (-en) **3** *library*
Biene die; (-n) **6** *bee*
bieten (ie,o,o) **3** *to offer*
Bild das; (-er) **2** *picture*
bilden **4** *to form, to constitute*
Billigung die **9** *approval*
binden **6** *to bind; also: to take up*
Biologie die **3** *biology*
Biomasse die **9** *biomass*
Biotonne die; (-n) **7** *bin for organic waste*
bis (+ Akk) **1** *until*
bis zu (+ Dat.) **5** *up to, as far as*
bislang *up to now, for the time being*
Blaue das; *uncertain destination*; ins Blaue fahren **1** Lit. *the blue; to go on a tour without a destination; to go on a mystery tour*
Blaue Umweltengel der **7** Lit. *blue environment angel; sign on products which indicates whether they are environmentally friendly*
bleibenlassen (sep.) **10** *to drop, not to do something*
bleifrei *lead-free*
Blick der; (e) (über + Akk.) **1** *view*
blicken **7** *to look, glance*
Lassen Sie sich hier nicht mehr blicken! *I don't want to see you here again!* (Lit. *Don't let yourself be seen here again)*
Blockheizkraftwerk das; (-e) **9** *central plant for district heating*
Blutalkoholgehalt der; **10** *blood alcohol level*
Blutfettwert (-e) **6** *blood cholesterol level*

Bluthochdruck der **6** *high blood pressure*
Böhmen das **8** *Bohemia*
Bösewicht der; (-e) **8** *bad person, villain*
Branche die; (n) **9** *industry*
Braunkohle die **9** *lignite*
brechen (i,a,o) **2** *to break*
Breite die; (-n) **9** *latitude*
Brenner der; (-) **9** *burner*
Brennwertgerät das; (-e) **9** *calorific value meter*
Brite der; (wk. n.) **8** *Briton*
Britin die *(female) Briton*
Brücke die; (-n) **1** *bridge*
brüllen **10** *to roar*
Buch das; (-¨er) **2** *book*
Bücherei die; (-en) **2** *library*
Buchstabe der; (wk. n.) **7** *letter (of the alphabet)*
Buckel der; (-) **7** *back*; Rutsch mir den Buckel runter! *(slang) Get lost!*
Bulldozer der; (-) **8** *bulldozer*
Bulle der (wk. n.) **7** *bull; (slang) policeman*
Bummel der; (-) **1** *stroll*
Bundesbahn die; (-en) **8** *German railway;* Lit. *federal railway*
Bundesjugendministerium das **5** *federal ministry for the youth*
Bundesland das; (¨-er) **2** *federal state of the Federal Republic of Germany*
Bundespräsident der (wk. n.) **9** *Federal President*
Bundestag der **7** *Federal Parliament*
Bundesverfassungsgericht das; **10** *Federal Constitutional Court*
Bundeswehr die **4** *German federal army*
Bürger der; (-) **8** *citizen*
Büro das; (-s) **3** *office*
Bushaltestelle die; (-n) **8** *bus stop*
Buttercremekuchen der; (-) **8** *butter-cream cake*
Chefin die; (-nen) **8** *(female) boss, head*
Chemie die **3** *chemistry*
chinesisch **2** *Chinese*
Cholesterin das **6** *cholesterol*
Cholesterinspiegel der **6** *cholesterol level*
Computer der; (-) **3** *computer*
Computerwissenschaft die **3** *computer science*
da vorne **7** *over there, further ahead*
dabeisein* (sep.) **2** *to be in the process of doing something*
Dach das; (-¨er) **6** *roof*
dagegen haben (+ Akk.) **10** *to mind*
dagegen sein* **10** *to be against it*
dagegen: dagegen haben **6** *against: to have nothing against this*
dahingehend, daß **2** *in so far as, in the respect that*
dahinvegetieren (sep.) **6** *to vegetate away*
dahinvegetieren (sep.) **4** *to drag out a miserable existence* (coll.)
danach **2** *after that, then*
danken (+ Dat.) **1**; nichts zu danken **2** *to thank; not at all*
dann **2** *then*
dasselbe wie **10** *the same as*
DDR die **2** *the former German Democratic Republic*
decken **9** *to cover*
der Deckel **5** *lid;* (slang for) *driving licence*
Demonstrant der (wk. n.) **7** *demonstrator*
denkbar **9** *conceivable*
denken (e,a,a); (über + Akk.) **6** *to think about*
deprimiert **6** *depressed*
derart **6** *such;* Lit.: *of that kind*
derartig **10** (Adj.) *such*
deswegen **9** *therefore, for this reason*
deutlich **10** *clear(ly)*
dichtbesiedelt **9** *densely populated*
dick **7** *fat, thick*
dienen (+ Dat.) **5** *to serve*
Dienst der: *service*; im Dienst sein **4** *be on duty*
Dienstleistung die; (-en) **9** *service*
Ding das; (-e) **6** *thing*
Direktor der (wk. n.) **7** *director, head teacher*
diskutieren **10** *to discuss*
Dokumentarfilm der; (-e) **2** *documentary (film)*

Dom der; (-e) **10** *cathedral*
doppelt soviel . . . wie **9** *twice as much as*
Dorf das; (¨-er) **6** *village*
Drachenfliegen das; **5** *hang-gliding*
dransein* (sep.): da ist 'was dran **6** *there is some truth in that*
draufgehen* (sep.); (e,i,a) **3** *to go on something*
dringend **9** *urgent(ly)*
Drogentote der/die (adj. n.) **6** *person who has died from drug-related problems*
drohen (+ Dat.) **5** *to threaten*
drosseln **6** *to reduce, cut;* Lit.: *throttle*
Druck der **9** *pressure*
Drucker der (-) **10** *print worker*
Duale System das **7** Lit. *dual system; system which puts re-usable material into two categories (a) glass / paper and (b) all other material*
Dummkopf der; (-¨e) **7** *idiot*
Dunkelziffer die; (-n) **10** *actual number, number of unrecorded cases*
durch (+ Akk.) **1** *through*
Durchblutungsstörung die; (-en) **6** *disturbance of the blood supply; circulatory problems*
durchfallen* (sep.); (ä,ie,a) **5** *to fail (an exam)*
durchführen (sep.) **3** *to conduct; carry out, implement*
durchgehend **2** *all day, all the time*
durchhalten (sep.); (ä,ie,a) **6** *to see (something) through*
durchkreuzen **4** *to thwart, frustrate*
Durchschnitt der **5** *average*
durchsetzten (sep.) **4** *to carry through, accomplish*
Dusche die; (-n) **2** *shower*
sich unter die Dusche stellen **2** *to take a shower*
düster **10** *gloomy*
ebensosehr **10** *just as much*
Ecke die; (-n) um die Ecke **1** *around the corner*
egal *sein (+ Dat.) **10** *not to care about*
ehemalig **8** *former*
eher **10** *rather*
Eheschließung die **10** *marriage, wedding (ceremony)*
Ehre die **10** *honour*
zu Ehren + Gen. *in honour of*
ehrlich **6** *honest*
ehrlich gesagt **3** *quite honestly*
eigen **10** *own*
Eigenschaft die; (-en) **8** *characteristic*
eigentlich **2** *actual(ly)*
eigentlich *actually*; eigentlich nicht **7** *not really*
einatmen (sep.) **7** *to breathe in*
eindeutig **9** *clear, unambiguous*
eindringen (sep.) (i,a,u) **8** *to penetrate*
einführen (sep.) **9** *to introduce*
Eingangshalle die (-n) **1** *lobby, foyer*
einen **10** *to unite*
einerseits **10** *on the one hand*
einfach **10** *simple, simply*
Einfluß der; (Einflüsse) **10** *influence*
eingebunden **5** *tied, constrained, bound*
eingehen* (e,i,a) auf + Akk. **10** *to go into, deal with*
eingeschränkt **10** *restricted, limited*
eingestellt sein; sie waren positiv eingestellt *they had a positive attitude*
einigermaßen **8** *more or less*
einiges **9** *a considerable amount*
Einigung die **4** *unification*
Einigungsvertrag der **10** *unification treaty*
Einkauf der; (¨-e) **7** *shopping*
Einkaufskorb der; (¨-e) **7** *shopping basket*
Einkommen das **7** *income*
einladen (ä,u,a) (sep.) **6** *to invite*
Einladung die; (-en) **4** *invitation*
sich einlassen auf + Akk. (ä,ie,a) (sep.) **10** *to let oneself in for, get involved in*
einlegen (sep.) **6** *to put in*
einleiten (sep.) **10** *to introduce, to start*
einleitend **10** *by way of introduction*

Einleitung die **10** *introduction*
einehmen (sep.) (i,a,o) **9** *to take up, adopt (of an attitude)*
einrichten (sep.) **1** *to arrange, to establish*
Einrichtung die; (-en) **10** *institution*
Einschätzung die; (-en) **5** *estimate, estimation*
einschließlich (+ Gen.) **1** *inclusive of*
einschneidend **9** *drastic, radical (of measures)*
einschreiten (ei,i,i) (sep.) *to intervene*
einsehen (sep.); (ie,a,e) **3** *to recognise, acknowledge, to realise, to understand*
einseitig **5** *one-sided*
einsichtig **8** *understandable*
einsparen (sep.) **7** *to save, to cut down*
einstellen (sep.) **10** *to stop, close down*
Einstellung die; **3** *appointment*
Einstieg der **9** *entry*
eintauchen (sep.) (in + Akk.) **1** *to immerse (oneself) in*
Einteilung die **2** *division*
eintreten* (sep.); (i,a,e) **5** *to join; to enter, come about*
eintreten* (sep.) für (+ Akk.) **9** *to stand up for*
eintrittsfrei **9** *free of charge*
Einvernehmen das **9** *agreement, harmony*
einwenden (sep.); (e,a,a) **6** *to object*
der Einwand (-¨) (gegen + Akk.) **5** *objection (to)*
einwickeln (sep.) **8** *to wrap*
Einwirkung die; (-en); (auf + Akk.) **6** *effect on*
einzigartig **8** *unique*
Eiskunstlauf der; **5** *figure skating*
elektrisch **9** *electrical*
Elektrogerät das; (-e) **7** *electrical appliance*
Elektrotechnik die **3** *Electrical Engineering*
Ell[en]bogengesellschaft die **10** Lit. *elbow society – a society in which the weak go to the wall*
Elternhaus das **10** *parental home*
Emission die; (-en) **9** *emission*
empfangen (ä,i,a) **10** *to receive*
Empfangsdame die; (-n) **1** *(female) receptionist*
empfehlen (ie,a,o) **1** *to recommend*
es empfiehlt sich *it is advisable*
empfehlenswert **8** *advisable*
Empfindung die; (-en) **6** *sensation*
Endspiel das; (-e) **5** *final*
Energie die; (-n) **9** *energy*
Energiebedarf der **9** *energy requirements*
Energiebedarf der **9** *energy requirements*
Energiequelle die; (-n) **9** *source of energy*
Energiesparen das **9** *saving of energy*
Energiesparlampe die; (-n) **9** *energy-saving bulb*
Energieversorgungsunternehmen das; (-) **9** *electricity (*Lit. *energy) generating company*
Englischkenntnisse die (pl.) **2** *knowledge of English*
entdecken **6** *to discover*
Ente die; (-n) **1** *duck; also used coll. for a Citroen 2CV*
entfernt *distant*
nicht im entfernstesten **8** *not in the remotest*
entgegenfiebern (sep.); (+ Dat.) **10** *to look forward to something with nervous anticipation*
entgegenstreben (sep.) **2** *to strive towards*
entgehen* (e,i,a) **2** *to escape*
enthalten (ä,ie,a) **6** *to contain, to include*
entlang (+ Akk./Dat.; + Gen.) **1** *along*
entrichten (Amtssprache) **7** *to pay*
sich entscheiden (ei,ie,ie) für + Akk. *to decide on*
Entschlossenheit die **6** *determination*
Entschlußkraft die; **3** *decisiveness*
sich entschuldigen für + Akk. **10** *to apologise for*
Entsetzen das **9** *horror*
entsetzlich **10** *dreadful, terrible*
entsetzt **10** *horrified*

entsorgen **7** *to dispose of*
Entsorgung die **9** *disposal*
Entsorgungsunternehmen das; (-) **7** *waste disposal company*
sich entspannen **6** *to relax*
entspannt **1** *relaxed*
entsprechend **9** *respective(ly)*
entsprechend (+ Dat.) **6** *corresponding (to)*
entstehen* (e,a,a) **8** *to occur, come about*
enttäuscht **10** *disappointed*
entwerfen (i,a,o) **9** *to design*
entwickeln (tr.) **9** *to develop*
sich entwickeln (intr.) **10** *to develop*
Entwicklung die (-en) **10** *development, tendency*
Entwöhnung die **6** *curing of an addiction*
entziehen (ie,o,o) **5** *to withdraw, take away*
Erachten das; meines Erachtens **6** *opinion; in my opinion*
erbitten (i,a,e) **9** *to request*
erbringen (i,a,a) **8** *to give, to produce*
Erdgas das **9** *natural gas*
Erdöl das **9** *oil*
Erdölindustrie die; (-n) **9** *oil industry*
sich ereignen **10** *to occur, happen*
erfahren (ä,u,a); am eigenen Leib erfahren **8** *to learn, to experience; to experience first hand*
Erfahrung die; (-en) **3** schlechte Erfahrungen machen *experience; to have bad experiences*
erfahrungsgemäß **9** *according to experience*
Erfolg der; (-e) *success;* mit Erfolg **9** *successfully*
erfolglos **4** *unsuccessful*
erfolgreich **4** *successful*
erforderlich **1** *necessary*
erforschen **6** *to explore*
Erforschung die **9** *research*
erfreulich **10** *pleasant, pleasing*
ergänzen **2** *to complete*
sich ergeben (i,a,e) *to arise, come about*
Ergebnis das; (-se) **10** *result*; zu einem Ergebnis kommen **6** *to reach a conclusion*
ergehen* (e,i,a) (jemandem) *to befall (s.o.)*; mir ist es ähnlich ergangen **4** *I was in a similar position*
ergreifen (ei,i,i) **9** *to take, adopt (of measures)*
erhalten (ä,ie,a) **3** *to receive*
erheben (e,o,o) **9** *to levy (a tax)*
erhöht **6** *above average, somewhat high, raised*
sich erinnern an + Akk. **3** *to remember*
Erkenntnisse (pl.) **10** *findings, knowledge*; neuesten Erkenntnissen zufolge *according to most recent evidence*
erklären **7** *to explain; declare*
sich erkundigen nach + Dat. **2** *to ask about, to inform oneself about*
erlangen **8** *to obtain, to gain*
erlassen (ä,ie,a) **6** *to enact, pass (of laws)*
erleben **10** *to experience*
erledigen **2** *to deal with, attend to*
erleichtern **6** *to facilitate, make easier*
sich ernähren von + Dat. **8** *to live on*
erneuerbar **9** *renewable*
erneuern **6** *to renew*
ernstnehmen (sep.) (i,a,o) **10** *to take seriously*
erreichen **10** *to reach*
erscheinen* (ei,ie,ie) **10** *to appear*
erschwinglich **4** *affordable*
ersetzen **6** *to replace, substitute*
erst **2** *only, not until*
erstaunt **9** *astonished*
ersticken **7** *to suffocate*
sich erstrecken auf + Akk. **8** *to stretch to, extend to*
Erwachsene der/die; (adj. n.) **6** *adult*
erwähnen **8** *to mention*
erwärmen **9** *to warm up*
Erwartung die; (-en) **8** *expectation*
erwecken **9** *to evoke, awaken*
Erwerbstätige/r die/der (-n) **2** *working woman / man*
erwiesenermaßen **9** *as has been proved*
erwünschen **9** *to desire, want*
erzeugen **9** *to generate, to produce*

Erziehungs- und Bildungsauftrag der **5** *task of educating*
Erziehungswissenschaft die **3** *Education*
erzielen **9** *to achieve*
der Esel; (-) **7** *donkey, ass*
essen (i,a,e) **2** *to eat*
Essen das *the meal;* beim Essen **6** *whilst eating*
Essensreste die: (m.pl.) **7** *leftovers (of food)*
Ethik die **10** *ethics*
eventuell **7** *possible, possibly*
Ewigkeit die; **1** *eternity*
exklusiv (+ Gen.) **1** *exclusive of*
EZ-Zuschlag der (¨-e) **1** *single room supplement; EZ is short for* Einzelzimmer
Fachkenntnisse (pl.) *specialist knowledge*
Fähigkeit die; (-en) **3** *ability*
fahren* (ä,u,a) **2** *to go (in a vehicle), drive*
Fahrerlaubnis die **5** *licence to drive*
Fahrgemeinschaft die **9** *carpool*
Fahrschule die; (-n) **5** *driving school*
Fahrverbot das; (-e) **9** *ban on driving*
Fahrzeug das; (-e) **6** *vehicle*
Fall der; (¨-e) *case*; auf keinen Fall **3**; das ist der Fall **8** *in no circumstances;* Lit.: *in no case; this is the case, this is true*
Fall der; (¨-e) **10** *fall*
sich fallenlassen (ä,ie,a) **2** *to let oneself fall*
Fallschirmspringen das; **5** *parachuting*
Farbe die; (-n) **9** *paint*
Farbrest der; (-e) **7** *left-over paint*
fassen **4**; *to formulate, conceive;* sich an die eigene Nase fassen **7** *(coll.) to attend to one's own business*
faul **6** *lazy*
FCKW (*abbr. of* Fluorchlorkohlenwasserstoff) der; **7** *CFC (abbr. of chlorofluorocarbon)*
Fechten das; **5** *fencing*
fehlen **3**; *to be lacking, missing;* Das würde mir fehlen *I would miss that*
Fehlverhalten das **9** *incorrect conduct*
Feier die; (-n) **4** *celebration, ceremony*
feierlich **10** *ceremonious(ly)*
Feierabend der **6** *time after work*
Feiertag der; (-e) **7** *public holiday*
fernhalten (sep.); (ä,ie,a) **8** *to keep away*
fernsehen (sep.) (ie,a,e) **2** *to watch TV*
Fernsehrat der (¨-e) **5** *TV councillors concerned with supervision of the programmes*
fertigwerden* (i,u,o) (sep.) **3** *to finish*
Fest das; (-e) **4** *party, celebration*
festlich **10** *festive(ly)*
feststellen (sep.) **6** *to ascertain*
fett **2** *fat; bold (or print)*
feucht *damp*
finanziell **1** *financial*
finden (i,a,u) **6** *to find, to consider, to think about*
sich fit halten **5** *to keep fit*
Fitneßverein der; (-e) **6** *health club*
Flegel der; (-) **7** *lout*
Fleisch das **2** *meat*
fleißig **4** *hard-working, industrious*
fließen* (ie,o,o) **1** *to flow*
fließend **3** *fluent(ly)*
flüchtig **9** *volatile (of chemicals)*
Flüchtling der; (-e) **8** *refugee*
Fluorchlorkohlenwasserstoff der; (-e) **7** *chlorofluorocarbon*
Fluß der; (Flüsse) **10** *river*
Flußpferd das; (-e) **9** *hippopotamus*
Flüssigreiniger der; (-) **7** *liquid detergent*
folgen* (+ Dat.) **5** *to follow*
Folgeschaden der; (¨) **6** *harmful effect*
fordern **6** *to demand*
fördern **8** *to promote*
Forderung die; (-en) **9** *demand*
Formulierung die; (-en) **8** *formulation*
Forderung die; (-en) **6** *demand*
Fortbildungskurs der; (-e) **4** *(further) training course*
fortgeschritten **9** *advanced*

Fotograf der (wk. n.) **7** *photographer*
Franzose der; (wk. n.) **7** *Frenchman*
Frauenbewegung die **9** *women's movement*
freisetzen (sep.) **9** *to free, to release, to emit*
Freizeitangebot das; **3** *range of leisure activities*
Freundeskreis der **3** *circle of friends*
Fremdsprache die; (-n) **4** *foreign language*
fressen (i,a,e) **7** *to eat (of animals), to swallow up*
sich freuen auf + Akk. **1** *to look forward to*
Freundeskreis der **4** *circle of friends*
Friede(n) der; (wk. n.) **7** *peace*
Frisur die; (-en) **5** *hair-style*
froh **8** *glad*
sich fühlen **10** *to feel*
führen **1** *to lead, to conduct*
Führerschein der; (-e) **5** *driving licence*
Führerscheinentzug der **10** *driving ban (*Lit. *driving licence withdrawal)*
Führung die (-en) **1** *guided tour*
für (+ Akk) **1** *for*
Furcht die; (vor + Dat.) **8** *fear (of)*
Fürst der; (wk. n.) **7** *prince*
Fürstin die; (-nen) **8** *princess*
Fuß der (Füsse); zehn Minuten zu Fuß **2**; Fuß fassen **10** *foot; a ten-minute walk;* Lit.: *ten minutes on foot; to find one's feet*
Fußgängerregel die; (-n) **8** *rule for pedestrians*
Galerie die; (-n) **2** *gallery*
Gammeln das **10** *loafing around*
Gang der; (-¨e) **6** *course (of a meal)*
ganz einfach **7** *very simple*
gar **8** *even*
gar nicht **7** *not at all*
Gast der; (-¨e) **8**; zu Gast sein *guest; to be someone's guest*
Gaststätte die; (-n) **2** *public house, restaurant, inn*
Gasturbine die; (-n) **9** *gas turbine*
gaswirtschaftlich **9** *pertaining to the gas industry*
Gattin die; (-nen) **9** *wife (formal)*
GAU der; (größter anzunehmender Unfall) *greatest imaginable accident (in a nuclear plant)*
Gebäude das; (-) **7** *building*
geben (i,a,e) **2**; eine Party geben *to give; to give, throw a party*
geboren sein* **10** *to be born*
Gebrauch machen (von + Dat.) **3** *to make use of*
Gebrauch der; (¨-e) **3** *usage, use; also: custom*
gebraucht **7** *used*
Gebühr die; (-en) **3** *fee*
Geburtenrate die; (-n) **3** *birth rate*
Geburtstag der; (-e) **2** *birthday*
Gedanke der; (wk. n.) **7** *thought*
gedenken **4** (e,a,a) *to have in mind, plan*
Gedicht das; (-e) **2** *poem*
geeignet **9** *suitable, appropriate*
Gefahr die; (-en) **6** *danger*
gefallen (sep.); (ä,ie,a); (+ Dat.) **1** *to be pleasing*
es gefällt mir **2** *I like it*
gefälligst **7** *kindly*
Gefühl das; (-e) **3** *feeling*
gegen (+ Akk.) **1** *about, towards; against*
gegenüber (von) (+ Dat.) **1** *opposite*
das Gehirn; (-e) **8** *brain*
das Gehirngewebe **8** *brain tissue*
gehorchen (+ Dat.) **5** *to obey*
Gehorsam der; **8** *obedience*
gehoben **4** *elevated, refined*
gehören **7** *to belong*
Geisteswissenschaften die **3** *Humanities*
geistig **4** *mental(ly), spiritually; concerning the mind*
gelangen* **5** *to get to, to reach, to arrive*
Gelassenheit die **5** *calmness*
Geld das **2** *money*
Geldstrafe die; (-n) **10** *fine*
gelegen: An der Lösung dieses Problems ist mir wirklich sehr gelegen *I am really keen for a solution to this problem*
Gelegenheit die; (-en) **5** *opportunity*
gelegentlich **2** *occasionally*

Gelenk das; (-e) **5** *joint*
gelingen* (i,a,u) **4**; Es ist mir nicht gelungen, . . . *to succeed; I didn't succeed in . . ., I didn't manage to . . .*
gelten (i,a,o) **9** *to be valid, apply*
gemächlich **2** *leisurely*
gemeinsam **1** *communal, common*
Gemeinsamkeit die (-en) **10** *common feature*
Gemüter die (pl.) **9**; *spirits, feeling;* das erhitzt die Gemüter *that makes feelings run high*
genau **4**; genau(er) hinschauen *exact(ly), precise(ly); to take a closer look*
Genauigkeit die **8** *exactness, meticulousness*
genauso gut **10** *just as well*
genießen (ie,o,o) **8** *to enjoy*
genug haben (+ Dat.) **5** *to have enough*
der Genuß **6** *enjoyment, consumption*
die Genußmittel (pl.) **6** *drinks and tobacco*
geöffnet **2** *open*
Geographie die **3** *geography*
Gepäck das **1** *luggage*
gepflegt **8** *well-kept*
gerade **8** *just*
gerade hier **3** *here of all places*
gerade dann . . . wenn **6** *precisely at a time when*
geradeaus **1** *straight on*
Gerät das; (-e) **9** *appliance, instrument*
geraten* (ä,ie,a) **6**; *to get, go;* in Schwierigkeiten geraten *to run into difficulties*
geregelt **7** *regulated*
Gericht das; (-e) *court*
gering **3**, **9**; *little, low;* nicht im geringsten **9** *not in the slightest*
Germanistik die **3** *German Language and Literature*
gerührt **10** *touched, moved*
gesamt **9** *total, whole*
geschädigt **7** *damaged*
geschäftlich **4** *concerning business*
Geschäftsreise die; (-n) **4** *business trip*
geschehen* (ie,a,e) **10** *to happen*
Geschenk das; (-e) **8** *present*
Geschichte die; **1** *history; story*
geschieden **3** *divorced*
Geschirr das; (-e) **9** *dishes*
Geschmack der **5** *taste*; je nach Geschmack; das ist nach meinem G. **5** *according to taste; this is to my taste, liking*
gesellig **5** *sociable*
gesellschaftlich **10** *social(ly)*
Gesellschaft die; (-en) **3** *society*
Gesellschaftskundelehrer der; (-) **10**; Gesellschaftskundelehrerin die (-nen) *teacher of social studies*
Gesellschaftswissenschaften die **3** *Social Sciences*
Gesetz das (-e) **9** *law*
gesetzlich **6** *legal(ly), statutory*
gesetzlich vorgeschrieben *regulated by law*
gesetzt **8** *staid*
Gesichtspunkt der; (-e) **10** *point of view*
gestalten **4** *to arrange, form, shape*
Gestaltung die **3** *design*
gestreßt **8** *stressed*
gesundheitlich **9** *from the health point of view*
Gesundung die **9** *recovery*
Getränk das; (-e) **6** *drink*
gewaltig *huge, enormous*
Gewalttat die; (-en) **9** *act of violence*
Gewicht das; (-e) **6** *weight*
Gewitter das; (-) **5** *storm*
gewöhnen *to familiarise*; an etwas gewöhnt sein **5** *to be used to something*
gewöhnlich **2** *usually*
Gezeiten die (pl.) **9** *tides*
Gezeitenkraftwerk das; (-e) **9** *tidal power-station*
giftig **7** *poisonous, toxic*
Giftmobil das; (-e) **7** *van for toxic waste*
Giraffe die; (-n) **9** *giraffe*
Glascontainer der; (-) **7** *glass container*
Glasampulle die; (-n) **7** *glass ampoule*
Glaube der; (wk. n.) **7** *belief, faith*

glauben (+ Dat.) **5** *to believe*
glauben (an + Akk.) **10** *to believe in*
glauben machen (+ Akk.) **8** *to make (someone) believe*
gleich **7** *same*
gleichmäßig **9** *regular(ly), equal(ly)*
Gliedmaße die; (-en) **6** *limb*
Glimmstengel der; (-) **6** *(coll.) ciggy, fag*
Glück das: Glück haben **3** *luck; to be lucky*
glücklicherweise **2** *fortunately*
Glücksspiel das; (-e) **5** *lottery*
Grad das; (-) **7** *degree*
Graf der; (wk. n.) **7** *count*
grasen **9** *to graze*
gratulieren (+ Dat.) **5** *to congratulate*
greifen (ei,i,i) **3** *to grasp, reach*; in die Tasche greifen *to dig into one's pockets*
Grenzbereich der; (-e) **6** *limit (upper or lower)*
Grenze die; (-n) **1** *border, frontier*
Greueltat die; (-en) **8** *atrocity*
grob **3** *rough(ly)*
groß *large, big;* im großen und ganzen **8** *by and large*
großartig **8** *magnificent, splendid*
großräumig **9** *over a large area*
großspurig **8** *bigheaded, boastful*
größtenteils **5** *for the greater part, mainly*
Großversuch der; (-e) **5** *large-scale test*
Grund der; (¨-e) **5** *reason, bottom*; im Grunde **10** *basically*
Grundgesetz das **10** *Basic Law (constitution of the Federal Republic)*
grundgesetzlich **10** *constitutional*
Grundlage die (-n) **10** *basis, foundation*
gründlich **8** *thorough*
Gründlichkeit die **8** *thoroughness*
Grundstein der; (-e) **8** *foundation stone*
Grüne das *the countryside;* Lit.: *the green*
ins Grüne fahren **1** *to take a trip into the countryside*
Grüne Punkt der **7** Lit. *the Green Dot; sign on products to indicate that a wrapping should be recycled once*
Gruppierung die; (-en) **8** *group, faction*
gucken **10** *to watch*
gutbürgerliches Essen **6** *good, plain food*
Gymnasiallehrer/in der/die (-/-nen) **3** *grammar school teacher*
Gymnasium das (-en) **10** *(West German) grammar school*
halten (ä,ie,a); (von + Dat.) **6** *to think of*
halten (ä,ie,a); (für + Akk.) **7** *to consider to be*
die Haltestelle **1** *(bus, train, tram) stop*
Haltung die; (-en) **9** *attitude*
Hand die; (¨-e) *hand;* seine Hand für etwas ins Feuer legen **8** *to swear to something;* Lit. *to put one's hand into the fire for something*
handeln **10** *to act*
Händler der; (-) **2** *tradesman, dealer*
Handwerker der; (-) **2** *craftsman*
handwerklich *technical (work done by a craftsman / woman)*
Hang der **8** *tendency*
hänseln **8** *to tease*
Hartplastik das **7** *hard plastic (cracks when squeezed)*
Haß der **10** *hatred*
hätte **1** *would have; conditional form of the verb* haben
Haufen der; (-) **8** *crowd, pile*
Hauptbereich der; (-e) **10** *main area*
Hauptgrund der; (-¨e) **3** *main reason*
Hauptniederlassung die; (-en) **8** *main branch, main line*
Hauptpunkt der; (-e) **10** *main point*
hauptsächlich **1** *mainly*
Hauptschulabgänger/-in der/die (-/-nen) **3** *secondary school leaver (after nine years)*
Hauptstraße die; (-n) **5** *main road; High Street, Main Street*
Hauptursache die; (-n) **10** *main cause*

Hausbrand der **9** *domestic burning of fuel*
Haushalt der; (-e) **7** *household*
Hausmüll der **7** *household waste*
Hausrat der **7** *household goods*
Haut die; (¨-e) **6** *skin*
Hausschlüssel der; (-) **6** *house key*
Hebel der; (-) **9** *lever*
Heimat die **8** *home country, home region*
heiter; das kann ja heiter werden **7** *funny, cheerful, bright; that will be fun (iron.)*
heizen **2** *to heat*
Heizkosten die; (pl.) **7** *heating costs*
Heizplatte die; (-n) **2** *hotplate*
Heizung die; (-en) **9** *heating*
helfen (i,a,o) (+ Dat.) **1** *to help*
herabblicken (sep.) (auf + Akk.) **1** *to look down on*
herausfinden (i,a,u) (sep.) **10** *to find out*
heraushören (sep.) **10** *to hear, to detect*
herausragend **10** *outstanding*
herausstellen (sep.) **3** *to stress, emphasise*
Herbst der; **2** *autumn, fall*
herholen; zu weit hergeholt **10** *to fetch, too far-fetched*
herkömmlich **9** *traditional*
Herr der; (wk. n; -n, -en) **7** *gentleman*
herrichten (sep.) **6** *to do up, tidy up*
herrschen **9** *to prevail*
herstellen (sep.) **4** *to produce, manufacture*
Hersteller der; (-) **7** *producer, manufacturer*
Herstellung die **7** *production*
hervorrufen (sep.); (u,ie,u) **9** *to cause*
Herz das; (wk. n.) **7** *heart*
Hessische Rechnungshof der **4** *audit office of the state of* Hesse
Hetzkampagne die; (-n) **8** *smear campaign*
Hilfe die; (n) **2** *help, assistance, aid*
Hin- und Rückflug der; (¨-e) **1** *return flight*
hinschauen (sep.) **4** *to look (at)*
Hinsicht die; (-en) **10** *respect, regard*
hinter (+ Akk./Dat.) **1** *behind*
hintereinander **8** *one after another*
hinterher **7** *afterwards*
Hinterhof der; (¨-e) **1** *courtyard*
hinweisen (sep.); (ei,ie,ie); (auf + Akk.) **6** *to point out*
Hirnabbau der **6** *brain damage;* Lit. *brain reduction*
Hirt der (wk. n.) **7** *shepherd*
historisch **10** *historic/al(ly)*
Hochschule die; (-n) **3** *institution of higher education*
Hochschulstudium das (-en) **3** *study at an institution of higher education*
hochspielen (sep.) **8** *to play up, to exaggerate*
höchstens **2** *at the most* .
Hochzeit die; (-en) **5** *wedding*
Hoffnung die; **10** *hope*
Höhlenforschung, die **5** *caving, pot-holing*
Holz das **9** *wood*
Honig der **2** *honey*
hören **2** *to hear, to listen to*
Hörsaal der; (Hörsäle) **3** *lecture theatre*
Hose die; (-n) *trousers*; in die Hose gehen **10** *to be a complete flop* (coll.)
immer **2** *always*
immerhin **9** *all the same, at least*
impfen **6** *to vaccinate*
imponieren (+ Dat.) **5** *to impress*
Inbegriff der **9** *epitome, quintessence*
Industriekaufmann/-frau der/die **3** *person with three years' business training*
Infarkt der; (-e) **6** *heart attack, coronary (infarction)*
Informatik die **3** *Computer Science*
Initiative die; (-n) **7** *initiative; also: citizens' action group*
inklusiv (+ Gen.) **1** *inclusive of*
innerhalb (+ Gen.) **1** *inside of*
innerlich **6** *inside, internal*
innerstädtisch **9** *inner-city*
insgesamt **6** *in total, in all*
installieren **9** *to install*
Integration die; **10** *integration*
sich interessieren für + Akk. **2** *to be*

interested in
Internationale Atomenergiebehörde die **9** *International Atomic Energy Agency*
irgendwelch- **2** *any . . . at all*
Isarschlamm der **9** *the mud of the river Isar*
italienisch **2** *Italian*
Jahr das; (-e) *year*; vor zwei Jahren **2**; zweimal im Jahr **2** *two years ago; twice a year*
vor anderthalb Jahren **6** *eighteen months ago (*Lit. *one and a half years ago)*
Jahresbericht der; (-e) **4** *annual report*
je **5** *per, in each case*
je nachdem **2** *according to*
jed- **7** *each, every*
jedenfalls **6** *in any case*
jen- **7** *that*
jenseits (+ Gen.) **1** *on the other side of*
jeweils *in each instance*
Journalist der; (wk. n.) **7** *journalist*
Jubel der **10** *enthusiasm*
jüdisch **8** *Jewish*
Jugendarbeitslosigkeit die **10** *youth unemployment*
Jugendliche der/die (wk.n.) **3** *young person*
Junge der; (wk.n.) **7** *boy*
Jura die **3** *Law*
Jutesäckchen das; (-) **7** *small jute sack*
Kaffee der **2** *coffee*
Kammer die; (-n) **6** *chamber*
Kandidat der; (wk. n.) **7** *candidate*
Kanufahren das; **5** *canoeing*
karren **10** *to cart*
Karte die; (-n) **5** *ticket*
Käsemeister der **8** *master at cheese-making*
Käserei die (-en) **8** *cheese-factory*
Kat der *abbr. of* Katalysator **9**
Katalysator der; (-en) **9** *catalytic converter*
Kater der; (-) **6** *cat; also: hangover* (coll.)
kaufen **2** *to buy*
kaufmännisch **3** *commercial, business . . .*
Kaugummi der; (-s) **6** *chewing gum*
Kegelclub der; (-s) **5** *bowling club*
Kehrseite die; (-n) **8** *the other side*
Kellner der; (-) *waiter*
Kellnerin die; (-nen) **2** *waitress*
Kenner der; (-) **9** *expert, authority*
Kernenergie die **9** *nuclear / atomic energy*
Kernkraftwerk das (-e) **9** *nuclear power-station*
Kette die; (-n) **6** *chain*
Kettenraucher/-in der/die (-/-nen) **6** *chain smoker*
Kfz-Werkstatt die; (-¨en) **4** *car repair workshop*
Kilowattstunde die; (-n) **9** *kilowatt-hour*
Kinderprogramm-Schiene die (-n) **5** *series of children's programmes covering the state TV channels*
Kindersendung die; (-en) *children's programme*
Kindesmißhandlung die **10** *mistreatment of children, child abuse*
Klamotten (f.pl.) **7** *(coll) clobber, gear*
klappen **4** *to turn out all right*
klar **7** *clear*
Klarheit die **9** *clarity*
Klettern das; **5** *climbing*
klingeln **2** *to ring*
Klischee das; (-s) **8** *cliché*
Kloß der; (-¨e) **8** *dumpling*
knackig **7** *crisp, crunchy*
Koalitionär der; (-e) **9** *coalition partner;* (here) *member of the ruling coalition*
kochen **2** *to cook, to make (coffee)*
Kochnische die; (-n) **2** *small cooking area;* Lit.: *cooking niche*
Kohle die **9** *coal*
Kohlekraftwerk das; (-e) **9** *coal-fired power station*
Kohlendioxid das **9** *carbon dioxide*
Kohlenwasserstoff der; (-e) **9** *hydrocarbon*
Kollege der; (wk. n.) **7** *colleague*
Kollegin die; (-nen) *(female) colleague*
Kolpingwerk das **1** *Kolping organisation*
komisch: das hört sich komisch an **7**

strange: that sounds strange
Kommilitone/-in der/die (-n/nen) **3** *fellow-student*
Kommunalverwaltung die; (-en) **7** *local administration*
Kommunikationstechnik die **5** *communication technology*
Komposthaufen der; (-) **7** *compost (heap)*
Konkurrenz die **3** *competition*
konkurrenzfähig **3** *competitive, viable*
konkurrieren **3** *to compete*
können (a,o,o) *to be able to*
sich konzentrieren auf + Akk. *to concentrate on*
Konzequenz die; (-en) **9** *consequence*
Körperbehinderte der/die (wk.n.) **3** *physically handicapped person*
körperlich **4** *physically, bodily; concerning the body*
korrekt **8** *correct*
kosten **1**; NB: Das hat **mich 200** DM gekostet *to cost; That cost me 200 marks*
Kosten die **9** *cost*
kostspielig **9** *expensive*
Kraft die; (¨-e) *force, power*; außer Kraft setzen **8** *to repeal, to countermand*
Kraftwerk das; (-e) **9** *power station*
Kran der; (¨-e) **8** *crane*
Krankenversicherung die; (-en) **6** *health insurance*
Kranzarterie die; (-n) **6** *coronary artery*
Krawall der; (-e) **8** *riot*
Krebs der **6** *cancer*
Krebserkrankung die; (-en) **6** *illness involving cancer*
Krebsrisiko das; (-en) **9** *cancer risk*
Kreislauf der **5** *circulatory system*
Kreisverwaltung die **10** *district authority*
Kreuz das; (-e) **1** *cross, motorway interchange*
Kreuzung die; (-en) **1** *crossroads*
kribbeln **6** *to tickle*; es kribbelt mir/mich *I have pins and needles*
Kriegsdienstverweigerer der; (-) **4** *conscientious objector (to military service)*
Kriminalität die **10** *criminality, crime*
krisenfest **10** *unaffected by crises*
krisengeschüttelt **9** *shaken by crisis, crisis-ridden*
Küchenabfall der; (¨-e) **7** *organic waste;* Lit. *kitchen waste*
Kühlschrank der; (¨-e) **2** *refrigerator*
kulturinteressiert **5** *interested in the arts*
sich kümmern um (+ Akk.) **6** *to take care of, look after, concern oneself with*
Kunde der; (wk. n.) **7** *customer, client*
kündigen **10** *to hand in one's notice*
Kündigungsschutz der **10** *protection against dismissal*
Kundin die; (-nen) **1** *(female) customer*
kundtun (sep.) **4** *to reveal, announce*
künftig **7** *in future*
Kunst die **2** *art*
Kunst-Galerie die; (-n) **2** *art gallery*
Kunstgeschichte die **3** *history of art*
Kunstmäzenin die; (-nen) **8** *patron(ess) of the arts*
Kunststoffverpackung die; (-en) **7** *plastic wrapping*
kursiv **2** *in italics*
Kurswechsel der **9** *change of course*
Kurzarbeit die **4** *short-time working, short time*
küssen **2** *to kiss*
Labor(atorium) das; (-s/-en) **3** *lab(oratory)*
lächerlich **10** *ridiculous*
Laib der;(-e) **8** *loaf (of bread);* ein Laib Käse *a whole cheese*
lallen **8** *babble, mumble*
Land das; (¨-er): an Land **5** *country, shore: ashore*
Land das; (¨-er) **2** *federal state (of the Federal Republic of Germany)*
Landbau der **3** *agriculture*
landen **5** *to arrive, to land*
Landespflege die **3** *landscape conservation*
Landschaft die **8** *scenery*

Landwirt der; (-e) **2** *farmer*
lang: am längsten **3** *long; longest*
langen **9** *to suffice*
langfristig **9** *long-term, in the long run*
langgehen (sep); man wußte, wo es langgeht **10** *to go in a certain direction; one knew the rules (coll.)*
langjährig **5** *of many years*
langsam **9** *slow(ly)*
längst **10** *long since*
langweilen **5** *to bore*
langweilig **1** *boring*; Wird Ihnen nicht manchmal langweilig? **2** *Don't you get bored sometimes?*
Langzeitschaden der; (¨) **9** *long-term damage*
laufen (ä,ie,au) **2** *to run, walk; to be on (TV)*
Laufende das; auf dem Laufenden sein **5** *the latest; to be up to date*
laut (+ Gen.) **1** *according to*
lauten **6** *to run, go (of text)*
Lebensart die **8** *way of life*
Lebensraum der; (¨-e) **9** *habitat*
Leberzirrhose die; (-n) **6** *cirrhosis of the liver*
Leck das; (-s) **9** *leak*
sich legen *to lie*; sich ins Bett legen **2** (Lit. *lay oneself) down; to go to bed*
Lehrkabinett das **10** *training workshop (East German expression)*
Lehrstelle die; (-n) **3** *training place, trainee post*
Lehrveranstaltung die; (-en) **2** *(higher education) class, seminar, lecture*
Leib der; (-er) **8** *body*
Leichenbeschauer der; **8** *doctor performing an autopsy*
Leichtathletik die; **5** *[track and field] athletics*
leiden (ei,i,i) **6** *to suffer*
leihen (ei,ie,ie) **2** *to lend; to borrow*
Leistung die; (-en) **1** *achievement; also: what is offered, included (in a package holiday), performance*
Leistungsanforderung die; (-en) **8** *demands on performance*
Leistungsdruck der **8** *pressure to perform, to work harder*
Leistungsprinzip das (-ien) **10** *achievement principle, competitive principle*
Leistungsschwimmer/-in der/die (-/-nen) **10** *competitive swimmer*
leitend *managing, leading*
leitende(r) Angestellte(r) (adj n.) *executive, manager*
Leitfaden der **8** *textbook; basic introduction*
letzthin **10** *recently*
letztlich **3** *ultimately*
Leukämie die **9** *leukemia*
lieben **7** *to love*
liebenswürdig **8** *kind, charming*
lieber; es ist mir lieber **5** *preferable; to prefer: I prefer (it)*
liegen (ie,a,e) (in + Akk.) **1** *to be situated (in), to lie (in)*
liegen (ie,a,e) **3** (+ Dat); *to be appropriate;* Das liegt mir nicht **3**; *That doesn't suit me; that doesn't appeal to me;* Das liegt mir am Herzen **9** *That is a matter of concern to me*
liegenbleiben* (sep.) (ei,ie,ie) *to be left over, undone*
Linienschiff das; (-e) **1** *company ship*
links (nach) **1** *to the left*
links **1** *on the left*
Liter der/das; (-) **7** *litre*
locker **10** *casual(ly)*
Lohn der; (-¨e) **3** *wage*
sich lohnen **1** *to be worthwhile*
Lohntüte die (-n) **10** *wage packet*
Lokal das; (-e) **6** *bar/pub*
Lokalbesitzer der; (-) **6** *bar/pub owner*
lösen **1** *here: to buy, to obtain (a ticket)*
losgehen* (e,i,a) (sep.) **2** *to start, set off*
Losung die;(-en) **10** *slogan*
Lösung die;(-en) **1** *solution*
lösungsmittelhaltig **9** *solvent-containing*
Lösungsmöglichkeit die **10** *possible solution*
Lösungsteil der **2** *solutions, answers*
losfahren* (ä,u,a) (sep.) **1** *to set out*

(in a vehicle)
los: Was ist denn los? **10** *What's going on then?*
loswerden* (i,u,o) (sep.) **3** *to be rid of*
Lücke die; (-n) **2** *gap*
Lückentext der; (-e) **2** *gapped text*
Luft die; (¨-e); dicke Luft **7** *air; polluted air;* Lit.: *thick air*
Luftbelastung die **9** *air pollution (*Lit. *burdening of the air)*
Lüneburger Heide die **9** *the Luneburg Heath*
Lunge die; (-n) **8** *lung*
Lust haben **6** *to be in the mood, to want to*
Luxus der **1** *luxury*
Macht die; (¨-e) **8** *power*
Mädchen das; (-) **7** *girl*
Magen der **8** *stomach*
Mahlzeit die; (-en) **1** *meal*
Malerei die; **5** *painting*
manches **10** *a number of things*
manchmal **2** *sometimes*
Marktwirtschaft die **4** *market economy*
marktwirtschaftlich **3** *concerning the principles of a market economy*
Marmelade die; (-n) **2** *jam*
Maß das; (-e): in Maßen **6** *measure: in moderation*
Maschinentechnik die **3** *Mechanical Engineering*
Maschinist der; (-en) **4** *machinist*
Maßnahme die; (-n) *measure*
eine Maßnahme ergreifen **6** *to take a measure*
massenhaft **6** *in large quantities*
Mathematik die **3** *Mathematics*
meckern (über + Akk.) **8** *to moan, grouse, bleat (about)*
Medaille die; (-n) **8**; die Kehrseite der Medaille *medal; the other side of the coin*
Medien die; (pl.) **10** *media*
medikamentös **6** *with drugs*
Mediziner/-in der/die; (-/-nen) **6** *medical expert*
mehrfach **9** *repeated(ly)*
Mehrheit die **6** *majority*
Mehrwegverpackung die; (-en) **7** *re-usable packaging*
Mehrzahl die **10** *majority*
meiden (ei,ie,ie) **8** *to avoid*
meinen (zu + Dat.) **6** *to think about, to have an opinion on*
Meinung die; (-en) **6** *opinion*
meistens **2** *mostly*
Meldebürokratie die; (-n) **5** *information bureaucracy*
Menge die; (-n) **6** *quantity*
Mensa die; (-en) **2** *refectory, university dining hall*
Mensch der; (wk. n.) **7**; Mensch! **3** *human being, person; wow!*
menschlich **9** *human*
merkwürdig; das erscheint mir merkwürdig **7** *strange, peculiar; that seems strange to me*
messen (i,a,e) **9** *to measure*
Meßfühler der; (-) **5** *sensor*
Meter der/das; (-) **5** *metre*
Metzger der; (-) **2** *butcher*
Metzgerei die; (-en) **2** *butcher's (shop)*
mies **10** *terrible, lousy*
Mietwagen die; (-) **6** *hire car*
Minderheit die; (-en) **4** *minority*
Mineralöl das; (-e) **9** *mineral oil*
Minna: die Grüne Minna **4** *German police car (coll.)*
Mißbrauch der **6** *abuse*
Misere die (-n) **10** *wretched, dreadful state*
Mißgeschick das **8** *misadventure*
Mist bauen **10** *to mess things up (coll.)*
mit sich bringen (i,a,a) **9** *to entail*
Mitbürger der; (-) **8** *fellow citizen*
miteinander **3** *with one another*
Mitfahrzentrale die; (-n) **9** *agency for people wanting or giving lifts*
Mitglied das; (-er) **8** *member*
mitkriegen (sep.) **7** (coll.) *to get, understand*
mitmachen (sep.); (bei + Dat.) **7** *to take part in, to participate*
Mitmensch der (-en) **6** *fellow human being*
Mittag der; zu Mittag essen **2** *midday; to have lunch*
mittags **2** *midday, lunchtime*
die Mitte **8** *middle*
Mittel das; (-) **6** *means*

mitten (durch + Akk.) **1** *(through) the middle of*
Mitternacht die **2** *midnight*
Mittlere Reife die **3** *secondary school leaving certificate taken after ten years of schooling*
mögen (Modalverb) *to like*
Möglichkeit die; (-en) **2** *possibility*
monieren **4** *to criticise*
Moralpredigt die; (-en) **7** *(moralising) lecture*
motiviert **4** *motivated*
Motorradrennen das; **5** *motor-cycle racing*
Müll der **9** *rubbish, garbage*
Müllabfuhr die **7** *refuse collection, garbage collection*
Mülldeponie die; (-n) **7** *rubbish tip*
Müllentsorgung die **8** *rubbish disposal, garbage disposal*
Müllhalde die; (-n) **7** *rubbish tip*
Mülltonne die; (-n) **7** *rubbish bin*
der Mund; (-¨er) **7** *mouth*
Musik die **3** *music*
Musikant der; (wk. n.) **7** *musician*
müssen (u,u,u) **1** *to have to, must*
Muttersprache die; (-n) **1** *mother tongue*
nach wie vor **8** *still, as always*
Nachbar der; (wk. n.) **7** *neighbour*
Nachbarschaft die **7** *neighbourhood*
Nachfrage die; (-n) **3** *demand*
nachfühlen (sep.) + Dat. **10**; *to empathise with;* Das kann ich dir nachfühlen! *I know what you mean!*
die Nachnahme: per Nachnahme **10** *delivery: cash on delivery (COD)*
Nachrichtensendung die; (-en) **2** *news*
Nachrüstung die **9** *upgrading*
nachsehen (ie,a,e) (sep.) **1** *to have a look*
nächstgelegen **9** *nearest*
Nachteil der; (-e) **3** *disadvantage*
Nachweis der; (-e); einen Nachweis erbrigen **8** *proof, evidence; to produce evidence*
Nähe die *proximity*
in der Nähe von (+ Dat.) **1** *near*
nahebringen (sep.); (Dat.) **8** *to bring something to life for someone*
sich nähern (+ Dat.) **5** *to approach*
nämlich **1** Lit. *namely; you see*
Name der; (wk. n.) **7** *name*
Naschwerk das **6** *sweets*
Nase die; (-n) *nose*
die N. voll haben **7** *to have had enough* (coll.)
Nationalhymne die **8** *national anthem*
Nationalstolz der **8** *national pride*
naturbelassen **8** *natural*
natürlich **7** *natural(ly)*
neben (+ Dat.) **1** *next to, near; also: in addition to*
nehmen (i,a,o) **8** *to take*
neidisch **3** *envious*
neigen (zu + Dat.) **8** *to tend to*
nervenaufreibend **4** *nerve-racking*
neulich **10** *recently*
nicht allzufern **9** *not too far off*
Nichtraucher der; (-) *non-smoker*
nie **2** *never*
Niedergang der **10** *fall, decline*
niedrig **3** *low*
normalerweise **2** *normally*
Note die; (-n) **9** *mark grade*
nötig sein **5** *to be necessary*
nötig *necessary*; etwas nötig haben **4** *to need something*
notwendig **9** *necessary*
Nulltarif der; (-e); *no charge*: zum Nulltarif **6** *free of charge*
nur **4** *only*
Nuß die; (Nüsse) **8** *nut*
nutzen **6** *use*
Nutzung die **9** *use*
Oase die: (-en) **1** *oasis*
Obdachlose der/die; (adj. n) **7** *homeless person*
obendrein **4** *above all, on top*
Oberdeck das; (-s) **1** *top deck*
offenkundig werden **10** *to become apparent*
offensichtlich **10** *apparent, clear*
Öffentlich-Rechtlichen die (pl.) **5** *state television channels*
Öffentliche Dienst der **4** *public service sector*
Öffentlichkeit die **6** *public*
öfters **2** *fairly often*
oftmals **8** *often (times)*
ohne (+ Akk) **1** *without*

Ohrensausen das **6** *ringing in the ears*
Opernsänger der; (-) **8** *opera singer*
Opfer das; (-) **8** *victim*
Optimist der; (wk.n) **10** *optimist*
ordentlich **8** *tidy*
Ordnung die **8** *order, orderliness, tidiness*
ordnungsliebend **8** *adj. (person) who likes to see things neat and tidy*
Orientierung die **8** *orientation*
orten **5** *to locate*
Ostseeküste die **2** *Baltic Coast*
Ozonwerte die (m.pl.) *ozone values, levels*
Pädagoge der; (wk.n.) **9** *teacher, educationalist*
Papiertonne die; (-n) **7** *paper bin*
Parfüm das; (-s) **7** *perfume, scent*
parken **3** *to park*
parlamentarisch **5** *parliamentary*
Partnerstadt die; (¨-e) **5** *twin town*
Party die; (-s) **2**; eine Party geben *party; to give a party*
passen (+ Dat.) **5** *to suit, match*
passieren lassen (ä,ie,a) **8** *to let pass*
passieren* **5** *to happen*
Pause die; (-n) *break:* eine Pause einlegen **6** *to take a break*
Pensum das **3** *amount of work, work quota*
personell **4** *concerning the personnel*
Pfandflasche die; (-n) **7** *returnable bottle (on which deposit is paid)*
pfeifen (ei,i,i) **8** *to whistle*
Pferderennen das; **5** *horse racing*
Pflanzenöl das; (-e) **9** *vegetable oil*
pflegen **8** *to care for*
Pflicht die **9** *compulsion; duty*
Pflichtfach das; (¨er) **9** *compulsory subject*
Phantasiebegabte der/die; (-n) **9** *person with a vivid imagination*
Photovoltaïkanlage die **9** *solar power plant*
Philosophie die **3** *Philosophy*
Phosphat das; (-e) **7** *phosphate*
Physik die **3** *Physics*
Podiumsdiskussion die; (-en) **2** *panel discussion*
Politiker der; (-) **9** *politician*
Polizist der; (wk. n.) **7** *policeman*
Polkappe die; (-n) **9** *the polar cap*
Postamt das; (¨-er) **1** *post office*
prägen **10** *to shape*
Praktikum das; (die Praktika) **3** *period of practical instruction / training whilst at school / studying*
Präsident der; (wk.n.) **6** *president*
Prinz der; (wk.n.) **7** *prince*
Problem das; (-e) **8** *problem*
Problemmüll der **7** *waste which is difficult to dispose of*
Produzent der (wk. n.) **4** *producer*
profitieren (von + Dat.) **10** *to profit from*
Prognose die; (-n) **4** *prognosis*
Promille das **10**; ein Lit. *per thousand* Blutalkoholgehalt von **2,00** Promille *a blood alcohol level of two parts per thousand*
Promotion die; **2** *gaining of a doctorate*
Prüfung die; (-en) *examination*
Prüfungsangst die **10** *fear of examinations*
PS das; (-) = Pferdestärke die *horse-power*; mit eigenen PS zur Arbeit reiten **2** *to take your own car to work;* Lit.: *to ride your own horse-power to work*
Psychologie die **3** *Psychology*
Punkt der; (-e) **8** *point, spot, dot*
pünktlich **8** *punctual, on time*
Puppe die; (-n) **7** *doll*
Qualifizierte Hauptschulabschluß der **3** *secondary school leaving certificate taken after nine years of schooling*
Quatsch der **7** *nonsense* (coll.)
quatschig **7** *nonsensical* (coll.)
Rabatt der; (-e) **5** *discount*
Radfahren das; **5** *cycling*
Rahmen der; (-) **1** *framework*
rasch **10** *speedy, quick*
raten (ä,ie,a) (+ Dat.) **5** *to advise*
Ratesendung die; (-en) **2** *panel game, quiz show*
rational betrachtet **10** *from a rational point of view;*

Lit. *rationally considered*
Raubtier das; (-e) **9** *predator, beast of prey*
Rausch der **10** *state of intoxication or exhilaration*
Rauschgift das *drugs, narcotics*
rauskommen* (sep.) **10** *to get out*
Realschule die; (-en) *school at which pupils sit the* Mittlere Reife *exam, which is roughly equivalent to GCSE in England & Wales*
rechnen mit **5** *to expect, to reckon with*
recht sein **6** *to be all right;* es ist mir recht *it's all right by me*
recht haben **6** *to be right*
Recht das; (-e); (auf + Akk.) **6** *right to*
rechts **1** *on the right*
rechts (nach) **1** *to the right*
Rechtschutz der **10** *legal protection*
rechtsextrem **8** *right-wing extremist*
rechtzeitig **1** *in good time, on time*
Recycling das **7** *recycling*
recyceln **7** *to recycle*
reden (über + Akk.) **4** *to talk about*
Referendariat das **3** *period of in-service training for Civil Servants, including teachers*
Regel die; (-n) **8** *rule*
regelmäßig **6** *regular(ly)*
regeln **8** *to regulate, to settle*
Regelstudienzeit die **3** *period within which a university course should be completed*
regional **7** *regional(ly)*
reichen **5**; *to suffice;* Das hat mir gereicht *That was enough for me*
reichhaltig **1** *substantial, full (breakfast)*
reichlich **4** *plenty, ample*
reifen **8** *to mature*
rein **6** *pure, clean*
reinhängen (sep.) **3** *to stick at* (coll.), *persist*
reinigen **5** *to clean*
Reinigungsmittel das; (-) **9** *cleaning agent*
reinschmeißen (sep.); (ei,i,i) **7** *to throw in* (coll.)
Reisebegleitung die; (-en) **1** *accompanied tour; Lit. tour accompaniment*
Reiseleiter der; (-) **7** *courier*
Reiseverlauf der **1** *tour plan; Lit. tour course*
Reiten das; **5** *riding*
reizbar **6** *irritable*
Religionswissenschaften die **3** *Religious Studies*
renommiert **8** *renowned*
renovieren **3** *to renovate*
Rentner/in der/die; (-/-nen) **2** *pensioner*
Rentnerdasein das **10** *life as a pensioner*
Reserve die; (-n) **7** *reserve*
Ressentiment das; (-s) **8** *resentment, antipathy*
Rezeptur die (-en) **8** *recipe*
Rheinauen die (pl.) **9** *the meadows along the river Rhine* (poetic)
sich richten nach + Dat. **2** *to depend on*
Richter der (-e) **7** *judge*
richtig **6** *right*
Richtung die; (-en) **1** *direction*
Riese der (wk. n.) **7** *giant*
Ringen das; **5** *wrestling*
Risiko das; (-en) **9** *risk*
Rodeln das; **5** *tobogganing*
Rohmilch die **8** *unprocessed milk*
Rohstoff der; (-e) **7** *raw material*
Rolle die (-n); (k)eine Rolle spielen **10** *role; to play a / no role, to be (un)important*
Rollschuhlaufen das; **5** *roller skating*
Romanistik die **3** *Romance Languages and Literature*
rückfällig werden* (i,u,o) **6** *to relapse*
Rücknahmepflicht die **7** *obligation to take back* (a purchased item)
Rücksicht nehmen auf (+ Akk.) **6** *to show consideration for*
Rückstand der; (-e) **7** *backlog, deficit;* im Rückstand sein *to be behind*
Rudern das; **5** *rowing*
die Ruhe **7** *peace, quiet*
ruhelos **6** *restless*
Ruhestörung die; (-en) **8** *disturbance (of the peace)*

rund **2** *around*
rundlaufen* (sep.); (äu,ie,au) *to circulate*
runtergehen* (sep.): den Berg r. **10** *to go down: to go downhill*
runterkommen* (sep.) **10** *to come down*
Rüschenbluse die; (-n) **8** *blouse with frills*
Russe der; (wk. n.) **7** *Russian*
Sache die; (-n) *affair, issue:* jemandes Sache sein **9** *to be of someone's concern*
Saft der; (¨-e) **2** *juice*
saftig **7** Lit. *juicy; also: hefty, big*
Sammelstelle die; (-n) **7** *collecting point*
Satz der: (-¨e) **1** *sentence*
Satzteil der; (-e) **2** *part of a sentence, sentence element*
sauber **8** *clean*
saubermachen (sep.) **2** *to clean*
Sauerkraut das **8** *sauerkraut, pickled cabbage*
schaden (+ Dat.) **5** *to harm, damage*
schädigen **6** *to harm, damage*
schädlich **7** *harmful*
Schadstoff der; (-e) **9** *harmful substance, pollutant*
schadstoffarm **9** *low in pollutants*
Schaf das; (-e) **7** *sheep*
Schäferhund der; (-e) **8** *Alsation (dog)*
schaffen **3** *to manage* (coll.)
Schaffner der; (-) **8** *ticket inspector*
Schalter der (-) **10** *cashpoint*
scharf **9** *sharp, tight, strict*
schätzen **3** *to estimate*
schätzen **8** *to appreciate*
schätzungweise **3** *roughly, approximately*
schauen (auf + Akk.) **1** *to look at*
Scheibe die; (-n) **2** *slice*
scheiden **10** *to divorce*
Scheißdeutsche die/der; (-n) (vulgar) **8** *bloody German*
Schenkel der; (-) **6** *thigh*
schenken **3** *to give (as a present)*
sich scheren um + Akk. **7** *to care about*
Schicht die; (-en) **2** *shift*
Schicht die; (-en) **10** *stratum, level*
schieben: eine ruhige Kugel schieben **4** *to take things easy; Lit. to push a quiet ball*
Schießübung die; (-en) **4** *shooting exercise*
Schild der; (-e) **4** *sign*; Was führst du im Schilde? *What are you up to?*
schlafengehen* (sep.) **2** *to go to bed*
Schlägertruppen (pl.) **10** *gangs of thugs*
Schlangestehen das **8** *queuing up*
schlank halten **7** *to keep slim, to keep low*
schlank **7** *slim*
schlecht **8** *bad*
Schlendrian der **4** *slackness* (coll.)
schlicht **7** *simple, plain*
schließen (ie,o,o) **4** *to shut, close*
schließlich **10** *after all, finally, in the end*
Schlittschuhlaufen **5** *ice skating*
Schluß der: zum Schluß **2** *finally*
Schlußfolgerung die; (-en) **10** *conclusion*
Schnellkurs der; (-e) **1** *rapid course, crash course*
Schnitt der (-e) **10** *cut; drastic change*
Schnupperlehre die; (-) **3** *short period of "trial" training in a company / workshop*
Schock der (-s) **10** *shock*
schon **2** *already*
schonen **9** *to treat with care, to protect, to conserve*
Schrank der; (-¨e) **7** *cupboard*; der hat nicht alle Tassen im Schrank *he's a few sandwiches short of a picnic*
schrecklich **10** *terrible*
Schreibtisch der; (-e) **2** *desk*
Schreiner der; (-) **3** *carpenter*
Schreinerlehre die; (-n) **3** *carpentry apprenticeship*
Schritt der; (-e): einen S. tun **5** *step: to take a step*
Schrott der **7** *scrap (metal)*
schrump(e)lig **7** *wrinkled, shrivelled*
Schulabgänger der; (-) **3** *school-leaver*
Schulbank die; (¨-e): die S. drücken **9**

school desk: to go to school
Schulnote die; (-n) **3** *school grades*
schwach **3** *weak*
schwafeln **7** *to waffle*
Schwede der; (wk. n.) **7** *Swede*
Schweinebraten der **8** *roast pork*
schwer wiegen (ie,o,o) **9** *to carry weight;* Lit. *to weigh heavily*
schwernehmen (sep.) (i,a,o) **10** *to take seriously*
Schwiegereltern die **2** *parents-in-law*
schwierig **1** *difficult*
Schwierigkeit die; (-en) **6** *difficulty*
Schwimmbad das; (-¨er) **2** *swimming pool*
Schwimmunterricht der **5** *swimming lessons*
Schwindelgefühl das **6** *feeling of dizziness*
Schwitzen das *sweating:* ins Schwitzen kommen **9** *to start sweating*
See der; (-n) **1** *lake*
See die; (-n) *sea*
Segeln das; **5** *sailing*
Sehenswürdigkeit die; (-en) **1** *sight (worth seeing)*
Sehnsucht die **10** *longing, yearning*
seit (+ Dat) **1** *since*
Seite die; (-n) **5** *side, aspect*
Sekundenschnelle die *high speed:* in S. **5** *in a matter of seconds*
selbständig **2** *self-employed; also: independent*
Selbstgefälligkeit die **10** *complacency*
selbstkritisch **8** *self-critical*
selten: nur selten **2** *rare(ly); only occasionally*
Semester das; (-) **3** *semester*
Seminar das; (-) **3** *seminar*
Sendeplatz der **5** *place in the TV schedule*
senken **9** *to lower, reduce*
setzen *to put, set*
sicher **9**; sich einer Sache sicher sein *safe, sure; to be sure of something*
sicher **2** *sure(ly), certain(ly)*
Sicherheit die; (-en) **9** *security*
Sicherheitsvorkehrung die; (-en) **9** *security precaution*
Sicherheitsvorschrift die; (-en) **9** *security regulation*
sicherlich **5** *certainly, no doubt*
sichern: gesichert **7** *to secure: secured*
Sichtweite die **5** *visibility*
Sinn der; *sense, mind:* in den Sinn kommen **5** *to come to mind*
sinnvoll **6** *sensible*
Sitzruhe die **6** *when sitting still;* Lit.: *rest while sitting*
Skilaufen das; **5** *skiing*
sofort **2** *immediately*
sogar **2** *even*
Solarenergie die; (-n) **9** *solar energy*
Solarzelle die; (-n) **9** *solar cell*
Solarzellenpanel das; (-e) **9** *solar panel*
Soldat der; (wk. n.) **7** *soldier*
sollen: Was soll das? **10** *(modal verb): What is all that about?* (coll.)
Sonderabgabe die; (-n) **6** *special deduction, special tax*
Sondermaßnahme die (-n) **10** *special measure*
Sondermüll der **7** *hazardous waste*
sonnabends **1** *on Saturdays*
Sonne die **9** *sun*
Sonnenenergie die; (-n) **9** *solar energy*
Sonnenkollektor der; (-en) **9** *solar panel*
Sonnenkraftwerk das; (-e) **9** *solar power plant*
sonst **2** *otherwise*
sorgen (für + Akk.) **7** *to see to it, to look after: to cause*
sich Sorgen machen um + Akk. **6** *to worry about*
sorgsam **8** *careful(ly)*
Sorte die; (-n) **7** *brand*
sowieso **6** *anyway, in any case*
Sozialarbeiter der; (-) **4** *social worker*
Sozialpädagoge/-in; (-n/-nen) **4** *person with a degree in Social Education*
Sozialversicherungssytem das; (-e) **8** *social security system*
Sozialwissenschaften die **3** *Social Sciences*
Soziologie die **3** *Sociology*

Spalte die; (-n) **7** *column*
Spannung die (-en) **10** *tension*
Spaß der; (¨-e); Es macht mir Spaß **3** *fun; I enjoy it*
Sperrmüll der **7** *(large items of) refuse, such as old TV sets, funiture, etc. – there is a special collection for this, usually once a month.*
speziell **9** *special(ly)*
Spiel das; (-e) *play, game:* ins Spiel kommen **9** *to come into play, to come into it*
spielen **3** *to play*
spontan **5** *spontaneous(ly)*
Sport der; *sport:* Sport machen *to do sports*
Sportplatz der; (¨-e) **5** *sports field*
Sportwissenschaft die **3** *Sports Science*
Sprach- und Literaturwissenschaften die **3** *Language and Literature*
Sprachfertigkeit die; (-en) **3** *linguistic skill, fluency*
Sprachinstitut das (-e) **4** *institute of languages*
sprechen (i,a,o) **2** *to speak*
Sprecher/-in der/die; (-/-nen) **5** *spokesman / -woman*
Sprit der **9** *petrol* (coll.)
spritzen **7** *to spray*
spurlos **3** *without trace*
Staatsbesuch der; (-e) **9** *state visit*
Staatsexamen das; (-) **3** *state exam; similar to the M.A. degree*
Staatsführung die **10** *government;* Lit.: *state leadership*
Staatssekretär/-in der/die (e-/nen) **5** *permanent secretary in parliament*
Stadt die; (-¨e) **1** *town, city*
Stadtbücherei die; (-en) **2** *town / city library*
Städteaustausch der; **6** *(town) twinning exchange*
Stadtrat der **10** *town / city council*
Stadtverwaltung die **8** *town / city council; municipal authority*
Stahl der **9** *steel*
Stahlkocher der; (-) **9** *steel producer*
Stall der; (¨-e) **2** *stable*
ständig **3** *constant(ly), all the time*
Standort der; (-e) **5** *location, position*
Standpunkt der; (-e) **10** *standpoint, view*
Stange die; *stick:* (-n) eine Stange Geld **7** *a small fortune:* Lit.: *a stick of money*
stark **6** *strong(ly)*
Starnberger See der **2** *large lake near Munich*
Start der; (-s) *start:* einen guten S. haben **8** *to have a good start, to be in a good starting position*
Station die; (-en) **6** *station; also: office, outlet*
statistisch: statistisch gesehen **4** *statistical(ly); statistically speaking*
stattfinden (sep.) (i,a,u) **2** *to take place*
Stau der; (-s) **2** *traffic jam, tailback*
Staub der **4**; man konnte sie vor Staub nicht mehr sehen *dust; they couldn't be seen for dust*
Staulage die **5** *situation concerning tailbacks*
staunen (über + Akk.) **4** *to be amazed at*
Stauung die; (-en) **1** *jam, tailback*
stehenlassen (ä,ie,a) (sep.) **7** *to leave (standing)*
steigen* (ei,ie,ie) **9** *to rise*
sich steigern **5** *to increase*
Steinkohle die **9** *[hard] coal*
stellen; *to put, place;* sich unter die Dusche stellen **2** *to have a shower*
Stellenwert der; *status:* einen hohen S. haben **5** *to have a high status*
Stellung die; (-en) **3** *position, job*
sterben* (i,a,o) **3** *to die*
Stereoanlage die; (-n) **6** *stereo (system)*
Steuer die (-n) **1** *tax*
Stickstoff der **9** *nitrogen*
stillegen (sep.) **4** *to close down*
Stillegung die; (-en) **4** *close-down*
stimmen **6** *to be correct*
stinken (i,a,u) **9** *to stink*
Stipendium das; (-ien) **3** *grant*
Stirnrunzeln das **5** *frowning*
Stoff der; (-e) **6** *substance*
stolz sein (auf + Akk.) **8** *to be proud of*

Stolz der **5** *pride*
stören **8** *to disturb*
Störung die; (-en) **6** *malfunction; also: interruption, disturbance*
stoßen* (ö,ie,o) auf + Akk. **7** *to come across*
Stoßstange die; (-n) **1** *bumper*
Strafe die; (-n) **7**; eine Strafe ausschreiben *fine; to impose a fine*
Strahlung die **9** *radiation*
stramm **6** *firm, strict, authoritarian*
Straßenbahn die; (-en) **1** *tram*
Straßenverkehr der **10** *road traffic*
Streik der; (-s) **2** *strike*
streng **8** *strict(ly)*
streßfrei **2** *free of stress*
stricken **2** *to knit*
Stroh der **9** *straw*
Strom der **9** *electricity*
Stromerzeuger der; (-) **9** *electricity producer*
Stromlieferant der; (wk. n.) **9** *electricity supplier*
Student der; (wk. n.) **7** *student*
Studienabschluß der; **3** *roughly equivalent to a degree* (Lit. *end of studies)*
Studiengebühr die; (-en) *study fee*
Studienzeit die **4** *period of study*
Stufe die; (-n) **4** *step, level*
Stunde die; (-n) **5** *hour, lesson*
Subvention die; (-en) **9** *subsidy*
subventionieren **9** *to subsidise*
suchen; *to search, to look for*: eine Stellung suchen **4** *to look for a job*
Süßigkeiten (pl.) **6** *sweets, confectionery*
sich suhlen **9** *to wallow*
Supermarkt der; (¨-e) **7** *supermarket*
Synagoge die; (-n) **8** *synagogue*
systematisch **8** *systematical(ly)*
Tagesablauf der **2** *daily routine*
Talent das; (-e) **9** *talent*
Tankstelle die; (-n) **9** *filling station*
Tanzclub der; (-s) **5** *dance club*
tanzen **2** *to dance*
Tanzkurs der; (-e) **5** *dancing classes*
Tarif der; (-e) **4** *agreed rate of pay*
Taschengeld das **10** *pocket money*
Tastatur die; (-en) **9** *keyboard*
Tat die; (-en) **4** *deed*
in die Tat umsetzen *to put into action, effect, to realise*
in der Tat **10** *in fact*
Tauchen das; **5** *diving*
sich täuschen **7** *to be wrong, to be mistaken*
Technische Umweltschutz der **3** *Technical Environmental Protection*
Technische Überwachungsverein der (TÜV) **7** *organisation which controls the implementation of recommended standards, i.e. in the case of cars; often compared with the MOT*
Teelöffel der; (-) **6** *teaspoon*
Teil der (-e); *to share:* zum Teil **5** *part; partly*
teilen; *to share*: eine Meinung teilen **6** *to share an opinion*
Teilerfolg der; **10** *partial success*
teilnehmen (sep.); (i,a,o); (an + Dat.) **2** *to take part in*
Teilnehmer/in der/die; (-/-nen) **1** *participant*
Tempolimit das; (-s) **9** *speed limit*
Termin der; (-e) **4** *date, deadline*
teuer **2** *dear, expensive*
Theaterstück das; (-e) **5** *play, drama*
Thema das; (-en) **8** *subject, topic*
Thüringen **2** *Thuringia – one of the five Eastern states* (Länder) *of Germany*
Tier das; (-e): *animal:* ein hohes Tier **9** *big shot* (coll.)
Tierart die; (-en) **9** *species*
tierisch **9** *bestial;* also: *unbearable*
Tierversuch der; (-e) **9** *animal experiment*
tödlich **6** *fatal*
toll **8** *fantastic* (coll.), *great;* Lit. *insane*
Tollhaus das **9** *madhouse*
torkeln* **6** *to stagger*
Tote der/die (adj. n.) **6** *dead person*
Tourist der; (wk. n.) **7** *tourist*
Toxikologe/-in der/die (-n/-nen) **6** *toxicologist*

traditionsreich **8** *rich in tradition*
Träne die; (-n) **10** *tear*
trauen (+ Dat.) **5** *to trust*
sich trauen **8** *to dare*
Traum der; (-¨e) **10** *dream*
treffen (i,a,o) **2** *to meet; to hit, to hurt*
Treffen das **8** *meeting*
Treibhaus das; (¨-er) *greenhouse*
Treibhausgas das; (-) **9** *gas which helps to cause the greenhouse effect*
Treibstoff der **6** *fuel*
trennen **10** *to separate*
Trennmüll der **7** *refuse, garbage which has been sorted into various categories*
Treppe die **3** *staircase, stairs*
Tresen der (-) **10** *counter*
Trott der; *routine:* in den Trott geraten **10** *to be dragged into a routine*
trotz (+ Gen./Dat.) **1** *despite, in spite of*
trügen **10** *to deceive*
Trunkenheitsdelikt das; (-e) **10** *drink-driving offence*
tumultartig **10** *turbulent*
tun (u,a,a) **2** *to do*
Türke der (wk.n.) die Türkin (-nen) **10** *Turk*
Turnen das; **5** *gymnastics*
Turnier das; (-e); *tournament;* auf Turnier gehen **5** *to take part in a tournament, competition*
typisch **8** *typical(ly)*
U-Bahn die; (-en) **1** *short for Untergrundbahn: tube*
übel **10** *bad*
über (+ Akk./Dat.) **1** *over, above*
Überbesetzung die **4** *excess in personnel*
überdurchschnittlich **3** *above average*
übereinstimmen (sep.); (mit + Dat.) **6** *to agree with*
überflüssig **7** *superfluous*
Überfüllung die **3** *overcrowding*
überhaupt nicht **6** *not at all*
überhöht **4** *excessively high*
überholt **10** *outmoded, outdated*
überlagern **9** *to interfere with*
sich etwas überlegen **6**; Ich habe es mir anders überlegt **4** *to think about, consider something; I've changed my mind*
übermächtig **8** *superior, very powerful*
übermäßig **8** *excessive(ly)*
übermorgen **2** *the day after tomorrow*
Übernahmeangebot das; (-e) **4** *takeover bid*
übernehmen (i,a,o) **3** *to take on, take over*
überprüfen **6** *to check (over)*
überraschen *to surprise*
sich überschneiden; (ei,i,i) **5** *to clash, overlap*
übersehen (ie,a,e) **10** *to ignore, overlook*
übersetzen **10** *to translate*
überspielen **6** *to cover up, gloss over*
überstülpen (sep.) **10** *to pull on*
übertreiben (ei,ie,ie) **8** *to exaggerate*
überwältigend **8** *overwhelming*
überwiegend **8** *predominantly*
überzeugen **3,9** *to convince*
üblich **9** *usual*
übrigens **5** *by the way*
um (+ Akk.) **1** *around*
um **2** *at (exact time)*
umdenken (sep.); (e,a,a) **7** *to rethink*
umfangreich **9** *extensive*
Umfrage die; (-n) **10** *survey, opinion poll*
Umgebung die; (-en) **2** *surrounding area*
umgehend **10** *immediate*
umsetzen (sep.) **4**; in die Tat umsetzen *to move, translate; to put into effect, realise*
umsonst **2** *free of charge*
Umstand der (¨-e) **3**; *circumstance;* unter keinen Umständen *in no circumstances*
umsteigen* (sep.) **1** *to change (buses, trains, etc.)*
sich umstellen (sep.) **9** *to adjust, change*
Umweg der; (-e) **5** *detour*
Umweltbehörde die **7** *environmental authority*
Umweltflegel der; (-) **7** *lout (in*

regard to environmental matters)
Umweltministerium das; (-en) **3** *Ministry of the Environment*
Umweltproblem das; (-e) **10** *environmental problem*
Umweltrisiko das; (-en) **9** *environmental risk*
Umweltschutz der **7** *environmental protection*
Umweltsteuer die **7** *environment tax*
unausgeschlafen **6** *still tired, not properly rested*
unbedingt **6** *by any means, at all costs*
unbemerkt **6** *unnoticed*
unbequem **1** *uncomfortable*
unbedingt **10** *absolutely*; unbedingt erforderlich *absolutely essential*
unbestritten **9** *indisputably*
undenkbar **4** *unthinkable*
uneingeschränkt **9** *unrestricted(ly), unreserved(ly)*
unerfreulich **8** *unpleasant*
unergiebig **8** *unrewarding, unproductive*
unerhört **10** *outrageous, scandalous;* Lit. *unheard of*
unerwartet **10** *unexpected*
Unfall der, (-¨e) **10** *accident*
ungeachtet (+ Gen.) **9** *irrespective of*
ungeheuer **3** *huge(ly), immense(ly)*
ungemütlich **6** *cheerless, uninviting*
ungespritzt **7** *unsprayed*
ungewöhnlich **8** *unusual*
unglaublich **10** *incredible*
unglückselig **10** *unfortunate*
unheimlich viel **5** *a great deal*
Unrecht das **6** *injustice*
unrein **10** *impure, dirty*
unruhig **6** *anxious, agitated*
Unsinn der **6** *nonsense*
unter (+ Akk./Dat.) **1** *under; among, beneath*
unterbewerten **10** *to underrate, undervalue*
sich unterhalten; (über + Akk.) **4** *to talk (about)*
Unterhaltungsserie die; (-n) **2** *soap opera*
Untermieter der; (-) **7** *lodger*
unternehmen (i,a,o) **9** *to do something about*
unterrichten **4** *to teach*
Unterrichtsraum der; (-¨e) **2** *teaching room*
unterschätzen **9** *to underestimate*
unterscheiden (ei,ie,ie) **10** *to distinguish*
Untätigkeit die (-en) **9** *lack of action, inactivity*
sich unterscheiden (von + Dat.) **2** *to be different from, to be distinguished from*
Unterschied der; (-e) (zwischen + Dat) **7** *difference between*
unterschiedlich **6** *different(ly), varying*
unterschreiben (ei,ie,ie) **7** *to sign*
unterstützen **3** *to support*
Unterstützung die; (-en) **6** *support*
untersuchen **10** *to examine*
Untertitel der; (-) **5** *subtitle*
unterwegs; *away*: unterwegs sein **5** *to be away, to be on a trip*
unverschämt **7** *outrageous*
unverständlich **8** *unclear*
unwahrscheinlich **10** *improbable*
Unwirtschaftlichkeit die **4** *economic inefficiency*
Uran das **9** *uranium*
Urenkel/in der/die (-/-nen) **2** *great-grand / daughter*
Urkunde die; (-n) **9** *document*
Urlaub der; (-e); Urlaub machen *holiday, vacation; to go on holiday, vacation*
urlaubsreif **8** *ready for / in need of a holiday*
Ursache die; (-n) **9** *cause*
ursprünglich **8** *original(ly)*
verabredet **2**: Ich bin verabredet *I have an appointment / date*
verabschieden **9** *to adopt, pass (of a law or policy)*
veraltet **4** *outdated, outmoded*
Veränderung die; (-en) **9** *change, alteration*
veranstalten **4** *to organise, hold*
Veranstaltung die; (-en) **1** *event*
verantwortlich (für + Akk.) **10** *responsible for*
verantwortungsvoll **9** *responsible*

verbessern **10** *to improve*
verbieten (ie,a,o) **6** *to prohibit, to ban*
verbinden **2** *to join, combine*
Verbindung die (-en) **9** *compound*
Verbindung die (-en) **10** *link*
Verbot das; (-e); *ban:* ein V. verhängen **6** *to impose a ban*
Verbrauch der **7** *consumption*
verbrauchen **7** *to consume, use*
verbrauchsgerecht **9** *favourable to consumers*
verbreiten **8**; weit verbreitet **10** *to spread; widespread*
verbrennbar **7** *burnable*
Verbrennen das **7** *burning*
Verbrennung die **9** *burning, combustion*
verbringen (i,a,a) *to pass;* Zeit verbringen **3** *to spend time*
verbunden sein (mit + Dat.) **9** *to be linked with; also: to cause*
verdanken **4** *to owe*
verdeutlichen **10** *to make clear, clarify*
verdienen **10** *to earn*
Verfassung die **10** *constitution*
Verfechter der; (-) *advocate, champion*
Verfechterin die; (-nen) **9** *(female) advocate, champion*
verfliegen* (ie,o,o) **10** *to pass (of emotions)*
verfolgen *to follow, to watch*
Verfolgung die **9** *persecution*
Verfügung die; (-en) **10** *order, decree*
zur Verfügung stehen **2** *to be available, at someone's disposal*
Vergangenheit die **8** *past*
vergeben (i,a,e) **8** *to forgive*
vergessen (i,a,e) **8** *to forget*
vergeßlich **6** *forgetful*
Vergiftung die **8** *poisoning*
Vergleich der; (-e) **10** *comparison*
im Vergleich zu *compared with*
vergleichen **10** *to compare*
Vergütung die; (-en) **4** *pay (of a state employee)*
verhaften **7** *to arrest*
verhallen **10** *to wane, faint away*
sich verhalten **3** *to behave, to act*
das Verhalten **6** *behaviour*
Verhaltenstherapie die; (-n) **6** *behavioural therapy*
Verhandlung die; (-en) **4** *negotiation*
verheerend **9** *devastating*
Verkalkung die **6** *calcification;* (coll.) *senility*
Verkehr der **1** *traffic*
Verkehrsamt das; (¨-er) **1** *tourist information office*
Verkehrsaufkommen das **9** *volume of traffic*
Verkehrsbeschränkung die; (-en) **9** *traffic restriction*
Verkehrsdichte die **1** *traffic density*
Verkehrsflughafen der; (¨) **6** *commercial airport*
Verkehrsfunk der **5** *radio traffic service*
Verkehrsmeldung die; (-en) **1** *traffic news (*Lit. *traffic announcement)*
Verkehrsredaktion die **1** *traffic information staff*
verkennen (e,a,a) **6** *to fail to appreciate, recognise*
verkennbar **10** *deniable*
verkünden **10** *to announce, proclaim*
verlangen; *to demand:* nicht zuviel verlangt **6** *(this is) not asking too much*
verlängern **5** *to extend*
sich verlassen auf + Akk. **5** *to rely on*
verlaufen* (äu,ie,au) **4** *to go, elapse*
Verlegenheit die **6** *embarrassment*
verletzen **7** *to injure*
verlieren (ie,o,o) **8** *to lose*
vermeiden (ei,ie,ie) **7** *to avoid*
vermeintlich **5** *supposed*
vermindern **9** *to decrease, reduce*
vermissen **10** *to miss*
vermitteln **8** *to give, to pass on (knowledge)*
vernünftig **9** *reasonable, rational*
Verordnung die; (-en) **7** *regulation*
Verpackung die; (-en) **7** *wrapping*
Verpackungsverordnung die; (-en) **7** *regulation for dealing with packaging material*
verpesten **6** *to pollute*

verpflichten **7** *to oblige, commit*
Verpflichtung die; (-en) **10** *obligation, commitment*
verplanen **5** *to book out completely, to plan every minute*
sich verprügeln **10** *to beat each other up*
verrecken* **10** *to die a miserable death*
verregnet **8** *rainy, wet, spoilt by rain*
verringern **9** *to reduce*
verrückt **1** *mad, insane*
Versagen das **9** *failure, error*
Versammlung die; (-en) **2** *meeting*
verschieden **6** *various, different*
verschwinden* (i,a,u) **3** *to disappear*
Versicherungspolice die; (-n) **8** *insurance policy*
Versicherungsvorschrift die; (-en) **8** *insurance regulation*
versprechen (i,a,o) **5** *to promise*
sich verständigen **9** *to reach agreement*
Verständnis das *understanding*: V. haben (für + Akk.) **5** *to understand (smth.)*
verstecken **10** *to hide*
Versuch der; (-e) **3** *experiment, attempt*
versuchen **2** *to try*
Verteuerung die; (-en) **6** *price increase*
Vertrag der; (-¨e) **10** *contract; treaty*
vertrauen (auf + Akk.) **3** *to trust (in)*
Vertrauen das **3** *trust, confidence*
vertraut; *familiar:* v. sein (mit + Dat.) **3** *to be familiar with*
Vertreter der; (-) **9** *representative*
Verursacher der; (-) **9** *causer, originator*
verurteilen **10** *to sentence*
vervollständigen **3** *to complete*
Verwaltungsgericht das **10** *administrative court*
Verwandte der/die (adj. n.) *relative*
verweisen (auf + Akk.) **5** *to point to*
verwenden **6** *to use*
Verwertung die; (-en) **7** *recycling*
Verzicht der (auf + Akk.) **6** *the giving up (of)*
verzichten (auf + Akk.) **7** *to do without*
verzeichnen **10** *to note, record*
vierzehntägig **7** *fortnightly*
Volk das; (-¨er) **8** *people, nation*
Volkswirtschaft die **9** *economics*
voll (+ Gen.) **7** *full (of)*
vollkommen **10** *complete(ly)*
vollständig **4** *complete*
von (+ Dat.) **1** *from, of*
vor (+ Akk./Dat.) **1** *in front of*
vor allem **2** *above all*
vorangehen* (sep.) **10** *to proceed, go ahead*
voraussichtlich **4** *probably*
vorbehalten (ä,ie,a) (sep.) **1** *to reserve (the right)*
vorbereiten (sep.) **2** *to prepare*
sich vorbereiten (sep.) (auf + Akk.) **10** *to prepare (for)*
vorbeugen (sep.) (+ Dat.) **5** *to prevent*
sich vordrängeln **8** *to jump the queue*
Vorgeschmack der **10** *first taste*
vorgesehen **3** *planned*
Vorhaben das; (-) **4** *intention*
vorhaben (sep.) **1** *to intend, to plan, to have in mind*
vorhanden sein **9** *to exist*
vorher **1** *in advance, beforehand, first*
Vorkehrung die; (-en) **9** *precaution*
Vorkehrungen treffen (i,a,o) *to take precautions*
vorkommen* (o,a,o) (sep.) **7** *to occur*
Vorkommen das **9** *deposit*
Vorläufer der **9** *precursor*
Vorlesung die; (-en) **3** *lecture*
Vorliebe die; (-n) **5** *preference*
Vorname der; (-n wk. n.) **6** *forename, first name*
vornehmen (sep.) (i,a,o) **9** *to make, undertake*
sich etwas vornehmen (sep.); (i,a,o) **5** *to plan something*
vornherein: von vornherein **8** *from the start*
Vorsatz der; (¨-e) **6** *intention, resolution*
Vorschlag der; (¨-e) **5** *proposal,*

suggestion
vorschlagen (ä,u,a) (sep.) **1** *to suggest*
Vorschrift die; (-en) **7** *regulation*
Vorsicht die; *care, guard:* es ist V. angeraten **8** *one should be careful*
Vorsitzende der; (adj. n.) *president, chairman*
vorstellen (sep.) **6** *to introduce*
sich vorstellen (sep.); (+ Akk.) **7** *to imagine (something)*
Vorstellung die; (-en) **8** *idea*
Vorstellungsgespräch das; (-e) **3** *job interview*
Vorteil der; (-e) **2** *advantage*
vorteilhaft **10** *advantageous*
Vortrag der; (¨-e) **8**; einen Vortrag halten **8** *lecture, talk; to give a lecture*
Vorurteil das; (-e) gegenüber + Dat. **8** *prejudice against*
vorziehen (sep.); (ie,o,o) **5** *to prefer*
wachsen* (ä,u,a) **6** *to grow*
Wade die; (-n) **6** *calf (of the leg)*
wagen **9** *to risk, dare*
wahlweise **5** *alternatively*
Wahnsinn der **3** *madness, insanity*
Wahre das; *the true thing, the truth:* da ist 'was Wahres dran **8** *there is some truth in that*
während (+ Gen.) **1** *during; while*
Wahrheit die; *truth:* ein Körnchen W. **8** *a grain of truth*
wahrnehmen (i,a,o) (sep.) **4** Diesen Termin kann ich leider nicht wahrnehmen *to carry out, perform, fulfil; I'm afraid I cannot make this date*
wahrscheinlich **4** *probably*
währungspolitisch **10** *concerning monetary policy*
Währungsunion die **10** *monetary union*
Wald der; (-¨er) **7** *forest*
Waldsterben das **9** *forest death*
wandern* **2** *to ramble, hike*
Wandern das; **5** *rambling, hiking*
Wanderung die; (-en) **6** *walking tour, ramble*
Wanken das; *wavering:* ins Wanken geraten **9** *to become shaky, begin to totter*
wäre **1** *would be; conditional form of the verb* sein
Warendschungel der **7** Lit.: *jungle of products; mass of products*
warnen (vor + Dat.) **6** *to warn against*
wartungsfrei **6** *without check-ups*
was: was für ein(e) **4** *what: what kind of (coll.)*
Wäsche die **2** *laundry, washing*
waschen (ä,u,a) **2** *to wash*
sich waschen **2** *to wash (oneself)*
Waschsalon der; (-s) **2** *launderette*
Wasser das; ins Wasser fallen **4** *to fall through, be a washout*
Wasserkraftwerk das (-e) **9** *hydroelectric power station*
Wechsel der; (-); *change:* im Wechsel **7** *alternately*
wechseln **2** *to change*
Wechselverkehrszeichenanlage die; (-n) **5** *commuter traffic information system*
weder ... noch **6** *neither ... nor*
wegen (+ Gen./Dat.) **1** *because of, on account of*
wegfließen* (ie,o,o) (sep.) **10** *to flow away*
wegkommen* (sep.); (o,a,o) (von + Dat.) **9** *to get away from*
wegschmeißen (ei,i,i) (sep.) **7** *to chuck away*
Wegweiser der; (-) **7** *signpost*
Weihnachten das **2** *Christmas*
weinen **10** *to cry, weep*
Weißblech das; (-e) **7** *tin plate*
weiter **2** *further*
weitaus **2** *by far*
weitgehend **8** *largely, mostly*
weiträumig **9** *over a wide area, extensively*
Welt die; (-en) aus der W. schaffen **8** *world; to resolve (a problem);* Lit.: *to eliminate something from the face of the earth*
Wende die **3** *turning point; used to refer to the absorption of the former GDR into the Federal Republic*
Werk das; (-e) **5** *work*
Werkstatt die; (¨-en) **2** *workshop*

werktäglich **5** *during the (working) week*
Werktätige der/die (adj. n.) **10** *working man / woman*
Werkzeugmaschine die; (-n) **4** *machine tool*
Wert der; (-e); *value:* W. legen (auf + Akk.) **8** *to attach importance to*
werten **8** *to assess, to judge*
Wertstofferfassung die; (-en) **7** *registration of re-usable material*
Wertstoffhof der; (¨-e) **7** *collection point for re-usable material*
Wertstoffsammlung die; (-en) **7** *collection of re-usable material*
wertvoll **7** *valuable, precious*
wesentlich **9** *essential*
wesentlich **10** *considerably*
Wesentliche das **8** *the essential*
wichtig *important*
Wichtigkeit die **10** *importance*
widersprechen (i,a,o) (+ Dat.) **5** *to contradict*
Widerspruch der (¨-e) **10** *contradiction*
Wiederaufbereitung die **9** *reprocessing*
Wiederaufbereitungsanlage die; (-n) **9** *reprocessing plant*
Wiederholung die; (-en) **5** *repetition*
Wiedervereinigung die **10** *re-unification*
wiederverwertbar **7** *recyclable*
wiederverwerten (sep.) **7** *to recycle*
wieviel **1** *how much, how many*
wildfremd **10** *totally strange*
Wille, der; (wk. n.) **4** *will, wish, intention*
Willkommensbrief der; (-e) **6** *letter of welcome*
Wind der **9** *wind*
Windkraftanlage die; (-n) **9** *wind power plant*
Windpark der; (-s) **9** *wind park*
wirksam **6** *effective*
wirkungsvoll **10** *effective*
wirtschaftlich **9** *economic / al(ly)*
Wirtschaftsklima das **4** *economic climate*
Wirtschaftswissenschaften die **3** *Economics*
Wirtschaftswunder das **8** *economic miracle*
wissen (ei,u,u) **1** *to know*
Wissenschaftler/-in der/die; (-/-nen) **6** *scientist, scholar, academic*
Wissenschaftlicher Assistent; der **2** *assistant lecturer at a German institution of higher education*
wissentlich **6** *knowingly*
Witwe die; (-n) **2** *widow*
Witz der; (-e) **6** *joke*; Machen Sie Witze? **7** *Are you joking?*
Woche die; (-n) *week*: einmal in der Woche **2** *once a week*
wohin **8** *where to*
wohin damit **7** *(coll) where shall it be put, where shall it go*
wohingegen **8** *whereas*
Wohnstube die (-n) **10** *living room*
womöglich **1** *possibly*
wund **8** *sore*
wunderschön **6** *really beautiful*
wünschenswert **9** *desirable*
Wurstwarenstand der; (¨-e) **8** *meat / sausage counter*
Zahl die; (-en) **1** *number*
Zähler der; (-) **9** *meter*
Zähneputzen das **9** *brushing of one's teeth*
zart *delicate*
Zeichen das; (-) **10** *sign,indication*
zeigen (+ Dat.) **8** *to show*
Zeitabstand der; (-¨e) **6** *interval*
zeitaufwendig **7** *time-consuming*
Zeitbombe die; (-n) **9** *time bomb*
zeitig **2** *early, in good time*
Zeitlang die; *duration of time:* eine Zeitlang **6** *for a while*
Zeitmangel der **4** *lack of time*
zeitweise **8** *from time to time*
Zensur die; (-en) **3** *mark, grade*
Zeuge der (wk. n.) **7** *witness*
ziehen* (ie,o,o) **2** *to move*
ziehen (ie,o,o) **2** *to pull*
Ziel das (-e) **4** *goal*; Was hast du dir zum Ziel gesetzt? *What aim have you set yourself?*
ziemlich **10** *considerable, rather*
zirka **1** *about*
zitieren **8** *to quote, cite*
Zivildienst der **4** *a kind of community service instead of doing military service*

Zivildienstleistende der (adj. n.) **4** *person doing community service (instead of military service)*
zu (+ Dat) **1** *to, for*
zu tun haben (sep.) **3** *to have to do*
zu spüren bekommen (o,a,o) **8** *to feel the effects of the fact that ...*
zuckerkrank **6** *diabetic*
zuerst **2** *at first*
zufrieden **3** *satisfied*
Zug der; (¨-e) **6** *train; also: draught; drag (on a cigarette)*
zugeben (i,a,e) (sep.) **7** *to admit*
zugehen* (sep.); (e,i,a) **10** *to go on*
zügig **9** *quickly, without delay*
zugleich **8** *at the same time*
zuhören (sep.) **7** (+ Dat.) *to listen to*
zum einen ... zum anderen **9** *on the one hand ... on the other hand*
zumachen (sep.) **4** *to close*
Zumutung die; (-en) **6** *imposition, unreasonable demand*
zunächst **2** *at first, initially*
zunehmen (i,a,o) (sep.) **6** *to increase*
zuordnen (sep.) **2** *to assign, attribute*
zurückgehen* (sep.); (e,i,a) **9** *to go down, become less*
zurückkehren* (sep.) **9** *to return*
zurückliegen (sep.); (ie,a,e) **10** *to be in the past*
zusagen (+ Dat.) **5** *to be to one's liking*
zusammenfassen (sep.) **10** *to put together, to unite; summarise*
zusammenfassend **10** *by way of summarising*
zusammengehören (sep.) **10** *to belong together*
Zusammenhang der; (¨-e) **6** *connection*
zusammenpressen (sep.) **8** *to squeeze*
zusammenschließen (sep.) **10** *to unite, to put together*
sich zusammentun; (sep.) (u,a,a) **10** *to get together*
zusätzlich **7** *additional(ly)*
Zustand der; (-¨e) **10** *state*
zuständig **9** *responsible*
Zusteigemöglichkeit die; (-en) **1** *pick-up point;* Lit.: *getting-on possibility*
Zustimmung die **9** *approval*
zuviel werden **5** *to become too much*
zuvorkommend **8** *obliging*
Zwangsabgabe die **7** *compulsory return, handling in*
zwar **1** *admittedly*
Zweck der; (-e); *purpose:* zu diesem Zweck **2** *for that purpose*
Zweigstelle die; (-n) **3** *branch, subsidiary*
zwischen (+ Akk/Dat) **1** *between*
Zwischenfall der; (-¨e) **10** *incident*
Zwischenzeit die; *meantime:* in der Z. **6** *in the meantime*

INDEX TO GRAMMAR NOTES

The first number in each entry refers to the unit (**Lektion**), the second to the section within the **Grammatische Hinweise**.

Abbreviation: **Rdw.** = **Redewendungen**

— ACKNOWLEDGEMENTS —

The author and publishers would like to thank the following for their permission to reproduce material:

BUNTE; Deutsche Presseagentur d.p.a.; FOCUS; Frankfurter Allgemeine Zeitung; GLOBUS Kartendienst GmbH; Informationszentrale der Elekrizitäts-Wirtschaft E.V.; The New York Times Syndication; Der Spiegel; Zeitverlag GmbH.

Every effort has been made to trace copyright holders of material reproduced in this book. The publishers will be glad to make suitable arrangements with any copyright holder not acknowledged within this printing.